D0421097

INTRODUCTION TO TRADE POLICY

Introduction to Trade Policy provides a comprehensive overview of the rules and regulations that govern trade flows. It discusses the trade policy formulation process of major international economic players, and analyzes existing trade policy tools that countries may resort to in order to take advantage of the benefits of international trade and to protect themselves against its dangers, as well as their implications for trade policy, law and negotiations.

In Section I, the book explores the ways in which interest groups interact with government and legislators to shape trade policies. By developing an analytical view of trade policy formulation systems in the U.S., European Union, the BRICS countries (Brazil, Russia, India, China and South Africa), Canada, Mexico and Australia, the book will help the reader to gain a better understanding of these countries' trade policy developments and also to apply such learning to the analysis of the trade policy formulation of any other countries. Section II goes on to explain how governments use trade policy tools to achieve trade and other policy objectives, while Section III analyses trade in services and the multilateral trade rules on Intellectual Property. Finally, Section IV uses hypothetical case studies in simulation exercises to illustrate trade policy decision-making and trade agreement negotiations in a bilateral, plurilateral and multilateral setting.

This is the ideal introduction to international trade policy formulation for students and professionals in the areas of law, politics, economics and public policy who are seeking to develop a global view of international trade, gain insights into trade negotiations and understand the motivations behind the policies and actions of governments regarding international trade issues. This book, the result of documental research by the authors spanning ten years, is also the ideal companion to any traditional legal casebook on international trade or on international economic law.

Aluisio de Lima-Campos is an Adjunct Professor at the School of Law at the American University, the Washington College of Law in Washington, D.C., U.S.A., where he teaches courses on trade policy and regional trade agreements in the Trade, Investment and Development Program. He has over 30 years' experience as a trade policy specialist and economic advisor to the Brazilian Embassy in Washington, D.C., and established the ABCI Institute in 2007, which offers trade policy study and training for Brazilian government and private sector professionals. He is also a former instructor for the Regional Trade Policy courses of the WTO, delivering training to government officials worldwide.

Juan Antonio Gaviria is a Doctor of Juridical Science from American University, the Washington College of Law in Washington, D.C., U.S.A. He holds a LL.M. with an emphasis on International Business Law from the same university and was an Adjunct Professor there for the course on Advanced Issues in International Trade Policy. He has over 15 years' experience as a legal practitioner in trade and business law and also as a professor and academic researcher. Besides trade law, his main academic interests lie in the intersection of legal and economic topics. He is a tenured Professor and Researcher at Universidad Pontificia Bolivariana, School of Law (Medellín, Colombia) and member of the Research Group on Legal Studies (GRID) at the same university.

INTRODUCTION TO TRADE POLICY

Aluisio de Lima-Campos and
Juan Antonio Gaviria

LONDON AND NEW YORK

First published 2018
by Routledge
2 Park Square, Milton Park, Abingdon, Oxon, OX14 4RN

and by Routledge
711 Third Avenue, New York, NY 10017

Routledge is an imprint of the Taylor & Francis Group, an informa business

© 2018 Aluisio de Lima-Campos and Juan Antonio Gaviria

The right of Aluisio De Lima-Campos and Juan Antonio Gaviria to be identified as authors of this work has been asserted by them in accordance with sections 77 and 78 of the Copyright, Designs and Patents Act 1988.

All rights reserved. No part of this book may be reprinted or reproduced or utilised in any form or by any electronic, mechanical, or other means, now known or hereafter invented, including photocopying and recording, or in any information storage or retrieval system, without permission in writing from the publishers.

Trademark notice: Product or corporate names may be trademarks or registered trademarks, and are used only for identification and explanation without intent to infringe.
British Library Cataloguing in Publication

British Library Cataloguing in Publication Data
A catalogue record for this book is available from the British Library

Library of Congress Cataloging-in-Publication Data
Names: Lima-Campos, Aluisio de, author. | Gaviria, Juan Antonio, author.
Title: Introduction to trade policy / Aluisio de Lima-Campos,
Juan Antonio Gaviria.
Description: Abingdon, Oxon [UK]; New York : Routledge, [2017] |
Includes bibliographical references and index.
Identifiers: LCCN 2017026187 | ISBN 9781138676756 (hardback) |
ISBN 9781317196631 (adobe reader) | ISBN 9781317196624 (epub) |
ISBN 9781317196617 (mobipocket)
Subjects: LCSH: Trade regulation. | Foreign trade regulation. |
International trade. | General Agreement on Trade in Services (1994
April 15) | Agreement on Trade-Related Aspects of Intellectual Property
Rights (1994 April 15)
Classification: LCC K3840. L56 2017 | DDC 382—dc23
LC record available at https://lccn.loc.gov/2017026187

ISBN: 978-1-138-67675-6 (hbk)
ISBN: 978-1-138-67676-3 (pbk)
ISBN: 978-1-315-55989-6 (ebk)

Typeset in Galliard by
Keystroke, Neville Lodge, Tettenhall, Wolverhampton

CONTENTS

FIGURES

TABLES

ABBREVIATIONS

AB	Appellate Body
ACFTA	ASEAN–China Free Trade Area
ACP	African, Caribbean and Pacific countries
ADA	Antidumping Agreement
AGOA	African Growth and Opportunity Act
ALADI	Asociación Latino Americana de Integración
APEC	Asia-Pacific Economic Cooperation
APTA	Asia Pacific Trade Agreement
ATPA	Andean Trade Preference Act
ATPDEA	Andean Trade Promotion and Drug Eradication Act
Art.	Article
ASCM	Agreement on Subsidies and Countervailing Measures
ASEAN	Association of Southeast Asian Nations
ASEM	Asia–Europe meeting
BAT	Border Adjustment Tax
BII	Chinese Bureau of Industry Injury
BIT	Bilateral Investment Treaties
BOFT	Chinese Bureau of Fair Trade for Imports and Exports
BREXIT	Britain's exit (from the E.U.)
CACEX	Carteira de Comércio Exterior do Banco do Brasil S.A.
CAFTA-DR	Central American Free Trade Agreement and Dominican Republic
CAN	Community of Andean Nations
CAP	Common Agricultural Policy
CBERA	Caribbean Basin Economic Recovery Act
CBI	Caribbean Basin Initiative
CBTPA	Caribbean Basin Trade Initiative Act
CCU	Countervailing Currency Intervention

CEB	Coalizão Empresarial Brasileira
CEP	Constructed export price
CEPAL	United Nations Economic Commision for Latin America and the Caribbean
CETA	The Comprehensive Economic and Trade Agreement
CFSP	The Common Foreign and Security Policy
CIS	Commonwealth of Independent States
CISA	Division of Commerce and Investment in South Africa
CAN	Confederação Nacional de Agricultura
CNI	Confederação Nacional da Indústria
CUT	Central Única dos Trabalhadores
DCFTA	Deep and Comprehensive Free Trade Agreement
DITE	Division of International Commerce and Economics (South Africa)
DoC	U.S. Department of Commerce
DSB	Dispute Settlement Body
DSU	Dispute Settlement Understanding
DTI	South African Department of Commerce and Industry
DTT	Treaties to avoid double taxation
EEA	European Economic Association
EFTA	European Free Trade Association
E.U.	European Union
FEER	Fundamental equilibrium exchange rate
FGV	Fundação Getulio Vargas
FIESP	Federação das Indústrias do Estado de São Paulo
FTAA	Free Trade Area of the Americas
GATS	General Agreement on Trade and Services
GATT	General Agreement on Tariffs and Trade
GDP	Gross domestic product
GPA	Government procurement agreement
GSP	Generalized system of preferences
IADB	Inter-American Development Bank
IBRD	International Bank for Reconstruction and Development
ICSID	International Center for Settlement of Investment Disputes
IMF	International Monetary Fund
ITA	U.S. International Trade Administration
ITA	Information Technology Agreement
ITAC	International Trade Administration Commission of South Africa
ITC	U.S. International Trade Commission
ITEDC	International Trade and Economic Development Commission
MEFTI	Middle Eastern Trade Initiative
MERCOSUR	Mercado Común del Sur
MFN	Most-Favored Nation
MOFCOM	Ministry of Commerce of China
NAAEC	North American Agreement on Environmental Cooperation

NAALC	North American Agreement on Labor Cooperation
NAFTA	North America Free Trade Agreement
NEDLC	National Economic Development and Labor Council of South Africa
NPC	National People's Congress of China
NTC	National Trade Council
OECD	Organization for Economic Co-operation and Development
OTMP	Office of Trade and Manufacturing Policy
Para.	Paragraph
PBT	Punitive Border Tax
PFS	Policy Formulation System
PIIE	Peterson Institute for International Economics
PJCC	Police and Judicial Cooperation in Criminal Matters
PSC	Politburo Standing Committee
PTA	Preferential Trade Agreement
RCEP	Regional Comprehensive Economic Partnership
S	Section
SACU	South African Customs Union
SADC	Southern African Development Community
SCMA	Subsidies and Countervailing Measures Agreement
SGA	Safeguards Agreement
SOEs	State-owned Enterprises
SPS	Agreement on the Application of Sanitary and Phytosanitary Measures
TBR	Trade Barrier Regulation
TBT	Agreement on Technical Barriers to Trade
TFA	Trade Facilitation Agreement
TIEA	Canada–E.U. Trade and Investment Enhancement Agreement
TiSA	Trade in Services Agreement
TPP	Trans-Pacific Partnership
TRIMs	Agreement on Trade-Related Investment Measures
TRIPS	Trade-related aspects of intellectual property rights
TRQ	Tariff-rate-quota
TTIP	Trans-Atlantic Trade and Investment Partnership
U.K.	United Kingdom
U.N.	United Nations
UNCTAD	United Nations Conference on Trade and Development
U.S.	United States
USTR	The Office of the United States Trade Representative
VAT	Value added tax
VRA	Voluntary restraint agreements
WB	World Bank
WIPO	World Intellectual Property Organization
WTO	World Trade Organization

SECTION I

Trade policy

This section, besides making some introductory remarks about the pros and cons of international trade, analyzes the trade policy formulation systems of the largest WTO members: The United States, The European Union, China, Brazil, India, Russia, South Africa, Mexico, Canada, and Australia. The chapters discussing such systems will give the reader a useful understanding about how trade policy is formulated in practice and how the different actors interact in such processes.

1

INTRODUCTION TO TRADE POLICY

1.1 The purpose of this book

This book, as its title suggests, is about what trade policy is, how it is made in different countries and what legal and economic tools policy formulators may use to do it. This book's purpose, in turn, is to give the reader the basic knowledge related to the formulation of international trade policy. Many books have been written about either the economics[1] or the legal aspects of international trade.[2] To the best of the authors' knowledge, however, books analyzing the rules of international trade not only from the legal and economic standpoints but also from a policy perspective are scarce and, when they exist, follow a different approach.[3] This book intends to fill this gap by providing a holistic and comprehensive view of trade policy.

For this purpose, this book is divided into four sections: the first about trade policy formulation, the second focusing on trade policy tools, the third discussing the GATS and TRIPS Agreements, and the fourth introducing simulations that put into practice the combined knowledge of trade policy formulation and instruments. The first section, besides making some introductory remarks in the present chapter, will discuss how the trade policy systems of selected countries and supranational organizations[4] account for the largest share of international trade. Such countries and regions are: the United States – Chapter 2; the European

1 See, e.g., Paul R. Krugman and Maurice Obstfeld, *International Trade* (10th ed.) (2014).

2 The classic text is John H. Jackson et al., *Materials and Texts on Legal Problems of International Economic Relations* (6th ed.) (2013).

3 For some of the few books about International trade policy, see, e.g., Geza Feketekuty, *Policy Development and Negotiations in International Trade: A Practical Guide to Effective Commercial Diplomacy* (2013).

4 Since the European Union will be analyzed in Chapter 3 *infra*.

Union – Chapter 3; China – Chapter 4; Brazil – Chapter 5; India – Chapter 6; Russia – Chapter 7; South Africa – Chapter 8; and other countries (Mexico, Canada and Australia) – Chapter 9.

The second section, in turn, analyzes the main trade policy tools that countries may resort to in order to make the most of the benefits of international trade, on the one hand, and to prevent or mitigate any potential issues derived from the increased and global competition, on the other. This section is divided into the following chapters: Market access (tariffs, customs procedures and trade facilitation) – Chapter 10; Trade remedies (antidumping, countervailing duties and safeguards) – Chapter 11; Currency manipulations and trade – Chapter 12; Regulatory measures (technical barriers to trade, sanitary and phytosanitary measures, rules of origin, trade related investment measures, preference programs and government procurement) – Chapter 13; Dispute settlement – Chapter 14; Trade agreements – Chapter 15; and Advanced analysis of international trade negotiations – Chapter 16.

The third section discusses the legal rules of the multilateral trade agreements other than the GATT and the DSU: the GATS in Chapter 17 and the TRIPS in Chapter 18. Finally, the fourth section is about case simulations, i.e., exercises based on specific trade policy hypothetical cases about the following items: (1) Trade policy decision-making process – Chapter 19, (2) Bilateral trade agreement negotiations – Chapter 20, (3) Plurilateral trade agreement negotiations – Chapter 21, and (4) Multilateral trade agreement negotiations – Chapter 22.

1.2 The notion of trade policy

Before starting the study of trade policy, it is obviously necessary to define this term, describe its objectives, and mention the pros and cons of international trade.

Regarding the first topic, hundreds of definitions of trade policy exist. Among them, the most precise and illustrative are the following ones: first, and from an economic standpoint, trade policy is the science of finding the efficient point of import and export policies in a spectrum whose extremes are total "government intervention" and total "free trade."[5] Finding this efficient point, needless to say, is a complex task. In any event, some countries might implement trade policies characterized by a high degree of government intervention and a restriction of international trade while other countries might consider that the opposite approach is better for macroeconomic purposes. That countries might follow different approaches does not entail that some of them are on the right track and the remaining countries are on the wrong track; after all, one-size-fits-all policies do not exist in international trade. Otherwise, books on trade policy would not be necessary or would not be longer than a very few pages. Thus, each trade policy

5 See Stephen D. Cohen et al., *Fundamentals of U.S. Foreign Trade Policy: Economics, Politics, Laws, and Issues* (2nd ed.) 1 (2002).

must be tailored to the particular legal, political and economic features of a given country at a given historical time.

Trade policy might also be defined, from a legal standpoint, as the set of laws and regulations that affects the foreign trade of a country. To put it another way, trade policy is the ensemble of legal rules which impact and influence a certain country's foreign trade.[6] This meaning is similar to the former; after all, legal rules are the instruments that allow a country to choose how far or how near it is going to be from the extremes of total government intervention and total free trade. This definition also reminds us that governments[7] are the ones which formulate trade policies through legal rules which, in turn, influence endogenous economic variables such as trade balances and balance of payments.

Once the concept of trade policy has been defined, this book turns to trade policy's goals. Two main objectives exist. First, trade policy, if a country believes in the benefits of international trade, intends to integrate a country in the global economy by strengthening the economic links among nations under the rationale, that many scholars including this book's authors agree with, but that other people are against, that a more interconnected world will make all countries better off.

As a second and related goal, trade policy spurs socio-economic development and growth by, for instance, stimulating GDP's growth, decreasing the unemployment rate, and reducing the disparities of income distribution among the population of a given country.[8] In any event, economic growth is not and should not be the only target of any trade policy. Quite to the contrary, a well-formulated trade policy should promote not only the improvement of pure economic indicators such as economic growth, but also the enhancement of other indicators with a social impact, such as a decrease in poverty (i.e., reducing the number of people below the line of poverty) or an improvement in the Gini coefficient.[9] In other

6 See Wordnet Princeton, https://wordnet.princeton.edu/ (last visit, April 30, 2017).

7 In this context, the term government includes not only the Executive (which enforce trade legal rules) but also the Legislative (which enact such rules) and the Judiciary branches (which may withdraw some trade legal rules if they are in breach of some superior rules, such as the Constitution).

8 But see Dani Rodrik, *The Globalization Paradox*, p. 57 (2012) (stating that the size of the redistribution might be so large in comparison with the benefits resulting from international trade. For example, a move from 5 percent tariffs to complete free trade "would reshuffle more than $50 of income among different groups for each dollar of efficiency or net gain created!" In other words, "we are talking about $50 of redistribution for every $1 of aggregate gain. It's as if we give $51 to Adam, only to leave David $50 poorer.").

9 The Gini index, named after the Italian statistician Corrado Gini, measures the dispersion of income distribution in a given territory. A country where everybody receives the same income would have a Gini index of 0 while a country with the worst inequality (one individual having all the country's wealth) will have a Gini of 1. Thus, the farther the indicator is from 0, the worse the inequality in a given country (although the ideal Gini is not 0 – absolute equality might distort incentives to create wealth). For figures about the GINI, see The World Bank, http://data.worldbank.org/indicator/SI.POV.GINI (last visit, April 30, 2017).

words, a trade policy having as its main effect an economic growth which is only beneficial to the wealthiest layers of the population might be not only incomplete but also counterproductive. This, by the way, has been one of the main criticisms of trade liberalization since the last decades of the twentieth century (although the authors of this book do not share such a view). International trade, the argument goes, has promoted economic growth and efficiency gains but has not necessarily alleviated poverty or reduced social inequalities.[10]

After explaining the meaning and goals of trade policy and before turning to the role of multilateral organizations in the formulation of trade policies, a brief analysis of the pros and cons of free trade is warranted. The notion of trade is not new. Indeed, human beings have been trading for millennia. In the words of Adam Smith in *The Wealth of Nations*:

> Nobody ever saw a dog make a fair and deliberate exchange of one bone for another with another dog. Nobody ever saw one animal by its gestures and natural cries signify to another, this is mine, that yours; I am willing to give this for that.[11]

In the same book, Smith made his famous remark about the market's invisible hand. Smith explained that the individual's pursuit of his/her self-interest goals makes possible the improvement in the collective welfare. The following quote explains this rationale:

> It is not from the benevolence of the butcher, the brewer, or the baker that we expect our dinner, but from their regard to their own interest. We address ourselves, not to their humanity but to their self-love, and never talk to them of our necessities but of their advantages.[12]

Smith also applied the rationale in this quote to international trade:

> If a foreign country can supply us with a commodity cheaper than we ourselves can make it, better buy it of them with some part of the produce of our own industry, employed in a way in which we have some advantage.[13]

Another Scottish economist, David Ricardo, also applied 200 years ago the notion of the invisible hand to international trade and introduced the concepts of comparative and absolute advantage through an example of international trade

10 See, e.g., Joseph E. Stiglitz and Andrew Charlton, *Fair Trade for All: How Trade Can Promote Development*, p. 1 (2007).

11 See Adam Smith, *The Wealth of Nations* Book IV, Section II, p. 12 (2014).
See also Xavier Sala-i-Martin, *Economía en Colores [Economics through Colors]* 15 (2016).

12 Adam Smith, *The Wealth of Nations* Book IV, Section II, p. 12 (2014).

13 *Id.*

between two countries.[14] In Ricardo's example, both England and Portugal produce two goods: cloth and wine, labor being the only input. If England produces cheaper cloth than Portugal and the latter country harvests cheaper wine than England, it is straightforward to conclude that England should specialize in the manufacturing of cloth, amounting the total output to the requirements of both the internal market and the Portuguese market, while Portugal should focus on the harvesting of wine, selling some of it domestically and exporting the remaining part to England. Under these facts, England has a comparative advantage in cloth and Portugal has such advantage in wine. Tables 1 and 2 explain the concept of comparative advantage assuming that each country produces and consumes one unit of cloth and another unit of wine and using some hypothetical figures regarding their costs.

In these tables, it is assumed that England manufactures two units of cloth and exports one of them to Portugal while Portugal harvests two units of wine and exports one of them to England. In both cases, the export prices are equal to the goods' costs.

Ricardo's real contribution was to show that even if one country produces both goods at cheaper costs, trade would still be advantageous due to the theory of absolute advantage. For instance, while Portugal might produce both goods more

TABLE 1 Comparative advantage without international trade

Country	*Cost*		
	Cloth	*Wine*	*Total*
England	$50	$80	$130
Portugal	$70	$60	$130
Total	*$120*	*$140*	*$260*

TABLE 2 Comparative advantage with international trade

Country	*Product*	*Cost – two units (a)*	*Imports – one unit (b)*	*Exports – one unit (c)*	*Total cost (a + b – c)*	*Benefits in comparison with Table 1*
England	Cloth	$100	$0	$50	$50	$0
	Wine	$0	$60	$0	$60	$20
	Total	*$100*	*$60*	*$50*	*$110*	*$20*
Portugal	Cloth	$0	$50	$0	$50	$20
	Wine	$120	$0	$60	$60	$0
	Total	*$120*	*$50*	*$60*	*$110*	*$20*
Benefits of free trade						$40

14 David Ricardo, *On the Principles of Political Economy and Taxation*, p. 1 (2014).

TABLE 3 The case when one country is more efficient in the production of both goods (without international trade)

Country / cost	*Cloth*	*Wine*	*Total*
England	$100	$120	$220
Portugal	$90	$80	$170
Total	*$190*	*$200*	*$390*

TABLE 4 Absolute advantage with international trade

Country	*Product*	*Cost – two units (a)*	*Imports – one unit (b)*	*Exports – one unit (c)*	*Total cost (a + b – c)*	*Benefits in comparison with Table 3*
England	Cloth	$200	$0	$90	$110	$-10
	Wine	$0	$100	$0	$100	$20
	Total	*$200*	*$100*	*$90*	*$210*	*$10*
Portugal	Cloth	$0	$90	$0	$90	$0
	Wine	$160	$0	$100	$60	$20
	Total	*$160*	*$90*	*$100*	*$150*	*$20*
Benefits of international trade						$30

cheaply, Portugal and England might reap benefits if Portugal specializes in manufacturing the good that can be produced at a lowest cost (relative to the other good) and England focuses on the production of this other good. Tables 3 and 4 show this analysis, again using hypothetical costs.

In such tables, assume that England specializes in the manufacturing of cloth (two units) while Portugal focuses on the harvest of wine (two units). Suppose also that Portugal exports its wine at $100 per unit (i.e., obtaining a profit of $20) and that England exports the cloth at $90 per unit (i.e., obtaining a loss of $10 which makes sense because it may import the wine at $100 instead of harvesting it at $120).

As Tables 3 and 4 show, the total costs when each country produces one unit of cloth and another of wine (without international trade) is $390, an amount that is reduced to $360 when England specializes in the manufacturing of cloth (in spite of the fact that Portugal might produce it more cheaply) and Portugal focuses on the harvesting of wine with each country exporting to the other the quantities not required at home. Of course, the figures might vary in reality, according to the economics of scale and cost characteristics of each industry in not only two places, but in the more than two hundred countries that exist nowadays.

In the twentieth century, Swedish Professors Eli Heckscher and Bertil Ohlin developed a trade model – the so-called Heckscher–Ohlin model or simply the H-O model – that builds on the theory of comparative and absolute advantages that David Ricardo described two centuries before.[15] The H-O model predicts

15 See Eli Heckscher, *The Effect of Foreign Trade on the Distribution of Income*, Ekonomisk Tidskrift, 497 (1919). Reprinted as Chapter 13 in *Readings in the Theory of International*

that countries with cheap labor will produce and export goods requiring a significant amount of this input and will import goods intensive in capital, such as machinery.[16] Countries with expensive labor and cheap capital will have the opposite characteristics.[17]

In response of some criticisms of the H-O model, such as its failure to precisely predict the patterns of international trade, Professor Raymond Vernon introduced the so-called Product Life-Cycle theory.[18] Professor Vernon attempted to understand why many products were manufactured in the United States, despite the fact that such goods required a significant amount of labor and, therefore, according to the H-O model, should be fabricated in developing countries.

The Product Life-Cycle theory states that the place where a product is manufactured depends on its stage of development. At the first stage, the product is manufactured in the country where it was invented (usually a developed country) and exported to other countries. In later stages, production moves to countries where the manufacturing processes are cheaper (generally, developing countries). Thus, in contrast to both Ricardo's theory and the H-O model, the place where a good is manufactured is not constant during its life (hence, the name of this theory). Some empirical studies in diverse industries have demonstrated that some products follow a cycle similar to the one that Vernon's model describes.[19]

A final model related to the topics discussed above which might go against the tenets of the Ricardo's theory is the so-called Stolper-Samuelson theorem, named after the two creators of this theory: Wolfang Stolper, an American economist working for the Nigerian Government during the 1960s, and, widely regarded as one of the most brilliant economists of all time, Paul Samuelson.[20] In their famous

Trade, pp. 272–300 (1949); and Bertil Ohlin, *Interregional and International Trade* (1933). This book was based in the Ohlin's doctoral dissertation whose supervisor was Eli Heckscher. See *The Concise Encyclopedia of Economics*, Bertil Gotthard Ohlin (1899–1979), available at: www.econlib.org/library/Enc/bios/Ohlin.html (last visit, April 30, 2017). See also Robert E. Baldwin, *The Development and Testing of Heckscher-Ohlin Trade Models: A Review*, p. 1 (2008), and Edward A. Leamer, *The Craft of Economics: Lessons from the Heckscher-Ohlin Framework*, p. 1 (2012). Bertil Ohlin was jointly awarded the Nobel Memorial Prize in Economics in 1977 together with the British economist James Meade for their path-breaking contribution to the theory of international trade and international capital movements. See Nobel Prize Organization, www.nobelprize.org/nobel_prizes/economic-sciences/laureates/ (last visit, April 30, 2017).

16 See *id.*

17 See *id.*

18 See Raymond Vernon, *International Investment and International Trade in the Product Cycle*, LXXX Q. J. Econ., 190 (1966).

19 See, e.g., Gary C. Hufbauer, *Synthetic Materials and the Theory of International Trade*, p. 1 (1966), and Seev Hirsch, *Location of Industry and International Competitiveness*, p. 1 (1967).

20 See Wolfang Stolper and Paul Samuelson, *Protection and Real Wages* 9(1) Rev. Econ. Stud. 58 (1941). See also *Tariffs and Wages, An Inconvenient Iota of Truth*, The Economist, August 6th, 2016, available at: www.economist.com/news/economics-brief/21703350-third-our-series-looks-stolper-samuelson-theorem-inconvenient-iota (last visit, April 30, 2017).

papers, these economists showed that international trade with low-wage nations, such as Nigeria, could hurt workers in a high-wage country (such as the United States), because unskilled workers in a wealthy country might be replaced with workers in the poorer country. In sum, very cheap labor might not be so cheap since low wages might reflect poor productivity, as Wolfang Stolper observed in some Nigerian mills. In other words, "some groups will *necessarily* suffer long-term losses in income from free trade. In a wealthy country such as the United States, these are likely to unskilled workers such as high school dropouts."[21]

After describing its benefits, this chapter turns now to some objections that have been made to international trade. An early criticism states that international trade leads to an economic globalization that is only beneficial to wealthier countries and people, widening the gap between them and poor countries and individuals and, therefore, worsening inequality. Thus, and according to this criticism, unrestricted international trade and, more generally, globalization are processes with few winners taking all the benefits and many losers. Some of such losers would be developing countries lacking the infrastructure necessary to take advantage of the benefits of international trade, as well as workers in such countries helplessly observing their jobs move elsewhere.[22]

This criticism does not stop there. Globalization, according to the people against it, is a process whose effects go beyond the economic impacts.[23] For instance, globalization, as the argument goes, might banish the cultural differences among regions and countries and might expand, as a monoculture, the Western traditions.[24]

Naturally, since this is a pro-international trade book, its authors do not share these criticisms. First, the evidence shows a positive correlation and even a cause-and-effect relationship between openness to trade and economic growth.[25]

21 Dani Rodrik, *The Globalization Paradox,* p. 56 (2012).

22 While believers of international trade consider that the benefits of it greatly outweigh their costs, the criticism described here should not be overlooked. It might have been one of the reasons why the majority of people in the United Kingdom voted in favor of this country leaving the European Union (see *infra* Chapter 3) and also why Donald J. Trump was elected as the 44th U.S. President. Regarding the latter, see generally Katherine J. Cramer, *The Politics of Resentment: Rural Consciousness in Wisconsin and the Rise of Scott Walker,* p. 1(2016). Recall that one of the bases of the campaign of the current U.S. President was making sure that no more jobs would move from the United States to countries with lower labor costs such as Mexico and China. See Donald J. Trump Official Web page, www.donaldjtrump.com/ (last visit, April 30, 2017).

23 See, e.g., Peter Iadicola, *Globalization and Empire,* 1(2) Int'l J. Social Inquiry 1 (2008). But see, e.g., John Muthyala, *Dwelling in American: Dissent, Empire, and Globalization,* p. 1 (2012).

24 See *id.*

25 As examples of countries whose economics have recently thrived in part as a result of the benefits of international trade, see, e.g., Chile and Hong-Kong. Indeed, since Hong Kong was a capitalist regime that the United Kingdom controlled until 1997 but, at the same time, its main market was Communist China and its culture was Chinese, it was a natural experiment and perhaps the best empirical example of the benefits of international trade until it came under Chinese control.

For instance, the most recent winner of the John Bates Clark medal, which the American Economic Association grants annually to a leading economist under 40 years old, has empirically tested the benefits of international trade and, in particular, the empirical performance of Ricardo's theory of comparative advantage.[26] In a paper written with Professor Arnaud Costinot, the authors use agricultural data related to the productivity in 17 crops of 1.6 million parcels of land in 55 countries around the world to prove that Ricardo's theory is not only mathematically correct but also empirically valid.[27] Thus, this paper finds that integration during the period analyzed there contributed as much to agricultural output as did the increase in productivity.[28]

Second, while it is true that international trade might not only benefit some people but also harm other individuals, it is not a zero-sum game. To put it another way, the benefits of international trade are greater than its drawbacks.[29] Third, it is the role of governments to enact and implement public policies, mainly related to public expenditure, such as legal subsidies, and progressive taxation, to help people and companies which international trade might negatively affect. In other words, governments helping people and companies harmed by international trade is a better solution than going back to the times of mercantilism and autarchy and, therefore, closing the border and sacrificing the significant gains resulting from international trade in order to avoid the minor losses resulting from it.

On top of that, the concern about a cause-and-effect relationship between international trade and inequality seems unfounded. Studies indicate that domestic factors such as productivity and infrastructure and not competition for world markets

26 See Arnaud Costinot and Dave Donaldson, *Ricardo's Theory of Comparative Advantage: Old Idea, New Evidence*, National Bureau Econ. Research, Working Paper 17969 (2012), available at: www.nber.org/papers/w17969.pdf (last visit, April 20, 2017).

27 See *id.*

28 See *id.* See also 'Free Exchange, A trade economist wins the John Bates Clark medal', The Economist, April 20, 2017, available at: www.economist.com/news/finance-and-economics/21721136-law-comparative-advantage-200-still-winning-prizes-trade-economist (last visit, April 20, 2017). Other papers empirically showing such correlation and even causation between trade and economic growth are legion. See, e.g., Anne O. Krueger, *Why Trade Liberalization is Good for Growth*, 108 Econ. J. 1513 (1998); Bülent Ulaşan, *Openness to International Trade and Economic Growth: A Cross-Country Empirical Investigation* Discussion Paper No 2012-25, Econ., Open-Access, Open-Assessment E-J., available at: www.economics-ejournal.org/economics/discussionpapers/2012-25 (last visit, April 30, 2017); Jeffrey A. Frankel and David Romer, *Does Trade Cause Growth?* 89(3) Am. Econ. Rev. 379 (1999); and Joseph E. Stiglitz, '*Towards a New Paradigm for Development: Strategies, Policies, and Processes*', Prebisch Lecture, UNCTAD, Geneva (1998). The literature, however, is not uniform since some experts are sceptic about this cause–effect relationship. See, e.g., Francisco Rodríguez and Dani Rodrik, *Trade Policy and Economic Growth: A Skeptic's Guide to the Cross-National Literature* Cambridge, MA: National Bureau of Economic Research. NBER Working Paper 7081 (1999).

29 See *id.*

are the main drivers of national living standards.[30] Also, trade liberalization seems to increase inequality within countries (an issue that, as the last paragraph indicated, might be mitigated through domestic policies) but not between countries.[31] In the same sense, the Kuznets curve, named after the economist who created it (Simon Kuznets) predicts that international trade and more generally market forces first increase inequality and, at a later stage of development, decrease it.[32]

As a second criticism, trade liberalization might have harmful environmental consequences, which are especially worrisome at a time when slowing climate change is a priority. Free trade requires countries to be competitive; otherwise, they would not be able to export goods to other countries and imported goods would prevail over their national output. Thus, in the race – to the bottom – to be competitive, the argument goes, increasing the output is the priority and environmental protection ends up being the least of the problems. This line of reasoning, indeed, is not restricted to environmental issues; it might be extended to health and safety issues as well.

There is an environmental version of the above-mentioned Kuznets curve.[33] According to this theory, economic growth and international trade contribute to environmental degradation at least until some degree of development is reached. After that point, the environmental standards tend to improve.[34] Thus, plotting a curve in a chart whose X-axis is income per capita and its Y-axis is pollution, the environmental Kuznets curve has the shape of an inverted U. If this theory is true, international trade-led growth is especially harmful for developing countries.[35] The results estimating whether the theory underlying the environmental Kuznets curve holds in the empirical world are mixed.[36]

30 See Robert J. Barro, *Determinants of Economic Growth: A Cross-Country Empirical Study*, p. 1 (1998). See also Xavier Sala-I-Martin, *I Just Ran Two Million Regressions* 87(2) Am. Econ. Rev. 178 (1997), and Chapter 4, 'The Theory of Economic Growth', available at: http://eml.berkeley.edu/~webfac/trehan/e100b_sp05/chap4.pdf (last visit, April 30, 2017).

31 See *supra* note 23.

32 See Simon Kuznets, *Economic Growth and Income Inequality* 45(1) Am. Econ. Rev. 1 (1955).

33 See Gene M. Grossman and Alan B. Krueger, *Environmental Impacts of a North American Free Trade Agreement.* National Bureau of Economic Research Working Paper 3914, NBER, Cambridge MA (1991); and Nemat Shafik and Sushenjit Bandyopadhyay, *Economic Growth and Environmental Quality: Time Series and Cross-Country Evidence.* Background Paper for the World Development Report 1992, The World Bank, Washington, D.C. (1992).

34 See *id.*

35 See *id.*

36 See, e.g., Richard T. Carson, *The Environmental Kuznets Curve: Seeking Empirical Regularity and Theoretical Structure* 4(1) Rev. Environmental Econ. & Policy, 3 (2010); James Van Alstine and Eric Neumayer, 'The Environmental Kuznets Curve', in *Handbook on Trade and the Environment* (Kevin P. Gallagher Ed.) 55 (2008); Christoph Martin Lieb, *The Environmental Kuznets Curve – A Survey of the Empirical Evidence and of Possible Causes*, Discussion Paper Series No 391, Department of Economics, University of Heideberg, available at: www.uni-heidelberg.de/md/awi/forschung/dp391.pdf; and Matthew Cole,

In any event, this book contends that trade liberalization triggers forces protecting the environment that are stronger than the forces harming it. This is especially true if trade liberalization is not a chaotic phenomenon but, on the contrary, a process subject to an international rule of law. As an illustration supporting this reasoning, there is significant WTO case law upholding domestic measures intended to protect the environment.[37]

A third objection states that international trade may adversely impact labor standards and human rights. In particular, and as part of the above-mentioned race to the bottom, countries might relax such standards in order to be more competitive in the global stage. Such a race may have been one of the causes of the surge of the so-called sweatshops in Bangladesh and neighboring countries where labor conditions in certain industries are not very far from slavery.[38]

While this concern is not completely unfounded, international trade might raise the bar of labor and human rights standards rather than lowering it on the following grounds: (i) studies show not only that trade liberalization promotes economic growth (and, therefore, a higher income) but also that human rights are income-elastic or, in other words, that an increase in income improves human right indicators,[39] and (ii) trade liberalization promotes globalization and this process makes human rights violations more visible. For instance, human rights violations in a closed country such as North Korea are very likely but, at the same time, very difficult to detect and, therefore, to punish. In contrast, human rights violations in the manufacturing of goods which are sold globally might become public which, in turn, would allow countries and companies to impose sanctions (for instance, some multinationals might stop buying raw materials from the companies violating human rights). More importantly, visibility also allows consumers to stop purchasing such goods.

Anthony J. Rayner and John M. Bates, *The Environmental Kuznets Curve: An Empirical Analysis* 2(4) Environment and Development Economics 401 (1997).

37 Examples of these cases are: (i) Australia – Measures Affecting Importation of Salmon (DS18); (ii) European Communities – Measures Concerning Meat and Meat Products (Hormones) (DS26); (iii) United States – Standards for Reformulated and Conventional Gasoline (DS52); (iv) United States – Import Prohibition of Certain Shrimp and Shrimp Products (DS58); and (v) US – Tuna II (DS381).

38 See, e.g., 'Two years ago, 1,129 people died in a Bangladesh factory collapse. The problems still haven't been fixed' (April 23, 2015), The Washington Post, www.washingtonpost.com/news/wonk/wp/2015/04/23/two-years-ago-1129-people-died-in-a-bangladesh-factory-collapse-the-problems-still-havent-been-fixed/ (last visit, April 30, 2017). See generally Jennifer Bair, Doug Miller and Marsha Dickson (Eds), *Workers' Rights and Labor Compliance in Global Supply Chains: Is a Social Label the Answer?* p. 1 (2016).

39 See *supra* note 23. See also Alan O. Sykes, 'International Trade and Human Rights: An Economic Perspective', in *Trade and Human Rights: Foundations and Conceptual Issues* (Fredereick M. Abbott, Christine Breining-Kaufmann and Thomas Cottier Eds), p. 45 (2006); and Todd Landman and Marco Larizza, *Inequality and Human Rights: Who Controls What, When, and How?* 53(3) Int'l Stud. Q. 715 (2009).

As a final objection,[40] international trade is said to constrain national sovereignty by creating an international organization (WTO) and by limiting the rights of the countries which adhere to its agreements and which cannot, therefore, enact domestic rules in contravention of the multilateral legal rules. While this statement is true, it does not make sense if coming from countries that signed those agreements. If they did, they must have realized that it was not necessarily a bad outcome. If they think differently today, they can withdraw. In sum, and in the view of this book's authors, moving the decision-making process from domestic legislatures to international trade meetings and substituting the WTO for national agencies is the price that has to be paid for a regulated international trading system – a system that has served all WTO members well, by bringing discipline to international trade, discouraging unilateral protectionist actions and, thereby, preventing trade wars.

1.3 The World Trade Organization and other multilateral institutions that affect trade policies

Before the mid-twentieth century, international rules governing trade among countries were almost inexistent. As a result, diplomacy or military expeditions, if the former method was unsuccessful, were the usual methods of settling trade disputes.

This scenario changed during the years following the end of the Second World War, which was a turning point. At this time, the emerging consensus was that some international trade organizations were necessary to avoid protectionist and domestic measures such as the ones taken during the interregnum between the world wars.[41] As a result, the creation of two financial organizations was decided at a gathering of Allied Nations delegates in a New Hampshire town named Bretton Woods: the IMF, the main purpose of which was to avoid global financial crisis by controlling exchange rates and payment imbalances; and the IBRD, established with the main goal of financing the reconstruction of the areas that the Second World War had devastated. Some years after its creation, this organization was re-baptized as the WB and its purpose was widened and updated in order to include the funding of programs intended to spur the economic growth of both developing and under-developed countries.

A set of international financial organizations was incomplete without an international trade system. Being aware of this fact, negotiations of a multilateral trade

40 There are, of course, other objections to international trade. For instance, international trade might be detrimental to infant industries since its incipient development might make them an easy prey for global competition. The reader who is interested in learning more about these objections might consult, for instance, Michael Trebilcock and Robert Howse, *The Regulation of International Trade* (4th ed.), p. 1 (2012).

41 For an account of these facts, see Liaquat Ahamed, *The Bankers Who Broke the World*, p. 1 (2009).

agreement began shortly after the Bretton Woods agreements. The negotiations, which ended in 1948 with the Havana Charter, provided for the establishment of the International Trade Organization. The outcome, however, was not successful. While 53 countries signed the Havana Charter, the U.S. Government's decision not to submit the treaty to the U.S. Senate for its ratification, an example that some other countries followed, entailed that the charter never entered into legal force.[42]

While the establishment of the International Trade Organization failed, another less ambitious trade agreement, the GATT, succeeded.[43] While the GATT was basically a tariff agreement, the ITO charter was closer to that of the WTO. It allowed for international cooperation and rules against anticompetitive business practices, and encompassed agreements in many areas besides tariffs, such as labor standards, investment and preferential agreements. Twenty-three countries signed the GATT in 1947, intended to facilitate trade by reducing tariffs and other barriers, with many other countries following suit over the following decades. The GATT agreement was expanded during its seven rounds of negotiations and it was the only legal rule governing international trade until the establishment, as a result of the so-called Uruguay Round and of the Marrakesh Agreement, of the World Trade Organization, which came into legal force on January 1, 1995. As of 2016, the WTO has 157 members accounting for about 96 percent of world trade.[44]

WTO legal rules are composed of four annexes. Annex 1 is, in turn, divided into three sub-annexes: (i) Annex 1A, which includes GATT 1994 plus other agreements on topics such as agriculture, textiles, clothing and, more important for this book, antidumping, subsidies and countervailing duties, safeguards, and technical, sanitary and phytosanitary barriers; (ii) Annex 1B, GATS, governing trade in services; and (iii) Annex 1C, TRIPS, including the rules on intellectual property. Annex 2 comprises the rules governing the settlement of trade disputes (DSU). Annex 3 is about the trade policy review mechanism (a "regular collective appreciation and evaluation of the full range of individual Members' trade policies and practices and their impact on the functioning of the multilateral trading system").[45] Finally, Annex 4 includes some plurilateral agreements (e.g., the Government Procurement Agreement), which only binds some WTO Members.

42 Almost 60 years later, something similar might happen to the TPP. In both cases, the international agreement might not make sense without the U.S. membership.

43 For an informal summary of its texts, see The Havana Charter for an International Trade Organization, An Informal Summary, available at: https://docs.wto.org/gattdocs/q/GG/SEC/53-41.PDF (last visit, April 30, 2017). For the legal texts regarding the Havana Charter, see www.wto.org/english/docs_e/legal_e/havana_e.pdf.

44 See The WTO, www.wto.org/english/thewto_e/acc_e/cbt_course_e/intro_e.htm. Indeed, the largest economy outside the WTO measured by the GDP, is only the twenty-eighth largest economy (Iran). See The World Bank, http://data.worldbank.org/indicator/NY.GDP.MKTP.CD?order=wbapi_data_value_2014+wbapi_data_value+wbapi_data_value-last&sort=asc (last visit, April 30, 2017).

45 See WTO, www.wto.org/english/docs_e/legal_e/29-tprm_e.htm (last visit, April 30, 2017).

The WTO agreements are based on two main pillars: the Most Favored Nation clause and the National Treatment. MFN treatment (GATT Art. 1) means that any advantage that a WTO member concedes to another member shall be extended to all the other WTO members, unless a legal exception applies (for instance, when the advantage is granted to the countries belonging to the same Preferential Trade Agreement).[46] National treatment (GATT Art. 3), in turn, means that barriers (for instance, taxes) shall not favor domestic goods over foreign goods.

WTO rules are not the only legal rules governing international trade. Many countries have entered into hundreds of preferential trade agreements during the last decades, most of them bilateral or even having few but more than two signatories (e.g., NAFTA). Chapter 14 will discuss these preferential trade agreements in depth.

Before turning to the next section, it is worth mentioning that, nowadays, a significant amount of tariff barriers has disappeared and, therefore, the challenge is the enactment and enforcement of new WTO rules reducing non-tariff barriers.

1.4 Trade policy formulation systems (Trade PFS)

Governments have a variety of trade policy instruments to take advantage of international trade, on the one hand, and to avoid or at least minimize its harmful effects, on the other. Some of these instruments, to be discussed later on in this book, are: (i) negotiations intended to increase trade among some countries (multilateral, regional or bilateral); (ii) import tariffs whose reduction might escalate international trade and, conversely, whose increase might protect a domestic industry from foreign competition; (iii) trade remedies, intended to provide relief for domestic industries being severely injured by unfair trade practices from foreign competitors (antidumping and countervailing duties) or by a sudden upsurge in imports even if foreign competitors have not done anything wrong from a legal standpoint (safeguards); (iv) rules of origin; (v) technical barriers to trade; (vi) sanitary and phytosanitary measures; and (vii) Tariff Preference programs, such as GSP and AGOA.

Governments, of course, not only must implement the appropriate mix of trade policy measures but also should estimate whether or not they are performing well; that is, whether they are achieving their goals. Three kinds of indicators to measure such performance exist: (i) policy, (ii) economic, and (iii) socio-economic indicators. Policy indicators take into account the direction, intensity, coverage and sustainability of trade policies, their effect in the political processes both within a given country and abroad and the degree of involvement of such country in integration mechanisms such as preferential trade agreements.

Economic indicators, in turn, measure the effect of trade policies on economic variables such as economic growth (i.e., changes in GDP), the growth of exports

46 See *infra* Chapter 14.

and imports, the share of world trade, and the terms of trade. Finally, socio-economic indicators measure the impact of trade policies and, therefore, of increased trade flows on non-trade variables, such as poverty, income inequality, environmental protection, human rights protection, and human development.

National constitutions usually grant the authority to formulate the trade policy jointly to the Executive and the Legislative branches. Generally speaking, the Executive has the power to negotiate trade agreements and to impose trade remedies (subject to the review of the Judicial branch) while the Legislative might approve or reject such agreements. The precise powers of each branch depend on the constitutional rules of each country. That the Legislative and the Executive branches jointly have the power to formulate the trade policy of a country does not mean that the participation of the civil society is not important, especially in democratic regimes. Both the private and the public sectors usually suggest trade policy measures, protest if their suggestions are not taken into account, and impart legitimacy to the actions and decisions of a government. These sectors also verify that the trade policy-making is coupled with domestic public policies ensuring that the gains from international trade improve the welfare of a significant population and not only of a few sectors. If such verification concludes that the trade policy is neither well formulated nor implemented, such sectors might vote for a change in the Legislative and in the Executive branches.

Trade policy is the result of the interaction of four actors, no matter the country or political regime scrutinised. They are the Executive, the Legislative, the Private Sector, and the Public Interest. These four functions are performed in all forms of government, in one way or another. In democratic regimes, a president heads the **Executive**, comprised of ministers of State or cabinet secretaries responsible for specific areas. The **Legislative** is generally represented by a Congress, typically formed by an upper house – the Senate – and a lower house for deputies or the equivalent – the House of Representatives.

Under a monarchy, the king or queen may fulfill a dual role of legislating and executing, or determine that his closest advisor(s) act as legislator(s) or other. Parliamentary systems allow the monarch to transfer legislative responsibility to Parliament, while delegating Executive duties to the prime minister. In a purely dictatorial regime, the head of State assumes both Legislative and Executive duties. In other, less radical dictatorships, a junta may perform both Executive and Legislative functions or have a legislating body that is not entirely independent or other.

The Public Interest and the Private Sector are also present in all regimes, exerting varying degrees of influence. The political regime of a given country usually determines the level of freedom of action afforded to those groups. At one extreme, their activities may be entirely hindered while, on the other side of the spectrum, they may operate freely and unrestricted.

For the purposes of this book, the **Public Interest** consists of the civil society plus all international organizations that may affect trade policies, such as the World Trade Organization (WTO), the United Nations Conference on

Trade and Development (UNCTAD), the Organization of Economic Co-operation and Development (OECD), the International Bank for Reconstruction and Development (World Bank), and the International Monetary Fund (IMF). The Public Interest also includes social, environmental, and union concerns, as well as national and public safety concerns and other interests not directly related to the Private Sector. Finally, the **Private Sector** encompasses all for-profit businesses that are not owned or operated by the government.

How these four groups interact in order to generate a country's trade policies is called a **trade policy formulation system** or, in short, trade PFS. Trade policy, on the other hand, is the product of the interaction of the four above-mentioned groups and the various influencing factors that warrant consideration throughout the process. A discussion of trade PFS in the United States, the European Union, the so-called BRICS countries (Brazil, Russia, India, China and South Africa), Mexico, Canada and Australia follows in the next chapters.

2

THE U.S. TRADE POLICY SYSTEM

2.1 How players influence trade policy in the United States

This chapter describes the structure of the U.S. trade policy formulation system so as to assist the reader in understanding, on the one hand, how the four trade players (the Executive and the Legislative Branches, the Private Sector, and the Public Interest) influence public policies and, on the other hand, the U.S. perspective on trade issues and negotiations.

As the previous chapter indicated, and for any country, this book divides the players who may influence trade policy into four categories: The Executive Branch (or just the "Executive"), the Legislative Branch (or just the "Legislative"), the Private Sector, and the Public Interest. Needless to say, all four players interact among themselves in the international trade game. Therefore, as game theory indicates,[1] the decisions and strategies of any group influence the other players' moves, as Figure 1 shows.

Pursuant to the U.S. Constitution Art. 1, Section 8, Para. 3, the U.S. Congress has the power "[t]o regulate commerce with foreign nations." In other words, the Congress is the highest U.S. authority in trade matters. The reasons for this are not fortuitous and go back to some centuries ago. Recall that until not some many decades ago, tariffs were not only a barrier to protect domestic industries from foreign competition but also a method to raise revenues; that is, tariffs used to be regarded as taxes on imports. Recall also that "no taxation without representation" is a universal principle since the enactment of *Magna Carta* in the thirteenth century.[2] Indeed, taxes were one of the reasons leading to the U.S. independence

1 See Drew Fudenberg and Jean Tirole, *Game Theory* (1991).

2 Such *Magna Carta* was a charter that King John of England (known as John Lackland) was forced to sign in 1215 in order to avoid a rebellion of some barons. See generally Dan Jones, *Magna Carta: The Birth of Liberty* (2015).

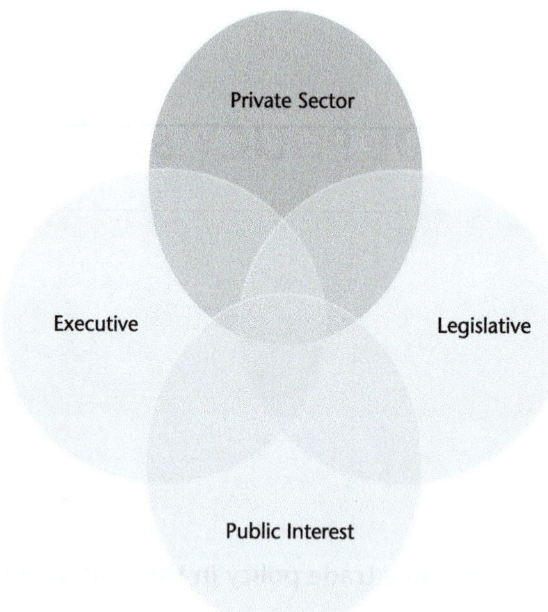

FIGURE 1 The four players in trade policy[3]

since the British Parliament was imposing them on the colonies without accepting individuals born there in its legislative branch.[4] The principle of no taxation without representation is part of the U.S. Constitution, whose Art. 1, Section 8, Para. 1 provides that "Congress shall have power to lay and collect taxes, duties, imposts and excises."

In spite of being the highest U.S. trade authority, Congress has temporarily delegated trade power to the Executive. The latter branch may start and conduct trade negotiations and, therefore, sign trade agreements, although these are not self-executing since Congress may either approve or reject them. For instance, the U.S. executive reached a preferential trade agreement with Colombia in 2006 but the U.S. Congress only approved it in 2011, entering in legal force on May 15, 2012.[5]

The U.S. Congress's power over a trade agreement is not, however, unlimited. On the contrary, and pursuant to the Trade Promotion Authority (the so-called Fast-Track), the U.S. Congress may approve or reject an agreement in its entirety but cannot either approve only part of it or modify it.

3 Figure made by the authors.

4 See generally Charles Adams, *Those Dirty Rotten Taxes: The Tax Revolts that Built America* (1998).

5 See USTR, United States-Colombia Trade Promotion Agreement, https://ustr.gov/trade-agreements/free-trade-agreements/colombia-tpa (last visit, April 30, 2017).

Self-imposed restrictions like this one, reminding of Odysseus putting wax in his ears to avoid yielding to the temptation of joining the sirens after listening to their enchanting songs,[6] make sense: trade negotiations are very complex and any agreement on a given issue depends on an agreement on all the other issues. After all, trade negotiations usually progress through a give-and-take approach. Thus, if the negotiated approach to one issue is modified or rejected (a topic where, for instance, the United Stated made a concession), there is no deal anymore regarding the other issues (topics where the United States might have received concessions from its counterparts), even if Congress left them unchanged. Other countries, anticipating this undesired outcome, might refrain from entering into negotiations in the first place.

As an additional self-imposed restriction, the U.S. Congress shall take a decision about whether or not to approve a trade agreement within a limited period once the Executive files it before the Legislative. This is also logical – market conditions might change very fast and the interest of the other parties to a trade agreement might decrease if the U.S. Congress lingers over the decision of whether or not to approve it for years.[7]

The Trade Promotion Authority has been in legal force during three stages. The first one was the Trade Act of 1975, which was in legal force from 1975 to 1994 and which allowed, for instance, the negotiation and approval of NAFTA. The second stage, the Trade Act of 2002, was in legal force from 2002 to 2007, although it was applicable to trade agreements that were already in negotiations in 2007 and that were signed by 2011. This Trade Act, for instance, was applicable to the preferential trade agreements with Peru and Colombia (in legal force since 2009 and 2012, respectively).[8] The first and current stage, the Trade Act of 2015, goes from 2015 to 2018, with a possible extension to 2021.

In any event, the U.S. trade policy is not the exclusive territory of the Executive and the Legislative Branches. On the contrary, it is the result of continuous and hard negotiations among diverse and seasoned political actors over a growing number of issues not restricted to purely trade topics such as tariff and non-tariff barriers but also related to international trade-related matters such as foreign investment, regulatory measures, impact of trade policies in the labor market, enforcement of intellectual property rights, human rights, and global warming and other environmental issues.

The political process described above, although very complex, might reach efficient outcomes. Each group (for instance, advocates of labor rights of domestic companies' personnel, free trade believers, politicians defending the rights of their constituents, etc.) fights for its own interests, emerging a great variety of proposals

6 See Homer, *The Odyssey* (Robert Fagles, Translator), p. 1 (1997).

7 See generally I. M. Destler, *American Trade Politics* (4th ed.), p.1 (2005).

8 See USTR, Western Hemisphere, https://ustr.gov/countries-regions/americas/ (last visit, April 30, 2017).

TABLE 5 The U.S. Executive Branch

The U.S. President			
President's offices	*Agencies and departments*		*Coordinating inter-agency groups*
Office of Trade and Manufacturing Policy (OTMP)	Department of State	Agency for International Development	Trade Policy Review Group
USTR	Department of the Treasury	Department of Defense	Trade Policy Advisory Committee
Domestic Policy Council	Department of Commerce	Department of Transportation	Trade Promotion Coordination Committee
National Security Council	Department of Agriculture	Department of Justice	Others
Council of Economic Advisers	Labor Department	Department of Interior	
Office of Management and Budget	Energy Department	Other departments and executive agencies	
	Environmental Protection Agency	Independent agencies/ International Trade Commission/ Export-import Bank/ Others	

that the Executive and the Legislative might take into account before formulating any trade policy. The complexity of this continuous interaction among many groups also entails that trade policy formulation requires highly qualified and experienced staff with backgrounds in law, politics and economics not only in the Executive and in the Legislative, but also in the Private Sector and in the Public Interest.

Before turning to a deeper explanation of the Private Sector and the Public Interest in the United States, some additional comments about the structure of the U.S. Executive Branch are needed. Table 5 lists the offices, agencies and groups that might be involved in the trade policy formulation within the U.S. Executive.

As its location in Table 5 suggests, the Office of the United States Trade Representative Office (USTR) has traditionally been the most important agency regarding U.S. trade policy. The U.S. Department of State was the entity in charge of trade matters until 1962, when the U.S. Congress rightly considered that a less bureaucratic, more efficient, more specialized, and more trade-sensitive agency should formulate and implement the U.S. trade policy. Thus, and under the Trade Expansion Act, the Kennedy administration established the Special Trade Representative whose purpose was "to balance foreign and domestic economic interests, coordinate the executive branch as a whole, and bargain with both

Congress and foreign governments."[9] Some years later and during the Nixon administration, the Trade Act of 1974 (the same act that established the already mentioned fast-track procedure), elevated the Special Trade Representative to cabinet level and made it accountable to both the President and the Congress.[10] In turn, the Executive Order 12188 of 1980 renamed the Special Trade Representative as the Office of the United States Trade Representative, or simply the USTR.

The USTR, through its about 200 employees,[11] leads the negotiations of trade agreements with foreign governments (either bilateral or plurilateral), oversees the Generalized System of Preferences, participates in meetings and negotiations related to WTO issues, interacts with international organizations, such as the OECD and UNCTAD, in trade-related matters, promotes the expansion of market access for U.S. goods and services, settles trade disputes with other countries, participates in global trade policy organizations, and interacts with members of the Executive, the Legislative, the Private Sector and the Public Interest both in the United States and abroad through its offices in, of course, Washington, D.C., Geneva (since the WTO is located there), Brussels (the seat of the most important institutions of the European Union), and Beijing (since China is one of the top three U.S. trade partners).[12]

Since 2017, however, and under Trump's administration, the USTR lost its leadership role in trade policy formulation to the Secretary of Commerce. In addition, a new Office of Trade and Manufacturing Policy (OTMP), substituting the short-lived National Trade Council, was created at the White House and tasked with proposing innovative strategies in trade negotiations and coordinating with other government agencies the assessment of the country's industrial capacity, among others.[13] As a result, and at the time of this writing, it is not clear whether the USTR will continue to coordinate trade policy formulation discussions within the Executive. Another change in 2017 is that trade policy will cease to be reactive to the wishes of the Private Sector and become proactive, with the initiative coming from the Executive.

It is now time to describe the importance of both the Private Sector and the Public Interest in the formulation of the U.S. trade policy. Before doing that, Figure 2 shows the interaction between these two players with the Legislative and the Executive.

9 U.S. Trade Expansion Act of 1962.

10 Trade Act of 1974 S 141.

11 See USTR, https://ustr.gov/about-us (last visit, April 30, 2017).

12 See United States Census Bureau, www.census.gov/foreign-trade/statistics/highlights/top/top1312yr.html (last visit, April 30, 2017).

13 See The White House, Presidential Executive Order on Establishment of Office of Trade and Manufacturing Policy, www.whitehouse.gov/the-press-office/2017/05/01/presidential-executive-order-establishment-office-trade-and (last visit, May 18, 2017). See also The Wall Street Journal, *Despite Setbacks, Trump's Trade Warrior Peter Navarro Is Fighting On*, www.wsj.com/articles/despite-setbacks-trumps-trade-warrior-peter-navarro-is-fighting-on-1494275645 (last visit, May 18, 2017).

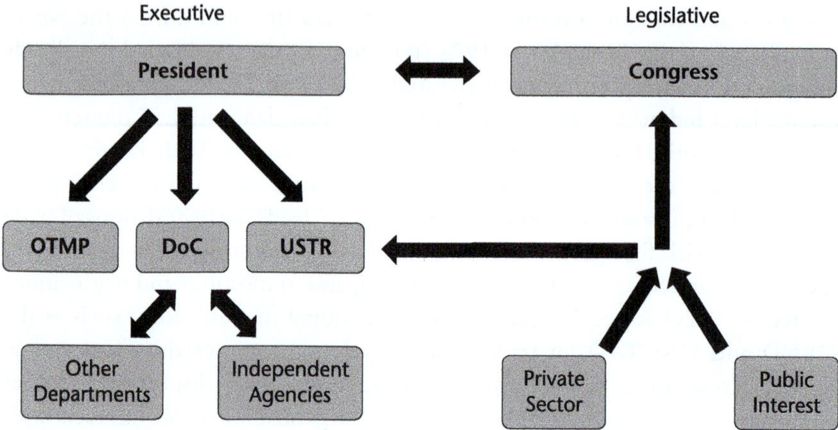

FIGURE 2 Interaction of players in U.S. trade policy[14]

The Private Sector is a set of diverse interest groups. This book, in turn, defines an interest group as an organization of people with shared ideas and attitudes in trade-related matters and whose purpose is to influence public policies or, more particularly, to change the trade policy in accordance with the group's views. To put it differently, interest groups engage in lobby activities intended to persuade the Legislative, the Executive or both of them of enacting laws or other kinds of legal rules, abrogating them, approving (or rejecting) a trade agreement, protecting a given domestic industry through trade remedies, eliminating such trade remedies in order to benefit some importers, etc. Interest groups in particular, and the Private Sector in general, are aware that the Legislative and the Executive are institutions that react to stimuli. Thus, the stronger the lobby and the pressure in favor (or against) a given trade policy, the higher the odds that the Legislative or the Executive approves (or rejects) it.

Given the complexities of the U.S. trade policy, it is not surprising that, at the time of writing this book, over 11,000 interest groups exist in Washington, D.C., the seat of both the U.S. Executive and the U.S. Legislative branches. In any event, such a figure and the money spent in lobby activities as well have been steadily decreasing since at least 2008, as Table 6 indicates.[15]

Nonetheless, Table 6's figures might be very conservative since many groups engaged in lobby activities are not registered. Thus, the real number of lobbyists in 2015 might have been up to eight times the figure reported in Table 6.[16]

14 Figure made by the authors.

15 See Center for Responsive Politics, www.opensecrets.org/ (last visit, April 30, 2017). The Center for Responsive Politics is a non-profit, nonpartisan research group based in Washington, D.C., that estimates the effects of lobbying on public policies. See *id.*

16 See The Nation, *Where Have All the Lobbyists Gone?*, www.thenation.com/article/shadow-lobbying-complex/ (last visit, April 30, 2017).

TABLE 2 The U.S. lobby industry

Year	*Registered groups*	*Expenditures (in US$ billion)*
2008	14,206	3.3
2009	13,767	3.5
2010	12,949	3.5
2011	12,628	3.3
2012	12,183	3.3
2013	12,118	3.2
2014	11,818	3.2
2015	11,169	2.4

In the same vein, the total expenses related to lobby activities might be in the order of 9 billion U.S. dollars.[17] Put it another way, while at first sight the size of the lobby industry might have decreased, a closer look reveals that part of it has gone underground.

As the above-mentioned figures indicate, lobbying is a well-developed industry in the United States. It hires communication people and public relations firms, technicians, lawyers, former politicians, economic advisors, and experts in several areas. It is also a complex industry since its activities, related with many sectors of the economy, deal with a wide variety of issues, such as protection of industries, labor standards, pollution and human rights.

The best way to graphically represent the Private Sector and its lobby activities, not only in the United States but also in other countries, is by drawing a tree. The tree's deepest roots are influential individuals, local groups and local associations. The opinions of these individuals and entities filter to state associations, which may be drawn as shallower roots. Federal associations, the tree's trunk, adopt the most important of these opinions and make them national. As a tree needs a root to take nutrients from the soil and a trunk to transport them to other parts of it, groups and associations take ideas from their members and, by employing experts in several areas, communicate them to the media, the Executive and the Legislative (the tree's branches), intending to influence their decisions. The leaves and fruits are the final outcome that national associations seek: making sure that the interest of the group is reflected in a law, a regulation, any other kind of a governmental decision or, in general, a public policy (either against or pro trade). Figure 3 shows the U.S. tree.

17 See *id.*

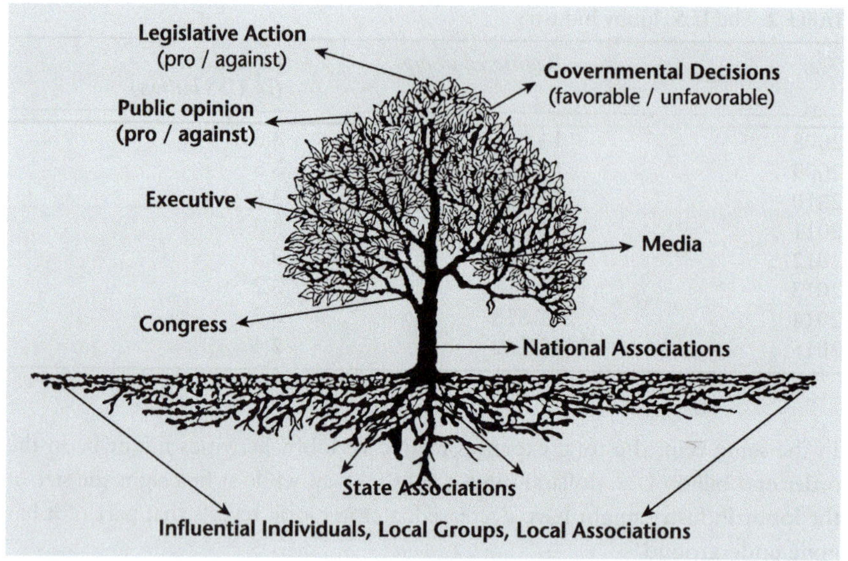

FIGURE 3 The U.S. tree[18]

The fourth and final participant in the formulation of any trade policy is the Public Interest. This player is composed of all organizations not included in the other roles (the Executive, the Legislative, and the Private Sector). In other words, the Public Interest is composed of non-profit organizations that might be either in favor of or against international trade but that does not represent a given group or industry. Such organizations might be: (i) think tanks, such as the American Enterprise Institute for Public Policy Research,[19] the Brookings Institution,[20] the Cato Institute,[21] the Carnegie Endowment for International Peace,[22] the Center for Global Development,[23] the Peterson Institute for International Economics,[24] and the Inter-American Dialogue[25]; (ii)labor organizations such as the American Federation of Labor – Congress of Industrial Organizations,[26] the Congress of Industrial Organizations (which merged with the American Federation of Labor in 1955),[27]

18 Figure made by the authors.
19 See www.aei.org (last visit, April 30, 2017).
20 See www.brookings.edu (last visit, April 30, 2017).
21 See www.cato.org (last visit, April 30, 2017).
22 See www.carnegieendowment.org (last visit, April 30, 2017).
23 See www.cgdev.org (last visit, April 30, 2017).
24 See https://piie.com/ (last visit, April 30, 2017).
25 See www.thedialogue.org (last visit, April 30, 2017).
26 See www.aflcio.org/ (last visit, April 30, 2017).
27 See Encyclopedia of Chicago, available at: www.encyclopedia.chicagohistory.org/pages/326.html (last visit, April 30, 2017).

the International Labor Organization,[28] and the International Brotherhood of Teamsters (a trade union)[29]; (iii) Non-governmental organizations whose purpose is the defense of human rights, the environment, the alternative forms of energy, the consumers, etc.; and (iv) international organizations such as, of course, the WTO,[30] the UNCTAD,[31] the WB,[32] the IMF,[33] the IADB,[34] The UN,[35] the United Nations Food and Agriculture Organization,[36] and the International Progress Organization.[37] As a general rule, the more organized the Public Interest, the stronger its influence in the formulation of trade policy. For instance, consumers are rarely politically organized and, therefore, they often end up suffering the negative consequences of new trade policies.

2.2 The U.S. perspective on trade issues and negotiations

Once the four participants in the formulation of U.S. trade policy have been described, this chapter turns to, first, the decision process; second, the trade policy instruments; and third, some comments on the U.S. international trade policy.

The decision process in the United States is complex and lengthy. Both the Private Sector and the Public Interest submit many trade policy proposals to the USTR. This entity, through two inter-ministerial committees and several sub-committees, leads the discussion of such proposals with the agencies and departments in the Executive that might have a say on the matter. This is done through the Trade Policy Review Group.

The decision making within the Executive is usually by consensus, an approach which, needless to say, slows the process and facilitates protectionism since the negative vote of only one agency might block a pro-trade policy. The bright side of this approach is its contribution to transparency. If consensus arises and the Executive has the power to enact a new trade legal rule, it does so. Sometimes, however, the Congress has the last say, especially if the proposal relates to changes in tariffs or to the ratification of a trade agreement (recall that Congress holds the highest authority on those issues). Regardless of whether or not a proposal succeeds, decisions are always the result of the interaction of the four players and,

28 This, as its name suggests, is not an U.S. but an international organization. See The International Labor Organization, www.ilo.org (last visit, April 30, 2017).

29 See The International Brotherhood of Teamsters, https://teamster.org/ (last visit, April 30, 2017).

30 See The World Trade Organization, www.wto.org (last visit, April 30, 2017).

31 See The United Nations Conference on Trade and Development, www.unctad.org/en (last visit, April 30, 2017).

32 See The World Bank, www.worldbank.org (last visit, April 30, 2017).

33 See The International Monetary Fund, www.imf.org (last visit, April 30, 2017).

34 See The Inter-American Development Bank, www.iadb.org (last visit, April 30, 2017).

35 See The United Nations, www.un.org/en/ (last visit, April 30, 2017).

36 See The United Nations Food and Agriculture Organization, www.fao.org (last visit, April 30, 2017).

37 See The International Progress Organization, www.i-p-o.org (last visit, April 30, 2017).

TABLE 7 The rank of players' influence on U.S. trade PFS (1 = more influence)

Player	*2009–2016*	*2017–*
Executive	3.0	1.0
Legislative	2.0	3.0
Private sector	1.0	2.0
Public interest	4.0	4.0

more generally, the outcome of a political process highly influenced by the priorities of the industries and people that the new trade policy might benefit or affect.

It is possible to rank the influence of the main actors in the U.S. trade policy formulation, as Table 7 shows. There, changes from the previous administration to the present one can be observed, ranking ranges from 1 (strongest influence) to 4 (least relative influence). As mentioned earlier, there was a major change in the U.S. trade policy formulation in 2017. In addition to the change in leadership (from the USTR leadership to a 'troika'), trade policy ceased to be reactive (to the wishes of the U.S. Private Sector), to be proactive with the initiative originating in the Executive.

In the previous eight years, the Private Sector had the most influence in negotiations. The recommendation then was that an understanding with the Private Sector should be sought prior to negotiations with the Executive in order to guarantee an agreement. In 2017, the Private Sector shifts to a secondary place in terms of influence, but continues to be more influential than Congress. This makes sense, since the Private Sector plays an important role in the election of senators and House representatives.

On the other hand, Section 301 of the Trade Act of 1974,[38] about the authorities and procedures to enforce legal trade rules, is one of the main U.S. trade policy instruments. The goal of this section is to enforce U.S. rights when foreign countries breach trade agreements or engage in unjustifiable, unreasonable or discriminatory foreign trade practices which burden or restrict U.S. commerce.[39] When the USTR determines that a foreign act, policy or practice breaches or is inconsistent with a trade agreement, or is unjustifiable, the Executive shall impose sanctions.[40] If, on the contrary, the foreign legal rule or practice is unreasonable or discriminatory, the measure is discretionary.[41]

The sanctions that the Executive might impose are, among others, the following ones:(i) to suspend, withdraw, or prevent the application of trade concessions to the foreign country involved; (ii) to impose duties or other import restrictions on the goods or services coming from the foreign country during the period that

38 19 U.S.C. § 2411.
39 See *id.*
40 See *id.*
41 See *id.*

the USTR deems appropriate; or (iii) to withdraw or suspend preferential duty treatment under the Generalized System of Preferences.[42]

Section 337 of the Trade Act of 1930 is also relevant for the understanding of the U.S. trade policy.[43] The goal of this section is to protect U.S. industries from foreign unfair competition, such as violations of U.S. patents, copyrights or other intellectual property rights.[44] If there is evidence of a breach of such rights, the International Trade Commission might issue an exclusion/cease and desist order (i.e., and order to stop the acts that are in breach of the U.S. legal rules), which the U.S. President might validate or disapprove.[45] For instance, the United States might impose sanctions against countries breaching intellectual property rights which are within the scope of a trade agreement.[46]

Trade remedies, which will be analyzed in detail in Chapter 11, are another and very common kind of trade policy instrument. These remedies might be antidumping duties (the most common kind), countervailing duties, or safeguards. The purpose of antidumping duties is to protect a U.S. industry against the imports coming from a country where one or more companies export goods at a price below their fair value (domestic price or cost of production). Once some companies accounting for the 25 percent or more of the industry's output have filed a petition to impose these kind of duties, the Department of Commerce evaluates whether or not the alleged dumping exists (i.e., whether or not the price is less than the fair value of the product) while the international Trade Commission establishes whether or not the dumping causes material injury (or the threat of) to the affected U.S. industry.[47] If the investigation is favorable for the domestic industry, an additional duty is applied on top of the existing tariffs for imports coming from the companies engaged in the dumping activities.[48] These additional duties are applied retrospectively, i.e., once they are imposed they may be reviewed one year later. The review takes about one year and if the duties are modified, either upwards or downwards, they are implemented retroactively to the date when they were first imposed, which could be two or two and a half years earlier.

Antidumping and countervailing duties share the same goal: to protect a domestic industry from unfair competition from abroad. The similarities do not stop there: countervailing duties, as its name suggests, also consists of a duty on top of the existing tariff. Countervailing duties, however, do not intend to offset the sale of goods at a price below its fair value but to offset the granting of subsidies from a foreign government to the companies where the imports come from. The procedure to establish a countervailing duty is very similar to the one

42 See *id.*
43 19 U.S.C. §1337.
44 See *id.*
45 See *id.*
46 See *id.*
47 See Trade Act of 1974.
48 See Trade Act of 1974.

to establish an antidumping duty: the Department of Commerce evaluates whether or not another country has granted a subsidy that the WTO legal rules regards as illegal while the International Trade Commission establishes whether such subsidy causes material injury (or threat of).[49]

Safeguards are the third and less common kind of trade remedies. Similar to antidumping and countervailing duties, safeguards consist of a temporal extra tariff to the imports of some goods. In contrast to antidumping duties (which might be imposed even to only one company) and countervailing duties (which are imposed to the imports coming from the country where the government grants the subsidy), safeguards shall be imposed across the board, i.e., to all other WTO Members, with few exceptions.[50] Indeed, this is one of the reasons explaining why safeguards are scarcer than antidumping and countervailing duties[51]; after all, its imposition might annoy some foreign governments which, as a result, might politically retaliate. As another reason for its less frequent imposition, a safeguard can only be levied if there is evidence of both a sudden and significant import increase and the existence of a serious injury, or threat thereof (another difference with dumping and subsidies, where the standard is lower – material injury).[52]

A fourth and very controversial U.S. trade policy instrument is the imposition of tariff-rate quotas. Under this kind of quota, the imports below some threshold (e.g., the first 10,000 tons) are subject to a low tariff (the so-called inside tariff) while any amount in excess of this limit shall pay a much higher tariff (the outside tariff). If, as sometimes happens, the outside tariff is prohibitive, the tariff-rate quota is equivalent to an absolute quota, which GATT Art. XI para. 1 prohibits. The evident and perhaps illegal purpose of tariff rate quotas is to protect a domestic industry by limiting the quantity of the imports of like products. Thus, and according to microeconomic theory,[53] the domestic industry may consider at least part of the domestic consumers as a captive market and, therefore, charge higher prices.

The trade policy instruments indicated above are intended to protect domestic industries and therefore, might restrict rather than promote international trade. Preferential trade agreements and preference programs, in contrast, are trade policy instruments whose main purpose is to increase both exports and imports. Tables 8 and 9 show the trade agreements which the United States are currently a party to. It is worth mentioning that the Trans-Atlantic Trade and Investment Partnership is not included there because it is still under negotiation. Although an agreement was reached in 2015, the Trans-Pacific Partnership is also not

49 See Trade Act of 1974. See also the WTO Agreement on Subsidies and Countervailing Measures.

50 See the WTO Agreement on Safeguards, Art. 2, para. 2.

51 For some statistics, see *infra* Chapter 11.

52 See WTO Agreement on Safeguards, Art. 2, para. 1. *Cfr.* WTO Agreements on Antidumping duties and on Subsidies and Countervailing Measures.

53 See generally, Hal R. Varian, *Intermediate Microeconomics: A Modern Approach* (9th ed.), p. 1 (2014).

TABLE 8 U.S. preferential trade agreements (regional)

Regional trade agreements	
Treaty	*Parties other than the United States*
NAFTA	Canada and Mexico
CAFTA – DR	Costa Rica, Dominican Republic, El Salvador, Guatemala, Honduras, and Nicaragua
MEFTI	Middle Eastern countries
Enterprise for ASEAN Initiative	Brunei, Cambodia, Indonesia, Laos, Malaysia, Myanmar, Philippines, Singapore, Thailand and Vietnam
APEC	Pacific Rim countries

TABLE 9 U.S. preferential trade agreements (bilateral)

Bilateral trade agreements
Australia
Bahrain
Chile
Colombia
Israel
Jordan
Korea
Morocco
Oman
Pakistan
Panama
Peru
Singapore

included because, at the time of writing this book, the U.S. Congress had not approved it and President Donald J. Trump filed the 180 days' advanced notice of withdrawal from the agreement.[54]

On the other hand, and under preference programs, developed countries usually grant preferential tariff rates to imports from some developing countries and least-developed countries. The drawback of these programs, in comparison with preferential trade agreements, is that they are temporary and, therefore, less useful to serve as the basis for the expansion of some industries in other countries since the preferences may phase out before an entrepreneur has recouped its investment.

54 See The USTR, *The United States Officially Withdraws from the Trans-Pacific Partnership*, https://ustr.gov/about-us/policy-offices/press-office/press-releases/2017/january/US-Withdraws-From-TPP (last visit, April 30, 2017).

At first sight, preference programs would be against one of the WTO pillars: the MFN principle, embodied in GATT Art. I. The Contracting Parties to the GATT, however, allowed this kind of program by carving out an exception to this principle through the so-called enabling clause. This exception is logical. After all, preference programs seek to improve economic and social indicators and alleviate poverty in countries struggling with slow or elusive economic growth or with other kinds of issues through the concession of trade advantages. Since these developing and least-developed countries are usually not very competitive from a trade standpoint, it is unlikely that such advantages might alter the checks and balances of global trade or that might materially harm a domestic industry. To put it differently, developed and wealthy countries are not going to suffer a strong impact (or they might not suffer an impact at all) because of the advantages granted to countries with a marginal participation in global trade. Chapter 10 analyzes in more depth trade preference programs, which are not only trade policy tools but also geopolitical and strategic tools as well.[55]

The United States currently grants trade advantages through the following preference programs: (i) GSP – General System of Preferences (currently expired), (ii) AGOA – African Growth and Opportunity Act, (iii) ATPDEA – Andean Trade Promotion and Drug Enforcement Act, and (iv) CBI – Caribbean Basin Initiative (which comprises the Caribbean Basin Economic Recovery Act or CBERA, the Caribbean Basin Trade and Partnership Act or CBTPA, and the Haiti Hemispheric Opportunity through Partnership Encouragement or the HOPE Act).

As a summary, this chapter ends with some positive and negative comments on the U.S. trade policy. On the bright side, the U.S. trade policy: (i) has a well-defined and robust structure, (ii) is transparent, with actors whose roles have been clearly divided, and with a structure enabling both the Private Sector and the Public Interest a swift access to the right authority, and (iii) is the result of the interaction of the four players and, in general, of very well-qualified personnel in diverse areas of expertise, which gives an advantage to the United States in trade negotiations since most other countries lack this access to seasoned trade professionals.[56]

On the negative side, the United States might have abused its strong position in international trade by the adoption of several strategies. First, the United States has granted huge and perhaps illegal subsidies and imposed trade distorting tariff rate quotas on certain imports in order to protect its agricultural industry. Second, antidumping and countervailing duties might have been applied in ways that could be considered excessive or domestic-industry biased by taking advantage of some loopholes in the WTO legal rules. For instance, the U.S. antidumping duties

55 See *infra* Chapter 10.

56 See I. M. Destler, *American Trade Politics* (4th ed.), p. 1 (2005). This feature is positive regarding the U.S. trade policy but less-favorable if such policy is considered under a global approach.

usually are in legal force for many years, regardless of five-year reviews (designed to revoke duties, except if the U.S. authorities decide that it can lead to recurrence of dumping and injury) or whether the market conditions of the protected industry have changed.[57] Third, the United States have omitted or delayed the compliance with some rulings of the Appellate Body that have considered some U.S. measures to be against the WTO legal rules. Some examples are the Byrd amendment,[58] the cotton subsidies,[59] and the zeroing practices.[60]

57 See Aluisio de Lima-Campos and Adriana Vito, *Abuse and Discretion*, 38(1) J. World Trade 34 (2004).

58 See United States – Continued Dumping and Subsidy Offset Act of 2000 (DS 217).

59 See United States – Subsidies on Upland Cotton (DS 267).

60 See United States – Laws, Regulations and Methodology for Calculating Dumping Margins (Zeroing) (DS 294).

3

THE E.U.'S TRADE POLICY SYSTEM

3.1 The E.U.'s system

This chapter describes how trade policy is formulated in the European Union. Before discussing trade issues and taking into account that this is the only chapter of this section whose subject is not a country but a supranational organization composed of 28 countries, the text first summarizes the history and evolution of the European Union. Indeed, the European Union is an economic union, the deepest form of integration as far as trade agreements are concerned. It goes beyond a simple trade agreement and a customs union (equivalent to a trade agreement plus a common external tariff) to include also common economic policies. The European Union is also one of the three largest players in international trade (alongside the United States and China).[1]

Once the generalities of the European Union have been described, this chapter explains the structure of the European trade PFS; how the four players (the Executive, the Legislative, the Private Sector and the Public Interest) influence the E.U.'s trade policy; and the European perspective on trade issues and negotiations.

Some figures confirm the importance of the European Union as a significant trade policy maker. Its GDP is the largest in the world ($18.5 trillion dollars in 2014),[2] accounting for 23 percent of the world GDP.[3] The European Union is also the second-largest exporter and importer of goods, accounting for around 20 percent of the global trade in spite of only having 7 percent of the world's

1 See The World Bank, http://data.worldbank.org/indicator/NE.EXP.GNFS.ZS (last visit, April 30, 2017).

2 See The World Bank, http://data.worldbank.org/region/EUU (last visit, April 30, 2017). See also European Union, http://europa.eu/about-eu/facts-figures/economy/index_en.htm (last visit, April 30, 2017). In spite of this chapter focusing on the European Union, all figures are in U.S. dollars. This comment is applicable to all the other chapters of this book.

3 See The World Bank, http://data.worldbank.org/region/EUU (last visit, April 30, 2017).

population.[4] On top of that, the European Union is both the major source of foreign direct investment in the world ($210 billion in 2013) and the largest recipient of it ($342 billion in 2013).[5]

With the advent of Brexit (short for Britain's exit – an in-depth discussion of Brexit ahead in this section), the United Kingdom's withdrawal from the European Union should be concluded by April 2019, if the regular two-year process period runs through. In such a case, new statistics for the European Union, without the United Kingdom, will be needed.

3.2 The E.U.'s background and institutions

The first attempts of integrating some European countries happened in 1948, shortly after the end of the Second World War, when Belgium, France, Luxembourg, the Netherlands, and the United Kingdom entered into the Brussels Treaty establishing the Western European Union and providing a mutual defense clause. A few years later (in 1951), Belgium, France, Italy, Luxembourg, the Netherlands, and West Germany signed the Treaty of Paris establishing the European Coal and Steel Community. The purpose of this treaty was to share the production and distribution of the two main inputs of any war at this time: coal and steel and, as a result, to prevent a new and devastating global conflict. The Treaty of Paris was in legal force from July 23, 1952 until the same date 50 years later.

Six years after the signing of the Treaty of Paris, the six original members entered into another agreement: the Treaty of Rome, which established the European Economic Community. This treaty reduced the tariffs levied on goods coming from other members and intended to establish a customs union and even a common market in the short term. It also encouraged in the short term the coordination of national trade policies and, by establishing the European Commission, even intended, in the long term, to consolidate trade policy formulation in one supranational body.

Some further steps in the process of trade liberalization and, more generally, in the process of a deeper integration among the members of the European Economic Community were taken during the following years. First, the Treaty of Brussels of 1965, also known as the Merger Treaty, substituted the Commission and the Council of the European Economic Communities for not only the former executive bodies of this organization but also the former bodies of both the European Coal and Steel Community and the European Atomic Energy Community.

Second, an external common tariff was adopted in 1968 (fulfilling one of the goals of the Treaty of Rome of establishing a customs union).[6] Third, the Single

4 See European Union, http://europa.eu/about-eu/facts-figures/economy/index_en.htm (last visit, February 20, 2016).

5 See European Union, http://ec.europa.eu/economy_finance/international/globalisation/fdi/index_en.htm (last visit, April 30, 2017).

6 For the definition of a custom union, whose main feature is an external common tariff, see *infra* Chapter 11.

European Act was enacted in 1987. This Act, which amended the Treaty of Rome, set the basis for the establishment of a single or common market (another goal of the Treaty of Rome). Fourth, the Treaty of Maastricht, also known as the Treaty on European Union, was signed in the Dutch city of the same name in 1992. This treaty paved the way for the adoption of a single European currency: the euro, which was launched as an accounting and virtual currency in 1999 and as legal tender in 2002.[7] Nowadays, 16 of the 28 E.U. Member States are part of the so-called Eurozone (Austria, Belgium, Cyprus, Finland, France, Germany, Greece, Ireland, Italy, Luxemburg, Malta, the Netherlands, Portugal, Slovakia, Slovenia, and Spain).[8]

The Treaty of Maastricht also established the E.U.'s three pillars. The first one, the European Communities pillar, relates to unified policies regarding: (i) a customs union and a single market, (ii) a Common Agricultural Policy or CAP, and also a common fisheries policy, (iii) E.U.'s legal rules on competition and consumer protection, (iv) an economic and monetary union, (v) an E.U.'s citizenship, (vi) common policies on education and culture, (vii) healthcare, and (viii) environmental laws. This pillar's purpose was to move the process of public policies' formulation from the national echelons to the supranational level in search of a unique and stronger speaker representing E.U. Members in multilateral and regional arenas.

The Common Foreign and Security Policy (CFSP) is the second pillar. As its name indicates, this pillar deals with two main topics: foreign policy (human rights, democracy, and foreign aid), and security policy (European security and defense policy). The Police and Judicial Cooperation in Criminal Matters (PJCC), the third pillar, relates to the prevention and control of illegal activities such as drug trafficking, money laundering, weapons smuggling and terrorism.

The Treaty of Maastricht has been amended three times. The Treaty of Amsterdam of 1997, which was the first amendment, entered into legal force in 1999 and granted more powers to the European Parliament. The Treaty of Nice, signed in 2001 and in legal force since 2003, prepared the European Union for receiving some Central and Eastern European countries as new members. In particular, the Treaty of Nice:

> established a new base line for the exercise of trade policy powers by the Commission, by including most areas of services as exclusive supranational competence, but excluding a number of sensitive sectors and still retaining certain rights of national action for member states.[9]

Finally, the Treaty of Lisbon, signed in 2007 and in legal force since 2009, not only amended the Treaty of Maastricht but also the Treaty of Rome by making

7 See Euro, *Everything related to Euro and European Union and Schengen Visa*, www.euro-dollar-currency.com/history_of_euro.htm (last visit, April 30, 2017).

8 See *id.*

9 Andrea C. Bianculli and Andrea Ribeiro (Eds), *Regional Organizations and Social Policy in Europe and Latin America. A Space for Social Citizenship?* p. 405 (2015).

some changes to the E.U.'s institutions. In particular, the Treaty of Lisbon changed the name of this supranational organization from the European Communities to the European Union; further strengthened the role of the European Parliament; granted major competences to the European Union in topics related to services, intellectual property rights, and foreign direct investment; ended the three pillars' system by merging them and giving legal personality to the European Union.

The membership of the European Union has significantly grown since its establishment. As already stated, its six initial members were Belgium, France, Italy, Luxembourg, the Netherlands, and West Germany (Germany since the reunification in 1990). The first enlargement happened in 1973 when Denmark, Ireland and The United Kingdom were accepted as members. Greece was the tenth member in 1981, and Spain and Portugal the eleventh and twelfth countries belonging to this supranational organization in 1986. Nine years later, Austria, Finland and Sweden were new members. The fifth, largest and most controversial enlargement happened in the first decade of the twentieth century when the European Union expanded to Eastern Europe, integrating, among others, some countries which had previously been behind the so-called Iron Curtain. Thus, the European Union grew from 14 to 24 members when Cyprus, the Czech Republic, Estonia, Hungary, Latvia, Lithuania, Malta, Poland, Slovakia, and Slovenia were accepted into the organization in 2004. The second part of this fifth enlargement came with the accession of Bulgaria and Romania in 2007 and of Croatia in 2013, which was the last one of the current 28 members. Albania, Montenegro, Serbia, the Former Yugoslav Republic of Macedonia, and Turkey are the current candidates, although it is unclear when their accession will be approved since such process is a complex one, especially after Brexit.[10] Turkey, because of the size of its economy and also due to some political and religious issues, might be the most complicated case. Besides these countries, Bosnia and Herzegovina and Kosovo are potential candidates, although its accession to the European Union would likely not occur in the short- or mid-term.[11]

However, the E.U.'s developments do not stop with the Treaty of Lisbon. After years of deepening integration, the United Kingdom in 2017 decided to initiate exit procedures from the European Union. Before describing the results of the referendum in the so-called Brexit process, it is worth mentioning some background. First of all, recall that the United Kingdom was not one of the original members of the European Coal and Steel Community and only became a member of the European Economic Community in 1973. The British people approved such membership in a referendum held in 1975.[12] Nevertheless, the

10 See European Union http://europa.eu/about-eu/countries/index_en.htm (last visit, April 30, 2017).

11 See *id.*

12 See Council on Foreign Relations, *What Brexit Means*, www.cfr.org/united-kingdom/debate-over-brexit/p37747?cid=ppc-Google_grant-brexit_backgrounder-061315&gclid=CKD0k7WNj88CFVVahgodX5wMnQ (last visit, April 30, 2017).

U.K.'s integration with the European Union was not as deep as in the case of most other E.U. Members. The United Kingdom, for instance, never joined either the border-free Schengen area[13] or the euro currency market, keeping the pound sterling as its currency.[14]

Indeed, opposition to the European Union has always been strong in the United Kingdom based on at least two grounds. First, the possibility that such union could be in the future and through the adoption of a constitution, more a supra-state (i.e., the United States of Europe) than a supranational organization. Such deepening of European integration would entail more power for international organizations in Brussels, whose processes are regarded as bureaucratic, not accountable, and not very transparent by some British players.[15] Second, some British politicians, companies and people were not satisfied with the E.U.'s enlarging process, which enabled the access of Eastern Europe countries whose population might migrate to wealthier areas within the European Union such as, of course, the United Kingdom.[16]

These issues, in addition to other heated topics such as the allocation of people from Africa and the Middle-East seeking asylum in E.U. Member States and the coordination of fiscal policy in the wake of the financial crises of some E.U. Members such as Greece led the U.K.'s government, chaired by the former Prime Minister David Cameron, to request changes to the E.U.'s structure in four major areas: national sovereignty, immigration policy, financial and economic regulation, and competitiveness.[17] In spite of the fact that the E.U.'s leaders accepted some but not all of these changes, opposition to the membership of the European Union did not decline and, as a result, Mr. Cameron decided to comply with his campaign promise of holding a referendum about whether the United Kingdom should stay in or leave the European Union.

On June 23, 2016, a referendum was held in which the voters were asked the following question: "Should the United Kingdom remain a member of the European Union or leave the European Union?"[18] More than 30 million people voted (71.8 percent out of the total registered voters) with a close result that was

13 Named after the Schengen agreement, signed in 1985 in a town with the same name in Luxembourg, this treaty harmonized visa procedures and eliminated border and passport controls for people from the signatory countries. See Schengen Visa Info, www.schengenvisainfo.com/schengen-visa-countries-list/ (last visit, April 30, 2017).

14 See generally http://ec.europa.eu/economy_finance/euro/index_en.htm (last visit, April 30, 2017).

15 See, e.g., Julian Birkinshaw, *Three Bureaucracy Busting Lessons from Brexit*, Forbes, July 7 2016, available at: www.forbes.com/sites/lbsbusinessstrategyreview/2016/07/07/three-bureaucracy-busting-lessons-from-brexit/#31146cde445f (last visit, April 30, 2017).

16 See Council on Foreign Relations, What Brexit Means, www.cfr.org/united-kingdom/debate-over-brexit/p37747?cid=ppc-Google_grant-brexit_backgrounder-061315&gclid=CKD0k7WNj88CFVVahgodX5wMnQ (last visit, April 30, 2017).

17 See *id.*

18 See Official Website of the United Kingdom Government, www.gov.uk/government/topical-events/eu-referendum/about (last visit, April 30, 2017).

surprisingly different from what recent polls had predicted: 52 percent in favor of the United Kingdom leaving the European Union and 48 percent voting for this country staying as a member of this supranational organization.[19]

The results had a significant and revealing variance among ages. Most older people voted for the leaving option while younger individuals favored the remaining option. The results also differed along geographical areas: while England and Wales voted for leaving the European Union (53.4 percent versus 46.7 percent and 52.5 percent and 47.5 percent, respectively), Scotland and Northern Ireland voted for remaining in this supranational organization (62.0 percent versus 38.0 percent and 55.8 percent and 44.2 percent, respectively).[20] The Scotland case is the most striking not only because the double digit difference between the remain and leave options but also because on September 18, 2014 55.3 percent of Scottish people voted *No* in a referendum to the question "Should Scotland be an independent country" (44.7 percent for *Yes*).[21] Some of the people voting *No* may have based their decisions on the fact that an independent Scotland, at the time of this referendum, would not have been an automatic member of the European Union.

On top of that, no provision of the Treaty of Lisbon or of any other E.U. treaties grants legal significance to the referendum results. In spite of not only this legal background but also of some people asking for a new referendum and on the fact that she was in favor of the remain option, the new Prime Minister Theresa May has clearly stated that "Brexit means Brexit" and that there will not be any attempt to remain in the European Union.[22]

Besides the political consequences that led to the resignation of David Cameron (who, despite calling the referendum, campaigned for the remain option) and the appointment of Theresa May as his successor, the referendum has significant legal and economic consequences. Legally speaking, the referendum's results are not mandatory since the Parliament, and not the people, is the only authority which can opt the United Kingdom out of the European Union.[23] Indeed, this was what

19 See BBC (British Broadcasting Corporation), *Brexit: All You Need to Know about the UK Leaving the E.U.* (April 25, 2017), www.bbc.com/news/uk-politics-32810887 (last visit, April 30, 2017).

20 See BBC, www.bbc.com/news/politics/eu_referendum/results (last visit, April 30, 2017).

21 See BBC, www.bbc.com/news/events/scotland-decides/results (last visit, April 30, 2017).

22 See *Theresa May says 'Brexit means Brexit' and there will be no Attempt to Remain Inside EU* (July 11, 2016), www.independent.co.uk/news/uk/politics/theresa-may-brexit-means-brexit-conservative-leadership-no-attempt-remain-inside-eu-leave-europe-a7130596.html (last visit, April 30, 2017). See also *Exiting the European Union: Ministerial Statement* 5 November 2016, www.gov.uk/government/speeches/exiting-the-european-union-ministerial-statement-5-september-2016 (last visit, April 30, 2017) (reporting the statement of the Secretary of State, David Davis, who said before the House of Commons that, since the instructions from the British people were clear, the United Kingdom will leave the European Union and that there will be "[n]o attempt to delay, frustrate or thwart the will of the British people" and also "[n]o attempt to engineer a second referendum."

23 See *Can the United Kingdom Government Legally Disregard a Vote for Brexit?* (June 14, 2016), http://blogs.ft.com/david-allen-green/2016/06/14/can-the-united-kingdom-government-legally-disregard-a-vote-for-brexit/ (last visit, April 30, 2017).

a High Court in London ruled after considering that the 1972 European Communities Act, which gives legal effect to British membership in the European Union, is a matter of domestic and not of international law.[24] The Government appealed this ruling before the U.K. Supreme Court, which upheld the decision of the High Court, ruling, in a 8–3 decision, that the British Government must hold a parliamentary vote before triggering the E.U. exit process.[25] In any event, such ruling was not a big issue, since the House of Commons passed legislation authorizing the Prime Minister to begin the Brexit process.[26]

Once this approval was obtained, the U.K. Government notified the European Council of the United Kingdom's intention to withdraw from the European Union.[27] Given its historical importance, the complete text of the letter is transcribed below:

> Dear President Tusk. On 23 June last year, the people of the United Kingdom voted to leave the European Union. As I have said before, that decision was no rejection of the values we share as fellow Europeans. Nor was it an attempt to do harm to the European Union or any of the remaining member states. On the contrary, the United Kingdom wants the European Union to succeed and prosper. Instead, the referendum was a vote to restore, as we see it, our national self-determination. We are leaving the European Union, but we are not leaving Europe – and we want to remain committed partners and allies to our friends across the continent. Earlier this month, the United Kingdom Parliament confirmed the result of the referendum by voting with clear and convincing majorities in both of its Houses for the European Union (Notification of Withdrawal) Bill. The Bill was passed by Parliament on 13 March and it received Royal Assent from Her Majesty the Queen and became an Act of Parliament on 16 March. Today, therefore, I am writing to give effect to the democratic decision of

24 See R (Miller) v Secretary of State for Exiting the European Union [2016] EWHC 2768 (Admin) Case No CO/3809/2016 and CO/3281/2016 3 November 2016. See also The Article 50 Case, Taking Back Control, The Economist, November 6th, 2016, available at: www.economist.com/news/britain/21709589-high-court-rules-parliament-must-vote-trigger-brexit-process-taking-back-control (last visit, April 30, 2017).

25 See *UK Supreme Court Rules MPs Must Vote on Triggering Brexit*, Financial Times, January 24, 2017, available at: www.ft.com/content/af707ac0-e216-11e6-8405-9e5580d6e5fb (last visit, April 30, 2017). See also *The Article 50 Case, Taking Back Control*, The Economist, November 6, 2016, available at: www.economist.com/news/britain/21709589-high-court-rules-parliament-must-vote-trigger-brexit-process-taking-back-control (last visit, April 30, 2017).

26 See U.K. Parliament, www.parliament.uk/ (last visit, April 30, 2017). See also *Parliament Passes Brexit Bill and Opens Way to Triggering Article 50*, The Guardian, March 13, 2017, available at: www.theguardian.com/politics/2017/mar/13/brexit-vote-article-50-eu-citizens-rights-lords-mps (last visit, April 30, 2017).

27 See *Brexit: The UK's Letter Triggering Article 50*, BBC News, March 29, 2017, available at: www.bbc.com/news/uk-politics-39431070 (last visit, April 30, 2017).

> the people of the United Kingdom. I hereby notify the European Council in accordance with Article 50(2) of the Treaty on European Union of the United Kingdom's intention to withdraw from the European Union. In addition, in accordance with the same Article 50(2) as applied by Article 106a of the Treaty Establishing the European Atomic Energy Community, I hereby notify the European Council of the United Kingdom's intention to withdraw from the European Atomic Energy Community. References in this letter to the European Union should therefore be taken to include a reference to the European Atomic Energy Community.[28]

The first consequences of this decision were on the domestic side. On April 19, 2017 and by an overwhelming vote of 522 to 13, the U.K. Parliament agreed to hold elections on June 8, 2017 at the request of Prime Minister Theresa May.[29] While the UK Prime Minister intended to strengthen her parliamentary support in order to have a better bargaining position during the Brexit negotiations with the European Union, the results of this election were disappointing for the Conservative Party, which fell well below the 326 seats needed to keep its majority in Parliament. In a so-called hung parliament (no party holds the majority), the Conservative Party needed to resort to an alliance with the minority Democratic Unionist Party (from Northern Ireland) in order to form a minority government.

The relevant legal rule regarding the Brexit process is Article 50 of the Treaty of Lisbon (reproduced below), which does not enter into the procedural details of an exit process (it only has 261 words):

> 1. Any Member State may decide to withdraw from the Union in accordance with its own constitutional requirements.
> 2. A Member State which decides to withdraw shall notify the European Council of its intention. In the light of the guidelines provided by the European Council, the Union shall negotiate and conclude an agreement with that State, setting out the arrangements for its withdrawal, taking account of the framework for its future relationship with the Union. That agreement shall be negotiated in accordance with Article 218(3) of the Treaty on the Functioning of the European Union. It shall be concluded on behalf of the Union by the Council, acting by a qualified majority, after obtaining the consent of the European Parliament.
> 3. The Treaties shall cease to apply to the State in question from the date of entry into force of the withdrawal agreement or, failing that, two years

28 See *id.*

29 See U.K. Parliament, www.parliament.uk/ (last visit, April 30, 2017). See also *U.K. Parliament Approves Theresa May's General Election Call*, The New York Times, April 19, 2017, available at: www.nytimes.com/2017/04/19/world/europe/uk-general-election.html (last visit, April 30, 2017).

after the notification referred to in paragraph 2, unless the European Council, in agreement with the Member State concerned, unanimously decides to extend this period.

4. For the purposes of paragraphs 2 and 3, the member of the European Council or of the Council representing the withdrawing Member State shall not participate in the discussions of the European Council or Council or in decisions concerning it.
   A qualified majority shall be defined in accordance with Article 238(3)(b) of the Treaty on the Functioning of the European Union.
5. If a State which has withdrawn from the Union asks to rejoin, its request shall be subject to the procedure referred to in Article 49.

Pursuant to the third paragraph of this legal rule, the United Kingdom would be out of the European Union no later than two years after this country has officially notified the European Council of its intention to leave the European Union (unless there is a positive consensus to extend the term). In the meantime, the United Kingdom and the European Union would negotiate an agreement. The key question is which would be the scope and features of such an agreement.

At least four options exist, which are described below, ordered from the most to the least degree of integration.[30] The first one consists of the United Kingdom, once it is outside the European Union, joining the European Economic Area, whose members are the E.U.'s members plus Iceland, Liechtenstein and Norway.[31] These three countries, by paying a financial contribution, currently enjoy access to the E.U.'s market and, in reciprocity, E.U.'s companies have access to the markets of Iceland, Liechtenstein and Norway.

A second route is to follow the Swiss model. Switzerland is a member of EFTA but not of the EEA.[32] As a result, the access of Swiss goods to the E.U.'s market is governed by some bilateral agreements between Switzerland and the European Union that covers some but not all areas of trade (for instance, the banking sector is not part of such agreements).[33]

The third model consists of the European Union and the United Kingdom entering into a preferential trade agreement giving both parties access to the other

30 See generally Swati Dhingra and Thomas Sampson, *Life after BREXIT: What are the UK's Options Outside the European Union?* (2016), available at: http://cep.lse.ac.uk/pubs/download/brexit01.pdf (last visit, April 30, 2017).

See also BBC, *Five Models for Post-Brexit UK Trade*, June 27, 2016, www.bbc.com/news/uk-politics-eu-referendum-36639261 (last visit, April 30, 2017).

31 See European Economic Area, www.efta.int/eea (last visit, April 30, 2017).

32 See EFTA, www.efta.int/ (last visit, April 30, 2017). Indeed, the Swiss people voted against joining the EEA in 1992. See European Parliament, The European Economic Area (EEA), Switzerland and the North, www.europarl.europa.eu/atyourservice/en/displayFtu.html?ftuId=FTU_6.5.3.html (last visit, April 30, 2017).

33 See European Commission, http://ec.europa.eu/trade/policy/countries-and-regions/countries/switzerland/ (last visit, April 30, 2017).

party's market but without imposing some of the requirements under the EEA or the Swiss model, which are mainly related to the free movement of people and labor, a topic very sensitive for the British Government. Thus, the trade agreement might either establish a custom union between the European Union and the United Kingdom, following the Turkey model,[34] or just to enter into a preferential treaty reducing both tariff and non-tariff barriers, in a similar way to the preferential trade agreement between the European Union and Canada (CETA).[35]

The last option is following the default rule. That is, the tariff and non-tariff barriers applicable to British goods being exported to the European Union and to E.U.'s goods being exported to the United Kingdom would be those that the WTO agreements establish. If none of these options is agreed, the U.K.'s economy might significantly suffer the consequences of leaving the European Union.[36] After all, almost 50 percent of the U.K.'s goods and services are exported to E.U. countries.[37]

In any event, neither route would be easy for the United Kingdom. This country will have to negotiate new trade agreements with major partners such as China, India and Brazil. Since those countries will be looking for a new set of concessions, it will take a long time to reach the end of negotiations. Meanwhile, it is likely that the United States will stay behind the lines, observing the baselines of the new trade agreements, especially those with the WTO and the European Union, before negotiating a U.K.–U.S. deal.

There are other legal, economic and political consequences for the United Kingdom in leaving the European Union. Regarding the legal issues, many questions arise in topics such as the necessary amendments to local legislation, which up to now has been in sync with European Union directives, the potential for investor-state disputes, and the new set of legal trade rules that the United Kingdom will require.[38]

On the political realm, such a decision is a heavy blow to the global integration or, more precisely, to globalization. The referendum, therefore, may encourage people in other parts of the world, who are already against globalization, to stop integrating efforts or, even worse, to move the clock backwards by rejecting some trade agreements already in legal force. From the legal perspective, there is a lot

34 See European Commission, http://ec.europa.eu/trade/policy/countries-and-regions/countries/turkey/ (last visit, April 30, 2017).

35 See European Commission, http://ec.europa.eu/trade/policy/in-focus/ceta/ (last visit, April 30, 2017).

36 See generally, John Springford and Simon Tilford, *The Great British trade-off. The impact of leaving the E.U. on the UK's trade and investment.* Centre for European Reform (2014), www.cer.org.uk/sites/default/files/publications/attachments/pdf/2014/pb_britishtrade_16jan14-8285.pdf (last visit, April 30, 2017).

37 See Fullfact.org, *Do Half the UK's Exports go to Europe?*, November 9, 2015, https://fullfact.org/europe/do-half-uks-exports-go-europe/ (last visit, April 30, 2017).

38 See Jennifer A. Hillman and Gary Horlick, *Legal Aspects of Brexit: Implications of the United Kingdom's Decision to Withdraw from the European Union*, p. 1 (2017).

of work to be done, at least in the United Kingdom, since it will need to replace hundreds of European legal instruments with local legal rules.[39]

From an economic standpoint, the consequences would not be good. On the one hand, and besides the fall of the pound sterling following the Brexit decision,[40] some studies predict that its GDP will not grow as much as it would if the United Kingdom would have remained in the European Union.[41] According to the OECD, "Brexit would be akin to a tax on GDP, imposing a persistent and rising cost on the economy that would not be incurred if the UK remained in the EU."[42] Thus, and by 2020, the U.K.'s GDP might be 3 percent smaller than if this country had kept its E.U. membership while, in the long term, the impact will be even larger: a GDP 5 percent smaller in 2030.[43]

In any event, one of the most-affected sectors will be the financial industry, which has been so important for the City of London. Such services currently are subject to the so-called passport rule, by which U.K. based financial institutions might operate freely in any of the E.U. Member States.[44] If such benefit disappears as a result of the United Kingdom leaving the European Union, some financial institutions might have incentives to move their European headquarters to a country that still belongs to such supranational organization.

On the other hand, and besides the already mentioned European Economic Area, there are several preferential trade agreements that are in legal force between the European Union and other countries, such as Canada (CETA), Chile, Mexico, South Korea, and Turkey.[45] The United Kingdom, of course, will not be a part of these trade agreements once it leaves the European Union. Therefore, if the United Kingdom intends to have preferential access to such markets, it will have to negotiate new trade agreements with such countries going back to square one.

39 See Financial Times, *Can the United Kingdom Government Legally Disregard a Vote for Brexit?*, June 14, 2016, http://blogs.ft.com/david-allen-green/2016/06/14/can-the-united-kingdom-government-legally-disregard-a-vote-for-brexit/ (last visit, April 30, 2017).

40 See *The Economic Impact of Brexit, Straws in the Wind*, July 16, 2016, www.economist.com/news/britain/21702225-forget-financial-markets-evidence-mounting-real-economy-suffering (last visit, April 30, 2017).

41 See Iain Begg and Fabian Mushövel, *The Economic Impact of Brexit: Jobs, Growth and the Public Finances*, www.lse.ac.uk/europeanInstitute/LSE-Commission/Hearing-11---The-impact-of-Brexit-on-jobs-and-economic-growth-sumary.pdf (last visit, April 30, 2017).

42 See Rafal Kierzenkowski1, Nigel Pain, Elena Rusticelli and Sanne Zwart, *The Economic Consequences of Brexit, A Taxing Decision* (2016), www.oecd-ilibrary.org/economics/the-economic-consequences-of-brexit_5jm0lsvdkf6k-en (last visit, April 30, 2017).

43 See *id.*

44 See European Banking Authority, www.eba.europa.eu/regulation-and-policy/passporting-and-supervision-of-branches (last visit, April 30, 2017).

45 See European Commission, http://trade.ec.europa.eu/doclib/docs/2012/june/tradoc_149622.pdf (last visit, April 30, 2017).

3.3 How players influence trade policy in the European Union

The players are those already mentioned in the chapter about trade policy in the United States: the Executive, the Legislative, the Private Sector, and the Public Interest. The European Commission is the Executive while the Legislative is composed of both the European Parliament and the Council of Ministers. These three bodies are described below.

The European Commission is a "college" composed of 28 commissioners (one from each E.U. Member State) and an administrative body of around 20,000 European civil servants. As the E.U.'s Executive Body, the European Commission is independent from its members. Its purposes are: (i) to file legislative proposals before the European Parliament and the Council of Ministers, (ii) to be the guardian of the E.U. treaties (i.e., to verify its compliance), (iii) to manage the budget, (iv) to settle competition cases, and (v) to represent the European Union and its members in trade negotiations.[46]

With respect to this last purpose, the Commission is the coordinator of the trade policy formulation and the only authorized negotiator in international trade on behalf of E.U. members although, for that purpose, it follows the Council of Ministers' instructions. This Council, moreover, may either approve or reject the results of the negotiations.[47] Pursuant to the Treaty of Lisbon new Art. 207 (former Art. 133 TEC) and 218 (former Art. 300 TEC), the negotiations of international trade agreements are confidential, the deliberations of the Council of Ministers are unpublished, and no formal votes are recorded. While this confidential treatment of information might contribute to the advance of trade negotiations, it has been criticized for its lack of transparency.

On the other hand, and as the Legislative, both the European Parliament and the Council of Ministers approve or reject legislation. The Parliament is composed of 751 members that nationals of the E.U.'s members elect for five-year terms. The Parliament, pursuant to the Treaty of Lisbon, has a key role in trade negotiations since the Commission is now formally obliged to consult with it on the conduct of negotiations, it has to give its consent to the adoption of results of trade negotiations on a "take it or leave it" basis, and the Parliament and the Council of Ministers must jointly agree on regulations defining the framework for implementing the E.U.'s trade policy.

The Council of Ministers, in turn and as its name suggests, is composed of the ministers of the 28 E.U. Member States. The precise ministers representing E.U.

46 "Individual Member States have transmitted their competence for trade policy to the collective Council of Ministers of the EU, accepting the aggregate decisions emerging from it. Then, the Council of Ministers delegates to its executive body, the EC, the capability of engaging in international trade negotiations, within boundaries clearly established by the Council." Andrea C. Bianculli and Andrea Ribeiro (Eds), *Regional Organizations and Social Policy in Europe and Latin America: A Space for Social Citizenship?* p. 394 (2015).

47 See European Union http://europa.eu/about-eu/countries/index_en.htm (last visit, April 30, 2017).

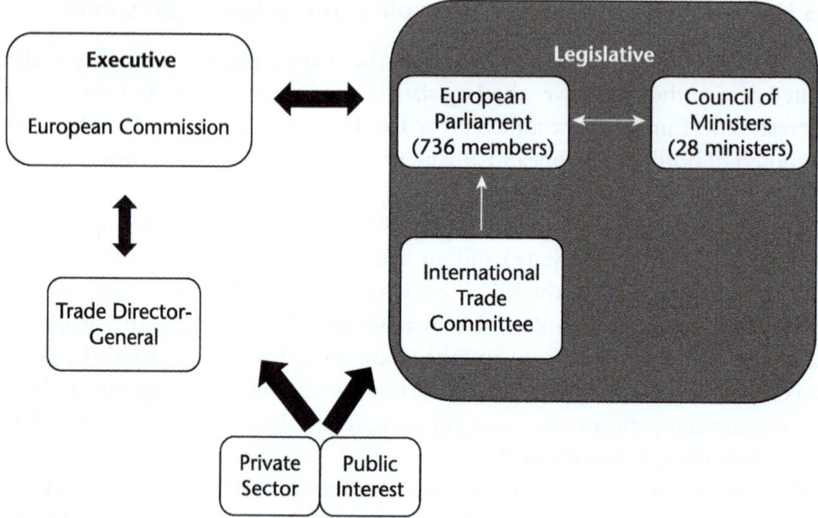

FIGURE 4 The E.U.'s Executive and Legislative[48]

Member States depend on the topic under consideration; i.e., if the topic is health, the ministers whose powers relate to this issue are the ones who vote. The Council's decisions, which are public, are adopted by qualified majorities save the cases of cultural services, audiovisual, social matters, education, and health, which requires unanimity.[49] The qualified majorities entail that a decision, to be passed into law, requires the affirmative vote of at least 55 percent of E.U. Member States (currently, 16 out of the 28) accounting for at least 65 percent of the E.U.'s population (i.e., around 330 million since the current population of the E.U. is about 500 million).[50] Figure 4 summarizes the structure of the Executive and the Legislative branches in the European Union.

On the other hand, and similar to the analysis made in the chapter about U.S. trade policy, a "tree" is useful to illustrate and assist in comparing the Private Sector *modus operandi* from country to country. In the E.U.'s tree, prominent individuals, local groups and local associations influence state associations which, in turn, have an impact on the decisions of national and supranational associations (which do not exist in the United States).

These kinds of associations engage in lobby activities in order to influence not only public opinion, either for or against a given public policy, but also the decisions of the media, the European Commission, the Council of Ministers and the European Parliament. Figure 5 plots the E.U.'s tree.

48 Figure made by the authors.

49 See Treaty of Lisbon Art. 207.

50 See European Union, http://europa.eu/about-eu/facts-figures/living/index_en.htm (last visit, February 20, 2016).

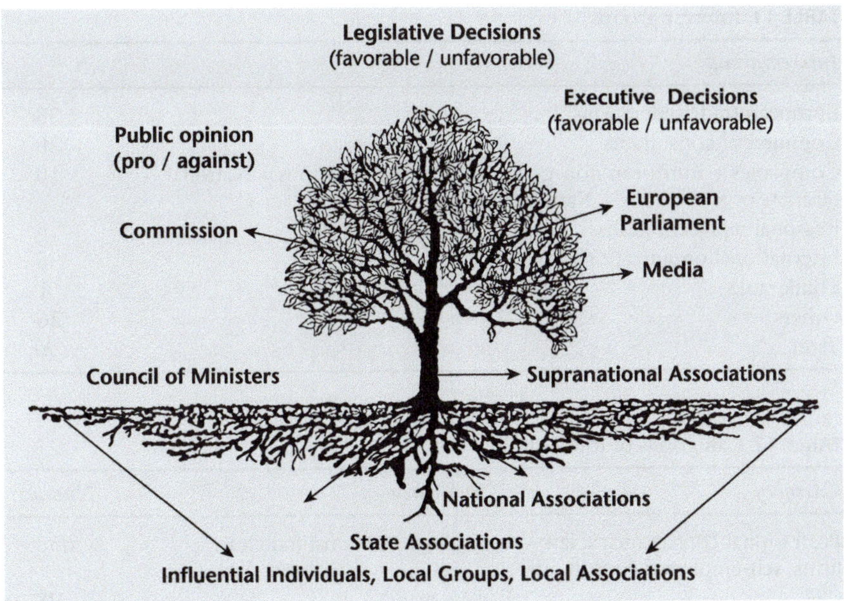

FIGURE 5 The E.U.'s tree[51]

Some additional figures illustrate the relevance of the Private Sector in the European Union. First, Table 10 shows the distribution of lobby groups regarding their country of origin. Second, Table 11 shows the main interest groups.[52] Third and finally, Table 12 indicates the categories of lobbyists.

TABLE 10 Distribution of lobby groups regarding their country of origin[53]

Country of origin	*Lobby groups*	*%*
Germany	380	17.2
United Kingdom	294	13.3
France	292	13.2
Belgium	171	7.8
United States	173	7.8
Switzerland	73	3.3
Others	826	37.4
Total	*2,209*	*100.0*

51 Figure made by the authors.

52 Andrea C. Bianculli and Andrea Ribeiro (Eds), *Regional Organizations and Social Policy in Europe and Latin America: A Space for Social Citizenship?* p. 405 (2015).

53 Arndt Wonka et al., *Measuring the Size and Scope of the E.U. Interest Group Population* (2011), http://eup.sagepub.com/content/11/3/463 (last visit, April 30, 2017).

TABLE 11 Interest groups[54]

Interest group	*%*
European trade federations	33
Commercial consultants	20
Companies + European non-governmental organizations + National business organizations + National labor organizations	10
Regional representations	5
International organizations	5
Think tanks	1
Others	26
Total	*100*

TABLE 12 Categories of lobbyists[55]

Category	*Sub-category*	*Number*
Professional consultancies, law firms, self-employed consultants	Professional consultancies	653
	Law firms	98
	Self-employed consultants	318
	Total	*1,069*
In-house lobbyists and trade/ business/professional associations	Companies and groups	1,626
	Trade and Business Associations	2,213
	Trade Unions and professional associations	546
	Other organizations	283
	Total	*4,668*
Non-governmental organizations, think-tanks, research, and academic institutions	Non-governmental organizations, think tanks and research institutions	2,365 463
	Academic institutions	186
	Total	*649*
Organizations representing churches and religious communities	Organizations representing churches and religious communities	39
Organizations representing local, regional and municipal authorities, other public or mixed entities	Organizations representing local, regional and municipal authorities, other public or mixed entities	427
	Grand Total	*9,217*

54 See *id.*

55 See European Union, *Statistics for the Transparency Register*, http://ec.europa.eu/transparencyregister/public/consultation/statistics.do?locale=en&action=prepareView (last visit, April 30, 2017)..

On the other hand, and similar to the United States, the Public Interest is composed of all non-profit organizations; i.e., organizations that might be either for or against international trade but that do not represent an industry.

Also similar to what happens in the United States, the interaction between the Executive, the Legislative, the Private Sector, and the Public Interest is a complex and lengthy process on the following grounds: (i) consensus building is the norm in the European Union and that means that negotiations progress slowly; (ii) every stage of the negotiation and formulation of the E.U.'s trade policy exhibits an intricate pattern of institutional structures and procedures; (iii) intense and continuous bargaining within each of the institutions occurs all the time; (iv) the process is full of tensions, conflicts and competition among the involved parties; and (v) informal but regular contacts are predominant since there are no formal structures of consultative committees at the E.U.'s level. Such informal contacts did take place between the private sector and the Commission, not with the Council of Ministers. That informal contacts may still exist in the European Union means that the odds are against small private associations influencing trade policy in comparison with their counterparts in the United States, where formal contacts are the norm.

On top of that, the participation of the different groups in the E.U. Commission's Civil Society dialogue on trade contributes toward achieving high standards of transparency. This participation involves regular meetings that the European Commissioner for Trade usually chairs, which are held every two months, whose purpose is to discuss trade policy issues, and which usually have a broad representation of diverse sectors of civil society.[56] This interchange of views is very important since, as already mentioned, the Commission represents the European Union in the negotiation of preferential trade agreements and, from a multilateral standpoint, before the WTO.

Within the E.U. trade PFS, the Executive ranks first in influence since only the Commission can propose rules and regulations on trade and it is in charge of international trade negotiations, even though instructions to European negotiators are decided in the Legislative branch (Council and Parliament). The Council and the Parliament comes next as the top legislative authorities for approval of laws, regulations and trade agreements. The Public Interest, unlike its counterpart in the United States, is as influential as the Private Sector because Europeans are,

TABLE 13 The rank of players' influence in E.U. trade PFS (1 = more influence)

Player	*Rank*
Executive	1
Legislative	2
Private Sector	3
Public Interest	3

56 See European Union, http://trade.ec.europa.eu/civilsoc/csd_proc.cfm (last visit, April 30, 2017).

generally speaking, more sensitive to environmental and social concerns than their peers in the United States.

On the other hand, an analysis of the sectors which comprise the E.U.'s economy is useful to understand the most sensitive issues and industries. The services sector is the backbone of the E.U.'s economy, accounting for over 73 percent of its GDP and employment.[57] Manufacturing is the second most-important industry, accounting for about 20 percent of the E.U.'s GDP and for around three-quarters of its merchandise exports.[58] The manufacturing industry share has been steadily declining during the last decades as a result of the trend to move some industrial activities to geographical areas with lower labor costs.[59] To avoid a steeper decline, the manufacturing sector remains a major beneficiary of state aid.[60] One of the staples of the manufacturing industry is the energy sector: the European Union is the world's largest energy importer, the second largest consumer and it is about 50 percent self-sufficient in energy.[61]

Agriculture, in turn, contributes less than the 3 percent of the E.U.'s GDP.[62] To improve the competitiveness of this sector, the E.U.'s agricultural ministers adopted on June 26, 2003 a fundamental reform of the Common Agricultural Policy (CAP), which is the E.U.'s agricultural policy. The amended CAP decoupled payments from production of particular crops; to put it differently, the granting of a subsidy does not require harvesting a given crop anymore but just evidence of having complied with some environmental, food safety, and animal welfare standards. In November 2010, the Commission discussed three options regarding the CAP: (i) keeping the program, (ii) starting a gradual reform, or (iii) overhauling the program, i.e., doing a complete reform. Having chosen the second road, the European Commission made some proposals in October 2011, still not approved, to make the CAP more effective and competitive. In general terms, the E.U.'s traditional agricultural policies have made subsidies indispensable for the export of some of the surpluses, something that the proposed reforms aim to change.[63]

57 See Eurostat, http://ec.europa.eu/eurostat/statistics-explained/index.php/National_accounts_and_GDP (last visit, April 30, 2017).

58 See *id.*

59 See *id.*

60 See Roman Stöllinger and Mario Holzner, *State Aid and Export Competitiveness in the EU*, Working Paper 106, The Vienna Institute for International Economics Studies (2013), https://wiiw.ac.at/state-aid-and-export-competitiveness-in-the-eu-dlp-3092.pdf (last visit, April 30, 2017). See also European Commission, Compilation of State Aid Rules in Force, http://ec.europa.eu/competition/state_aid/legislation/compilation/index_en.html (last visit, April 30, 2017).

61 See Eurostat, http://ec.europa.eu/eurostat/statistics-explained/index.php/Energy_production_and_imports (last visit, April 30, 2017).

62 See Eurostat, http://ec.europa.eu/eurostat/statistics-explained/index.php/National_accounts_and_GDP (last visit, April 30, 2017).

63 See European Union, http://trade.ec.europa.eu (last visit, April 30, 2017).

3.4 The European perspective on trade issues and negotiations

The E.U.'s trade policy instruments may be divided into offensive and defensive tools. Trade Barriers Regulation, or simply TBR, is the main offensive instrument. TBR is an instrument aimed at opening third countries' markets by eliminating obstacles to trade for the benefit of E.U. exporters. Pursuant to Council Regulation No 3286/94, E.U. companies, acting either individually or through their industry associations, as well as Member States may file a TBR complaint. Once the process has finished, the European Commission investigates any form of unfair barrier to the European exports of goods or services and, if necessary, takes measures intended to offset such trade barrier.

In turn, and similar to the U.S. trade policy discussed in the previous chapter,[64] antidumping measures, countervailing duties and safeguards are the defensive measures. The 1996 Antidumping regulation (Council Regulation (EC) No 384/96), in accordance with the WTO Antidumping Agreement, requires the following three conditions to allow the imposition of these kinds of duties: (i) evidence of dumping, (ii) a damage (or threat thereof) to a substantial part of the E.U.'s industry, and (iii) a cost-benefit analysis. According to the last prong of this test, antidumping measures are only adopted if they are in the broader E.U. interest; i.e., the measure is analyzed taking into account its effect on all the 28 countries and not only on the E.U. member or members that alleged material injury from dumped imports.[65]

The E.U.'s industries have two avenues to request the imposition of an antidumping duty: to request it directly to the European Commission or to make the petition through its national government. In any event, and once the petition is filed, the European Commission conducts the investigation and might impose provisional measures. The Council of Ministers might, later on, impose the resulting definitive measures, if any.

On the other hand, the imposition of countervailing duties requires the existence of: (i) a subsidy than a country not belonging to the European Union has granted to one of its industries, (ii) a damage (or threat thereof) to a substantial part of an E.U. industry, and (iii) a cost-benefit analysis. As observed, the second and the third requirements are the same than in the case of antidumping. The proceedings to impose antidumping and countervailing duties are also very similar. Regarding such proceedings, and unlike the United States, both the provisional and definitive measures in antidumping and countervailing cases are imposed in a prospective and not in a retrospective way, i.e., they are only in legal force from the date of its enactment forward in both investigations and reviews. Most countries adopt this prospective system.

64 See *supra* Chapter 2.

65 Andrea C. Bianculli and Andrea Ribeiro (Eds), *Regional Organizations and Social Policy in Europe and Latin America: A Space for Social Citizenship?*, p. 392 (2015).

Sometimes, it is the European Union that grants a subsidy (which another WTO member might countervail in case such subsidy does not comply with the WTO Agreement on Subsidies and Countervailing Measures). The European Union provides a significant amount of export subsidies, mainly to the agricultural sector.[66] While such subsidies are in decline, they remain relatively high.[67] Overall, export subsidies that the European Union has notified to WTO account for about 90 percent of all the WTO members' notified subsidies.[68] In any event, take into account that under the Ministerial Decision on Export Competition (WT/MIN(15)/45) adopted in the 10th WTO Ministerial Conference held in Nairobi in December 2015, "developed countries will immediately remove export subsidies, except for a handful of agriculture products, and developing countries will do so by 2018, with a longer timeframe in some limited cases."[69]

Finally, safeguards are only imposed in case of sudden import surges that cause serious injury to an E.U.'s industry. Since safeguards are a more extraordinary measure, only an E.U. member, but not an industry, is allowed to request it (this is one of the reasons why safeguards are rarer than both antidumping and countervailing duties). Once the petition to impose a safeguard is filed, the European Commission conducts the investigation and may impose provisional measures, which will be in legal force until the Council of Ministers decides whether or not to impose definitive measures.

Between 1995 and 2014, the European Union has imposed 298 antidumping measures (being the third most active WTO Member after India and the United States)[70] and 35 countervailing measures (being the second most active WTO Member after the United States).[71] It has been less active in safeguards, having imposed only three safeguards during the above-mentioned period, well behind the WTO leaders in this topic: India, Indonesia, and Turkey, with 19, 16, and 14 safeguards, respectively.[72]

Trade remedies are not the only defensive trade policy instruments. The European Union maintains import licenses for surveillance, quota management,

66 See Reform the CAP, www.reformthecap.eu/issues/policy-instruments/export-subsidies (last visit, April 30, 2017).

67 See *id.*

68 See WTO *Notifications under the Agreement on Subsidies and Countervailing Measures*, www.wto.org/english/tratop_e/scm_e/notif_e.htm (last visit, April 30, 2017). See also *Enforcement and Compliance, WTO Subsidies Notifications*, http://enforcement.trade.gov/esel/notify/ESEL_notification_country_02-04-04.html (last visit, April 30, 2017).

69 See *Briefing Note: Agricultural Issues*, WTO, www.wto.org/english/thewto_e/minist_e/mc10_e/briefing_notes_e/brief_agriculture_e.htm (last visit, April 30, 2017).

70 See *Statistics on Antidumping*, WTO, www.wto.org/english/tratop_e/adp_e/AD_MeasuresByRepMem.pdf (last visit, April 30, 2017).

71 See *Statistics on Countervailing duties*, WTO, www.wto.org/english/tratop_e/scm_e/CV_MeasuresByRepMem.pdf (last visit, April 30, 2017).

72 See *Statistics on Safeguards*, WTO, www.wto.org/english/tratop_e/safeg_e/SG-MeasuresByRepMember.pdf (last visit, April 30, 2017).

and safeguard purposes.[73] Also, almost 100 tariff lines, mainly related to agricultural goods, are subject to tariff quotas.[74]

Regarding the multilateral level, the European Union is a key player in the WTO and was very active in the Doha Development Round negotiations until they came to a standstill, and also during the last two WTO Ministerial Conferences when some commitments were reached regarding trade facilitation and the removal of agricultural subsidies. The European Union also remains one of the most active members in the WTO dispute settlement mechanism, having participated in 96 cases as a complainant, 82 cases as a respondent, and in 155 cases as a third party.[75]

In its Preferential Trade Agreements with developing countries, liberalization is usually undertaken asymmetrically, with the European Union liberalizing at a faster speed.[76] Lately, the European Union has shown interest in environmental matters as a result of the influence of the Public Interest. The European Union also considers that its Preferential Trade Agreements are part of a wider policy of promoting multilateralism and, in that connection, it recently announced its intention to launch new preferential trade negotiations with market access as the main criterion.[77]

On the other hand, the European Union grants MFN treatment to all WTO Members[78] and, to some developing and least-developed countries, unilateral preferences through its GSP scheme, which means "partial or entire removal of tariffs on two thirds of all product categories."[79] There are three kinds of preferences:[80] (i) the standard GSP agreement, which offers significant tariff reductions to some developing countries (e.g., those countries which do not have another preferential access to the European Union); (ii) the GSP+ enhanced preferences which means "full removal of tariffs on essentially the same product categories as those covered by the general arrangement" and which "are granted to countries which ratify and implement core international conventions relating

73 See Regulation 738/94.

74 See Treaty of the Functioning of the European Union. See also European Commission, https://ec.europa.eu/taxation_customs/business/calculation-customs-duties/what-is-common-customs-tariff/tariff-quotas_en (last visit, April 30, 2017). *Cfr.* GATT Art. XI.

75 See *Disputes by Country/Territory*, WTO,www.wto.org/english/tratop_e/dispu_e/dispu_by_country_e.htm (last visit, April 30, 2017).

76 See, e.g., the PTAs between the European Union and Colombia and Peru, which have been in legal force since 2013.

77 See European Commission, http://ec.europa.eu/trade/policy/accessing-markets/ (last visit, April 30, 2017). For a list of the PTAs where the European Union is a party or that is entity is negotiating, see European Commission, http://trade.ec.europa.eu/doclib/docs/2006/december/tradoc_118238.pdf (last visit, April 30, 2017).

78 See GATT Art. I.

79 See European Union, http://ec.europa.eu/trade/policy/countries-and-regions/development/generalised-scheme-of-preferences/index_en.htm (last visit, April 30, 2017).

80 See European Union, http://ec.europa.eu/trade/policy/countries-and-regions/development/generalised-scheme-of-preferences/index_en.htm (last visit, April 30, 2017).

to human and labor rights, environment and good governance"[81]; and (iii) the so-called Everything but Arms program which "grants duty-free quota-free access to all products, except for arms and ammunitions"[82] to least-developed countries.

Finally, some criticisms of the E.U.'s trade policy are the following ones: (i) its agricultural sector is highly protected and with an excessive use of export subsidies, which might be, at least in some cases, against the provisions of the WTO Agreement on Subsidies and Countervailing Duties, (ii) it has a strong dependence on energy imports, which might be a serious issue at any time the prices of oil and similar commodities are on the rise; (iii) its trade PFS may still allow for some informal contacts between the Private Sector and the Executive; and (iv) the confidentiality of trade negotiations may affect transparency.

81 See European Union, http://ec.europa.eu/trade/policy/countries-and-regions/development/generalised-scheme-of-preferences/index_en.htm (last visit, April 30, 2017).
82 See *id.*

4

BRICS PART 1

The Brazilian trade policy system

4.1 The Brazilian trade policy system

Chapters 4 to 8 analyze the trade policy systems of the countries belonging to the so-called BRICS,[1] that is: Brazil, Russia, India, China, and South Africa (although the order in this book will not be exactly this). The first chapter of the part dealing with the BRICS countries focuses on Brazil and intends to answer questions such as how the Brazilian trade policy system is structured, how the trade players influence the Brazilian trade policy, and what is Brazil's perspective on trade issues and negotiations.

Before explaining the Brazilian trade policy, however, some introductory comments related to the economic history of this country are granted. Taking into account its size and population,[2] it is not surprising to know that Brazil is the seventh world economy with a GDP close to $2.5 trillion.[3] Brazil is also the largest economy in Latin America.[4] Its international trade in 2014 amounted to around $454 billion, which is almost the 20 percent of its GDP.[5] Brazil is a member of

1 Jim O'Neill, from Goldman Sachs, coined the term BRICS in 2001 in a paper entitled Building Better Global Economic BRICs. See Jim O'Neill, *Building Better Global Economic BRICs* (2001), www.goldmansachs.com/our-thinking/archive/archive-pdfs/build-better-brics.pdf (last visit, April 30, 2017). See also Financial Times, *The Story of the BRICS*, January 15, 2010, www.ft.com/content/112ca932-00ab-11df-ae8d-00144feabdc0 (last visit, April 30, 2017). Later on, South Africa joined this group and, therefore, the BRIC countries became the BRICS ones.

2 Brazil has over 200 million inhabitants. See World Population Review, http://worldpopulationreview.com/countries/brazil-population/ (last visit, April 30, 2017). See also Countrymeters, http://countrymeters.info/en/Brazil (last visit, April 30, 2017).

3 See World Bank Data. http://databank.worldbank.org/data/reports.aspx?Code=NY.GDP.MKTP.CD&id=af3ce82b&report_name=Popular_indicators&populartype=series&ispopular=y (last visit, April 30, 2017).

4 See *id.*

5 See *id.*

Mercosur, a customs union whose other members are Argentina, Bolivia, Paraguay, Uruguay, and Venezuela.[6] Mercosur has also entered into trade agreements with Chile, Colombia, Cuba, Ecuador, India, Israel, Mexico, and Peru.[7] Other three agreements, with SACU (Southern African Customs Union), Egypt and Palestine, were successfully negotiated but they are still not in force.[8] An additional agreement with the European Union is under negotiation.[9]

Brazil is also a member of ALADI (Latin American Integration Association), whose members, as its name suggests, are Latin American countries.[10] ALADI countries have entered into specific trade agreements, such as the agreement on Trade in Seeds and the Agreement on Trade in Cultural Goods.[11] Brazil has also entered into some trade agreements on its own, such as the treaties with Mexico, Guinea, Suriname, and Venezuela.[12]

On the other hand, and between 1953 and 1991, CACEX (Carteira de Comércio Exterior do Banco do Brasil S.A.) was the public entity administering Brazilian trade policy and congregating all trade-related matters.[13] In the early days of CACEX, Brazil adopted an industrial and protectionist policy of import substitution.[14] In the 1970s, however, there were some policies targeting export promotion.[15] During the 1980s and the beginning of the 1990s, Brazil endured an economic and political crisis that led to hyperinflation and, in the trade sector, to a lack of dynamics regarding exports of goods.[16]

6 See Mercosur, www.mercosur.int/ (last visit, April 30, 2017). Venezuela has been suspended as a member of this organization. See *id.*

7 See Mercosur, www.mercosur.int/innovaportal/v/5271/2/innova.front/tratados-protocolos-y-acuerdos (last visit, April 30, 2017).

8 See *id.*

9 See *id.*

10 See ALADI, www.aladi.org/sitioAladi/index.html (last visit, April 30, 2017).

11 See *id.*

12 See SICE Foreign Trade Information System, Organization of American States, www.sice.oas.org/ctyindex/BRZ/BRZagreements_s.asp (last visit, April 30, 2017).

13 See Mario Marconini, 'Brazil', in *The Political Economy of Trade Reform in Emerging Markets: Crisis or Opportunity* (Peter Draper, Phil Alves and Razeen Sally Eds), 149 (2009). See also Gregory C. Shaffer, Michelle Ratton, Sanchez Badin and Barbara Rosenberg, 'Winning at the WTO: The Development of a Trade Policy Community Within Brazil', in *Dispute Settlement at the WTO: The Developing Country Experience* (Gregory C. Shaffer and Ricardo Meléndez-Ortiz Eds), p. 30 (2010).

14 See *id.* Such trade policies were in accordance with the public policies that, at this time, the United Nations Economic Commission for Latin America and the Caribbean (CEPAL – the Spanish acronym) recommended. See generally CEPAL, www.cepal.org/en/ (last visit, April 30, 2017).

15 See Mario Marconini, 'Brazil', in *The Political Economy of Trade Reform in Emerging Markets: Crisis or Opportunity* (Peter Draper, Phil Alves and Razeen Sally Eds), p. 149 (2009). See also Gregory C. Shaffer, Michelle Ratton, Sanchez Badin and Barbara Rosenberg, 'Winning at the WTO: The Development of a Trade Policy Community Within Brazil', in *Dispute Settlement at the WTO: The Developing Country Experience* (Gregory C. Shaffer and Ricardo Meléndez-Ortiz Eds), p. 30 (2010).

16 See *id.*

CACEX centralized all decisions, had a very low degree of transparency since only the inner circle was fully informed about how decisions were taken, and the contact with the Private Sector was informal and unpredictable.[17] Paradoxically, the period when CACEX led the Brazilian trade policy was also the time when most of the ALADI agreements were negotiated. Such agreements, however, were market opening commitments very limited in depth and scope and, as a result, did not pose any real threat to the Brazilian import-substitution model.

Due to the political and economic crisis summarized above, Brazilian trade policy suffered major changes during the 1990s. First of all, CACEX was terminated.[18] Also, Brazil initiated the integration with other countries of the Southern Cone of the Americas through the establishment of the customs union Mercosur, whose original members were Brazil, Argentina, Paraguay and Uruguay. During this time, Brazil also adopted other pro-trade measures such as a unilateral reduction of tariffs, which fell in average from 32 to 13 percent.[19] On top of that, the launching of the Plano Real in 1994, intended to eliminate the hyperinflation that was suffocating the economy, reinforced the Brazilian market orientation.[20]

Notwithstanding, the interaction between the government and the Private Sector did not significantly improve during the beginning of this new approach. While processes within the government were more democratic and transparent, the Private Sector still complained about being rarely consulted as to trade opening initiatives. Thus, there was still much room for improvement.

Partly as a result of this criticism from the Private Sector, the Brazilian Government significantly changed the trade policy in 1995 by beginning negotiations of some preferential trade agreements (in particular, the discussion of the Free Trade Area of the Americas or FTAA) and, more importantly, establishing CAMEX (Câmara de Comércio Exterior) as the most important trade authority in Brazil.[21] Since CAMEX corrected the lack of coordination among ministries and agencies, there was a more efficient division of labor within the government and the discussion of trade policies with the Private Sector significantly improved.

As the last paragraph indicated, not only CAMEX but also the negotiations of the FTAA were the two main features of Brazilian trade policies during

17 See *id.*

18 See Mario Marconini, 'Brazil', in *The Political Economy of Trade Reform in Emerging Markets: Crisis or Opportunity* (Peter Draper, Phil Alves and Razeen Sally Eds), p. 149 (2009). See also Gregory C. Shaffer, Michelle Ratton, Sanchez Badin and Barbara Rosenberg, 'Winning at the WTO: The Development of a Trade Policy Community Within Brazil', in *Dispute Settlement at the WTO: The Developing Country Experience* (Gregory C. Shaffer and Ricardo Meléndez-Ortiz Eds), p. 30 (2010).

19 See WTO, *Trade Policy Review Brazil: October 1996*, available at: www.wto.org/english/tratop_e/tpr_e/tp45_e.htm (last visit, April 30, 2017).

20 See Renato Baumann, Josefina Rivero and Yohana Zavattiero, *Tariffs and the Plano Real in Brazil*, www.cepal.org/en/publications/10671-tariffs-and-plano-real-brazil (last visit, April 30, 2017). See also Edmar L. Bacha, 'Brazil's Plano Real: A View from the Inside', in *Development Economics and Structuralist Macroeconomics* (Amitava Krishna Dutt Ed.), p. 120 (2003).

21 See CAMEX, www.camex.gov.br/ (last visit, April 30, 2017).

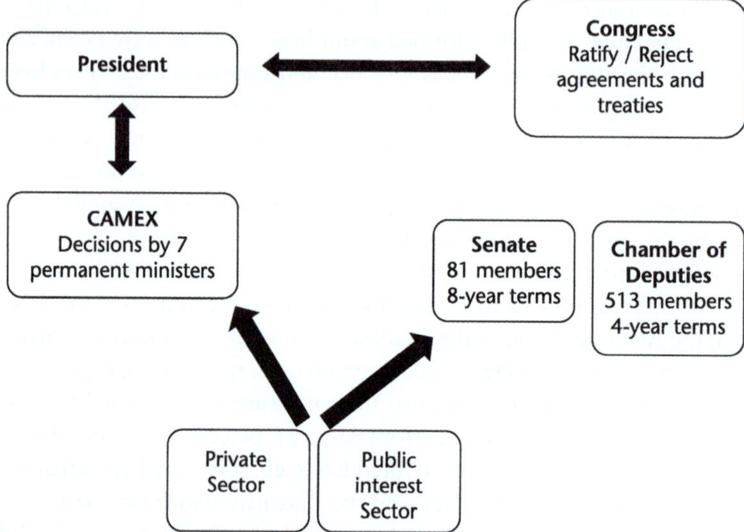

FIGURE 6 The Brazilian institutional framework[22]

the last decade of the twentieth century.[23] Such negotiations led to the following changes: (i) an internal restructuring of the Brazilian trade policy formulation system; (ii) a broader scope of the trade policy, focused on the coordination of domestic and international matters, substituted the previous emphasis on traditional commerce (the establishment of SENALCA – Secretaria Nacional da ALCA, which is the acronym of the National Secretary of the Free Trade Area of the Americas in Portuguese – was very helpful for this purpose); and (iii) the establishment of SENEUROPA, a similar instrument to SENALCA but focusing on trade negotiations with the European Union. Other instruments were also established: GICI, the Inter-Ministerial Working Group on International Trade in Goods and Services regarding the WTO and related matters, and the Forum of Economic and Social Consultation related to Mercosur. Having described the evolution of Brazilian trade policy, Figure 6 shows the Brazilian Institutional Framework.

4.2 How players influence the trade policy formulation in Brazil

Similar to the same sections in other chapters about trade policy systems, this section explains the role of the four players in the formulation of the Brazilian trade policy: the Executive, the Legislative, the Private Interest, and the Public Interest.

Regarding the Executive, and as Figure 6 indicates, the President delegates to CAMEX the formulation of Brazilian trade policy. CAMEX, in turn, interacts with the other trade policy players: The Legislative, composed of the Senate and the Chamber of Deputies; the Private Sector, and the Public Interest.

22 Figure made by the authors.

23 See generally Zuleika Arashiro, *Negotiating the Free Trade Area of the Americas*, p. 1 (2011).

CAMEX is a decision-making body where a collegiate of eight permanent ministers (Chief of Staff, Commerce and Industry, Foreign Affairs, Finance, Transportation, Agriculture, Planning, and General Secretary of Presidency)[24] meet once every two months under the chairmanship of the Chief of Staff and take decisions by majority, although in practice all parties reach an agreement on the issues discussed by consensus. Other ministers can attend meetings related to issues within their fields of interest and make their cases but they lack any voting rights. A minimum of five voting ministers is required for a decision.

On a related note, intra-governmental technical groups, composed of representatives of each ministry, are responsible for promoting studies and developing proposals within CAMEX. The results of their activities are submitted to the Council of Ministers, which could use them, but it is not obligated to do so, as the basis for a decision. CAMEX has also established a Technical Group on Analysis of the Public Interest (GTIP), whose purpose is to analyze the suspension, amendment or non-application of antidumping and countervailing duties, either on a definitive or on a temporary basis.[25]

The establishment of CAMEX in the 1990s has been positive in several ways. To begin with, its structure has encouraged a democratic debate among different players on the formulation of Brazilian trade policy. As a result, trade decisions are more decentralized, coherent and transparent. Trade decisions, nowadays, also take into account to a higher degree than before the views of the different ministers, the Private Sector, and the Public Interest. This higher degree of transparency and political participation, however, has understandably slowed the decision process. In any event, such a cost is worth the benefit of a more democratic and prudent mechanism than the existing one during a not too distant past. Figure 7 shows the CAMEX's structure.

CAMEX has the following purposes[26]: (i) to formulate and implement trade policy; (ii) to approve any change in actual tariffs; (iii) to establish the main goals for trade agreement negotiations; (iv) to approve the litigation strategies in the settlement of disputes before the WTO; (v) to approve trade measures such as those intended to boost exports, to enact non-tariff barriers or to increase the commercial defense; (vi) to approve official actions against protectionist measures by other countries; and (vii) to give support to the operations in Export Financing and Export Guarantees.

As to the Legislative, as Figure 6 indicates, it is composed of two chambers. The first one is the Senate, composed of 81 members elected for eight-year terms while the second one is the Chamber of Deputies, composed of 513 members elected for four-year terms. Both chambers, in accordance with the Brazilian

24 The number of permanent ministers was increased from seven to eight pursuant to Presidential Decree 9.029 of April 10, 2017. See www.planalto.gov.br/ccivil_03/_ato2015-2018/2017/Decreto/D9029.htm

25 See Resolution 13/2012.

26 See CAMEX, www.camex.gov.br/ (last visit, April 30, 2017).

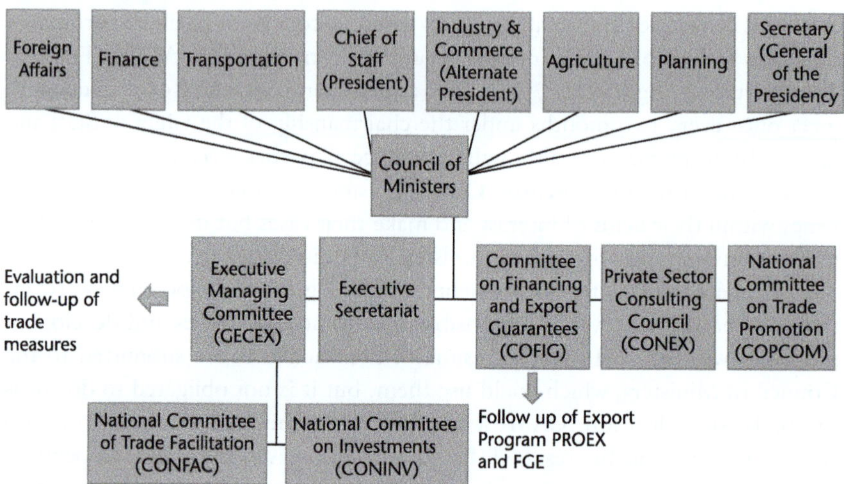

FIGURE 7 CAMEX's structure[27]

Constitution, are the main trade authority and have the capacity to approve or reject trade agreements that the Executive negotiates.[28]

The third actor in the formulation of Brazilian trade policy is the Private Sector. While the government representatives set the agenda for trade policies and negotiations, the Private Sector, especially in recent years, have a say regarding the determination of priorities. That is, the Private Sector was absent from trade policy consultations during the CACEX days but, since the inception of CAMEX, it has obtained growing influence with respect to both strategy and technical support for trade policies and negotiations. The increase in transparency standards, allowing stakeholders to be informed and consulted about the formulation of trade policies, has facilitated this surge in the Private Sector's participation. Nonetheless, transparency and formalization are not absolute, since some informal contacts between industries and government persist.

The Brazilian Private Sector is organized through the Coalizão Empresarial Brasileira (CEB) – Brazilian Business Coalition.[29] This coalition, bringing together the agricultural, industrial and service sectors, and departing from the sectorial approaches of the past, represents the business sector as a single entity in trade negotiations. The CEB maintains regular contact with officials on matters related to trade negotiations and informs its members through its website and/or recurrent meetings. Thus, CEB legitimized a broader representation of the Private

27 Figure made by the authors.

28 See Brazilian Constitution Arts 48–49.

29 See Portal da Indústria, www.portaldaindustria.com.br/cni/en/ (last visit, April 30, 2017). See also National Confederation of Industry (Confederação Nacional da Indústria), http://admin.cni.org.br/portal/data/pages/FF80808121B517F40121B54C1068470D.htm (last visit, April 30, 2017).

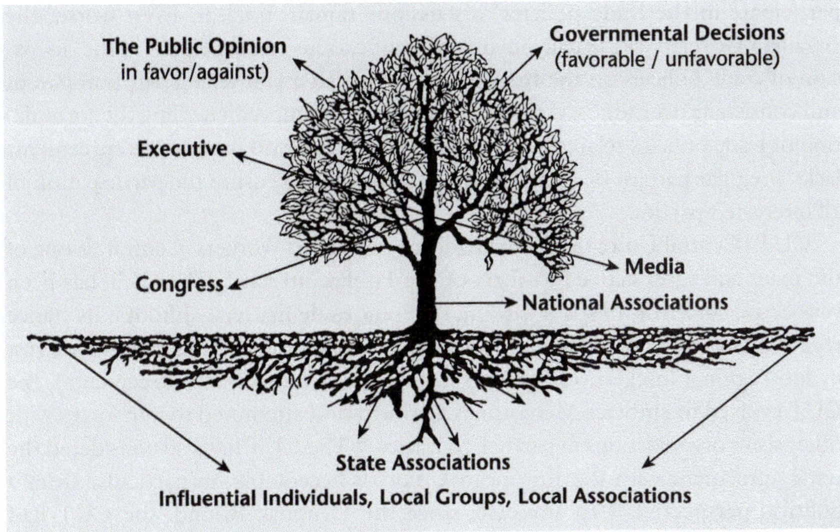

FIGURE 8 The Brazilian tree[30]

Sector in the formulation of Brazilian trade policy. On the negative side, however, such representation is still heavily industrial in its nature. The agricultural sector has also the Confederação Nacional de Agricultura (CNA) whose purpose is to promote and defend the interests of that sector.[31]

These major private sector associations follow the same model structure as those in the United States and in the European Union, as Figure 8 shows.

On the other hand, and like the rising influence of the Private Sector, the role and importance of the Public Interest has also grown since the last decades of the twentieth century, particularly in matters related to trade negotiations. On the regional level, the fact that the Economic and Social Consultative Forum of Mercosur is open to the so-called civil society has also contributed to the participation of the Public Interest in the formulation of trade policies. In practice, however, such trend is limited since the national sections of Mercosur members are the ones deciding, according to internal peculiarities, the institutions that may join in trade policy discussions.

The Brazilian Public Interest has two main features, neither of which is positive: informality and unpredictability. Regarding the first one, and even though the civil society's participation in the formulation of trade policies has increased and broadened during the last two decades, it is still carried out through informal contacts, i.e., the rules and procedures detailing how such civil society might

30 Figure made by the authors.

31 See Confederação Nacional de Agricultura (Brazilian National Confederation of Agriculture), www.cnabrasil.org.bra (last visit, April 30, 2017).

participate in the trade policies' discussions remain unclear. Even worse, the Brazilian Government usually invite different groups to participate in the discussion of trade policies on the basis of criteria which are anything but transparent and consistent over time. As to the second feature, unpredictability, the formulation of trade policies related to the WTO, the FTAA, and other trade agreements lacks a regular pattern of work and many times fails to ensure the participation of all interested parties.

CUT (Central Única dos Trabalhadores or Unified Workers' Central) is one of the main and most active members of the Public Interest.[32] The CUT has been very active since the 1990s regarding different trade matters, although its stance regarding international trade has evolved during this time.[33] From a lack of interest in sub-regional integration (or even from opposition to trade agreements), the CUT evolved to embrace Mercosur as a priority and attempted to join forces with other sister organizations in partner countries.[34] The CUT has also considered the trade agreement with the European Union as acceptable, in particular from a political perspective.[35] In any case, since the Uruguay Round, the CUT had campaigned for the inclusion of a social clause in trade agreements.[36]

The participation of NGOs in the formulation of trade policies has followed a pattern similar to the participation of trade unions.[37] The Belo Horizonte FTAA Ministerial Declaration of 1997[38] together with the Third WTO Ministerial Conference held in Seattle (the United States) in 1999[39] spurred the creation of both REBRIP (A Rede Brasileira Pela Integração dos Povos or the Brazilian Network for the Integration of Peoples)[40] and the WTO Network. Those two organizations merged in 2000 and now REBRIP congregates 35 NGOs, trade unions and other social movements.[41] In any event, REBRIP is openly against both the FTAA and the Mercosur-E.U. processes,[42] which contrasts with the trade unions' more flexible approach to those negotiations.

32 See Central Única dos Trabalhadores, www.cut.org.br/ (last visit, April 30, 2017).

33 See *id.*

34 See *id.*

35 See *id.*

36 See generally Bruno Ciccaglione and Alexandra Strickner, 'Global Crisis, the Need to Go Transnational Solidarity in the Struggle Against the Expansion of Free Trade', in *Free Trade and Transnational Labour* (Andreas Bieler, Bruno Ciccaglione, John Hilary and Ingemar Lindberg Eds), p. 146 (2010).

37 See generally Hannah Murphy, *The Making of International Trade Policy: NGOs, Agenda-Setting and the WTO,* p. 1 (2010).

38 See Belo Horizonte FTAA Ministerial Declaration, www.ftaa-alca.org/ministerials/belo/belo_e.asp (last visit, April 30, 2017).

39 See Third WTO Ministerial Conference, www.wto.org/english/thewto_e/minist_e/min99_e/min99_e.htm (last visit, April 30, 2017).

40 See REBRIP, A Rede Brasileira Pela Integração dos Povos (last visit, April 30, 2017).

41 See *id.*

42 See *id.*

TABLE 14 The rank of players' influence in Brazilian trade PFS (1 = more influence)

Player	*Rank*
Executive	1.0
Legislative	4.0
Private Sector	2.0
Public Interest	3.0

As it was done in previous chapters, the four players in the formulation of Brazilian trade policy are ranked in terms of influence in Table 14. The Executive, CAMEX mainly, holds most of the decision-making power, while Congress gets involved in specific circumstances such as for the ratification of treaties and approval of laws. Unlike in the United States, Congress is not a party to changes in tariffs, which is left entirely to CAMEX. The Private Sector is still more influential than the Public Interest, but the latter is catching up.

Some comments regarding the players that participate in the formulation of the Brazilian trade policy and the process of consultations with the Executive are necessary before ending this chapter. The purpose of consultations is to bring together the interested parties before negotiations; however, such a goal is rarely met. On a related note, the room-next-door is a strategy whose importance, not only in Brazil but also across the world, has been growing and it is now very common in entrepreneurial sectors. This strategy consists of business people going to the place where countries are negotiating trade agreements and, while they are not authorized negotiators, they obtain immediate knowledge about the progress of the deal. The CEB has been particularly involved with this kind of consultation. Other forms of communication, such as telephone, e-mail and various forms of instant messaging are also used to make sure that all sectors participate or, at least, immediately know the progress of trade negotiations. In any event, the most direct way to influence trade negotiations is becoming a member of the negotiating delegation, something that is not always possible either for the Private Sector or for the Public Interest.

Regarding the structure of the consultative process, some entities have a wide representation across a particular sector while other entities represent only aspects, activities or even geographical regions within a sector. To take one illustration, the CNI (Confederação Nacional da Indústria or National Confederation of Industry)[43] leads the representation of industrial sectors and hosts the CEB by providing organizational support and experts on some trade policies. Likewise, and during the last few years, the FIESP (Federação das Indústrias do Estado de

43 See Confederação Nacional da Indústria or National Confederation of Industry, www.portaldaindustria.com.br/cni/en/ (last visit, April 30, 2017).

São Paulo or the Industry Federation of São Paulo State) has become more vocal on these issues and could evolve further in that direction.[44]

4.3 Brazil's perspective on trade issues and negotiations

This section describes the main features of Brazilian trade policy. First, Brazil is becoming preeminent as both a user and a target of trade remedies.[45] Given the size and importance of the Brazilian economy, this is not a surprising fact. As of November 2014, Brazil is applying 65 measures, most them consisting of antidumping duties.[46] On the other hand, Brazil is the recipient of 37 trade remedies that other WTO members have imposed.[47]

Second, and nowadays, the national development's policy has become once again a major topic regarding foreign policy. This policy is related to (i) the concept of opposition between the North and the South (i.e., between developed countries in the Northern Hemisphere and developing countries in the Southern Hemisphere),[48] and (ii) the traditional function of foreign policy. Regarding the first item, Brazil intends to be the leader of the Southern block in trade matters and, in such regard, to support measures and policies favorable for this block, such as agribusiness. As to the second item, the main function of foreign policy is preserving the country from the threat that foreign commitments represent. As a result, Brazilian trade policy is subordinated to the objectives of foreign policy. This is why CAMEX is no longer chaired by the Ministry of Industry, Foreign Trade and Services but by the President's Chief of Staff.[49] On a related note, there is a present debate in Brazil regarding its political and economic strategies. Such debate is aggravated by the recent political crisis, which led to the impeachment of former President Dilma Rousseff.

The positive aspects of Brazilian trade policy might be divided into five categories. First, Brazil, as the seventh world economy, is a powerful player in the field of international trade. Second, and given such size, Brazil's GDP accounts for nearly two-thirds of the Mercosur's GDP, which means that Brazil is the

44 See Federação das Indústrias do Estado de São Paulo or the Industry Federation of the São Paulo State, www.fiesp.com.br/ (last visit, April 30, 2017).

45 See generally Trade Policy Review Brazil: 2013, www.wto.org/english/tratop_e/tpr_e/tp383_e.htm (last visit, April 30, 2017).

46 See Brazil and the WTO, www.wto.org/english/thewto_e/countries_e/brazil_e.htm (last visit, April 30, 2017).

47 See *id.*

48 See generally Bernard Hoekman, 'North-South Preferential Trade Agreements', in *Preferential Trade Agreements, Policies for Development, A Handbook* (Jean-Pierre Chauffour and Jean-Christophe Maur Eds), p. 107.

49 See Decree N° 9.029 (April 10, 2017), which amended Decree N° 8.807 (July 12, 2016), which, in turn, amended Decree N° 4.732 (June 10, 2003). See also *Diario Oficial da União*, http://pesquisa.in.gov.br/imprensa/jsp/visualiza/index.jsp?jornal=1000&pagina=1&data=12/07/2016 (last visit, April 30, 2017).

natural leader of this regional customs union. Third, the importance of both the Brazilian economy and of its agricultural sector allows it to pursue an offensive agenda in agriculture at the multilateral level, i.e., at the WTO. Fourth, Brazil is one of the leaders (if not the most important leader) of the dynamics of the so-called South-South trade, i.e., trade among developing countries located in the Southern Hemisphere. Fifth and finally, Brazil's trade policy is now focused on opening for trade with major partners.

The negative aspects of this trade policy might be divided in four topics. First, Brazil is not taking full advantage of potential gains resulting from both its WTO membership and the preferential trade agreements to which it is a party. Second, the negotiations of the South-South block have lacked the trade significance that had been envisioned some years ago. Third, while Brazil is clearly one of the leaders of the southern trade block, the real significance of such a block in international trade remains unclear, at best. Fourth, Brazil has had a defensive stance in trade negotiations, a tactic that has not always been successful.

The government of former President Dilma Rousseff implemented the so-called Bigger Brazil Plan, which incumbent President Michel Temer has continued. Its main measures have been credit stimulus (intended to spur economic growth, which has been very low during recent years),[50] a tweaking of the rules on innovation and a strengthening of the commercial defense, a broadening of tax incentives, and a facilitation of funding for domestic production in order to increase competitiveness. This plan, however, does not lack criticisms.[51] It has been said, for instance, that the current deficit has a negative impact on social welfare; that it might be against the WTO National Treatment principle[52]; that the agricultural sector lacks enough incentives to be more competitive; that the policies have been too focused on traditional economic sectors, forgetting sectors that are key to innovation and to the digital economy; and, finally, that the scope and number of trade policy measures are limited and too few.

50 See World Bank Data, http://data.worldbank.org/indicator/NY.GDP.MKTP.KD.ZG (last visit, April 30, 2017).

51 See, e.g., David Kupfer, *Case Studies of Successful and Unsuccessful Industrial Policies: The Case of Brazil* Powerpoint presentation at International Economic Association (IEA) – World Bank Roundtable May 22–23, Washington, D.C.: World Bank (2012); and Yasushi Ninomiya, 'Industrial Policy and the Post-New Brazil', in *The Post-New Brazil* (Ryohei Konta Ed.), p. 63 (2015).

52 GATT Art. III.

5

BRICS PART 2

The Chinese trade policy system

5.1 The Chinese trade policy system

Chapter 5 continues the analysis of the so-called BRICS countries. The turn is now to China, the world's second largest economy[1] and a leading merchandise trading nation in 2014 and 2015.[2] In particular, this chapter intends to answer questions such as how the Chinese trade PFS is structured, how trade players influence Chinese trade policy, and what is China's perspective on trade issues and negotiations.

China, as it is widely known, was a closed and centrally planned economy from the Chinese Revolution in 1949 until 1978. As a result, there was little role for international trade in this country during such time. Things began to change in 1978 under the leadership of Deng Xiaoping, who started the process of China's openness to international trade.[3] A major step in this direction was the creation between 1978 and 1986 of the so-called "special economic zones," which were delimited areas, most of them on the coast, intended to serve as a development hubs or, as they were known, as "windows to the world."[4]

The process of reform continued between 1986 and 1992 when the government enacted trade facilitation regulations, the so-called "twenty-two regulations," intended to create a beneficial environment for foreign investment.[5] Due to these changes and during the last decade of the twentieth century, China was not a

1 See World Bank Data, http://data.worldbank.org/indicator/NY.GDP.MKTP.CD (last visit, April 30, 2017).

2 See WTO Time Series (a database on international trade in merchandise and commercial services), http://stat.wto.org/StatisticalProgram/WSDBViewData.aspx?Language=E (last visit, April 20, 2017).

3 See generally Harry Harding, *China's Second Revolution: Reform after Mao*, p. 1 (2010).

4 See *id*.

5 See *id*.

centrally planned economy anymore but a hybrid: a socialist market economy.[6] On top of that, China was recognized as a global trading power.[7] An economy as large as the Chinese one which started to adopt market practices could not be out of the world trading system for too long. This would not have been good either for the WTO or for China itself. Thus, and after protracted and complex negotiations, China signed the Protocol of Accession to the WTO in 2001, and became a full member of this international trade organization in 2015.[8]

The openness of China to international trade has not been limited to its accession to the WTO 15 years ago. China is a full member of the following trade agreements: (i) Asia Pacific Trade Agreement (APTA, 2007)[9]; (ii) ASEAN – China Free Trade Area (ACFTA, 2003)[10]; (iii) Asia – Europe Meeting (ASEM, 1996)[11]; and (iv) Asia Pacific Economic Cooperation (APEC, 1991).[12]

China is not a member of the TPP, but it is negotiating a competing initiative: The Regional Comprehensive Economic Partnership (RCEP), which involves more countries, including three signatories of the TPP (Australia, Japan and New Zealand).[13] RCEP negotiations were launched by ASEAN leaders in November 2011 at the 19th ASEAN Summit and it includes the ten ASEAN member (Brunei, Cambodia, Indonesia, Laos, Malaysia, Myanmar, the Philippines, Singapore, Thailand and Vietnam) and the six countries with which ASEAN has existing free trade agreements (Australia, China, India, Japan, South Korea and New Zealand).[14] RCEP has the potential to transform the region into an integrated market of more than 3 billion people (over 45 percent of the world's population), with a combined GDP of about US$17.23 trillion, which is about a third of the world's current annual GDP.[15]

6 See *id.*

7 Arguably, China was a global trading power before, from around the year 130 BC to the fifteenth century (from the opening of the Silk Road to its closing by the Ottoman Empire). It brought economic prosperity to cities and towns along the route. More recently, China has been investing heavily in Central Asia, in a process that has been called a revival of the Silk Road. See *The New Trade Routes: Silk Road Corridor China seeking to revive the Silk Road*, Financial Times, May 9, 2016, www.ft.com/content/e99ff7a8-0bd8-11e6-9456-444ab5211a2f (last visit, April 20, 2017).

8 See *China and the WTO*, www.wto.org/english/thewto_e/countries_e/china_e.htm (last visit, April 30, 2017). See also *Permanent Mission of China to the WTO, China in the WTO: Past, Present and Future*, www.wto.org/english/thewto_e/acc_e/s7lu_e.pdf (last visit, April 30, 2017).

9 See generally United Nations Economic and Social for Asia and the Pacific, www.unescap.org/apta (last visit, April 30, 2017).

10 See ASEAN, http://asean.org/?static_post=asean-china-free-trade-area-2# (last visit, April 30, 2017).

11 See ASEM, www.aseminfoboard.org/ (last visit, April 30, 2017).

12 See APEC, www.apec.org/ (last visit, April 30, 2017).

13 See Asia Regional Integration Center, https://aric.adb.org/fta/regional-comprehensive-economic-partnership (last visit, April 20, 2017).

14 See *id.*

15 See *id.*

Indeed, China was one of the reasons the United States decided to pursue the TPP negotiations in 2008 as a way to outweigh the Chinese influence in its own backyard, the Asian southeast.[16] But that objective no longer stands in face of the U.S. withdrawal from TPP.

Regarding bilateral agreements, China has entered into economic partnership agreements with the Special Administrative Regions of Hong Kong[17] and Macau (2004),[18] and into agreements in commerce and economy with Australia (2003), New Zealand (2004), and the Cooperation Gulf Council whose members are Bahrain, Kuwait, Oman, Qatar, Saudi Arabia and the United Arab Emirates (2004).[19] China has also entered into preferential trade agreements with Korea (2015), Australia (2015), Iceland (2014), Switzerland (2014), Peru (2010), Taiwan (2010), Singapore (2009), Costa Rica (2008), New Zealand (2008), Chile (2005), Thailand (2003) and Pakistan (2003).[20] Some other preferential trade agreements are in the negotiation stage: China – Gulf Cooperation Council (whose members are the Kingdom of Bahrain and Saudi Arabia, the States of Kuwait and Qatar, the Sultanate of Oman, and the United Arab Emirates),[21] China – Norway, China-Japan-Korea, Regional Economic Comprehensive Partnership,[22] China – Sri Lanka, China – Maldives, and China – Georgia.[23]

China is also a beneficiary of GSP from Japan[24] and New Zealand.[25] The European Commission and Canada also used to grant these unilateral preferences but they were suspended as of 2015 taking into account the Chinese economic

16 See Gary C. Hufbauer, *The Evolving US View on TPP*, Working Paper No 484 (2013), http://ycsg.yale.edu/sites/default/files/files/hufbauer_TPP.pdf (last visit, April 30, 2017). See generally the USTR, https://ustr.gov/tpp/ (last visit, April 30, 2017).

17 See Trade and Industry Department, the Government of Hong Kong Special Administrative Region, www.tid.gov.hk/english/cepa/ (last visit, April 30, 2017). Hong Kong was a colony of the United Kingdom until 1997 and it is now a Chinese special administrative zone.

18 See CEPA, www.cepa.gov.mo/cepaweb/front/eng/index_en.htm (last visit, April 30, 2017). Macau was a territory dependent on Portugal until 1999. It is now a special administrative zone of China.

19 See China FTA Network, http://fta.mofcom.gov.cn/english/index.shtml (last visit, April 30, 2017).

20 See *id.*

21 See Gulf Cooperation Council, www.gcc-sg.org/en-us/Pages/default.aspx (last visit, April 30, 2017).

22 A trade agreement among the ten ASEAN Members (Brunei, Cambodia, Indonesia, Laos, Malaysia, Myanmar, the Philippines, Singapore, Thailand, Vietnam) and the six states with which ASEAN has existing PTAs (Australia, China, India, Japan, South Korea and New Zealand). See China FTA Network, http://fta.mofcom.gov.cn/english/index.shtml (last visit, April 30, 2017).

23 See *id.*

24 See Generalized System of Preferences, Japan, http://ptadb.wto.org/ptaHistoryExplorer.aspx (last visit, April 30, 2017). But see Nikkei Asian Review, http://asia.nikkei.com/Politics-Economy/International-Relations/Japan-to-take-China-Thailand-off-reduced-tariff-list (last visit, November 30, 2016) (mentioned that Japan is considering to exclude China from its GSP due to its economic development).

25 See Generalized System of Preferences, New Zealand, http://ptadb.wto.org/ptaHistoryExplorer.aspx (last visit, April 30, 2017).

growth in the former case[26] and CETA, which is already in legal force in the latter case. On the other hand, China offers preferential tariffs to around 40 least developed countries on 60 percent of its products.[27]

Speaking of tariffs, they continue to be the main Chinese trade policy instrument; its overall average applied MFN tariff was 9.5 percent in 2015, a percentage very similar to previous years.[28] This figure might be decomposed in an average tariff of 14.8 percent for agricultural products and of 8.6 percent for non-agricultural products.[29] Given the importance of the Chinese agricultural sector, it is not surprising that the former figure is almost double the latter. Of course, tariffs are lower when they are applied under preferential trade agreements. Tariffs are used to protect the national industry and not to raise revenues since they only amount to a very low percentage of total revenues.[30]

5.2 How players influence trade policy in China

In spite of its transition from a centrally planned economy to a market economy, the Executive and the Legislative are still the two main actors in China, with the Private Sector and the Public Interest having reduced roles. Figure 9 shows the structure of the Executive and the Legislative.

The most relevant authority in trade issues is the Ministry of Commerce (MOFCOM), established in 2003, which coordinates and implements trade-related policies.[31] Its main responsibilities are drafting and formulating laws, regulations and policies on domestic and international trade and on foreign investment as well; harmonizing domestic laws and regulations on trade and economic affairs; adopting, amending or abrogating controls of imports and exports, quotas, licenses and trade remedies; and promoting and facilitating trade.[32] Besides the MOFCOM, other governmental institutions that have influence on the international trade agenda include the National Development and Reform Commission,[33] which is in charge of formulating trade and economic policies, the Ministry of Finance,[34] and the General Administration of Customs.[35]

26 See European Commission, http://ec.europa.eu/trade/policy/countries-and-regions/development/generalised-scheme-of-preferences/ (last visit, April 30, 2017).

27 See generally WTO Tariffs, www.wto.org/english/tratop_e/tariffs_e/tariff_data_e.htm (last visit, April 30, 2017).

28 See WTO Trade Policy Review: China, www.wto.org/english/tratop_e/tpr_e/tp442_e.htm (last visit, April 30, 2017).

29 See *id.*

30 See *id.*

31 See Ministry of Commerce, http://english.mofcom.gov.cn/ (last visit, April 30, 2017).

32 See *id.*

33 See National Development and Reform Commission, http://en.ndrc.gov.cn/ (last visit, April 30, 2017).

34 See Ministry of Finance, http://english.gov.cn/state_council/2014/09/09/content_281474986284115.htm (last visit, April 30, 2017).

35 See General Administration of Customs, http://english.customs.gov.cn/ (last visit, April 30, 2017).

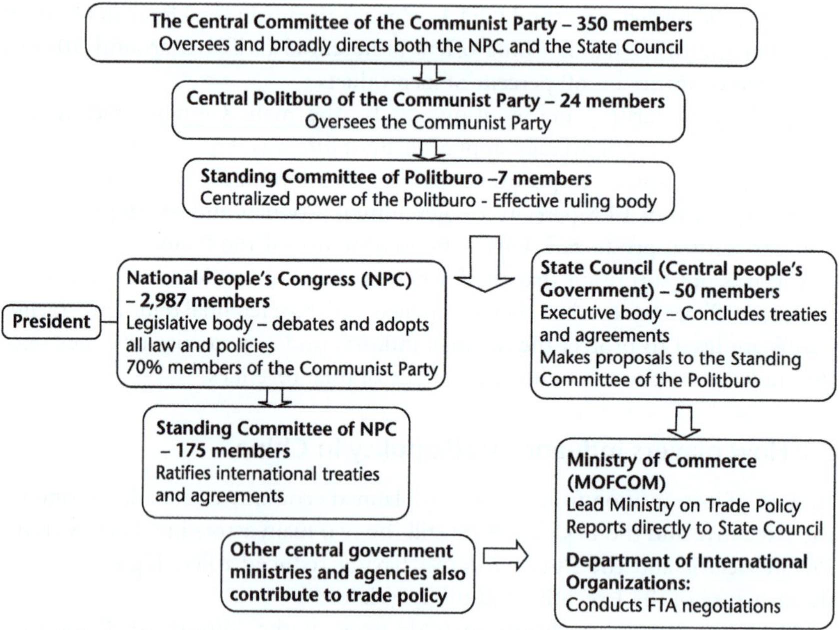

FIGURE 9 The Chinese institutional framework[36]

The ultimate authority, however, rests with the Politburo Standing Committee (PSC), composed, historically, of five to nine members, but presently of seven. How the PSC operates is unknown outside its walls. According to free press accounts,

> its meetings are thought to be regular and frequent, often characterized by blunt speaking and disagreement. Senior leaders speak first and then sum up, giving their views extra weight. The emphasis is always on reaching a consensus, but if no consensus is reached, the majority holds sway.[37]

Its decisions are routinely unopposed by the National People's Congress, something that virtually guarantees that what the NPC decides, goes.

The Legislative Body is the National People's Congress (NPC), composed of almost 3,000 members (around 70 percent of them are affiliated to the Communist Party), and which is in charge of enacting legislation.[38] Notwithstanding, it is one committee of this Congress, the NPC Standing Committee, composed of

36 Figure made by the authors.

37 *Inside China's Ruling Party*, BBC News, http://news.bbc.co.uk/2/shared/spl/hi/asia_pac/02/china_party_congress/china_ruling_party/how_china_is_ruled/html/politburo.stm (last visit, April 30, 2017).

38 See The National People's Congress, www.npc.gov.cn/englishnpc/news/ (last visit, April 30, 2017).

175 members, which ratifies international treaties.[39] Rarely, if ever, the NPC or its Standing Committee vote against decisions from the PSC.

As to the Private Sector, it is still young in China, as Figure 10 indicates, but growing very fast. Some numbers confirm this statement. To begin with, the number of small business that individuals opened increased from 140,000 in 1978, when economic changes began, to 25,000,000 in 2005.[40] On top of that, while only 24 percent of Chinese companies were private in 2000, this percentage increased to 53 percent in 2005 and to 78 percent in 2008.[41] Not all news, however, has been good for the Private Sector. In 2008, as a result of the financial crisis, a large number of private companies closed.[42] To ameliorate the impact of the financial meltdown, the Chinese government-financed state enterprises with the purpose of acquiring small business.[43] As a consequence, the market share of state enterprises has increased since 2008.[44] According to one source, "data from 2013 show the public sector still accounting for only 30 per cent of total firms but roughly 55 per cent of assets, 45 per cent of revenue and 40 per cent of profits" (Scissors, Derek, AEI, May 17, 2016). Finally, the Public Interest is almost nonexistent in China, but has grown in response to human rights, environmental and social concerns.

As Figure 10 depicts, the Chinese Private Sector tree is relatively small so as to represent the small but growing private concerns in China and their still small but increasing influence in trade policy formulation. The focus of Private Sector advocacy is on the Executive (PSC, MOFCOM and State Council), since other government branches, state press and civil society would either have no influence in policy or be immune to non-state advocacy.

5.3 China's perspective on trade issues and negotiations

As the size of its economy suggests, China is one of the most active WTO Members regarding the imposition of trade remedies.[45] Antidumping duties are the most

39 See The National People's Congress Standing Committee, www.npc.gov.cn/englishnpc/Organization/node_2847.htm (last visit, April 30, 2017).

40 See Hongliang Zheng and Yang Yang, *Chinese Private Sector Development in the Past 30 Years: Retrospect and Prospect*, Discussion Paper 45 (2009), www.nottingham.ac.uk/cpi/documents/discussion-papers/discussion-paper-45-hongliang-zheng-chinese-private-sector.pdf (last visit, April 30, 2017).

41 See *id*. Chinese Statistical Year Book 2009 (2009), www.stats.gov.cn/tjsj/ndsj/2009/indexeh.htm (last visit, April 30, 2017).

42 See *id*.

43 Hongliang Zheng and Yang Yang, *Chinese Private Sector Development in the Past 30 Years: Retrospect and Prospect*, Discussion Paper 45 (2009), www.nottingham.ac.uk/cpi/documents/discussion-papers/discussion-paper-45-hongliang-zheng-chinese-private-sector.pdf (last visit, April 30, 2017).

44 See *id*.

45 See WTO Trade Policy Review: China, www.wto.org/english/tratop_e/tpr_e/tp442_e.htm (last visit, April 30, 2017).

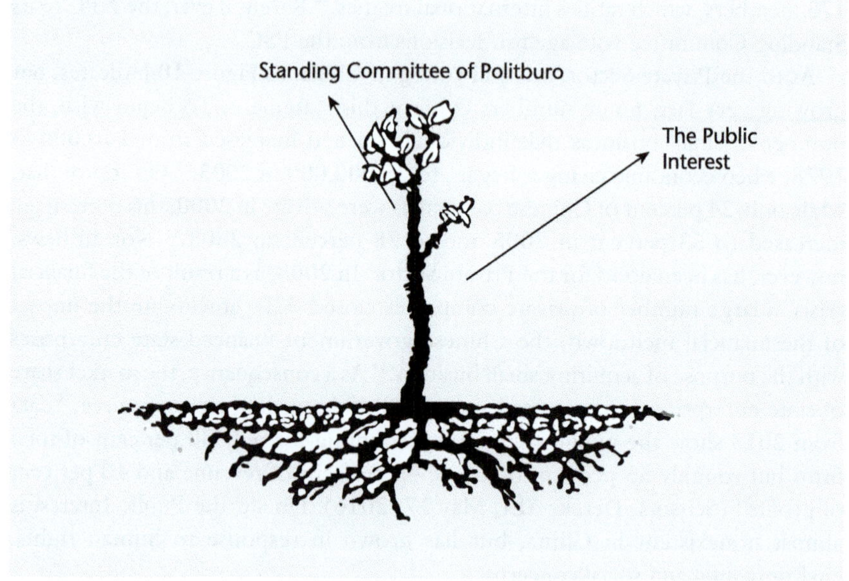

FIGURE 10 The Chinese tree

common trade remedy in China.[46] The proceedings to impose trade remedies in China are similar to those of the European system.[47] Such proceedings usually begin upon the request of the injured domestic industry or, less often and if some circumstances are met, the government initiates the proceedings *ex officio*.[48] The investigation cannot last more than one year although special circumstances in complex cases might allow for an extension of up to six months.[49]

Two governmental entities within the MOFCOM participate in antidumping proceedings (the process is very similar regarding countervailing duties and safeguards).[50] The Bureau of Fair Trade for Imports and Exports (BOFT) is in charge of the investigation and, in such capacity, determines whether or not dumping has occurred.[51] The Bureau of Industry Injury Investigations (BIII), in turn, investigates and determines whether or not the industry has suffered material

46 See *id.*

47 See *supra* Chapter 3.

48 See WTO Trade Policy Review: China, www.wto.org/english/tratop_e/tpr_e/tp442_e.htm (last visit, April 30, 2017). See also WTO Agreement on Antidumping Duties.

49 See *id.*

50 See Ministry of Commerce, http://english.mofcom.gov.cn/ (last visit, April 30, 2017). See also The Decision of the State Council on Amending the Antidumping Regulations of the People's Republic of China (2004), www.lawinfochina.com/Search/SearchLaw.aspx (last visit, April 30, 2017).

51 See *id.*

injury.[52] Both entities (BOFT and BIII) are jointly responsible for determining the causal link between dumping and injury.[53] A special rule applies when the investigation is related to agricultural products: in such a case both the MOFCOM and the Ministry of Agriculture jointly conduct the investigation.[54]

Once the steps indicated in the previous paragraph are completed, MOFCOM determines in a preliminary investigation if any antidumping duties, or alternatively, any guarantee such as a deposit or a bond can be applied.[55] The Tariff Commission of the State Council, based on the recommendation of the MOFCOM, establishes whether or not to levy provisional antidumping duties.[56] In any case, provisional measures shall not be applied within the 60 days following the date when the decision to initiate the investigation was published and, more importantly, such provisional measures shall not exceed four months, although this timeframe might be extended up to nine months under special circumstances.[57] Similar to the procedures to establish provisional measures, the Tariff Commission of the State Council, based on the MOFCOM's suggestions, establishes whether or not to levy definitive antidumping duties, which might be in legal force for up to five years, extendable for a longer time following a review process.[58] If any party is not satisfied with the decision, the case might be appealed and reviewed under the Administrative Reconsideration Law.[59]

Table 15 ranks the influence of each of the four main actors in Chinese trade policy formulation. The Executive, as represented by the PSC, MOFCOM and the State Council, is the most influential by far, with the Public Interest and Private Sector coming in third (influence = 3) and second places (influence = 2), respectively.

TABLE 15 The rank of players' influence in China's trade PFS (1 = more influence)

Player	*Rank*
Executive	1.0
Legislative	4.0
Private Sector	2.0
Public Interest	3.0

52 See *id.*

53 See *id.*

54 See *id.* See also Ministry of Agriculture, http://english.agri.gov.cn/ (last visit, April 30, 2017).

55 See Ministry of Commerce, http://english.mofcom.gov.cn/ (last visit, April 30, 2017). See also The Decision of the State Council on Amending the Antidumping Regulations of the People's Republic of China (2004), www.lawinfochina.com/Search/SearchLaw.aspx (last visit, April 30, 2017).

56 See *id.*

57 See *id.*

58 See *id.*

59 See *id.* See also Chinese Administrative Law, The National People's Congress, www.npc.gov.cn/englishnpc/Law/2007-12/11/content_1383562.htm (last visit, April 30, 2017).

The Legislative, constituted by the NPC, which basically rubber-stamps decisions of the PSC, comes in last.

Before ending this chapter, a brief comparison between the Chinese trade policy system and the other systems discussed so far in this book is warranted. First, China is not part of a supranational body, as happens regarding the countries belonging to the European Union.[60] Second, and as mentioned above, the Executive is very powerful in China, certainly more than in the United States,[61] the European Union,[62] and Brazil.[63] Third, and due to its past as a communist country, the influence of the Private Sector on China's trade PFS is much lower than in the United States,[64] the European Union,[65] and Brazil.[66] This fact, however, might be misleading since the Chinese Private Sector is growing fast and might be a force to be reckoned with in a not too distant future. Fourth, the Public Interest is almost nonexistent in China, a fact that is closely related to the not very high standards of transparency in this country.

60 See *supra* Chapter 3.
61 See *supra* Chapter 2.
62 See *supra* Chapter 3.
63 See *supra* Chapter 4.
64 See *supra* Chapter 2.
65 See *supra* Chapter 3.
66 See *supra* Chapter 4.

6

BRICS PART 3

The Indian trade policy system

6.1 The Indian trade policy system

Chapter 6 discusses the trade policy system of the third member of the so-called BRICS group, India. The purpose of this chapter, similar to the previous ones, is to understand how the Indian trade policy system is structured, how trade players influence Indian trade policy, and India's perspective on trade issues and negotiations.

India was part of the British Empire until 1947, when it became two independent states: one Muslim state (Pakistan, which later on divided into Pakistan itself and Bangladesh) and another state with a Hindu majority, India.[1] During the first decades of independence and under the view that international trade was only beneficial to developed regions of the world, India was an almost autarchic country.[2] Exports were minimal, the government aimed at local self-sufficiency through import substitution and, generally speaking, there was a strict control of trade and foreign exchanges.[3] As a result of this policy, India's participation in international trade, which was already low in 1951 (2.4 percent), fell to almost zero in 1980 (0.4 percent).[4]

This trade policy began to change in the 1970s when the balance of payments problems that the well-known oil shock triggered led to policies focused on export

1 See BBC, *The Hidden Story of Partition and its Legacies*, www.bbc.co.uk/history/british/modern/partition1947_01.shtml (last visit, April 30, 2017).

2 See generally Jayanta Roy, Pritam Banerjee and Ankur Mahanta, *The Evolution of Indian Trade Policy: State Intervention and Political Economy of Interest Groups. Historical Development of Indian Trade Policy and the Impact of Institutional Choices on Present Time* (2012), www.ipekpp.com/admin/upload_files/Report_3_54_The_2552084041.pdf (last visit, April 30, 2017).

3 See *id.*

4 See *id.*

promotion during the 1980s and 1990s.[5] Such exports were required to obtain the foreign currency to import oil, tech and other vital goods that were not locally produced.[6] Thus, and with the support of the IMF Structural Adjustment Program in 1991, most restrictions to the participation of private companies in key sectors were repealed and, more generally, significant progress was made regarding trade liberalization, deregulation, and privatization.[7]

As a result of the reduced control from government over international trade during the early 1990s, exports rose.[8] For instance, handcrafters, stone makers, and jewelers, on the one hand, and textiles and apparel, on the other hand, respectively accounted for around 22.2 percent and 18.5 percent of exports in 1993 (around US$4.9 billion and US$4.1 billion).[9] Other significant exports were related to industrial equipment, leather goods, and chemical products.[10]

India adopted a stimulus package during the 2008 financial crisis.[11] While the economy did not grow too much, it continued its expansion process.[12] Notwithstanding, inflation pressures led the government to repeal some measures of this stimulus package.[13] The fiscal deficit, in turn, has been reduced in recent years although not in the expected amount under the fiscal consolidation process, which began in 2004.[14]

6.2 How players influence trade policy in India

The President and the Prime Minister are the highest authorities of the Executive.[15] Under such authority, the Ministry of Commerce and Industry is the entity in charge of formulating and implementing the trade policy.[16] As to the Legislative, the Indian Parliament is the authority in charge of approving or rejecting trade agreements.[17] It is divided into two houses: the lower house (*Lok Sabha*) and the upper house

5 See *id.*

6 See *id.*

7 See The World Bank Group, Independent Evaluation Group, 2012, http://lnweb90.worldbank.org/oed/oeddoclib.nsf/DocUNIDViewForJavaSearch/0586CC45A28A27498 52567F5005D8C89 (last visit, April 30, 2017).

8 See *id.*

9 World Integrated Trade Solution, India Trade Summary 1993, http://wits.worldbank.org/CountryProfile/en/Country/IND/Year/1993/Summarytext (last visit, April 30, 2017).

10 See *id.*

11 See WTO Trade Policy Review: India 2011, www.wto.org/english/tratop_e/tpr_e/tp349_e.htm (last visit, April 30, 2017).

12 See *id.*

13 See *id.*

14 See WTO Trade Policy Review: India 2015, www.wto.org/english/tratop_e/tpr_e/tp413_e.htm (last visit, April 30, 2017).

15 See Constitution of India, available at: http://indiacode.nic.in/coiweb/welcome.html (last visit, April 30, 2017).

16 See Ministry of Commerce and Industry of India, http://commerce.nic.in/DOC/index.aspx (last visit, April 30, 2017).

17 See Constitution of India, http://indiacode.nic.in/coiweb/welcome.html (last visit, April, 30, 2017).

(*Rajya Sabha*).[18] The Indian President has the authority to dissolve the lower house.[19] The Private Sector, in turn, is not as strong as in the United States,[20] the European Union,[21] or Brazil,[22] but has a more significant role than in China.[23] The Private Sector influences the policies that the Executive implements, through the Ministry of Commerce and Industry, especially in the most sensible sectors, such as agriculture, textiles, and jewelry.[24] Finally, the Public Interest, whose participation is facilitated by reasonable standards of transparency, has a high influence on topics related to poverty and nutrition.[25]

This last point is mainly related to agriculture, upon which 58 percent of India's population depend for their livelihood.[26] It has been more the rule rather than the exception that every time farmers are unable to produce and repay loans as a result of weather conditions or competition from imports, they commit suicide.[27] In 2013, more than 11,000 farmers killed themselves.[28] This is a major problem for the government, which in such situations must provide support for the families left behind and for agricultural production.[29] This quandary, to a significant extent, is what is behind India's resistance in agricultural market access negotiations.

Table 16 ranks the degree of influence of each of the four main players in India's trade policy formulation system. The Executive is the most influential, followed by Legislative, Private Sector and Public Interest. However, if the policy involves poverty and nutrition, the Public Interest will be more influential than the Private Sector.

India's trade policy is formulated for five-year periods, with yearly adjustments. The most recent trade policy is for the period 2015–2020.[30] The trade policy's main

18 See *id.*
19 See *id.*
20 See *supra* Chapter 2.
21 See *supra* Chapter 3.
22 See *supra* Chapter 4.
23 See *supra* Chapter 5.
24 See Asian Development Bank, *Trade Policy, Industrial Performance, and Private Sector Development in India,* p. 1 (2008). See also John Schaus, *Private Sector Development in India's Foreign Policy* (2015), https://csis-prod.s3.amazonaws.com/s3fs-public/legacy_files/files/publication/150504_Schaus_PrivateSecDevelIndia_Web.pdf (last visit, April 30, 2017).
25 See Asian Development Bank, *Trade Policy, Industrial Performance, and Private Sector Development in India,* p. 1 (2008). See also WTO Trade Policy Review: India 2015, www.wto.org/english/tratop_e/tpr_e/tp413_e.htm (last visit, April 30, 2017).
26 See India Brand Equity Foundation, www.ibef.org/industry/agriculture-india.aspx (last visit, April 30, 2017)
27 See *Why India's Cotton Farmers are Killing Themselves*, CNN, www.cnn.com/2015/04/19/asia/india-cotton-farmers-suicide/ (last visit, April 30, 2017).
28 See *Thousands of farmer suicides prompt India to set up $1.3bn crop insurance scheme*, The Guardian, available at: www.theguardian.com/world/2016/jan/14/india-thousands-of-farmer-suicides-prompt-1bn-crop-insurance-scheme (last visit, April 30, 2017).
29 See *id.*
30 See Foreign Trade Policy, Ministry of Commerce and Industry Department of Commerce (India), http://dgft.gov.in/exim/2000/ftp2015-20E.pdf (last visit, April 30, 2017).

TABLE 16 The rank of players' influence in India's trade PFS (1 = more influence)

Player	*Rank*
Executive	1
Legislative	2
Private Sector	3
Public Interest	4

goals are the simplification of import proceedings (India has implemented electronic customs proceedings and other facilitating trade measures), the increase of exports and the use of trade to reduce unemployment rates, and the reduction of tariffs, which went from 32 percent in 2001 to 15 percent in 2007 and to 12 percent in 2011.[31] On a related note, and while foreign investment is allowed in a significant number of industries, recent decisions have slowed the pace of privatizations in some other sectors.[32] Since the number of state-owned enterprises is still high and they are not always very profitable, these companies require significant financial resources from the government.[33] On the other hand, India grants duty free tariff preference to over 30 lesser-developed countries across the globe.[34]

6.3 India's perspective on trade issues and negotiations

The WTO in its Trade Policy Report from 2015 pointed out some new changes in the Indian economy such as the following ones.[35] First, economic growth has triggered an improvement in social indicators.[36] Second, India has implemented structural reforms in some sectors which have contributed to services being the fastest growing sector.[37] Manufacturing has also performed well, although infrastructure and other constraints such as access to credit and lack of qualified personnel have impeded further growth.[38] Reforms in this sector have focused on simplifying the tax regime and reducing trade restrictions.[39] On the other hand,

31 See *id.* See also WTO Trade Policy Review: India 2015, www.wto.org/english/tratop_e/tpr_e/tp413_e.htm (last visit, April 30, 2017).

32 See K. S. Vataliya and Bhanupen N. Parmar, *An Article on Foreign Capital and Foreign Investment (Foreign Direct Investment)* 1(3) Int'l J. Advance Res. Computer Sci. & Mgmt. Stud. 1 (2013), http://ijarcsms.com/docs/paper/volume1/issue3/V1I3-0005.pdf (last visit, April 30, 2017). See also U.S. Department of State, 2015 Investment Climate Statement: India, www.state.gov/e/eb/rls/othr/ics/2015/241595.htm (last visit, April 30, 2017).

33 See *id.*

34 See also WTO Trade Policy Review: India 2015, www.wto.org/english/tratop_e/tpr_e/tp413_e.htm (last visit, April 30, 2017).

35 See WTO Trade Policy Review: India 2015, www.wto.org/english/tratop_e/tpr_e/tp413_e.htm (last visit, April 30, 2017).

36 See *id.*

37 See *id.*

38 See *id.*

39 See *id.*

and regrettably, agricultural growth continues to be slow, erratic and dependent on increasingly unpredictable weather, causing considerable distress, especially among small and marginal farmers.[40] India has also entered into several bilateral and regional preferential trade agreements and is negotiating some more, intended to increase market access for its exports.[41] However, the Indian export regime continues to be complex.[42]

Third, the process of tariff reduction continued until 2011, since tariffs fell from 15 percent in 2006–2007 to 12 percent in 2010–2011.[43] However, the average MFN tariff increased to 13 percent in 2014–2015, an upsurge mainly due to the rise in the tariffs of some agricultural products.[44] Fourth, and since 2010, India has been an observer of the WTO Agreement on Government Procurement (GPA).[45] Last but not least, India is one of the most active countries regarding the imposition of antidumping duties. During the last period of the trade policy review, India began 80 investigations against 23 countries in sectors such as chemicals, plastics, rubber and textiles.[46] The Ministry of Commerce and Industry conducts trade remedies cases under the prospective system.[47]

On the other hand, the WTO Ninth Ministerial Conference held in Bali (Indonesia) in December 2013 approved the so-called Bali package, which is part of the Doha Development Round.[48] This package included measures lowering tariffs and agricultural subsidies, abolishing quotas on the same goods, and other rules related to trade facilitation (i.e., reduction of customs bureaucracies and formalities).[49] There were also other measures related to cotton and to preferential

40 See *id.*

41 India is a member of the South Asian Free Trade Area (SAFTA) whose other members are Afghanistan, Bangladesh, Bhutan, Maldives, Nepal, Pakistan and Sri Lanka. India has also entered into a Comprehensive Economic Cooperation Agreement (CECA) with ASEAN. See Ministry of Commerce and Industry, http://commerce.nic.in/doc/writereaddata/trade/FAQ_on_FTA_9April2014.pdf?id=9&trade=i (last visit, April 30, 2017). See also The Asia Digest, *Free Trade Agreements of India*, November 16, 2016, www.theasiadigest.com/message/statement-industry/labour/psus/12739/free-trade-agreements-and-india.htm#.WEcL4s09mZQ (last visit, April 30, 2017).

42 See WTO Trade Policy Review: India 2015, www.wto.org/english/tratop_e/tpr_e/tp413_e.htm (last visit, April 30, 2017).

43 See *id.*

44 See *id.*

45 See WTO Agreement on Government Procurement, Parties, Observers and Accessions, www.wto.org/English/tratop_e/gproc_e/memobs_e.htm (last visit, April 30, 2017).

46 See WTO Trade Policy Review: India 2015, www.wto.org/english/tratop_e/tpr_e/tp413_e.htm (last visit, April 30, 2017). In sheer contrast, India initiated only one countervailing investigation during the period under review and no one definitive countervailing measure is in place. During such period, India also initiated 18 safeguard investigations. See *id.*

47 For a deeper explanation of trade remedies, see *infra* Chapter 10.

48 See 9th WTO Ministerial Conference, Bali, 2013 and After, Bali Package and November 2014 Decisions, www.wto.org/english/thewto_e/minist_e/mc9_e/balipackage_e.htm (last visit, April 30, 2017).

49 See *id.*

measures for least developed countries.[50] After this WTO Ninth Ministerial Conference and previous to the local presidential elections, India effectively held the Bali package hostage, refusing to reduce the subsidies to its agricultural sector.[51] After some additional negotiations with other WTO Members, India eventually accepted to ratify the Trade Facilitation Agreement that was part of the Bali package.[52]

At least another two trade topics are very important for India right now. First, and although India is not a party to the GPA, the United States challenged Indian policies for the solar energy sector under the GATT, the TRIMs and the ASCM WTO agreements.[53] The Appellate Body, whose report was adopted by the DSB on October 14, 2016, held that certain measures of India relating to domestic content requirements under the Jawaharlal Nehru National Solar Mission (NSM) for solar cells and solar modules were inconsistent with WTO non-discrimination obligations under Art. III:4 of the GATT1994 and Art. 2.1 of the TRIMs Agreement, and not justified under GATT Art. XX(j), applicable to measures that are essential to the acquisition or distribution of "products in general or local short supply," or Art. XX(d), which establishes a general exception for measures necessary to "secure compliance" with a WTO member's "laws or regulations" which are not themselves GATT-inconsistent.[54] Second, compulsory licenses on patents and access to medicines remains a hot-button issue with the United States and the European Union.[55]

50 See *id.*

51 See WTO: 2016 News Items, *Trade Facilitation, India ratifies Trade Facilitation Agreement* (April 22, 2016), www.wto.org/english/news_e/news16_e/fac_21apr16_e.htm (last visit, April 30, 2017).

52 See *id.*

53 See DS456, India – Certain Measures Relating to Solar Cells and Solar Modules.

54 See *id.*

55 See Section 11 A of the Indian Patent Act, whose pertinent part reads:

> the patent-holder shall only be entitled to receive reasonable royalty from such enterprises which have made significant investment and were producing and marketing the concerned product prior to the 1st day of January, 2005 and which continue to manufacture the product covered by the patent on the date of grant of the patent and no infringement proceedings shall be instituted against such enterprises.

The Indian Patents (Amendments) Act 2005, www.ipindia.nic.in/ipr/patent/patent_2005.pdf (last visit, April 30, 2017).

7

BRICS PART 4

The Russian trade policy system

7.1 The Russian trade policy system

Chapter 7 discusses the trade policy system of the fourth BRICS member: Russia, which was also the latest large country to accede to the WTO.[1] For this purpose, this chapter analyzes the structure of the Russian trade policy system, the influence of the trade players on the Russian trade policy, and Russia's perspective on trade issues and negotiations.

The former Soviet Union was a centrally planned economy between the Russian Revolution in 1917, which overthrew the Czarist regime, and its demise in 1991. Under the leadership of Mikhail Gorbachev, some political and economic changes began in the early 1980s, which went deeper during the 1990s.[2] As a result, not only of such reforms but also of the fall of the Berlin Wall in 1989, the Soviet Union split up into 15 countries in 1991, Russia being the largest of them.[3]

Boris Yeltsin, the first president of the new Russian republic, started in 1991 a program of radical economic reforms, whose flagship was the privatization of the most important stated-owned enterprises.[4] As a consequence of this process and only five years after its beginning, Russia resembled more a developed market economy than a centrally planned economy.[5] Nonetheless, and although the

1 See WTO: 2012 Press Releases (August 22, 2012), www.wto.org/english/news_e/pres12_e/pr671_e.htm (last visit, April 30, 2017).

2 See generally Vladimir Mau and Robert Skidelsky, *The Political History of Economic Reform in Russia, 1985–1994* (1995).

3 See *id.*

4 See *id.*

5 See generally Marie Lavigne, *The Economics of Transition: From Socialist Economy to Market Economy* (2nd ed.), p. 1 (2007).

Russian economy seemed strong in 1996, it suffered the effects of the financial crisis of 1998, when the ruble, the Russian currency, precipitously fell.[6]

Nowadays, more than 25 years after the demise of the Soviet Union, Russia is still attempting to develop its market economy and to obtain more consistent growth,[7] although some political decisions might be against this goal.[8]

Besides the privatization program, other priorities of the reforms have been both the integration of Russia to international trade and the promotion of foreign investment.[9] For that purpose, the Russian Federation became an IMF member in 1992[10] and a World Bank member in the same year.[11] In the same sense, the OECD Council in 2007 decided to open accession discussions with, among other countries, the Russian Federation, although little progress has been made and the same Council postponed the activities related to such accession in March 2014.[12] On the political side, Russia belonged to the so-called G8 (an informal bloc of developed countries whose other members are Canada, France, Germany, Italy, Japan, the United Kingdom and the United States) from 1998 to 2014, when its membership was suspended after the Russian annexation of Crimea in the early months of that year (as a result, the name of the group is now the G7).[13]

Russia requested accession to the WTO in 1993 and, after an obviously lengthy and complex process, the WTO completed the terms in November 2011, the Ministerial Conference's approval was granted in the following month, and Russia joined the WTO in 2012 (Russia ratified the accession package on July 23 and 30 days later, on August 22, Russia became a full member).[14] Although the years that have elapsed since its accession are too few to determine the effects of this decision not only for Russia but for all other WTO Members, it is expected that Russia's accession to the WTO will bring benefits such as the opening of a huge market for foreign companies and amendments to domestic legal rules.[15]

6 See generally Martin Gilman, *No Precedent, No Plan: Inside Russia's 1998 Default* 1 (2010).

7 See International Monetary Fund, www.imf.org/external/country/RUS/index.htm (last visit, April 30, 2017).

8 See, e.g., Bill Browder, *Red Notice: A True Story of High Finance, Murder, and One Man's Fight for Justice,* p. 1 (2015).

9 See WTO Trade Policy Review: Russian Federation, www.wto.org/english/tratop_e/tpr_e/tp445_e.htm (last visit, April 30, 2017).

10 See International Monetary Fund, www.imf.org/external/np/sec/memdir/memdate.htm (last visit, April 30, 2017).

11 See World Bank, www.worldbank.org/en/about/leadership/members (last visit, April 30, 2017).

12 See Organization for Economic Cooperation and Development, www.oecd.org/about/membersandpartners/ (last visit, April 30, 2017).

13 See Council on Foreign Relations, www.cfr.org/international-organizations-and-alliances/group-seven-g7/p32957 (last visit, April 30, 2017).

14 See WTO: 2011 News Items, *Ministerial Conference approves Russia's WTO membership,* www.wto.org/english/news_e/news11_e/acc_rus_16dec11_e.htm (last visit, April 30, 2017).

15 See, e.g., Sergei Kirsanov and Evgeny Safonov, *The Consequences of Russia's Accession to WTO: Conclusions and Recommendations* 10(16) Eur. Sci. J. 195 (2014).

Russia made several commitments in its Protocol of Adhesion, such as the following ones.[16] Tariffs shall not exceed 7.8 percent (its average was 10 percent in 2001 and the reductions are gradual).[17] Tariffs ceilings depend on the sector: (i) 10.8 percent for agricultural goods (the average in 2011 was 13.2 percent), (ii) 7.3 percent for industrial goods (the average in 2011 was 9.5 percent), and (iii) zero for goods related to the information technology sector (the average in 2011 was 5.4 percent) and for cotton as well.[18] More generally, Russia will reduce the maximum tariff from 100,000 to 30,000 rubles and will simplify customs proceedings.[19]

Regarding the import of some goods, licenses shall be granted to import alcoholic and pharmaceutical products, Russia shall eliminate preferential tariffs for car makers with significant investments in this country and, while Russia does not intend to be a party to the WTO Agreement on Trade of Civil Aircrafts, airplanes manufactured abroad will have the same rights as Russian aircraft.[20] As to the services sector, international insurance companies have been able to incorporate subsidiaries in Russia as of 2012 while foreign companies are able to hold shares in Russian banks provided that their participation remains not higher than 50 percent.[21]

On sundry topics related to this Protocol of Adhesion, Russia (i) intends to be a party to the WTO Voluntary Agreement of Government Procurement no later than four years after the accession[22]; (ii) jointly with Belarus and Kazakhstan, Russia makes some sanitary and phytosanitary requirements regarding imports[23]; (iii) guarantees that the market will determine gas prices (one of the main Russian exports) save the case of non-commercial uses, who will pay regulated prices[24]; (iv) will not grant subsidies to agricultural exports and will eliminate all industrial subsidies or will guarantee that these subsidies will not be conditioned on exports and that they will not favor domestic goods to the detriment of imported goods[25]; (v) eliminated non-contractual administration of Intellectual Property Rights in

16 See Russian Protocol of Adhesion. See also WTO Report of the Working Paper on the Accession of the Russian Federation to the World Trade Organization, https://docsonline.wto.org/dol2fe/Pages/SS/DirectDoc.aspx?filename...doc& (last visit, April 30, 2017).

17 See *id.*

18 See *id.*

19 One U.S. dollar is approximately equivalent to 65 rubles. See Bloomberg, www.bloomberg.com/quote/USDRUB:CUR (last visit, April 30, 2017). See also International Monetary Fund, www.imf.org/external/np/fin/data/param_rms_mth.aspx (last visit, April 30, 2017).

20 See Russian Protocol of Adhesion. See also WTO Report of the Working Paper on the Accession of the Russian Federation to the World Trade Organization, https://docsonline.wto.org/dol2fe/Pages/SS/DirectDoc.aspx?filename...doc& (last visit, April 30, 2017).

21 See *id.*

22 See *id.*

23 See European Commission, http://ec.europa.eu/food/safety/international_affairs/eu_russia/sps_requirements_en (last visit, April 30, 2017).

24 See Russian Protocol of Adhesion. See also WTO Report of the Working Paper on the Accession of the Russian Federation to the World Trade Organization, https://docsonline.wto.org/dol2fe/Pages/SS/DirectDoc.aspx?filename...doc& (last visit, April 30, 2017).

25 See *id.*

2013[26]; and will continue the privatization of some state-owned enterprises (e.g., the United Grain Company in 2012 and Rosneft in the short term).[27] More generally speaking, and while the outlook in recent years has been the opposite,[28] Russia promised in its Protocol of Adhesion to offer a transparent and predictable environment for trade and investment.[29]

In respect of trade agreements, Russia is a member of the Eurasian Economic Union, a customs union whose other members are Armenia, Belarus, Kazakhstan and Kyrgyzstan.[30] Consequently, trade remedies cases are conducted by a supranational authority, the Eurasian Economic Commission (Eurasian EC), where common external tariffs and other trade policies are also discussed and implemented.[31] Russia also intends to establish a preferential trade area within the Commonwealth of Independent States – CIS (the countries which comprised the former Soviet Union).[32] Notwithstanding, the future of this trade agreement is anything but promissory after the tensions between Russia and Ukraine escalated as a result of, on the political side, the invasion of Crimea and, on the trade side, the signature of the Deep and Comprehensive Free Trade Agreement (DCFTA) between Ukraine and the European Union, which has been in legal force since January 1, 2016.[33] Russia is also a member of APEC[34] and, besides the former Soviet Union's countries, it has entered into a preferential trade agreement

26 See *id.*

27 See Reuters, Russia Aiming for Over $11 Billion from Rosneft Stake Sale (September 2, 2016), www.reuters.com/article/us-russia-rosneft-privatisation-idUSKCN1181A9 (last visit, April 30, 2017).

28 See Bill Browder, *Red Notice: A True Story of High Finance, Murder, and One Man's Fight for Justice*, p. 1 (2015).

29 See Russian Protocol of Adhesion. See also WTO Report of the Working Paper on the Accession of the Russian Federation to the World Trade Organization, https://docsonline.wto.org/dol2fe/Pages/SS/DirectDoc.aspx?filename...doc& (last visit, April 30, 2017).

30 See Eurasian Economic Union, www.eaeunion.org/?lang=en (last visit, April 30, 2017).

31 See Eurasian Economic Commission, www.eurasiancommission.org/en/Pages/default.aspx (last visit, April 26, 2017)

32 Eight CIS Members (Russia, Ukraine, Belarus, Kazakhstan, Armenia, Kyrgyzstan, Moldova and Tajikistan) signed this trade agreement on October 18, 2011. The remaining three CIS nations – Uzbekistan, Azerbaijan, and Turkmenistan – have not yet signed it. The 2011 CIS FTA will come into force following the ratification of three signatories. See World Bank, http://wits.worldbank.org/GPTAD/PDF/archive/CIS.pdf (last visit, April 30, 2017). See also USDA Foreign Agricultural Service, http://gain.fas.usda.gov/Recent%20GAIN%20Publications/Commonwealth%20of%20Independent%20States%20FTA%20_Moscow_Russian%20Federation_4-5-2012.pdf (last visit, April 30, 2017).

33 See European Commission, http://ec.europa.eu/trade/policy/countries-and-regions/countries/ukraine/ (last visit, April 30, 2017). See also The Moscow Times, *Russia Suspends Free Trade Agreement with Ukraine* (December 16, 2015), https://themoscowtimes.com/articles/russia-suspends-free-trade-agreement-with-ukraine-51261 (last visit, April 30, 2017).

34 See APEC, www.apec.org (last visit, April 30, 2017). See also RANEPA, The Russian Presidential Academy of National Economy and Public Administration, Russia in APEC, http://apec-center.ru/en/russia-in-apec/ (last visit, April 30, 2017).

with Serbia.[35] The Eurasian Economic Union has also recently entered into a trade agreement with Vietnam, although it is still not in legal force since Armenia and Vietnam's ratifications are still pending.[36]

7.2 How to influence trade policy in Russia

The highest authority in the Executive is, of course, the President and, then, the Prime Minister, who delegates the trade policy formulation to the Ministry of Economic Development.[37] The Legislative or the Federal Assembly, which has the power to ratify or reject trade agreements, is composed of the State Duma and the Federation Council.[38] Due to the low standards of transparency and to the recent past of Russia as a communist state, it is not surprising that the role of the Private Sector in the formulation of the country's trade policy is quite limited while the influence of the Public Interest is minimal or almost non-existent.[39]

It should be noted that state-owned enterprises (SOEs) play a big role in Russia. According to 2007 data, approximately 4,100 enterprises that have some degree of state ownership accounted for 39 percent of all employment in 2007 (down from over 80 percent in 1990).[40] In that same year, SOEs controlled 64 percent of the banking sector, 47 percent of the oil and gas sector and 37 percent of the utility sector.[41] This still significant participation of SOEs in the Russian economy is an important factor in fueling corruption, resisting privatization and undermining the influence of the Private Sector in the country's trade PFS. The next quote confirms this understanding:

> According to a [2013] government list, Russia has approximately 4,100 state-owned enterprises (SOEs), which play a prominent role across much of the Russian economy. The public sector accounted for a considerable share of economic activity with revenues of at least 71 percent of GDP, expenditures of at least 68 percent of GDP, and an estimated surplus of 3 percent of GDP in 2014. Russia is not yet party to the WTO Government Procurement Agreement, which would have an impact on the benefits enjoyed by SOEs in Russia. The Russian Government appears to be

35 See WTO Trade Policy Review. Russian Federation 2016, www.wto.org/english/tratop_e/tpr_e/s345_sum_e.pdf (last visit, April 30, 2017).

36 See Export.gov, *Russia – Trade Agreements*, www.export.gov/article?id=Russia-Trade-Agreements (last visit, April 30, 2017).

37 See Ministry of Economic Development, http://economy.gov.ru/en/home (last visit, April 30, 2017).

38 The Federal Assembly, www.gov.ru/main/page7_en.html (last visit, April 30, 2017).

39 See generally Vladimir Banacek and Mihaly Laki, *The Private Sector after Communism: New Entrepreneurial Firms in Transition Economies*, p. 1 (2013).

40 See Export.gov, *Russia – Competition from State-Owned Enterprises*, www.export.gov/article?id=Russia-Competition-from-State-Owned-Enterprises (last visit, April 26, 2017).

41 See *id.*

increasing state control over the country's leading economic institutions as the economy continues to weaken.

The Russian Government owns controlling stakes in major Russian energy firms and plays a large role in the energy sector. For example, the Russian Government owns a 50.23 percent stake in the natural gas firm Gazprom, which produced 67.5 percent of Russia's total natural gas output as of 2014. Similarly, the oil company Rosneft, in which the Russian state owns a 69.5 percent stake, accounted for 36.2 percent of oil output in Russia. In December 2014, Prime Minister Medvedev relaxed a 2011 regulation that had prohibited senior government officials from serving on SOE boards. Senior officials (deputy prime ministers and ministers) now have seats on the boards of the major state-owned companies Rosneft, Gazprom, Russian Railways, RusHydro, Rostelecom, Russian Grids, Bashneft, and Transneft.

The Government, in its latest count in January 2013, listed 4,132 SOEs, divided into 1,795 federal unitary enterprises and government stakes in 2,337 joint-stock companies. The Government also maintains a list of 176 "strategic companies" that are either wholly or partially owned by the Russian state and that cannot be privatized due to their national significance. This list includes 128 federal unitary enterprises (100 percent government-owned) and 48 joint stock companies, which have varying percentages of state ownership. A specific variant of SOE, state corporations (there are currently six: Rosatom, VEB, Fund for Communal Housing, Deposit Insurance Agency, Roskosmos, and Rostec), are 100 percent owned by the Russian Government and operate under separate legislation.[42]

Table 17 ranks the influence of each major actor in Russian trade policy formulation. At the top is the Executive, comprised by the President, Prime Minister and the Ministry of Economic Development. Without their support, especially from these two leaders, nothing goes. The Legislative comes second, since trade agreements depend on it to be ratified. The Private Sector comes in a distant third place, followed by the Public Interest.

TABLE 17 The rank of players' influence in Russia's trade PFS (1 = more influence)

Player	*Rank*
Executive	1
Legislative	2
Private Sector	3
Public Interest	4

42 Export.gov, *Russia – Competition from State-Owned Enterprises*, www.export.gov/article?id=Russia Competition from State Owned Enterprises (last visit, April 26, 2017).

7.3 Russia's perspective on trade issues and negotiations

While Russia signed the Accession agreement to the WTO in 2012, most of its current policies, especially on the political side, are in conflict with its alleged intention to become a more integrated country with the rest of the world. Thus, there are some trends to recentralize decisions, to buy back some privatized companies, and to constrain the freedom of entrepreneurship, which is so dear for any market economy.[43] Worse, Russia has escalated disputes with border countries, such as the conflict with Ukraine over Crimea,[44] and with the Private Sector as well.[45]

On top of that, a significant lack of transparency and a widespread corruption in all governmental levels are heavy obstacles to the path of Russia towards a place where people and authorities play by the rules and where investments thrive.[46] Unfortunately, fighting against corruption might be a very dangerous and even a deadly task in Russia.[47] A Russian lawyer named Sergei Magnitsky, who investigated some fraud involving tax officials, was imprisoned in 2009 and later died in a Russian jail.[48] Russian authorities were suspected of forging a criminal case against this lawyer and also of causing his death.[49] As a result, the U.S. Congress enacted the Russia and Moldova Jackson-Vanik Repeal and Sergei Magnitsky Rule of Law Accountability Act of 2012 (most usually known as the Magnitsky Act), which President Barack Obama signed in December 2012 and which punished Russian officials who were thought to be responsible for the death of Sergei Magnitsky by

43 *See* Uwe Becker and Alexandra Vasileva, *Russia's Political Economy Re-conceptualized: A Changing Hybrid of Liberalism, Statism and Patrimonialism*, J. Eurasian Stud. (2016), http://ac.els-cdn.com/S1879366516300276/1-s2.0-S1879366516300276-main.pdf?_tid=9ef623ac-bbfb-11e6-8f9f-00000aab0f01&acdnat=1481060186_82970d59426237301 16c771f6e68d3f1 (last visit, April 30, 2017). See also Russia Direct, *How the economic crisis hampers Russia's investment climate*, January 21, 2016, www.russia-direct.org/qa/how-economic-crisis-hampers-russias-investment-climate (last visit, April 30, 2017); and U.S. Department of State, Bureau of Economic and Business Affairs, *Investment Climate Statements for 2016: Russia*, www.state.gov/e/eb/rls/othr/ics/investmentclimatestatements/index.htm#wrapper (last visit, April 30, 2017).

44 See U.S. Department of State, Bureau of Economic and Business Affairs, *Investment Climate Statements for 2016: Russia*, www.state.gov/e/eb/rls/othr/ics/investmentclimatestatements/index.htm#wrapper (last visit, April 30, 2017).

45 See Bill Browder, *Red Notice: A True Story of High Finance, Murder, and One Man's Fight for Justice*, p. 1 (2015).

46 See U.S. Department of State, Bureau of Economic and Business Affairs, *Investment Climate Statements for 2016: Russia*, www.state.gov/e/eb/rls/othr/ics/investmentclimatestatements/index.htm#wrapper (last visit, April 30, 2017), and Bill Browder, *Red Notice: A True Story of High Finance, Murder, and One Man's Fight for Justice*, p. 1 (2015).

47 See Bill Browder, *Red Notice: A True Story of High Finance, Murder, and One Man's Fight for Justice*, p. 1 (2015).

48 See *id.* See also Stop the Untouchables, *Justice for Sergei Magnitsky*, http://russian-untouchables.com/eng/ (last visit, April 30, 2017).

49 See Bill Browder, *Red Notice: A True Story of High Finance, Murder, and One Man's Fight for Justice*, p. 1 (2015).

prohibiting their entrance to the United States and their use of its banking system. Russia retaliated by denying U.S. nationals the possibility of adopting Russian children, issuing a list of U.S. officials prohibited from entering Russia, and posthumously convicting Magnitsky as guilty.[50]

Last but not least, Russia has used its huge gas reserves as a political weapon, threatening to stop exports of this commodity if some concessions are not granted (a threat that is conveniently made in deep winter) or, in particular, if the European Union imposes sanctions in retaliation to the Russian invasion of Crimea.[51]

50 See Bill Browder, *Red Notice: A True Story of High Finance, Murder, and One Man's Fight for Justice*, p. 1 (2015).

51 See NATO Review Magazine, *Russian-Ukrainian – E.U. Gas Conflict: Who Stands to Lose Most?* www.nato.int/docu/review/2014/nato-energy-security-running-on-empty/Ukrainian-conflict-Russia-annexation-of-Crimea/EN/index.htm (last visit, April 30, 2017). See also European Union Newsroom, *E.U. sanctions against Russia over Ukraine crisis*, https://europa.eu/newsroom/highlights/special-coverage/eu_sanctions_en (last visit, April 30, 2017).

8

BRICS PART 5

The South African trade policy system

8.1 The South African trade policy system

Chapter 8 discusses the trade policy system of South Africa, the fifth and last member of the so-called BRICS, so as to answer the following questions: how the South African trade policy system is structured, how trade players influence South African trade policy, and what is South Africa's perspective on trade issues and negotiations.

South Africa was a closed and underdeveloped economy from the beginning of the twentieth century and at least until 1960.[1] This was a time when the dominant trade policy was based on imports substitution.[2] The next 30 years, from 1960 and until 1990, were a little better regarding economic growth, although the country continued being an almost autarchic economy.[3] While South Africa had been an original member of GATT 1947, the new rules of GATT 1994, combined with the end of apartheid and the subsequent reintegration of South Africa in the world, were the factors leading to the country's overhauling of its tariff system.[4] Thus, South Africa opened itself to the trading world by both reducing tariffs and non-tariff barriers.[5] Due to exports growth in sectors such as agribusiness, mining and manufacturing, the last decade of the twentieth century was a good one in terms of economic growth.[6]

South Africa is a member of the G20,[7] the Cairns Group (a "coalition of agricultural exporting countries with a commitment to reforming agricultural

1 See generally William Beinart, *Twentieth-Century South Africa*, p. 309 (2001).
2 See *id*.
3 See *id*.
4 See *id*.
5 See *id*.
6 See WTO Trade Policy Review: Southern African Customs Union (SACU): 1998, www.wto.org/english/tratop_e/tpr_e/tp72_e.htm (last visit, April 30, 2017).
7 See 2015 Turkey G20, http://g20.org.tr/about-g20/g20-members/ (last visit, April 30, 2017).

trade"),[8] and the Southern African Development Community, which is composed of 15 sub-Saharan countries and whose purposes

> are to achieve development, peace and security, and economic growth, to alleviate poverty, enhance the standard and quality of life of the peoples of Southern Africa, and support the socially disadvantaged through regional integration, built on democratic principles and equitable and sustainable development.[9]

8.2 How to influence policy in South Africa

As to the Executive, the President is the highest authority and the Department of Trade and Industry (DTI) is the executive body in charge of formulating trade policy.[10] The International Trade Administration Commission (ITAC)[11] and the International Trade and Economic Development Commission (ITEDC),[12] are divisions of the DTI. The National Treasury, in turn, might impose restrictions on the commercial agenda while the Department of International Relations and Cooperation has a marginal role.[13] Another relevant authority within the Executive is the National Economic Development and Labor Council – NEDLC.[14]

The South African Parliament is the Legislative, in charge of ratifying trade agreements.[15] The Private Sector, through entities such as the Chamber of Commerce and Industry,[16] exerts influence on the ITAC, the ITED, and the DTI. The Public Interest, in turn, is powerful in social matters.[17] Lastly, the levels of transparency are reasonable.[18]

8 The Cairns Group, http://cairnsgroup.org/Pages/default.aspx (last visit, April 30, 2017).

9 Southern African Development Community, www.sadc.int/about-sadc/overview/ (last visit, April 30, 2017).

10 See South African Constitution, www.gov.za/documents/constitution/constitution-republic-south-Africa-1996-1 (last visit, April 30, 2017).

11 See The International Trade Administration Commission, www.itac.org.za/ (last visit, April 30, 2017).

12 See The International Trade and Economic Development Commission, www.thedti.gov.za/about_dti/ited.jsp (last visit, April 30, 2017).

13 See *id*. See also The National Treasury, www.treasury.gov.za/ (last visit, April 30, 2017), and Department of International Relations and Cooperation, www.dirco.gov.za/ (last visit, April 30, 2017).

14 See The National Economic Development and Labor Council, http://new.nedlac.org.za/ (last visit, April 30, 2017).

15 See South African Constitution, www.gov.za/documents/constitution/constitution-republic-south-Africa-1996-1 (last visit, April 30, 2017).

16 See Chamber of Commerce and Industry, www.sacci.org.za/ (last visit, April 30, 2017).

17 For a list of South African NGOs, see Worldwide NGO Directory, www.wango.org/resources.aspx?section=ngodir&sub=region®ionID=18&col=BFB07D (last visit, April 30, 2017) and Rainbow Nation, www.rainbownation.com/directory/index.asp?category=1169 (last visit, April 30, 2017).

18 See generally Transparency International, www.transparency.org/country#ZAF (last visit, April 30, 2017).

In the Executive Branch, the structure of the DTI is the following one[19]: (i) a Division of International Commerce and Economics (DITE), in charge of international negotiations; (ii) a Division of Commerce and Investment in South Africa (CISA), which formulates the strategic industrial policies; and (iii) the already mentioned ITAC, which manages the trade policy and the commercial defense. ITAC was established in June 2003 pursuant to the International Trade Administration Act of 2002.[20] The main responsibilities of ITAC are the management of tariffs (including the Motor Industry Development Program and the Duty Credit Certificate System), the commercial defense (ITAC carries out the investigation regarding the imposition of antidumping and countervailing duties, and safeguards), and the control of imports and exports (ITAC issues exports and imports licenses on some goods).[21]

On the other hand, the aforementioned NEDLC (a forum for discussions on social and economic policies where people from government, companies, trade unions and civil society participate and which formulate trade policy recommendations, usually biased in favor of protectionism), is divided into the following four sub chambers: (i) the Chamber of the Labor Market, (ii) the Chamber of Commerce and Industry, (iii) the Chamber of Development, and (iv) the Chamber of Public Finance.[22] Figure 11 summarizes the main institutions within the South African Executive.

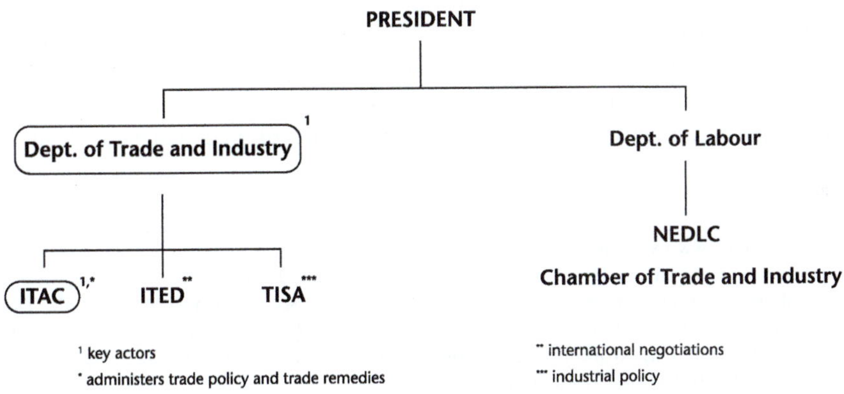

FIGURE 11 Trade policy institutional hierarchy in South Africa[23]

19 See Department of Trade and Industry (South Africa), www.thedti.gov.za/about_dti/ited.jsp (last visit, April 30, 2017).

20 See *id.*

21 See *id.*

22 See National Economic Development and Labor Council, http://new.nedlac.org.za/ (last visit, April 30, 2017).

23 Figure made by the authors.

TABLE 18 The rank of players' influence in South Africa's trade PFS (1 = more influence)

Player	*Rank*
Executive	1
Legislative	3
Private Sector	2
Public Interest	1

Table 18 ranks the influence of each major player in South Africa's trade policy formulation system. Most influential are the Executive and the Public Interest. The latter's high influence comes from significant concerns about social issues in policy decisions. Next is the Private Sector and, ranked last, the Legislative.

8.3 South Africa's perspective on trade issues and negotiations

South Africa is one of the five members of the Southern African Customs Union (SACU), whose other countries are Botswana, Lesotho, Namibia and Swaziland.[24] All these countries, except Botswana, have also formed a monetary union.[25] South Africa is the largest economy and main investor in the other SACU countries. It also dominates regional trade, with over 95 percent of trade flows within the customs union involving it as a destination or source.[26]

Some history of SACU is relevant.[27] The agreement creating this customs union, the oldest in the world, dates back to 1889.[28] More than two decades later, the SACU agreement was signed among South Africa and the territories of Basutoland and Swaziland, and the Protectorate of Bechuanaland.[29] Such

24 See SACU, www.sacu.int/ (last visit, April 30, 2017).

25 See Southern African Development Community, www.sadc.int/about-sadc/integration-milestones/single-currenc/ (last visit, April 30, 2017). See also Iyabo Masha et al., *The Common Monetary Area in Southern Africa: Shocks, Adjustment, and Policy Challenges*, WP/07/158, IMF Working Paper (2007), www.imf.org/external/pubs/ft/wp/2007/wp07158.pdf (last visit, April 30, 2017).

26 WTO, *Trade Policy Review: Southern African Customs Union* (2015), www.wto.org/english/tratop_e/tpr_e/tp424_e.htm (last visit, April 30, 2017).

27 See SACU, www.sacu.int/ (last visit, April 30, 2017). See also IBP USA, *South African Customs Union Sacu Business Law Handbook*, p. 1 (2009). According to the 2015 WTO TPR on SACU:

> The SACU agreement does not provide for harmonization of macroeconomic policies. However, by virtue of the membership of Lesotho, Namibia, and Swaziland of the Common Monetary Area (CMA), their currencies are pegged to the South African Rand, and their monetary policies are largely aligned on the policy pursued by the South African Reserve Bank (SARB).

See: WTO, www.wto.org/english/tratop_e/tpr_e/s324_sum_e.pdf (last visit, April 30, 2017).

28 See *id.*

29 See *id.*

agreement was reviewed in 1969, when Botswana and Lesotho joined it.[30] Lastly, negotiations of a new SACU agreement began at the time of the enactment of GATT 1994 and, after eight years of talks, was signed in 2002 among the five current members.[31] This new agreement provides some proceedings to take joint trade policies and a dispute settlement mechanism.[32]

Article 7 of the New SACU Agreement (2002 Southern African Customs Union or just the New SACU Agreement) establishes the following six institutions: (i) a Council of Ministers (the authority in charge of formulating the trade policy and of taking the decisions related to the SACU institutions, (ii) a Customs Union Commission (in charge of implementing the provisions of the new agreement), (iii) a Secretariat (which manages, coordinates and monitors the implementation of decisions that the Council and the Commission take), (iv) a Tariff Council (which makes recommendations to the Council regarding tariffs, antidumping and countervailing duties, and safeguards), (v) Technical Committees, and (vi) a Tribunal.[33] Figure 12 summarizes these authorities.

Applied MFN customs tariff, excise duties, duty and tax concessions (rebates, refunds and drawbacks), customs valuation, rules of origin, and contingency trade remedies remain harmonized within SACU. In practice, however, and in the absence of a regional authority, South Africa has been administrating the application of tariffs and duties through ITAC, which is currently responsible for managing the SACU common external tariff (CET); it is also mandated to recommend all rebates,

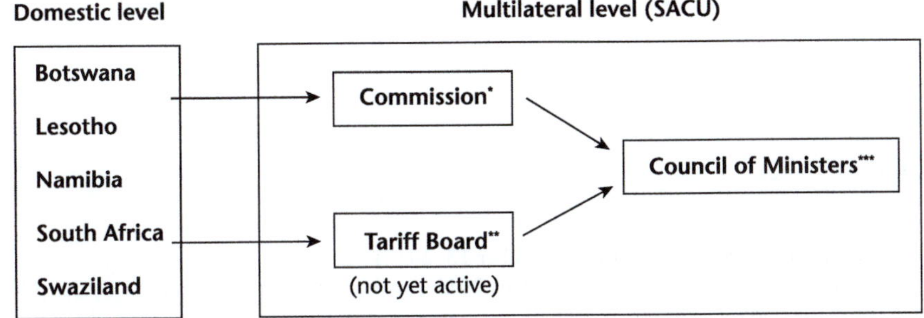

FIGURE 12 Decision-making in the SACU[34]

30 See *id.*
31 See *id.*
32 See *id.*
33 See 2002 Southern African Customs Union (SACU) Agreement, www.sacu.int/show.php?id=566 (last visit, April 30, 2017).
34 Figure made by the authors.

refunds, and drawbacks in SACU.[35] Pursuant to the New SACU Agreement, Members may keep treaties previously signed but new trade agreements must be negotiated with SACU as a block and not with individual members (unless a waiver is granted).

SACU's Council of Ministers met in 2011 in Swakopmund, Namibia.[36] The most important discussed topics were: (i) the formulation of a negotiation mechanism intended to establish a common stance regarding both trade policies and the negotiation of trade agreements, (ii) the redefinition of the institutional structure in accordance with the New SACU Agreement, (iii) the so-called Common Revenue Pool, intended to jointly manage the collection of taxes, and (iv) the establishment of a committee in charge of discussing topics such as information technologies, trade facilitation, and the involvement of the private sector in the formulation of trade policies.[37]

Besides being a SACU member, South Africa is a member of the Southern African Development Community (SADC) and has entered into a trade agreement with the European Union.[38] SACU has entered into trade agreements with Mercosur[39] and EFTA.[40] SACU also signed a Trade, Investment, and Development Cooperative Agreement with the United States in 2008.[41] There is also an Economic Partnership Agreement between the so-called SADC EPA Group (South Africa, Botswana, Namibia, Swaziland, Lesotho and Mozambique) and the European Union.[42] On the other hand, the European Union,[43] Canada, Japan, Norway, and Switzerland have granted South Africa preferential access to their markets through the GSP.[44] The United States did the same until 2015.[45]

35 See www.itac.org.za/ (last visit, September 13, 2017).

36 SACU Newsletter, Edition 1 (December 2011), www.sacu.int/newsletters/2011/dec.pdf (last visit, April 30, 2017).

37 See *id.*

38 See Department of Trade and Industry, www.thedti.gov.za/trade_investment/ited_trade_agreement.jsp (last visit, April 30, 2017).

39 See SACU Agreements, www.sacu.int/list.php?type=Agreements (last visit, April 30, 2017).

40 See *id.*

41 See the USTR, https://ustr.gov/countries-regions/africa/regional-economic-communities-rec/southern-african-customs-union-sacu (last visit, April 30, 2017).

42 See *id.*

43 See European Commission, Generalized Scheme of Preferences, http://ec.europa.eu/trade/policy/countries-and-regions/development/generalised-scheme-of-preferences/ (last visit, April 30, 2017).

44 See WTO, Preferential Trade Agreements, http://ptadb.wto.org/ptaList.aspx (last visit, April 30, 2017).

45 See The USTR, *U.S. to Suspend African Growth and Opportunity Act (AGOA) Benefits to South Africa*, https://ustr.gov/about-us/policy-offices/press-office/press-releases/2015/november/us suspend african growth and (last visit, April 30, 2017).

9

THE TRADE POLICY SYSTEM IN OTHER SELECTED COUNTRIES

This book, naturally, cannot cover the trade PFS for all WTO members. Notwithstanding, the trade policy analysis will be incomplete if at least some other relevant countries are not included. Thus, this chapter succinctly explains the trade policy systems of three other countries: Mexico, Canada and Australia. It is said succinctly because the analysis made is not as deep as the discussion of the trade policy systems in the United States, the European Union, Brazil, China, India, Russia, and South Africa.[1]

9.1 The Mexican trade policy system

According to the World Bank,[2] Mexico is the 15th largest world economy, with a GDP of around US$1,144,331. For a population of around 120 million,[3] the GPD per capita is slightly over US$10,000.[4] Due in part to its border with the United States and to the significant ties with this economy, Mexico was not immune to the Financial Crisis of the last decade, suffering a substantial GDP contraction in 2009.[5] Notwithstanding, and due to some countercyclical fiscal and monetary policies, the economic output has returned to pre-crisis levels.[6]

1 See *supra* Chapters 2 to 8.

2 See World Bank, http://data.worldbank.org/indicator/NY.GDP.MKTP.CD?year_high_desc=true (last visit, April 30, 2017).

3 See Worldometers, www.worldometers.info/world-population/mexico-population/ (last visit, April 30, 2017).

4 See *id.*

5 See WTO Trade Policy Review: Mexico (2013), www.wto.org/english/tratop_e/tpr_e/tp379_e.htm (last visit, April 30, 2017).

6 See *id.*

One of the reasons of the significant size of the Mexican economic output is the relevance of its international trade. Mexico is a party to at least 12 preferential trade agreements.[7] Of such agreements, the most significant ones are NAFTA (a trade agreement whose other members are Canada and the United States) and the so-called Pacific Alliance (in Spanish: Alianza del Pacífico).[8]

Besides Mexico, the Pacific Alliance Members are Colombia, Chile and Peru.[9] All these four countries have coasts in the Pacific Ocean; hence the name of this trade bloc. Mexico, however, is the only country in this Alliance that lacks any border with the other members, which are located in South America. Costa Rica might be the fifth member soon, pending some final procedures.[10] Panama is also interested in joining this Alliance in the short- or mid-term.[11] There are also 49 observer countries.[12] The Pacific Alliance was established in 2011 through the so-called Lima Statement (in Spanish: Declaración de Lima). Paradoxically, the Pacific Alliance Members trade more with countries outside this regional trade agreement such as the United States, China and the European Union than among themselves.[13] On a related note, and for better or worse, today Latin America is divided in two main trade blocs, each one having similar figures in terms of population and economic output,[14] the Pacific Alliance and Mercosur.[15]

The goals of the Pacific Alliance are the following ones: (i) the building of an integrated area with free (or at least, preferential) circulation of goods, services, money and people; (ii) the encouragement of higher economic growth, development and competitiveness, with a reduction of social inequality; and (iii) the establishment of a political, economic and trade platform projected to the world, with emphasis in the Asian-Pacific region.[16]

7 See WTO Trade Policy Review: Mexico (2013), www.wto.org/english/tratop_e/tpr_e/tp379_e.htm (last visit, April 30, 2017).

8 See *infra* Chapter 11 (about Preferential Trade Agreements).

9 See generally Alianza del Pacífico, https://alianzapacifico.net/ (last visit, April 30, 2017).

10 See Colombian Ministry of Commerce, Industry and Tourism, *Adhesión de Costa Rica a la Alianza del Pacífico, en la recta final*, www.mincit.gov.co/publicaciones.php?id=8931 (last visit, April 30, 2017). See also Colombian Ministry of Commerce, Industry and Tourism, *100 Preguntas de la Alianza del Pacífico* (Question 84), www.mincit.gov.co/tlc/publicaciones.php?id=7180 (last visit, April 30, 2017).

11 See Colombian Ministry of Commerce, Industry and Tourism, *100 Preguntas de la Alianza del Pacífico* (Question 84), www.mincit.gov.co/tlc/publicaciones.php?id=7180 (last visit, April 30, 2017).

12 See *id.*

13 See Cynthia J. Arnson, *Mercosur and the Pacific Alliance: Whither the Relationship*, www.wilsoncenter.org/article/mercosur-and-the-pacific-alliance-whither-the-relationship (last visit, April 30, 2017).

14 See The World Bank, http://data.worldbank.org/ (last visit, April 30, 2017).

15 See Osvaldo Rosales and Sebastián Herreros, *Mega-Regional Trade Negotiations: What is at Stake for Latin America?* The Inter-American Dialogue, http://archive.thedialogue.org/tradepp (last visit, April 30, 2017).

16 See *id.*

Mexico is also a member of the TPP, whose future, as of November 2016, is anything but clear after the U.S. President, Donald J. Trump, initiated withdrawal procedures from the agreement.[17]. This new Presidency, through its flag program ("Make America Great Again"),[18] which is against international trade and globalization, may be a serious threat to NAFTA and, in particular, to the Mexican economy. Given that over 80 percent of Mexican exports go to the United States through NAFTA, there is serious concern about the fate of the deal. The recently announced renegotiation could be a blessing (because it prevents termination) or it could be a curse (depending on to what extent its present favorable terms to Mexico are curtailed). Indeed, President Trump has several times stated that the United States has lost many jobs that have gone to countries such as China and Mexico.[19] On an unrelated note, Mexico was the first Latin American country to be accepted as a member of the OECD.[20]

On the other hand, and during recent years, Mexico has significantly lowered tariffs on a wide range of manufactured goods, simplified customs procedures and eliminated some import requirements.[21] At the same time, and while it has reduced its use, Mexico continues being an active user of anti-dumping measures, having 38 measures of this kind in legal force by June 2012 (in contrast, there was not one countervailing measure).[22]

Once the highlights of Mexican trade outlook have been mentioned, it is time to explain how Mexican key players influence trade policy. Mexico is a federal republic divided into 32 states (including its capital, Ciudad de México).[23] Pursuant to the Constitution enacted in 1917 (shortly after the end of the Mexican

17 See President's Executive Order of January 17, 2017, www.whitehouse.gov/the-press-office/2017/01/23/presidential-memorandum-regarding-withdrawal-united-states-trans-pacific (last visit, April 30, 2017)

18 See *id.*

19 See www.donaldjtrump.com/policies/trade/ (last visit, April 30, 2017). Indeed, after being elected as the 44th U.S. President but before taking office, Donald J. Trump announced a deal with Carrier, an air-conditioner company, by which this company changed its decision to move around 2,000 jobs from its plant in Indiana, the United States, to Mexico after the President Elect and its Vice President Elect (the current Indiana Governor) promised some economic incentives in exchange. See The New York Times, *Trump to Announce Carrier Plant Will Keep Jobs in U.S.*, November 29, 2016, www.nytimes.com/2016/11/29/business/trump-to-announce-carrier-plant-will-keep-jobs-in-us.html (last visit, April 30, 2017). Of course, all the U.S. people will have to pay this deal in the form of higher prices and higher taxes.

20 See generally OECD, Mexico, www.oecd.org/mexico/ (last visit, April 30, 2017).

21 See WTO Trade Policy Review: Mexico (2013), www.wto.org/english/tratop_e/tpr_e/tp379_e.htm (last visit, April 30, 2017).

22 See *id.*

23 See Constitución de los Estados Unidos de México [Constitution of the Mexican United States], Art. 43, www.sct.gob.mx/JURE/doc/cpeum.pdf (last visit, April 30, 2017). See also *Diario Oficial de México* (Official Mexican Gazette), www.dof.gob.mx/nota_detalle.php?codigo=5424043&fecha=29/01/2016 (last visit, April 30, 2017).

Revolution), the country has a presidential system.[24] The so-called PRI (Partido Revolucionario Institucional or Institutional Revolutionary Party) was the main political force and the governing party during the most part of the twentieth century in the so-called "perfect dictatorship" (in Spanish: dictadura perfecta).[25] While it is not now as powerful as some decades ago, it is still an important political party (indeed, the current president, Enrique Peña Nieto, is from this party) along with other parties such as the PAN (Partido de Acción Nacional or National Action Party, which held the presidency in the last term with Felipe Calderón) and the leftist Partido de la Revolución Democrática (Party of the Democratic Revolution).[26] While the Mexican President is the one in charge of formulating the trade policy,[27] this task is usually delegated in the Secretary of Economy (in Spanish: Secretaría de Economía).[28]

While Mexico is a presidential regime, the Legislative or Federal Congress is, of course, a force to be taken into account in the formulation of trade policy. After all, this legislative branch has the authority to ratify (or reject) trade agreements.[29] The Federal Congress is composed of two chambers: the Senate (128 members) and the Chamber of Deputies (500 members).[30]

The Private Sector is very active and, therefore, also an important player in the trade policy formulation. Given the size of the Mexican economy, it is not surprising to know that both entrepreneurs and workers have established some associations that permanently contribute to the discussion of Mexican trade policy. Some examples of entrepreneurial associations are Coparmex (Confederación Patronal de la República Mexicana or Employers Confederation of the Mexican Republic), that has more than 30,000 company members,[31] and many Chambers of Commerce, such as the Cámara de Comercio de la Ciudad de México (Chamber of Commerce of Mexico City).[32] Labor unions are equally strong. Some of them are the Confederación de Trabajadores de México (Mexican Confederation of

24 See Constitución de los Estados Unidos de México [Constitution of the Mexican United States], Art. 43, www.sct.gob.mx/JURE/doc/cpeum.pdf (last visit, April 30, 2017).

25 See generally Enrique Krauze, *La Presidencia Imperial* [*The Imperial Presidency*], p. 1 (2014).

26 See generally Jorge I. Domínguez et al. (Eds), *Mexico's Evolving Democracy: A Comparative Study of the 2012 Elections*, p. 1 (2014).

27 Constitución de los Estados Unidos de México [Constitution of the Mexican United States], Art. 43, available at: www.sct.gob.mx/JURE/doc/cpeum.pdf (last visit, April 30, 2017).

28 See Secretaría de Economía, www.gob.mx/se/ (last visit, April 30, 2017).

29 *Constitución de los Estados Unidos de México* [Constitution of the Mexican United States], Art. 43, available at: www.sct.gob.mx/JURE/doc/cpeum.pdf (last visit, April 30, 2017).

30 See *id.*

31 See Coparmex, www.coparmex.org.mx/ (last visit, April 30, 2017).

32 See Chamber of Commerce of Mexico City, www.ccmexico.com.mx/es/ (last visit, April 30, 2017).

TABLE 19 The rank of players' influence in Mexico's trade PFS (1 = more influence)

Player	*Rank*
Executive	1
Legislative	2
Private Sector	3
Public Interest	4

Workers)[33] and the Sindicato de Trabajadores Petroleros de la República Mexicana (Labor Union of Mexican Oil and Gas Workers).[34]

Last but not least, and regarding the Public Interest, several Non-Governmental Organizations contribute to the formulation of the Mexican trade policy through their analysis, comments and proposals. Most of them focus on the promotion and protection of human rights.[35]

Table 19 ranks the influence of each main actor in Mexico's trade policy formulation system. The Executive has traditionally been very strong. The Legislative is important but not as much as the Executive. The importance of the Private Sector has been growing recently but it is still not as organized as in more developed countries. Finally, the Public Interest has also been growing during the first two decades of the twenty-first century, but its relevance in the PFS is still marginal.

9.2 The Canadian trade policy system

In spite of its low population (fewer than 40 million people live in almost 4 million square miles),[36] Canada is another heavy player in the international trade arena. According to World Bank data, Canada is the world's tenth largest economy with a GDP of US$1.550.536,[37] with exports accounting for around 25 percent of such output.[38] The mining and energy sectors are the strongest manufacturing

33 See Mexican Confederation of Workers, www.ctmoficial.org (last visit, April 30, 2017).

34 See Portal Político [politics website], www.portalpolitico.tv/content/site/module/directorio/op/empresa/id_empresa/1792/format/html/ (last visit, April 30, 2017).

35 For a list of Mexican Non-Governmental Organizations, see, e.g., Directory of Mexican Non-Governmental Organizations, http://ongs.com.mx/directorio/ (last visit, April 30, 2017), and Cátedra UNESCO de Derechos Humanos de la Universidad Nacional Autónoma de México UNAM [UNESCO Cathedra of Human Rights at the UNAM], http://catedraunescodh.unam.mx/catedra/pronaledh/index70ed.html?option=com_content&view=article&id=148&Itemid=126 (last visit, April 30, 2017).

36 See Worldometers, www.worldometers.info/world-population/canada-population/ (last visit, April 30, 2017).

37 See World Bank Data, http://data.worldbank.org/indicator/NY.GDP.MKTP.CD?year_high_desc=true (last visit, April 30, 2017).

38 See World Top Exports, www.worldstopexports.com/canadas-top-exports/ (last visit, April 30, 2017).

industries.[39] In spite of that, service is the most relevant sector, accounting for around 70 percent of the GDP.[40]

Like the other U.S. neighbor (Mexico), the Financial Crisis of 2008–2009 also hit Canada, although this country has recovered well since then.[41] The so-called Economic Action Plans, implemented since 2009 and aimed at encouraging economic growth, creating jobs and promoting prosperity have been useful tools for achieving the goal of such recovery.[42]

Not surprisingly, the main Canadian trade partner is its unique neighbor, the United States, which buys almost three-quarters of its exports.[43] The remaining exports are atomized, with goods being sent to Asian countries (10 percent), the European Union (9 percent), Latin American countries (7 percent) and some other countries.[44] Paradoxically, and spite of sharing a membership in NAFTA, Canadian exports to Mexico account for only 1 percent of its total exports.[45] Perhaps the lack of a common border and lower trade complementarity with Mexico[46] explain this low percentage.

Canada has considered PTAs as a staple of its trade policies. As this book mentions in detail elsewhere,[47] Canada is a member of NAFTA, the precursor of modern PTAs. Also, and very recently (on October 30, 2016), the European Union and Canada ended the negotiations of the so-called Comprehensive Economic and Trade Agreement (CETA), the most important trade agreement for Canada since NAFTA. It is expected that CETA will increase jobs and investments in both sides of the Atlantic once it enters in legal force. The European Parliament voted in favor of CETA in February 2017, but national parliaments still need to ratify it before it goes into force.[48]

CETA negotiations began in 2009 although they already go back to some years earlier when the E.U. and Canadian leaders meeting in Ottawa in 2004 agreed to a framework for a new Canada–E.U. Trade and Investment Enhancement Agreement (TIEA).[49] Closing the deal was not an easy task since, besides the

39 See *id.*
40 See *id.*
41 See WTO, Trade Policy Review: Canada 2015, www.wto.org/english/tratop_e/tpr_e/tp414_e.htm (last visit, April 30, 2017).
42 See *id.*
43 See Trade Policy Review: Canada 2015 (Table A1. 4 Merchandise exports and re-exports by trading partner, 2011–14, 164), www.wto.org/english/tratop_e/tpr_e/tp414_e.htm (last visit, April 30, 2017).
44 See *id.*
45 See *id.*
46 See:Knoema,https://knoema.com/UNCTADMTC2015/merchandise-trade-complementarity-annual-1995-2013?exporter=1001260-mexico (last visit, April 30, 2017)
47 See *infra* Chapter 11.
48 See European Commission, http://ec.europa.eu/trade/policy/in-focus/ceta/ (last visit, May 2, 2017).
49 See SICE Foreign Trade Information System, www.sice.oas.org/TPD/CAN_EU/CAN_EU_e.ASP (last visit, April 30, 2017).

Canadian approval, it also required the positive vote of all 28 E.U. Member States. The French speaking Belgian region of Wallonia, heavily hit by agricultural competition and deindustrialization, only withdrew its veto to CETA after the Belgian Government made some economic concessions to its inhabitants.[50]

Indeed, and once CETA is in legal force, the European Union will remove tariffs on 98 percent of its goods (nowadays, only 25 percent of such goods are tariff free).[51] CETA will also eliminate restrictions on access to public contracts, liberalize the services market, offer more stable legal rules for investors, strengthen the protection of intellectual property rights, and uphold European standards in areas such as food safety and worker's rights.[52]

Naturally for a country that has been traditionally open to international trade, NAFTA and CETA are only two of the PTAs that Canada is a party to. Other PTAs that this country has successfully negotiated are those with the Republic of Korea, Colombia, Honduras, Jordan and Panama.[53] Indeed, around 61 percent of Canadian imports receive preferential treatment pursuant to a PTA, with NAFTA accounting for the lion's share of such percentage.[54]

On the other hand, the 1985 Investment Canada Act is the main legislation governing foreign investment.[55] Pursuant to this Act, most foreign investments require a previous approval in order to verify whether they bring benefits to Canada and whether they do not harm national security.[56] There are also some additional restrictions in the most sensitive sectors, such as fishing, mining, and oil and gas.[57]

Finally, and before describing how players influence its trade policy, Canada is an avid user of both antidumping and countervailing measures as the fact that 17 antidumping and 23 countervailing duties investigations were initiated in 2013 indicates.[58]

50 See European Commission, News Archive, *Malmström Met with the Minister-President of Wallonia* (October 2, 2015), http://trade.ec.europa.eu/doclib/press/index.cfm?id=1372 (last visit, April 30, 2017). See also The New York Times, *Canada and E.U. Sign Trade Deal, Bucking Resistance to Globalization* (October 30, 2016), www.nytimes.com/2016/10/31/business/international/canada-european-union-trade-agreement.html?_r=0 (last visit, April 30, 2017).

51 See Department of Global Affairs (Canada), Canada – European Union, Comprehensive Economic and Trade Agreement, www.international.gc.ca/gac-amc/campaign-campagne/ceta-aecg/index.aspx?lang=eng (last visit, April 30, 2017).

52 See European Commission, http://ec.europa.eu/trade/policy/in-focus/ceta/ (last visit, April 30, 2017).

53 See Trade Policy Review: Canada 2015, www.wto.org/english/tratop_e/tpr_e/tp414_e.htm (last visit, April 30, 2017).

54 See *id.*

55 See Investment Canada Act (R.S.C., 1985, c. 28 (1st Supp.)), Justice Laws Website, http://laws-lois.justice.gc.ca/eng/acts/I-21.8/ (last visit, April 30, 2017).

56 See *id.*

57 See *id.*

58 See Trade Policy Review: Canada 2015 (Table A1. 4 Merchandise Exports and Re-exports by Trading Partner, 2011–14, 164), www.wto.org/english/tratop_e/tpr_e/tp414_e.htm (last visit, April 30, 2017).

Canada has a federal system, meaning that the authority is divided into three levels: the federal, the provincial and the municipal government.[59] Canada is also a constitutional monarchy belonging to the Commonwealth of Nations, an association of countries that were part of or that had significant ties with the British Empire.[60] For this reason, the Queen of the United Kingdom is also the Queen of Canada and, furthermore, the head of state of this country.[61] The Governor General represents the Queen in Canada and acts as the head of state (thus, the Governor General is the equivalent of the president in other countries).[62] This Governor General, on behalf of the Queen, appoints the Prime Minister as well as the other ministers of the cabinet.[63] The Prime Minister is usually from the party holding the majority in the Legislative.[64] In turn, the Department of Global Affairs is the one which, besides deciding the foreign policy, also formulates Canada's trade policy.[65]

Speaking of the Legislative, this branch is divided into the House of Commons and the Senate.[66] The first one is in charge of approving the laws and proposing them to the Senate.[67] The Legislative has also the legal capacity to ratify preferential trade agreements.[68] While the 308 members of the House of Common are elected by popular vote,[69] it is the Governor General, on the Prime Minister's advice, who chooses the senators.[70]

The Private Sector is very strong in Canada since many entrepreneurs exist in this country and actively participate in the discussions about trade policies.[71] Some examples are the Canadian Chamber of Commerce,[72] the Canadian Association

59 See Constitution Act (1867), Justice Laws Website, at: http://laws-lois.justice.gc.ca/eng/const/ (last visit, April 30, 2017).

60 See *id.*

61 See *id.*

62 See *id.*

63 See *id.*

64 See *id.*

65 See Department of Global Affairs, www.international.gc.ca/international/index.aspx?lang=eng (last visit, April 30, 2017).

66 See Constitution Act (1867), Justice Laws Website, http://laws-lois.justice.gc.ca/eng/const/ (last visit, April 30, 2017).

67 See *id.*

68 See *id.*

69 See *id.*

70 See *id.*

71 See generally Graeme Douglas and Shannon Kindornay, *Development and the Private Sector: Canada's Approach*, Research Report, The North-South Institute (2013), www.nsi-ins.ca/wp-content/uploads/2013/10/Development-and-the-Private-Sector-Canada%E2%80%99s-Approach-updated.pdf (last visit, April 30, 2017).

72 See The Canadian Chamber of Commerce, www.chamber.ca/ (last visit, April 30, 2017).

TABLE 20 The rank of players' influence in Canada's trade PFS (1 = more influence)

Player	*Rank*
Executive	1
Legislative	3
Private Sector	2
Public Interest	4

of Petroleum Producers,[73] the Mining Association of Canada,[74] and the Fisheries Council of Canada.[75]

Regarding the Public Interest, labor unions are a significant force. If they align with Private Sector concerns they can form a powerful, influential block in trade policy formulation. The most noticeable examples are the Canadian Labor Congress,[76] representing over 3 million workers,[77] and the United Food and Commercial Workers International Union,[78] which represents over 1 million Canadian and U.S. workers laboring in industries such as agriculture, health care, food processing and manufacturing.[79] These are not, of course, the only labor associations in Canada, a country where around 30 percent of the total workforce belongs to a union.[80] On the other hand, there are many and diverse NGOs in Canada.[81]

Table 20 ranks the influence of each main actor in Canadian trade policy formulation. The Executive has the highest influence under the Prime Minister and the Department of Global Affairs, in addition to its power in appointing senators. In strong second comes the Private Sector while the Public Interest is still weak.

9.3 The Australian trade policy system

The size of the Australian economy is slightly smaller than the Canadian economy but slightly larger than the Mexican (Australia's GDP is around US$1.4 trillion).[82]

73 See The Canadian Association of Petroleum Producers, www.capp.ca/ (last visit, April 30, 2017).
74 See The Mining Association of Canada, http://mining.ca/ (last visit, April 30, 2017).
75 See The Fisheries Council of Canada, http://fisheriescouncil.com/ (last visit, April 30, 2017).
76 See The Canadian Labor Congress, http://canadianlabour.ca/ (last visit, April 30, 2017).
77 See *id.*
78 See UFCW Canada, www.ufcw.ca/index.php?lang=en (last visit, April 30, 2017).
79 See *id.*
80 See UFCW Canada, www.ufcw.ca/index.php?option=com_content&view=article&id=29&Itemid=49&lang=en (last visit, April 30, 2017).
81 For a list of such Canadian NGOs, see www.chatt.hdsb.ca/~menkac/classes/NGOs.htm (last visit, April 30, 2017).
82 2016 data. See World Bank Data, http://data.worldbank.org/indicator/NY.GDP.MKTP.CD?year_high_desc=true (last visit, April 30, 2017).

Service is the main sector of the economy, accounting for 71 percent of the Australian GDP.[83]

As to trade matters, Australia has preferential trade agreements in legal force with Chile, China, Japan, Korea, Malaysia, New Zealand, Singapore, Thailand and the United States.[84] As these country names indicate, the most important Australian trade ties are with Pacific rim countries while trade with African or European countries is less representative. Australia is also a member of both ASEAN[85] and the TPP,[86] although the latter is not in legal force and could be killed or at least delayed as a result of the United States withdrawal.[87]

On the other hand, and while tariffs are the main trade policy, they are not high: the average applied MFN tariff rate was 3 percent in 2014.[88] Non-tariff barriers might be a bigger issue for some countries: Australia has been the respondent country in several cases where other WTO Members, spurred by multinational tobacco companies such as the British Tobacco Company in Honduras, have requested the establishment of a panel.[89] The complaining countries state that Australian regulations are in breach of the TBT and other WTO agreements by banning any branding and advertising on cigarette packages other than the colorless and plain name of the respective brand.[90] On the

83 See Trade Policy Review: Australia, www.wto.org/english/tratop_e/tpr_e/tp412_e.htm (last visit, November 30, 2015).

84 See Department of Foreign Affairs and Trade, http://dfat.gov.au/trade/agreements/Pages/status-of-fta-negotiations.aspx (last visit, April 30, 2017).

85 See ASEAN, www.asean.org (last visit, April 30, 2017).

86 See The USTR, The Trans-Pacific Partnership, https://ustr.gov/tpp/ (last visit, April 30, 2017).

87 See Donald J. Trump webpage (Make America Great Again), www.donaldjtrump.com/policies/trade/ (last visit, April 30, 2017).

88 See Trade Policy Review: Australia 2015, www.wto.org/english/tratop_e/tpr_e/tp412_e.htm (last visit, November 30, 2015).

89 The cases are DS435, Australia – Certain Measures Concerning Trademarks, Geographical Indications and Other Plain Packaging Requirements Applicable to Tobacco Products and Packaging (www.wto.org/english/tratop_e/dispu_e/cases_e/ds435_e.htm), DS441, Australia – Certain Measures Concerning Trademarks, Geographical Indications and Other Plain Packaging Requirements Applicable to Tobacco Products and Packaging (www.wto.org/english/tratop_e/dispu_e/cases_e/ds441_e.htm), DS458, Australia – Certain Measures Concerning Trademarks, Geographical Indications and Other Plain Packaging Requirements Applicable to Tobacco Products and Packaging (www.wto.org/english/tratop_e/dispu_e/cases_e/ds458_e.htm), and DS467, Australia – Certain Measures Concerning Trademarks, Geographical Indications and Other Plain Packaging Requirements Applicable to Tobacco Products and Packaging (www.wto.org/english/tratop_e/dispu_e/cases_e/ds467_e.htm).

90 For a summary of such cases, see Department of Foreign Affairs and Trade, http://dfat.gov.au/international-relations/international-organisations/wto/wto-dispute-settlement/Pages/wto-disputes-tobacco-plain-packaging.aspx and http://dfat.gov.au/international-relations/international-organisations/wto/wto-dispute-settlement/Pages/summary-of-australias-involvement-in-disputes-currently-before-the-world-trade-organization.aspx (last visit, April 30, 2017).

other hand, antidumping and countervailing measures have been growing in Australia, having been the WTO's fourth largest user of antidumping duties in 2013.[91]

Like Canada, Australia is also a former member of the British Empire and, therefore, it is still a constitutional monarchy belonging to the Commonwealth of Nations.[92] Consequently, the Queen of the United Kingdom is also the head of the Australian state, at least symbolically.[93] The real executive power lies with the Governor General, who is advised by both the Prime Minister and the Federal Executive Council (composed of the Ministers).[94] The Prime Minister is usually the leader of the party holding the majority in the House of Representatives.[95] The Minister for Trade, Tourism and Investment is the one in charge of formulating the trade policy,[96] although this role is shared with the Department of Foreign Affairs and Trade.[97]

As to the Legislative, there are two chambers: the upper one or the Senate, composed of 76 members, and the lower one or the House of Representatives, composed of 150 members.[98] Australia is also a federal country divided into six states (New South Wales, Queensland, South Australia, Tasmania, Victoria and Western Australia) and two mainland territories (the Australian Capital Territory and the Northern Territory).[99]

As to the Private Sector, there are many trade and industry associations as well as some labor unions.[100] Some examples are the Association of Mining and Exploration Companies,[101] the Australian Chamber of Commerce and Industry,[102]

91 See Trade Policy Review: Australia 2015, www.wto.org/english/tratop_e/tpr_e/tp412_e.htm (last visit, April 30, 2017).

92 See Commonwealth of Australia Constitution Act, available at: Parliament of Australia, www.aph.gov.au/About_Parliament/Senate/Powers_practice_n_procedures/Constitution (last visit, April 30, 2017).

93 See *id.*

94 See *id.*

95 See *id.*

96 See Minister for Trade, Tourism and Investment, http://trademinister.gov.au/Pages/default.aspx (last visit, April 30, 2017).

97 See Department of Foreign Affairs and Trade, http://dfat.gov.au/pages/default.aspx (last visit, April 30, 2017).

98 See Commonwealth of Australia Constitution Act, Parliament of Australia, www.aph.gov.au/About_Parliament/Senate/Powers_practice_n_procedures/Constitution (last visit, April 30, 2017).

99 See *id.*

100 Regarding the former, see Australian Unions, www.australianunions.org.au/ (last visit, April 30, 2017).

101 See The Association of Mining and Exploration Companies, www.amec.org.au/ (last visit, April 30, 2017).

102 See The Australian Chamber of Commerce and Industry, www.acci.asn.au/ (last visit, April 30, 2017).

TABLE 21 The rank of players' influence in Australia's trade PFS (1 = more influence)

Player	*Rank*
Executive	1
Legislative	3
Private Sector	2
Public Interest	4

representing over 350,000 businesses,[103] the Australian Federation of Employers and Industries,[104] and the Australian Food and Grocery Council.[105]

Last but not least, the Public Interest is represented by many associations, such as the Fair-Trade Association.[106] There are also many Australian NGOs.[107]

Table 21 ranks the influence of each main actor in Australia's trade policy formulation system. The Executive is the most influential and the Public Interest, as in most of the countries previously examined, the least. The Private Sector is the second most influential, followed by the Legislative. Finally, the importance of the Public Interest is still marginal.

103 See Commonwealth Network, www.commonwealthofnations.org/sectors-australia/business/trade_associations_and_chambers_of_commerce/ (last visit, April 30, 2017).

104 See The Australian Federation of Employers and Industries, www.afei.org.au/ (last visit, April 30, 2017).

105 See The Australian Food and Grocery Council, www.afgc.org.au/ (last visit, April 30, 2017).

106 See The Fair-Trade Association, www.fta.org.au/ (last visit, April 30, 2017).

107 See Department of Foreign Affairs and Trade, http://dfat.gov.au/aid/who-we-work-with/ngos/Pages/list-of-australian-accredited-non-government-organisations.aspx (last visit, April 30, 2017).

SECTION II

Trade policy tools

After discussing trade policy formulation under the most relevant WTO members, Section II, covering Chapters 10 to 16, analyzes the trade policy tools that countries have use to make the most out of international trade, such as market access, trade remedies, regulatory measures, dispute settlement, trade agreements, and international trade negotiations. In essence, this section will cover all WTO agreements, preferential trade agreements and negotiations techniques.

10

MARKET ACCESS

Chapter 10 is a short text summarizing the main legal rules in international trade applicable to tariffs, customs procedures, trade facilitation, and tariff preference programs.

10.1 Tariffs

Tariffs can be *ad valorem* (expressed as a percentage to be applied over the value of imports) or specific (expressed as a value per kg or per lb or per unit etc.). They were the main subject of GATT 1947, where the most important goal was to reduce tariffs. Recall from Chapter 1 the notion of competitive advantage: even if a country is the most efficient at manufacturing two kinds of goods (i.e., fabricating them at the lowest expense), such a situation is not Pareto efficient.[1] That is, this country might obtain a benefit specializing in only one kind of product while importing the other good from another country, which will also obtain a net gain.[2] In any event, countries having different production costs is not enough to maximize the benefits resulting from eliminating or at least reducing barriers limiting the free movement of goods. Tariffs, needless to say, are the most common trade barrier.

Recall also that during the time elapsing between the two world wars, when the Great Depression heavily hit many people and businesses across the world, several countries attempted to encourage domestic growth and employment by raising tariffs, i.e., by making imports more expensive in comparison with local output.[3] In another illustration of the famous prisoner dilemma (where each player

1 See *supra* Chapter 1.
2 See *id.*
3 See *id.* See also Liaquat Ahamed, *The Bankers Who Broke the World*, p. 1 (2009).

adopts a strategy that maximizes its individual payoff but that, when other agents take the same decision, reduces the collective payoff),[4] this nationalistic trend significantly reduced international trade and, as a consequence, made countries worse off.[5]

Shortly after the end of the Second World War, many countries realized that restricting international trade was a bad idea.[6] As a result, several countries signed the Havana Charter which established the ITO. Nonetheless and since such treaty was never ratified, the ITO did not come into being and countries settled for a less ambitious trade agreement, GATT 1947.[7] Coupled with the national treatment principle (no discrimination between domestic and foreign output), the other pillar of this agreement was the so-called MFN principle, enshrined in GATT Art. 1, whose paragraph 1 reads (the original text is not underlined):

> With respect to customs duties and charges of any kind imposed on or in connection with importation or exportation or imposed on the international transfer of payments for imports or exports, and with respect to the method of levying such duties and charges, and with respect to all rules and formalities in connection with importation and exportation, and with respect to all matters referred to in paragraphs 2 and 4 of Article III, any advantage, favour, privilege or immunity granted by any contracting party to any product originating in or destined for any other country shall be accorded immediately and unconditionally to the like product originating in or destined for the territories of all other contracting parties.

In short, the MFN principle means that any trade concession that a GATT Member (nowadays, a WTO Member), such as a tariff reduction, makes to any other Member shall be immediately extended to all other WTO Members. Of course, there are some exceptions to this principle, such as Preferential Trade Agreements.[8]

4 In the prisoner dilemma, two accused men are jailed and offered two options: to confess a crime or to deny it. If both individuals confess, the penalty is ten years. If none of them confess, the penalty is only one year. If one of them confesses and the other one denies having committed any crime, the former goes free and the later pays a penalty of five years. Although both prisoners would be better off by denying the commission of any criminal offence, and they are isolated (i.e., they cannot communicate), the dominant strategy of this game is that both confess the crime. See generally William Poundstone, *Prisoner's Dilemma: John von Neumann, Game Theory, and the Puzzle of the Bomb*, p. 1 (1993).

5 See *id.*

6 See *id.* See also Liaquat Ahamed, *The Bankers Who Broke the World* (2009). See also Andreas F. Lowenfeld, *International Economic Law* (2nd ed.), p. 23 (2008).

7 See Andreas F. Lowenfeld, *International Economic Law* (2nd ed.), p. 23 (2008).

8 See *infra* Chapter 11.

In any event, notice that Art. I (the most favored nation principle) is not in itself granting any trade benefit or obligation to GATT or WTO Members. GATT Art. II is the legal rule that makes reference to a schedule of concessions, detailed in one of the annexes of this agreement, and by which GATT Members (nowadays WTO Members) have lowered their tariffs since this agreement entered in legal force.

Under the WTO, Member Countries are subject to bound tariffs, which are specific commitments made by individual member governments that represent the maximum MFN tariff a country can impose on a given product line.[9] Another type is the tariff rate quota (TRQ), which combines a lower tariff to be applied up to a certain product's import quantity with a much higher tariff to be applied to any quantity exceeding the previous limit.[10]

10.2 Customs procedures

By definition, international trade entails that goods must be transported from the exporting country to the importing one and, therefore, that some procedures must be followed at the importing countries' borders, i.e., the customs procedures.[11]

In particular, the authorities of the importing country usually verify if the goods being imported comply with all the legal requirements before authorizing their nationalization. Such requirements are, among others, evidence of the payment of tariffs, certificates of origin, compliance with sanitary and phytosanitary requirements, and transportation documents.[12]

Naturally, reducing tariffs might not increase international trade in the desired levels if traversing the customs areas is a burdensome, red-tape filled and time consuming task for exporters. Because of that, not only many countries have unilaterally streamlined their customs procedures but there is also a multilateral agreement on this topic,[13] which is explained in further detail in the next section.

10.3 Trade facilitation

Generally speaking, trade facilitation means the reduction of both the cost and time necessary for goods to move across national borders. Nowadays, and since there

9 See GATT Art. II.

10 See GATT Art. XI.

11 There might also be customs procedures in the exporting country, but since the goal of countries is to boost their exports, they are very rare (e.g., restricting or controlling exports when the goods are scarce and very important for the local people). An example of export tariffs are the taxes that the soya exported from Argentina triggers. See Decree 640, 2016.

12 A further detail of such procedures, in the case of the United States and the European Union, is available at: (i) the U.S. Customs and Border Protection, www.cbp.gov/trade/nafta/customs-procedures (last visit, April 30, 2017), and (ii) the European Taxation and Customs Union, http://ec.europa.eu/taxation_customs/business/customs-procedures_en (last visit, April 30, 2017).

13 See WTO Trade Facilitation Agreement, www.wto.org/english/thewto_e/20y_e/wto_tradefacilitation_e.pdf (last visit, April 30, 2017).

have been a significant progress in the reduction of tariffs since the inception of GATT almost 70 years ago, the so-called non-tariff barriers (as its name suggests, they are any barrier other than a tariff) are perhaps the main obstacle to international trade. Regardless of whether it is the result of inefficiency or, alternatively, purposely imposed to obtain an unfair advantage over imports, red tape is one of the leading examples of non-tariff barriers. Of course, customs procedures are not going to completely disappear since importing countries need to keep their rights to control the goods coming into their territories in order to make effective their regulatory and public policies, i.e., to avoid the importation of goods that do not comply with the payment of taxes, that are not safe for consumers or for the environment or, in general, that do not comply with other requirements. In any event, and needless to say, the expenses coming from a delayed importing process may vanish any gains obtained from the reduction of tariffs or, more generally, from international trade and, consequently, discourage many companies from conquering foreign markets.

The trade facilitation topic is so relevant that since many years ago, WTO members had been aware of the urgency of negotiating a multilateral agreement intended to enhance the efficiency of border procedures.[14] Thus, and at the Ministerial Conference held in Bali (Indonesia) in December 2013, the WTO Members approved the Trade Facilitation Agreement (TFA).[15] WTO members also adopted a Protocol of Amendment to insert the TFA into Annex 1A of the WTO Agreement.[16] The TFA entered into force on February 22, 2017.

The TFA provides legal rules intended to make more efficient the movement, release and clearance of goods, including goods in transit.[17] This agreement also contains provisions related to effective cooperation between customs and other appropriate authorities, technical assistance and capacity building.[18] According to the World Trade Report 2015, the TFA has the potential to increase exports of goods by up to $1 trillion per year.[19] Developing countries might be the most benefited from this agreement since they might capture more than half of such gains.[20] It is also expected that the TFA will reduce the total trade costs for low-income countries in 14.5 percent.[21]

The TFA is the first multilateral trade agreement since the establishment of the WTO at the end of the Uruguay Round in 1994. Notwithstanding, this agreement was in danger of being killed before it entered in legal force since one key WTO

14 See WTO Trade Facilitation: Background, www.wto.org/english/tratop_e/tradfa_e/tradfa_intro_e.htm (last visit, April 30, 2017).

15 See WTO, Trade Facilitation, www.wto.org/english/tratop_e/tradfa_e/tradfa_e.htm (last visit, April 30, 2017).

16 See *id.*

17 See WTO Trade Facilitation Agreement.

18 See *id.*

19 See World Trade Report 2015, available at www.wto.org/english/res_e/publications_e/wtr15_e.htm (last visit, April 30, 2017).

20 See *id.*

21 See WTO Trade Facilitation Agreement.

member, India, threatened to block the deal until other WTO members accept that the subsidies that this country grants to its farmers are not in contravention to the WTO legal rules.[22] Fortunately, the impasse was solved and India is now one of the WTO members that has ratified the Trade Facilitation Agreement.[23]

The TFA is divided into three sections.[24] The first one, intended to expedite the movement, release and clearance of goods, including goods in transit, complements GATT Arts V, VIII and X, and provides some legal rules on customs cooperation as well.[25] Pursuant to the second section, which is about special and differential treatment, the implementation of the agreement depends on the capacity of each WTO country to do this task.[26] Thus, any WTO member shall categorize any provision of the TFA and notify the other members of such choice within the established timeframe.[27] There are three categories: (i) A, including provisions that the WTO member shall implement by the time the TFA enters into legal force (unless the WTO member is a least-developed country, a case where the term is extended for one year); (ii) B, related to provisions that the WTO member shall implement after a transitional period; and (iii) C, regarding provisions that a WTO member shall implement only after a transitional period and, in addition, after the acquisition of assistance and support for capacity building.[28] The third TFA's section, in turn and besides some miscellaneous provisions, establishes a permanent committee on trade facilitation and requires WTO members to set up or maintain a national committee to facilitate both domestic coordination and the implementation of the agreement.[29]

The TFA also establishes the so-called Trade Facilitation Agreement Facility, by which the WTO Secretariat will provide technical assistance in order to help developing and least-developed WTO members in the implementation of this agreement.[30]

10.4 Tariff preference programs

Under preference programs, developed countries unilaterally grant preferential tariff rates to the goods coming from developing and least-developed countries

22 See WTO 2014 News Items, *Differences Remain on Deadlines and Forums for Post-Bali work on Agriculture* (September 16, 2014), www.wto.org/english/news_e/news14_e/agcom_16sep14_jmp_test_e.htm (last visit, April 30, 2017). See Chapter 6 *supra* to understand India's resistance in agricultural negotiations.

23 See WTO, Trade Facilitation: *India ratifies Trade Facilitation Agreement*, www.wto.org/english/news_e/news16_e/fac_21apr16_e.htm (last visit, April 30, 2017).

24 See WTO Trade Facilitation Agreement.

25 See *id.*

26 See *id.*

27 See *id.*

28 See *id.*

29 See *id.*

30 See *id.*

without requesting reciprocity (at least from the purely trade standpoint since sometimes the country receiving the trade benefits must apply some public policies).[31]

Preference programs are clearly inconsistent with the WTO MFN principle since they grant a more favorable tariff treatment to goods imported from some countries than the treatment granted to goods coming from other WTO members.[32] Indeed, preference programs are an example of agreements that might be illegal at first sight but, at the same time, necessary to reduce world inequality levels and to encourage the economic growth of poorest countries.

Notwithstanding the MFN principle and because preference programs have been viewed as trade expanding, in 1971, the GATT followed the lead of UNCTAD and enacted two waivers to the MFN obligation that permitted tariff preferences to be granted to developing country goods. Both these waivers were limited in time to ten years. In 1979, during the Tokyo Round, the GATT established a permanent exemption to the MFN obligation by way of the Enabling Clause (L/4903).[33] This Clause provided a legal basis for one-way tariff preferences and certain other preferential arrangements under the principles of generality, non-reciprocity, and non-conditionality. The Enabling Clause, as the AB held in 2004,[34] allows developed countries to offer preferential treatment to both developing and least-developed countries but only if an identical treatment is available to other countries under similar circumstances.

This clause also allowed developed countries to disregard Art. I of the GATT and discriminate in favor of developing countries, but under the following conditions: (i) the program must be general, i.e., what is given to one developing country must be given to all developing countries; (ii) it must be unconditional, i.e., preference cannot be dependent upon the beneficiary country fulfilling conditions established by the donor country; and (iii) it must be non-reciprocal, i.e., the donor country cannot request concessions from developing countries in exchange for the benefit.

This was the basis for the creation of the Generalized System of Preferences (GSP) that developed countries such as the United States, Japan, the European Union and others make available to developing countries. Nevertheless, it is worth

31 One example was the Andean Trade Promotion and Drug Eradication Act, in which the Andean countries receiving some trade benefits committed to cooperate in the fight against production and trade in drugs. This preference program is no longer in legal force. See Trade Act of 2002. See also The USTR, Andean Trade Promotion and Drug Eradication Act, https://ustr.gov/archive/Trade_Development/Preference_Programs/ATPA/Section_Index.html (last visit, April 30, 2017). The GSP+ is another example.

32 See GATT Art. I.

33 Officially called the "Decision on Differential and More Favourable Treatment, Reciprocity and Fuller Participation of Developing Countries." See the legal text at www.wto.org/english/docs_e/legal_e/enabling1979_e.htm (last visit, May 3, 2017)

34 See DS246, European Communities – Conditions for the Granting of Tariff Preferences to Developing Countries.

noting that none of these GSPs abide by the three Enabling Clause conditions described in the previous paragraph, which would make them vulnerable to challenges at the WTO Dispute Settlement System. Notwithstanding, which country wants to be responsible for terminating with GSP benefits to poor countries?[35]

The remaining part of this section will describe the main preference programs in which either the United States or the European Union have granted trade benefits to developing or least-developed countries. In the United States, the U.S. Generalized System of Preferences (GSP), which started on January 1, 1976 and was initially authorized for a 10-year period pursuant to the Trade Act of 1974,[36] provides preferential duty-free entry for more than 5,000 products from 122 designated beneficiary countries and territories.[37] The combined GSP-eligible product lists include most dutiable manufactures and semi-manufactures, and certain agricultural, fishery and primary industrial products.[38] The GSP, however, does explicitly exclude some goods from the preferential treatment, such as textiles made of cotton, wool, manmade fibers, other vegetable fibers (linen and ramie), watches, certain footwear and handbags, luggage, flat goods not make of silk, work gloves and other leather items.[39]

For the goods that may receive preferential treatment, some conditions apply: (i) the product cannot account for more than 50 percent of the U.S. imports (a condition that is easily complied with); (ii) the imports cannot be above US$150 million; (iii) any U.S. industry or any other country may file a petition of exclusion claiming non-compliance with the conditions of the program; and (iv) even if all conditions are met, the U.S. President may discretionally decide whether or not to give preferential treatment to a given good.[40]

The U.S. GSPs are: (i) the Caribbean Basin Initiative (CBI), (ii) the African Growth and Opportunity Act (AGOA), and (iii) the Andean Trade Promotion and Drug Eradication Act (ATPDEA).[41] The beneficiaries of CBI, as its name

35 In 2004, the WTO Appellate Body ruled that the Clause allows developed countries to offer different treatment to developing countries in a GSP program, but only if identical treatment is available to all similarly situated GSP beneficiaries.

36 See Trade Act of 1974.

37 See The USTR; Generalized System of Preferences, https://ustr.gov/issue-areas/trade-development/preference-programs/generalized-system-preference-gsp (last visit, April 30, 2017).

38 See The USTR; Generalized System of Preferences, https://ustr.gov/issue-areas/trade-development/preference-programs/generalized-system-preferences-gsp/gsp-program-i-0 (last visit, April 30, 2017).

39 See *id.*

40 See Trade Act of 1974. See also The USTR; Generalized System of Preferences, https://ustr.gov/issue-areas/trade-development/preference-programs/generalized-system-preference-gsp (last visit, April 30, 2017).

41 See The USTR; Caribbean Basin Initiative, https://ustr.gov/issue-areas/trade-development/preference-programs/caribbean-basin-initiative-cbi (last visit, April 30, 2017). See also the Caribbean Basin Economic Recovery Act (CBERA) and the U.S.-Caribbean Basin Trade Partnership Act (CBTPA).

suggest, are countries located in Central America or in the Caribbean Sea.[42] This program was launched in 1983 through the Caribbean Basin Economic Recovery Act (CBERA) and substantially expanded in 2000 through the U.S. Caribbean Basin Trade Partnership Act (CBTPA). CBPTA entered into legal force on October 1, 2000 and will continue in effect, for a given country, until September 30, 2020, or the date, if sooner, on which a trade agreement enters into force between the United States and a beneficiary country.[43] Currently, there are 17 countries that benefit from the CBI program.[44]

The African Growth and Opportunity Act (AGOA), in turn, provides duty-free access to the U.S. market for substantially all products exported from 38 sub-Saharan countries.[45] In 2013, about 91 percent of U.S. imports from AGOA eligible countries entered the United States duty-free.[46]

Finally, the Andean Trade Preference Act was enacted in 1991 to fight drug production and trafficking in the Andean countries: Bolivia, Colombia, Ecuador and Peru.[47] The rationale was that if these countries' exports grow, unemployment rates would decline and people will be less tempted to pursue illegal trades.[48] Thus, the program offered trade benefits to help these countries to develop and strengthen legitimate industries.[49] In particular, ATPDEA provided duty-free access to U.S. markets for approximately 5,600 products.[50] Peru and Colombia left this program once the trade agreements that these countries signed with the United States entered into legal force in 2006 and 2012, respectively.[51] In 2008, the United States removed Bolivia from the list of beneficiaries of this program contending its lack of cooperation in the eradication of drugs.[52] Having Ecuador as the only remaining beneficiary, ATPDEA expired on July 31, 2013.[53]

On the other hand, the European Community was the first one to implement a GSP scheme in 1971.[54] The E.U.'s scheme grants imported products from

42 See *id.*
43 See *id.*
44 See *id.*
45 See The USTR, AGOA, https://ustr.gov/issue-areas/trade-development/preference-programs/african-growth-and-opportunity-act-agoa (last visit, April 30, 2017).
46 See *id.*
47 See Andean Trade Preference Act. See also The USTR, Seventh Report to the Congress on the Operation of the Andean Trade Preference Act as Amended (June 20, 2013), https://ustr.gov/about-us/policy-offices/press-office/fact-sheets/archives/2001/september/new-andean-trade-benefts (last visit, April 30, 2017).
48 See *id.*
49 See *id.*
50 See *id.*
51 See *id.*
52 See *id.*
53 See *id.*
54 See Regulation 978/2012. See also European Commission, Generalized Scheme of Preferences, http://ec.europa.eu/trade/policy/countries-and-regions/development/generalised-scheme-of-preferences/ (last visit, April 30, 2017).

beneficiary countries either duty-free access or a tariff reduction, depending on which of the GSP arrangements a country enjoys.[55] On top of the benefits of the general arrangement, which all countries belonging to the GSP enjoy, the special incentive arrangement for sustainable development and good governance (the GSP+) provides additional benefits for countries implementing certain international standards in human and labor rights, environmental protection, the fight against drugs, and good governance (e.g., Bolivia, Ecuador, Georgia, Guatemala, and Sri Lanka).[56]

The most famous E.U. GSP is the ACP–EU Partnership Agreement, most commonly known as the Cotonou Agreement after the city in Benin where it was signed in 2003.[57] This agreement superseded the Lomé Conventions, which governed trade relations between the European Union and the African, Caribbean and Pacific states (ACP) from 1975 to 2000.[58] The Cotonou Agreement is based on five interdependent pillars: (i) enhanced political dimension, (ii) increased participation, (iii) more strategic approach to cooperation focusing on poverty reduction; (iv) new economic and trade partnerships, and (v) improved financial cooperation.[59]

55 See *id.*

56 See *id.*

57 See European Commission, ACP – EU Partnership Agreement, http://ec.europa.eu/europeaid/regions/african-caribbean-and-pacific-acp-region/cotonou-agreement_en (last visit, April 30, 2017).

58 See *id.*

59 See *id.*

11
TRADE REMEDIES

Chapter 11 discusses the trade remedies that WTO members may adopt to protect their domestic industries from foreign competition. Such remedies are safeguards (Section 11.1), antidumping duties (Section 11.2) and countervailing duties (Section 11.3).

11.1 Safeguards

Along with antidumping duties and countervailing measures, safeguards are one of the three types of contingent trade protection measures available to WTO members. Like the other two trade remedies, WTO members may challenge safeguards that other members have applied if, under the claimant's view, they are against WTO rules.[1] GATT Art. XIX and the WTO Agreement of Safeguards (hereinafter the SG Agreement or simply the SGA) set forth the rules that WTO members shall take into account before adopting or challenging safeguards.

Speaking of GATT Art. XIX, and because of its relevance, paragraph 1(a) of this legal rule is reproduced below:

GATT Art. XIX

Emergency Actions on Import of Particular Products

(a) If, as a result of unforeseen developments and of the effect of the obligations incurred by a contracting party under this Agreement, including tariff concessions, any product is being imported into the territory of that contracting party in such increased quantities and under such conditions as

1 See GATT Art. XIX, DSU Art. 6 and WTO Agreement on Safeguards Art. 15.

> to cause or to threaten serious injury to domestic producers in that territory of like or directly competitive products, the contracting party shall be free, in respect of such product, and to the extent and for such time as may be necessary to prevent or remedy such injury, to suspend the obligation in whole or in part or to withdraw or modify the concession.

In turn, and pursuant to Art. 2 of the SG Agreement, a WTO member may apply a safeguard if, and only if, it determines that the relevant product:

> is being imported into its territory in such increased quantities, absolute or relative to domestic production, and under such conditions as to cause or threaten to cause serious injury to the domestic industry that produces like or directly competitive products.

If these requirements are met, the injured country might impose, as a safeguard, a measure suspending trade concessions or obligations. Such suspension is usually in the form of quantitative import restrictions such as either tariff-rate-quotas (recall that GATT Art. XI prohibits absolute quotas[2]) or increased tariffs to a level higher than the respective country's WTO bound rates.[3]

The most relevant legal rules of the SG Agreement are the following ones. To begin with and since they are emergency measures, safeguards must be temporary.[4] They shall only be applied during the time required to prevent or to remedy the serious injury or threat thereof and to facilitate the adjustment of the domestic industry.[5] In particular, safeguards shall not be in legal force during more than four years,[6] a time considered enough for the surge in imports to alleviate or, alternatively, for the injured domestic industry to adapt to the new economic circumstances.[7] Some exceptions exist: a safeguard measure might be extended for up to another four years if it is found, through a new investigation, that its continuation is necessary to prevent or to remedy serious injury and if the evidence

2 GATT Art. XI paragraph 1 reads:

> No prohibitions or restrictions other than duties, taxes or other charges, whether made effective through quotas, import or export licenses or other measures, shall be instituted or maintained by any contracting party on the importation of any product of the territory of any other contracting party or on the exportation or sale for export of any product destined for the territory of any other contracting party.

3 See WTO Goods Schedules: Members' Commitments, www.wto.org/english/tratop_e/schedules_e/goods_schedules_e.htm (last visit, April 30, 2017). See *supra* Chapter 9.1.

4 See SGA Art. 7.1.

5 See *id.*

6 See SGA Art. 7.2. For developing countries safeguards may be applied for a total of ten years. See further explanation ahead in this chapter.

7 If the domestic industry is still not competitive in international markets after four years, the best course of action is to close down the companies belonging to it and to use the invested resources in other industries.

TABLE 22 Example of a safeguard that is gradually reduced

Year	*Tariff (Case 1)*	*Tariff (Case 2)*	*Tariff (Case 3)*
Before SG	5% (bound rate)	5% (bound rate)	5% (bound rate)
1	15%	15%	15.0%
2	13%	14%	14.9%
3	11%	13%	14.8%
4	9%	12%	14.7%
5	And so on	And so on	And so on

shows that the industry is still in the adjustment process.[8] In any event, the initial period of application plus any extension shall not exceed eight years.[9]

Safeguards shall not only be temporary but also, since they are only allowed as temporary safety valves, must be progressively liberalized.[10] Safeguards in place for longer than one year must be progressively reduced at regular intervals during the period of application,[11] while measures lasting more than three years shall be reviewed not later than at mid-term and, if appropriate, the measure shall be withdrawn or its pace of liberalization increased.[12] Table 22 shows an example of such liberalization (the legality of option three, since its degree of liberalization is minimal, is unclear).

As a second legal rule, WTO members are only allowed to impose safeguards provided that the imports from other WTO members cause or threaten to cause *serious* injury to a competing domestic industry.[13] This is a significant difference regarding antidumping and countervailing duties, which may be imposed when imports from other countries cause or threaten to cause *material* injury,[14] material injury being a lower standard than serious injury.

Third, SGA Art. 2.2 provides that "[s]afeguard measures shall be applied to a product being imported irrespective of its source." In other words, safeguards shall be applied across the board, in a non-selective or MFN basis, or to all WTO members without exceptions. This is another difference between safeguards and both (i) antidumping duties, which may be imposed surgically, i.e., directly to the company which is exporting goods below its normal value,[15] and (ii) countervailing measures, which might be exclusively imposed on the goods coming from the country granting the illegal subsidy.[16]

8 See SGA Art. 7.2.
9 See SGA Art. 7.3.
10 See SGA Art. 7.4.
11 See SGA Art. 7.4.
12 See *id.*
13 See GATT Art. XIX para. (a) and SGA Art. 2.1.
14 See Sections 11.2 and 11.3 *infra.*
15 See Section 11.1, *infra.*
16 See Section 11.2, *infra.*

Fourth, a country imposing a safeguard shall begin consultations with and pay compensation to the affected WTO members.[17] Compensation is intended to maintain a substantially equivalent level of concessions and other obligations with respect to other countries.[18]

If such compensation is not agreed within 30 days, the affected WTO members may individually suspend "the application of substantially equivalent concessions or other obligations under GATT 1994 [i.e., retaliate], to the trade of the Member applying the safeguard measure,"[19] unless the WTO Council for Trade in Goods rejects such approach.[20] To take an illustration, assume that country A imposes a safeguard by which all imports of good X coming from any country shall pay an extra tariff of 10 percent, that negotiations were unsuccessful and that country B, one of the largest exporters of good X, retaliates by imposing an extra tariff of 5 percent on all imports of good Y coming from country A.

In any event and if compensation is not agreed on, the right to retaliate cannot be exercised during the first three years of application of a safeguard measure if it has been taken based on an absolute increase on imports and otherwise conforms to the provisions of the SG Agreement.[21] This rule intends to protect countries that have been seriously hit by a surge in imports and that have imposed a safeguard under WTO rules but that have failed to reach an agreement regarding compensation due to the difficulties of negotiating such a deal with all the interested countries, of which there may be several. In such a case, retaliation would cause a harm equal to or even worse than the one that the safeguard is avoiding or offsetting.

Needless to say, WTO members cannot impose safeguards overnight. On the contrary, such measures shall be the outcome of a detailed investigation process that both the SG Agreement and domestic rules set forth. Thus, and to comply with the transparency standards that are so dear to the WTO Rules,[22] the investigation proceedings must be established and published prior to being used[23] while public hearings or other appropriate means must be held or be available to allow interested parties such as exporters, importers, domestic producers, and the Public Interest to make their cases regarding the proposed measures.[24] If the information that interested parties shall submit is confidential, they may replace it with a non-confidential summary thereof.[25]

Once the interested parties, which are usually the companies belonging to a domestic industry, comply with all the legal requirements, a WTO member may

17 See SGA Art. 8.1.
18 See SGA Arts 8.1 and 8.2.
19 SGA Art. 8.2.
20 See SGA Art. 8.2.
21 See SGA Art. 8.3.
22 See GATT Art. X.
23 See SGA Art. 3.1.
24 See *id.*
25 See SGA Art. 3.2.

or may not impose a definite safeguard measure, which, as already mentioned, might be either a tariff increase beyond the bound rates,[26] or, at first sight, a quantitative restriction. This second possibility requires a further explanation: safeguards in the form of quotas are an exception to GATT Art. XI and a key difference regarding other trade remedies, since WTO members are not allowed to impose quotas to offset the negative impact of either dumping or illegal subsidies. Quotas, in any case, are only allowed when serious injury has been found but not when just a threat thereof exists.[27]

On a related note, quotas might be either absolute ones or tariff-quotas. Absolute quotas exist, for instance, when a country enacts a legal rule providing that it will only import 50,000 tons in a first-come first-served basis. It is the authors' view that, pursuant to GATT Art. XI,[28] absolute quotas are not allowed in international trade and that safeguards are not an exception to such prohibition.[29] Even if such kind of quotas were allowed, they would generate practical problems, especially when the method to allocate them is a first-come first-served basis.[30] In such situations, exporters usually rush to fill the quota (the so-called quota race), crowding the importing ports during the first months or even the first weeks of the year if the quota is too low, favoring big companies with high levels of installed capacity, punishing smaller companies, and increasing storage costs (which the

26 If the tariff, after the increase, is still under the bound rates, the WTO member does not need either to comply with the investigation process or to impose a safeguard to achieve this purpose. See generally GATT Art. II.

27 See SG Art. 5.2(b), "The departure referred to above shall not be permitted in the case of serious injury."

28 Paragraph 1 of this legal rule reads:

> No prohibitions or restrictions other than duties, taxes or other charges, whether made effective through quotas, import or export licenses or other measures, shall be instituted or maintained by any contracting party on the importation of any product of the territory of any other contracting party or on the exportation or sale for export of any product destined for the territory of any other contracting party.

The rationale of this legal rule is not only that tariffs are more transparent than absolute quotas but also that it was easier to negotiate in future rounds the reduction of tariffs rather than the reduction of quotas (it is easier to value the concessions that countries make). See Michael Trebilcock and Michael Fishbein, 'International Trade: Barriers to Trade', in *Research Handbook in International Economic Law* (Andrew T. Guzman and Alan O. Sykes Eds), p. 15 (2008).

29 But see Arthur E. Appleton and Michael G. Plummer, *The World Trade Organization: Legal, Economic and Political Analysis*, p. 152 (2007) (stating that both GATT Art. XIX and the Safeguards Agreement add another legal exception to GATT Art. XI's prohibition on quantitative restrictions). There are, however, some valid exceptions to GATT Art. XI, such as GATT Arts XII.1 and XVIII.2 (allowing WTO members to impose quotas if they are suffering balance of payments problems).

30 See Roger B. Porter et al., *Efficiency, Equity, and Legitimacy: The Multilateral Trading System at the Millennium*, p. 119 (2004)

TABLE 23 Example of an absolute quota

Country	*Quota (thousands of tons)*
A	200
B	70
C	30
Other countries	0

TABLE 24 Example of a tariff-rate-quota

Country	*Quota (thousands of tons)*	*Intra quota tariff*	*Extra quota tariff*
A	200	5%	20%
B	70	5%	20%
C	30	5%	20%
Other countries	0	5%	20%
Total	*300*		

final consumer might end up paying).[31] Allocating the quota among different countries is not an efficient solution either.[32] Table 23 brings an example of absolute quotas.

According to Table 23, any country complying with its quota will pay a 10 percent tariff while imports exceeding the quota are not allowed.

Tariff-rate-quotas, in turn, are an additional tariff over the imports exceeding a threshold.[33] Table 24 shows an example of a tariff-rate-quota.

Pursuant to Table 24, any country complying with its quota will pay a 10 percent tariff while any country surpassing its quota shall pay a 25 percent tariff

31 See *id.* at p. 119:

(If the quota rights are extended to all exporters on a global first-come, first-served basis until the quota is exhausted, deadweight losses can arise because of the resulting 'quota race' where all foreign suppliers strive to be first in line. They may arrange their production schedule uneconomically to accelerate output, for example, or invest uneconomically in trying to locate and secure necessary import licenses before someone else does. Trade diversion can also occur because there is no reason to suppose that the lowest cost suppliers will always be first in line under the quota.).

32 See *id.* at p. 119, "If the quota is allocated by giving fixed shares to individual exporting nations, the danger arises that less efficient suppliers will be given an allocation (trade diversion)."

33 When a tariff-rate-quota is imposed, problems arise similar to those discussed in notes 607 and 608. Perhaps, the best method to avoid such issues is to auction the tariff-rate-quota. See David W. Skully, *Economics of Tariff-Rate Quota Administrations*, Market and Trade Economics Division, Economic Research Service, U.S. Department of Agriculture. Technical Bulletin No 1893 (2001).

TABLE 25 First example of a TRQ based on the import levels of recent years

Year	*Imports (thousands of tons)*
2010	500
2011	400
2012	600
Average = quota	500

TABLE 26 Second example of a TRQ based on the import levels of recent years

Year	*Imports (thousands of tons)*
2009	500
2010 (not relevant)[1]	1,100
2011	400
2012	600
Average of the last three years	700
Average of the last three representative years	500

[1] In any case, there is no legal rule providing a minimum difference between the imports of one year and the imports of other years to consider the former as a not representative year.

(e.g., if companies from country B exports 100,000 tons, they will pay 10 percent on the first 70,000 tons and 20 percent on the remaining 30,000 tons).

If a safeguard takes the form of a quantitative restriction, its level must not be below the actual import level of the most recent three representative years, unless *clear* justification is given for setting a lower level.[34] For instance, if imports were 5,000, 8,000, and 5,000 tons during the three previous years, the quota shall not be inferior to the three-year average, which is 6,000 tons. Tables 25 (an easy case), 26 (where one of the years is not representative because imports were too high), and 27 (where one of the years is not representative because imports were too low) are examples of tariff-rate-quotas based on import levels of recent years.

On top of that, if a quota is allocated among exporting countries, the importing WTO member shall negotiate an allocation agreement based on past market shares with the countries having a substantial interest.[35] The SG Agreement does not provide the meaning of substantial interest, but this does not seem a difficult notion. In the view of this book's authors, countries which have exported significant amounts of goods to the country applying the safeguard (e.g., at least 10 or 20 percent) have a substantial interest. Table 28 shows an example of this calculation, where countries A and B, covering 80 percent of imports, are deemed to have substantial interest.

34 See SGA Art. 5.1.

35 See SGA Art. 5.2(a).

TABLE 27 Third example of a TRQ based on the import levels of recent years

Year	*Imports (thousands of tons)*
2009	400
2010 (not relevant)[1]	100
2011	600
2012	500
Average of the last three years	400
Average of the last three representative years	500

[1] In any case, there is no rule providing the minimum difference between the imports of one year and the imports of other years to consider the former as a not representative year.

TABLE 28 TRQ allocated among exporting countries and based on past market shares

Country	*Imports*	*Market share*	*Relative market share*	*Quota*
A	500	50%	500/950 = 52.6%	526
B	300	30%	300/950 = 31.6%	316
C	150	15%	150/950 = 15.8%	158
Other countries (d)	50	5%	0%	0
Total	*1,000*	*100%*	*100%*	*1,000*
(a + b + c)/(a + b + c + d)	95%			

As a general rule and regarding that they are emergency measures and, therefore, temporary, a safeguard shall not be applied again to the same product until a period not inferior to two years or otherwise equal to the duration of the original measure has elapsed.[36] For instance, if a safeguard measure was applied for: (i) one year, (ii) four years, or (iii) six years, the minimum breaking term will be, respectively, two, four, and six years.

As an exception, and if the new measure has a duration of 180 days or less, it may be applied as long as the following two conditions are met: (i) at least one year has elapsed since the original measure was applied, and (ii) no more than two safeguard measures have been applied on the product during the five years immediately preceding the date of introduction of the new measure.[37]

While safeguards are usually definitive measures that a WTO member can only apply until a detailed investigation have been complied with, the SGA allows the imposition of provisional safeguard measures.[38] Such kind of measures are intended to protect a domestic industry which might have collapsed by the time the investigation has finished and the definitive measure has been applied. In any event, provisional safeguards must be more the exception than the rule. Thus, and

36 See SGA Art. 7.5.
37 See SGA Art. 7.6.
38 See SGA Art. 6.

only under critical circumstances where time is of the essence and any delay may cause an everlasting injury, provisional measures may be applied "pursuant to a preliminary determination that there is clear evidence that increased imports have caused or are threatening to cause serious injury."[39]

An interesting question is when such critical circumstances arise. While the WTO legal rules do not give an answer, it is logical to assume that such circumstances will be present whenever a seriously injured domestic industry, which greatly contributes to the economic output and employment of the affected country, may go beyond the rescue point before a definitive safeguard is applied. Such provisional measures, given their nature, shall not exceed 200 days,[40] being this time computed as part of the initial period of the definitive safeguard, if this is imposed.[41] Recall also that provisional safeguards cannot be quotas.[42]

The SG Agreement provides a special and different treatment for developing countries.[43] On the one hand, there is the so-called *de minimis* import exception.[44] Safeguards shall not be applied against imports coming from a developing country:

> as long as its share of imports of the product concerned in the importing member does not exceed 3 percent, provided that developing country members with less than 3 percent import share collectively account for not more than 9 percent of total imports of the product concerned.[45]

As an example, assume that total imports of good X being exported to country Y are 1,000,000 tons; that imports from country A (a developing one) are 20,000 tons; and that imports from nine other developing countries, all with the same market share, are 180,000. In other words, imports from developed countries are 800,000 or 80 percent of the total. In such a case, the imports from country A are 2 percent of the total, a percentage below the threshold of 3 percent; however, the *de minimis* import exception is not applicable because imports from developing countries (including country A) are individually lower than 3 percent and collectively 18 percent of the total, the double of the maximum percentage

39 SGA Art. 6.

40 See *id.*

41 See *id.*

42 See SGA Art. 6 - the underlined text is not part of the original legal rule:

> 'Such measures should take the form of tariff increases to be promptly refunded if the subsequent investigation referred to in paragraph 2 of Art. 4 does not determine that increased imports have caused or threatened to cause serious injury to a domestic industry'.

43 A list of developing countries does not exist. Such a list does exist regarding least-developed countries. See United Nations Committee for Development Policy, Development Policy and Analysis Division, Department of Economic and Social Affairs, List of Least Developed Countries (as of May 2016), available at: www.un.org/en/development/desa/policy/cdp/ldc/ldc_list.pdf (last visit, April 30, 2017).

44 See SGA Art. 9.1.

45 *Id.*

that the legal rule allows (9 percent). The *de minimis* exception would be applicable in this illustration if imports from developing countries were not higher than 90,000 tons.

On the other hand, developing countries may apply safeguard measures during a longer time in comparison with developed countries.[46] In particular, developing WTO members may extend the application of a safeguard for two years beyond the usually allowed time (i.e., the initial time is extended from four to six years). Thus, and after taking into account the possible extensions, developing countries may apply a measure for a total of ten years (six initial years extendable for other four years), in comparison with the usual eight years for developed WTO members (four initial years extendable for other four years).[47]

On the other hand, and for the purpose of complying with transparency requirements as well as to give enough time to other WTO members to adapt to the new rules, safeguard procedures shall be notified to the Committee on Safeguards in the following cases: (i) a WTO member has initiated an investigation regarding the existence of serious injury or threat thereof; (ii) a WTO member has found that either serious injury or threat thereof exists as a consequence of an increase of imports; and (iii) a WTO member has decided to either apply or extend a safeguard measure.

As indicated before, safeguards can only be imposed after some additional requirements have been met. The first one is the existence of increased imports. Needless to say, and since safeguards are emergency measures that should be sparingly used, not any increase is enough.[48] On top of that, the increase may be either absolute or relative. An absolute increase happens when the quantities of the imported goods were upward during a given time. An absolute increase occurs, for instance, when imports went from 200,000 to 900,000 tons per year. This is an easy case. Of course, the determination of the timeframe is strategic since imports could have gone up and down during the recent past. Thus, a more difficult case happens when imports went from 200,000 tons two years ago to 300,000, 100,000, 200,000, and 500,000 six months, one year, one year and a half and two years later. Table 29 shows a better example of imports which go up and down.

Naturally, the steepness of the increase depends on the selected timeframe. If such frame is a ten-month period, the graphic is the one that Figure 13 indicates.

If, in contrast, only the five last months are included in the graphic, the situation looks worse for the domestic industry, as Figure 14 depicts.

46 See SGA Art. 9.2.

47 See *id.*

48 See SGA Art. 2.1. See also DS121, Argentina – Safeguard Measures on Imports of Footwear, WT/DS121/AB/R, 14 December 1999, para. 131 (holding that both GATT Art. XIX and the SG Agreement Art. 2.1 "requires that the increase in imports must have been recent enough, sudden enough, sharp enough, and significant enough, both quantitatively and qualitatively, to cause or threaten to cause 'serious injury'," having the complainant party (Argentina) to meet this burden of proof). See generally DS98, Korea – Definitive Safeguard Measure on Imports of Certain Dairy Products.

TABLE 29 Example of increased imports

Month	*Imports (thousands of tons)*
March	200
April	300
May	500
June	600
July	900
August	700
September	1,000
October	1,200
November	1,300
December	1,800

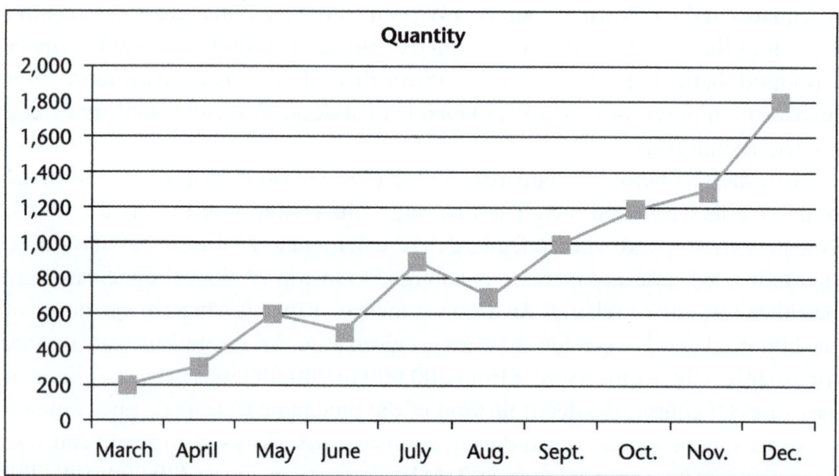

FIGURE 13 Timeframe of export increases (Case 1)

The slope may look steeper, which is useful to make the case for the domestic industry, if the ten months are registered in the graphic not individually as in Figure 13 but with the data clustered bimonthly. Figure 15 shows this trend.

An increase relative to domestic production, in turn, occurs when imports have remained stable or have gone down but domestic production has declined even further. Table 30 presents an example of a relative increase when imports are steady while domestic output is going down while Table 31 shows the opposite situation, when imports are going down but the decline of domestic output is steeper. Finally, Table 32 shows a case when domestic output is steady while imports are going up (in this case, there is both an absolute and a relative increase in imports). In all illustrations, imports are in thousands of tons.

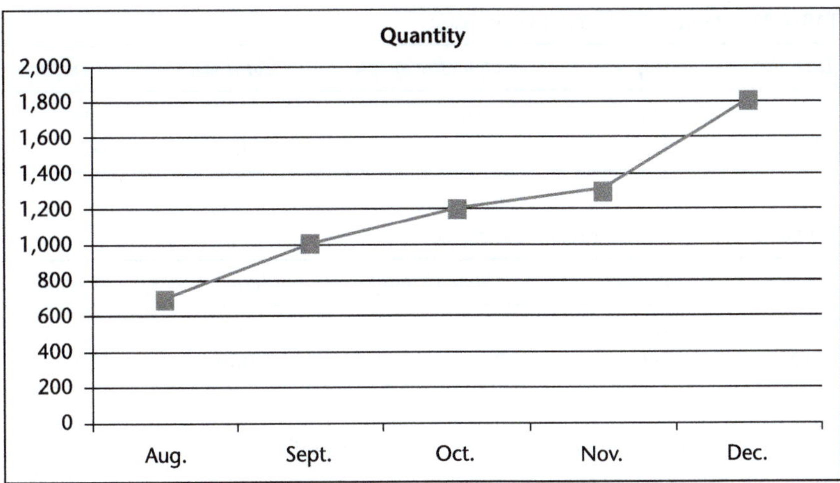

FIGURE 14 Timeframe of export increases (Case 2)

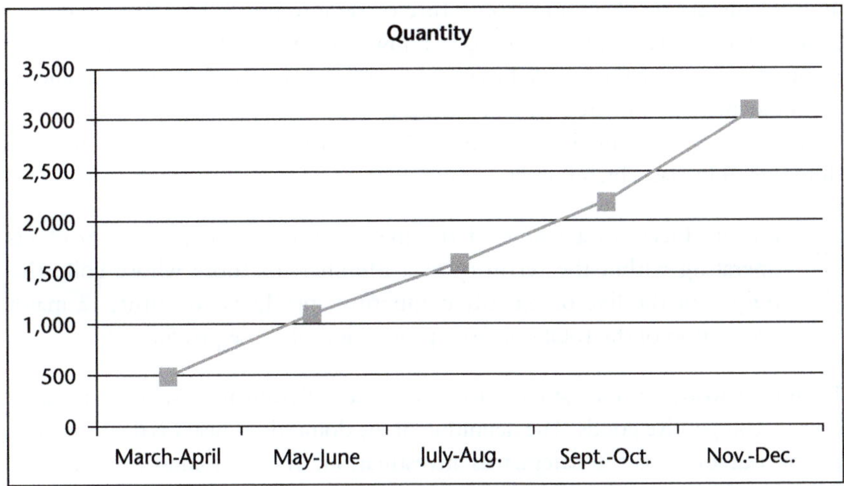

FIGURE 15 Timeframe of export increases (Case 3)

TABLE 30 Example 1 of a relative increase

Year	*Imports*	*Domestic output*	*Total sales*	*% imports*
2011	200	1,800	2,000	10%
2012	200	300	500	40%

TABLE 31 Example 2 of a relative increase

Year	*Imports*	*Domestic output*	*Total sales*	*% imports*
2011	200	1,800	2,000	10%
2012	180	320	500	36%

TABLE 32 Example 3 of a relative increase

Year	*Imports*	*Domestic output*	*Total sales*	*% imports*
2011	200	300	500	40%
2012	700	300	1,000	70%

The second requirement for the imposition of a safeguard is evidence of serious injury, or threat thereof, to a domestic industry.[49] Serious injury is a higher standard, i.e., requiring a higher burden of proof, than material injury, the standard required regarding antidumping and countervailing duties.[50] Serious injury is "a significant overall impairment in the position of a domestic industry"[51] while threat of serious injury is a clear imminent serious injury, "based on facts and not merely on allegation, conjecture or remote possibility."[52] Examples of serious injuries are plants operating at a low percentage of their capacities, the inability of domestic firms to do business at reasonable levels of profit, or significant unemployment or underemployment levels.

The third requirement is that the serious injury, or threat thereof, affects a domestic industry, which is defined as:

> the producers as a whole of the like or directly competitive products operating within the territory of a Member, or those whose collective output of the like or directly competitive products constitutes a major proportion of the total domestic production of those products.[53]

In simpler words, a domestic industry is the set of companies selling similar or directly competitive goods. The definition of the domestic industry is determinative of the outcome of the safeguards investigation. If the domestic industry is determined broadly (e.g., the companies producing soft beverages), its situation might not seem as distressed as if the domestic industry is composed of only a narrowly determined industry (e.g., companies bottling carbonated drinks).[54] Thus,

49 See SGA Art. 4.1.
50 See *infra* Sections 9.2 and 9.3.
51 SGA Art. 4.1 (a).
52 SGA Art. 4.1 (b).
53 SGA Art. 4.1 (c).
54 As the reader might have noticed, the determination of the domestic industry resembles the determination of the "relevant market" in antitrust proceedings. See generally Andrew I.

determining the approach is a strategic decision. In any case, safeguards should not be used to keep anticompetitive companies or industries forever; on the contrary, they are only safety valves intended to give time to firms that are competitive and profitable on a worldwide and long-term scale but that need some adjustment time before being ready to successfully fight an increased and fiercely foreign competition.

The fourth, final, most important, and also most difficult to prove requirement is causation.[55] The increase of imports must have caused the serious injury (or threat thereof).[56] While the cause does not need to be the only one generating the distress of the relevant industry,[57] it needs to be substantial.[58] Recessions, in turn, are not considered a valid cause since they usually affect a lot of industries across the economy and not a particular sector.[59] In any event, the WTO legal rules do not provide detailed guidelines since whether there is a causal link between increased imports and the serious injury is an empirical question that needs to be answered on a case-by-case basis.[60]

After describing the legal rules governing safeguard measures, it is relevant to mention some statistics about its application. Table 33 compares the number of investigations and final measures regarding antidumping duties, countervailing duties, and safeguards. As the figures indicate, safeguards are the least common trade remedy.

TABLE 33 Statistics on antidumping duties (AD), countervailing duties (CVD) and safeguards[61]

Measure	*AD*	*CVD*	*Safeguards*
Initiations	4,125	291	234
Measures	2,649	170	118
Percentage	64%	58%	50%

Gavil, William E. Kovacic and Jonathan B. Baker, *Antitrust Law in Perspective: Cases, Concepts and Problems in Competition Policy*, p. 1 (2002).

55 See generally Alan O. Sykes, *The Persistent Puzzles of Safeguards* 7(3) J. Int'l Econ. L. 523 (2004).

56 See SGA Arts 2.1 and 4.1(b).

57 See SGA Art. 4.1(b), "When factors other than increased imports are causing injury to the domestic industry at the same time, such injury shall not be attributed to increased imports."

58 See DS121, Argentina – Safeguard Measures on Imports of Footwear, WT/DS121/AB/R, 14 December 1999, para. 136; and DS98, Korea – Definitive Safeguard Measure on Imports of Certain Dairy Products, WT/DS98/AB/R, 14 December 1999, para. 108.

59 See DS121, Argentina – Safeguard Measures on Imports of Footwear, WT/DS121/R 25 June 1999, para. 8.269.

60 See, e.g., Douglas A. Irwin, *Causing Problems? The WTO Review of Causation and Injury Attribution in US Section 201 cases* 2(3) World Trade Rev. 297 (2003).

61 For statistics on antidumping duties, see Antidumping, www.wto.org/english/tratop_e/adp_e/adp_e.htm (last visit, April 30, 2017). For statistics on countervailing duties, see Subsidies and Countervailing Duties, www.wto.org/english/tratop_e/scm_e/scm_e.htm (last visit, April 30, 2017). For statistics on safeguards, see Safeguard Measures, www.wto.org/english/tratop_e/safeg_e/safeg_e.htm (last visit, April 30, 2017).

TABLE 34 Safeguard measures by WTO members[62]

Country	*Safeguards*
India	14
Turkey	13
Indonesia	13
Chile	7
Jordan	7
Philippines	7
United States	6
Argentina	4
European Union	3
Brazil	2
China	1
Other 19 countries	106
Total	*234*

Table 34, in turn, shows the countries that more often apply safeguards.

Before ending the section on safeguards, two policy questions and their answers are relevant. The first question relates to the differences between safeguards and antidumping and countervailing duties. As already mentioned, safeguards might be imposed when there is a surge in imports of a certain good, regardless of whether such imports are fair or unfair. They are, therefore, a safety valve intended to temporarily protect a domestic industry from increased foreign competition. As a result, safeguards shall be imposed across the board; i.e., to all the imports causing or threatening to cause material injury to the domestic industry.[63]

Antidumping duties, on the other hand, can only be imposed on imports coming from countries or, more precisely, companies which are selling at a price below the normal value of the goods.[64] As a result, antidumping duties may be surgically imposed: only to the company or companies incurring in this unfair trade practice.[65] Countervailing duties, in turn, can only be imposed to imports coming from the WTO member which is granting a prohibited or an actionable subsidy.[66]

On top of that, safeguards are usually imposed (or not imposed) based not only on technical but also political considerations since such measures might trigger issues that go beyond trade relations (they might have consequences in the realm of foreign affairs, for example). Antidumping and countervailing duties, in turn,

62 See Safeguard Measures, www.wto.org/english/tratop_e/safeg_e/safeg_e.htm (last visit, April 30, 2017).

63 See SG Agreement 2.2. "Safeguard measures shall be applied to a product irrespective of its source."

64 See *infra* Sections 11.2 and 11.3.

65 See *infra* Section 11.2.

66 See *infra* Section 11.3.

should be imposed based on technical reasons; i.e., after determining through sound methods whether the investigated foreign companies are exporting at prices below their normal values or whether they are receiving illegal subsidies.[67]

The second question enquires on the reasons why antidumping duties, and countervailing measures in a lower scale, but not safeguards, are the most common trade remedy. In other words, why are safeguards rarely applied? The differences indicated in the last paragraph are the answer. Antidumping duties are the most effective trade remedy since they can be imposed directly to the source generating the trade damage while safeguards need to be generally imposed, without distinguishing between countries and exporting companies, a feature that might adequately discourage some producers abroad from keeping a high level of exports but that, at the same time, might alienate some other industries in countries which might politically retaliate.

11.2 Antidumping duties

Antidumping rules exist in international trade since GATT 1947, whose Art. VI para. 1 states:

> The contracting parties recognize that dumping, by which products of one country are introduced into the commerce of another country at less than the normal value of the products, is to be condemned if it causes or threatens material injury to an established industry in the territory of a contracting party or materially retards the establishment of a domestic industry. For the purposes of this Article, a product is to be considered as being introduced into the commerce of an importing country at less than its normal value, if the price of the product exported from one country to another
>
> (a) Is less than the comparable price, in the ordinary course of trade, for the like product when destined for consumption in the exporting country, or,
> (b) In the absence of such domestic price, is less than either
>
>   (i) The highest comparable price for the like product for export to any third country in the ordinary course of trade, or
>   (ii) The cost of production of the product in the country of origin plus a reasonable addition for selling cost and profit.
>
> Due allowance shall be made in each case for differences in conditions and terms of sale, for differences in taxation and for other differences affecting price comparability.

67 See SG Agreement 2.2, "Safeguard measures shall be applied to a product irrespective of its source."

This legal rule is now coupled with the Antidumping agreement, officially known as the Agreement on Implementation of Art. VI of GATT 1994 (the AD agreement or just the ADA) that WTO members approved in 1994 at the end of the Uruguay Round. Before that, the first multilateral antidumping Code, the Agreement on Anti-Dumping Practices, had entered into force in 1967 as a result of the Kennedy Round. However, since the United States never signed the Kennedy Round Code, it had little practical significance. It was not until the Tokyo Round that a robust Code, which entered into force in 1980, was completed. The first national antidumping law is Canadian and dates back to 1904.

Generally speaking, dumping arises whenever a company located in a WTO member exports a product to another WTO member at a price below its normal value.[68] This formula is reproduced below, where NV is the normal value and EP is the Exporting Price. The normal value means the comparable price, in the ordinary course of trade, for a like product when it is destined for consumption in the exporting country.[69] In the absence of such domestic price (i.e., there is no domestic market for this product), the normal value is either: (i) the price for a like product available for export to any third country in the ordinary course of trade, or (ii) the cost of production of the product in the country of origin plus a reasonable addition for selling costs and profits.[70]

$Dumping = NV - EP > 0$, where NV = normal value and EP = export price

Before levying an antidumping duty, a WTO member must undertake a thorough investigation complying with both substantive and procedural requirements. Failure to respect any such requirements may entitle a WTO member to challenge the validity of the trade remedy either domestically[71] or before the DSU.[72] Regarding substantive requirements, it must be proved not only that dumping exists,[73] but also that it is causing material injury[74] or threat thereof,[75] i.e., that there is a causal link between the dumped imports and the injury to the domestic industry.[76]

On the other hand, both GATT Art. VI and AD Agreement set forth the procedural requirements. Any investigation shall be initiated based on a written request submitted by or on behalf of a domestic industry.[77] The written submission must give enough evidence of dumping, injury, and causal relationship between the dumped imports and the alleged injury.[78] The AD Agreement also

68 See ADA Art. 2.1.
69 See ADA Art. 2.1.
70 See ADA Art. 2.2.
71 See ADA Art. 13.
72 See ADA Art. 17.
73 See ADA Art. 2.1.
74 A lower standard than serious injury, the standard used in safeguards. See *supra* Section 11.1.
75 See GATT Art. VI and ADA Art. 3.
76 See ADA Art. 3.5.
77 See ADA Art. 5.
78 See ADA Arts 3, 5 and 6.

sets forth detailed rules on the process of investigation regarding matters such as confidentiality, transparency and public notice.[79]

Similar to safeguards, antidumping duties might be imposed as provisional measures.[80] In any event, domestic authorities must make a preliminary affirmative determination of dumping, injury and causality before applying such provisional measures.[81] On top of that and to avoid hasty measures, no provisional measures shall be applied sooner than 60 days after initiation of an investigation.[82]

Other procedural rules are the following ones. First, and even if all other requirements have been met, the imposition of antidumping duties is optional.[83] Indeed, the legal rules also indicate the desirability of applying the so-called "lesser duty" rule, i.e., applying the required duty to offset the dumping but not any additional basis point in order to minimize the harm to international trade.[84] Second, both provisional and final antidumping duties may be applied only as of the date on which the determination of dumping, injury and causality has been made.[85] Nonetheless, if the imposition of antidumping duties is based on a finding of material injury (and not on a finding of threat of material injury), antidumping duties may be collected as of the date when the provisional measures were imposed.[86] Third, antidumping duties shall normally terminate no later than five years after their application began (or five years after the most recent review) unless an investigation prior to that date indicates that expiration of the duty would likely entail the continuation or recurrence of both the dumping and the injury.[87] This safety valve, in practice, allows for the fact that a non-negligible number of antidumping measures stay in legal force indefinitely,[88] in sheer contrast to the principle that antidumping duties should be temporary remedies.[89]

Now, this section turns to the analysis of antidumping proceedings in the United States, the European Union, non-market economies, and other countries. The most interesting comparison is the one between the U.S. and the E.U. antidumping regimes taking into account that they apply the two existent systems to carry out antidumping investigations: the retrospective (the United States) and the prospective (European Union) systems.[90] Most countries follow the E.U.'s

79 See ADA Art. 6.
80 See ADA Art. 7.
81 See ADA Art. 7.1.
82 See ADA Art. 7.3.
83 See ADA Art. 9.1.
84 See ADA Art. 9.1.
85 See ADA Art. 10.1.
86 See ADA Art. 10.2.
87 See ADA Art. 10.3.
88 See Aluisio de Lima-Campos, *Nineteen Proposals to Curb Abuse in Antidumping and Countervailing Duties Proceedings* 39(2) J. World Trade 239, 250 (2005) (proposing to abolish sunset reviews and let antidumping expire after five years).
89 See ADA Art. 11.1.
90 See *supra* Chapters 2 and 3.

model.[91] This is not surprising taking into account that the E.U. system is easier to administer and thus more attractive to both new users and developing countries with limited budgets and personnel, at least in comparison with the more complex and detail-oriented U.S. system.

The United States adopts the retrospective system.[92] Under such scheme, importers do not pay antidumping duties at the time of entry; they pay deposits based on duty deposit rates that are subject to review, up or down, as much as two years after the entry date.[93] Pursuant to the retrospective system, the importer does not know the final cost of its investigated imports until around two and a half years later. This introduces a major uncertainty with regard to the import cost and, consequently, profit, which in turn may lead to a reduction of imports even before or at the outset of an investigation.[94] Consequently, in terms of domestic industry protection, the U.S. retrospective system is more efficient than the European.

The European Union, in contrast, employs an alternative prospective method, in use by most countries, by which authorities determine the amount of duties before the entry of the goods and impose such duties on imports of covered products.[95] Thus, the duties are final at the time of entry.[96] In this case, importers have no uncertainty about the final cost of the imported product and, by knowing the final cost ahead of time, have the choice of not buying the foreign product if the transaction does not look profitable.

In the United States, any industry may seek relief by filing a petition with the International Trade Commission (ITC) and the Department of Commerce (DoC).[97] As a procedural requirement, producers accounting for at least 25 percent of domestic output in the relevant industry must support this petition.[98] On top of that, the petition shall contain some evidence of dumping and injury (or threat thereof) to the domestic industry.[99]

Once an antidumping investigation is initiated, the ITC has 45 days to determine whether there is a reason to believe that dumped imports are causing or threatening injury to a domestic industry.[100] If the ITC reaches a preliminary affirmative finding, the DoC issues questionnaires to the largest known foreign

91 See Gary N. Horlick & Edwin Vermulst, *The 10 Major Problems with the Antidumping Instrument: An Attempt at Synthesis*, 39(1) J. World Trade 67 (2005).

92 See *supra* Chapter 2.

93 See U.S. Trade Act of 1974.

94 See Aluisio de Lima-Campos and Adriana Vito, *Abuse and Discretion: the impact of antidumping and countervailing duty proceedings on Brazilian exports to the United States* 38(1) J. World Trade 37–68 (2004).

95 See *supra* Chapter 3.

96 See *id.*

97 See U.S. Trade Act of 1930 19 U.S.C. §1673.

98 See *id.*

99 See Trade Act of 1930, Sections 1671–1677n, 19 U.S.C. §1673.

100 See *id.*

producers and exporters of subject merchandise from the countries in question.[101] Failure either to respond to the DoC's questionnaires or to fully cooperate in the proceedings typically result in the assignment of an adverse rate of duty.[102]

The DoC usually makes its preliminary determination within 140 days following the beginning of the investigation.[103] If the DoC's preliminary determination is affirmative, the liquidation is suspended for all future imports, and a bond must be posted to cover possible antidumping duties at the rate that such preliminary determination indicated.[104] The DoC then makes its final determination within 75 days following the preliminary determination.[105] During this period, the DoC conducts an on-site verification of the respondent's questionnaires and considers factual and legal arguments that petitioners and respondents submitted.[106]

Once the DoC has issued its final determination, and assuming that it was in the affirmative, respondents must pay cash deposits on possible antidumping duties at the rate announced in such decision.[107] The ITC usually has 45 days to determine whether or not dumping has caused injury (or threat thereof).[108] If the ITC finds injury (or threat thereof), an antidumping order is issued, which subjects prospective imports to antidumping duty deposits equal to the calculated rate of dumping.[109] Please keep in mind that the antidumping deposit rate is only an estimate of dumping liability based on dumping margins calculations for the period under investigation.[110]

Later on, the DoC determines through administrative reviews whether or not there is final liability.[111] The first period of review covers imports from the beginning of duty liability to the first anniversary of the antidumping order while any subsequent period of review covers imports from one anniversary date to the next one.[112] The DoC's final determination establishes the final dumping liability or the value of the deposits for imports during the period under review.[113] If the definitive amount of dumping is more than the cash deposits, the respondent owes the difference plus the interest; by contrast, if the amount of dumping is less, the respondent is entitled to a refund plus interest.[114]

101 See *id.*
102 See *id.*
103 See *id.*
104 See *id.*
105 See *id.*
106 See *id.*
107 See *id.*
108 See *id.*
109 See *id.*
110 See *id.*
111 See *id.*
112 See *id.*
113 See *id.*
114 See *id.*

Final antidumping measures are subject to administrative reviews that the DoC conducts every year.[115] On top of that, and under the so-called sunset review provision, an antidumping duty order is terminated automatically after five years unless a sunset review is requested.[116] Thus, every five years, in these sunset reviews, the DoC and the ITC determines whether or not termination of the order would be likely to lead to the continuation or resumption of dumping and injury, respectively.[117] If both entities make affirmative determinations, the order continues for other five years.[118] Most of the time, antidumping duties in the United States last for many years.[119] Figure 16 summarizes the U.S. administrative proceedings to determine antidumping duties.[120]

Needless to say, companies may appeal the DoC's final decisions regarding antidumping duties before the Court of International Trade, in the first instance, the Court of Appeals for the Federal Circuit, in the second instance and, only if a writ of *certiorari* is granted,[121] which is extremely rare,[122] before the U.S. Supreme Court.[123]

On the other hand, the U.S. antidumping proceedings are subject to several criticisms. To begin with, comparison of average prices may be skewed by price fluctuations over the period of investigation. Thus, the more volatile the price of the relevant good, the more likely the finding of dumping. In particular, the legal rules skew the calculation and comparison of net prices in the direction of higher dumping margins[124] because: (i) the arm's length test, used to determine whether sales to affiliated customers in the home market have been made at prices and on terms comparable with those granted to unaffiliated customers, eliminates low-priced sales to home-market affiliated companies, but not high-priced sales, thus inflating normal value and, consequently, dumping margins; (ii) the cost test, used to eliminate from consideration sales made in the home market at prices lower than the full cost of production, eliminates low-priced sales in the home market when they are found to be below cost, where the evidence for a sanctuary

115 See *id.*
116 See *id.*
117 See *id.*
118 See *id.*
119 See Greg Mastel, *Antidumping Laws and the U.S. Economy,* p. 123 (1998). See generally United States – Sunset Reviews of Antidumping Measures on Oil Country Tubular Goods from Argentina (WT/DS268/AB/R, 29 November 2004).
120 Figure made by the authors.
121 See 28 U.S. Code Section 1254.
122 But not non-existent. For such a case, see *United States v. Eurodif S. A.* 555 U.S. 305 (2009), holding that some sales of low enriched uranium which the DoC and the ICT subjected to antidumping duties were contracts for sale of goods (and, therefore, dumping was possible) and not contracts for sale of services (where dumping is not possible).
123 See U.S. Trade Act of 1930 19 U.S.C. §1673.
124 Brink Lindsey and Daniel J. Benson, *Reforming the Antidumping Agreement: A Real Map for WTO Negotiations*, 21 Trade Pol. Anal. (2002).

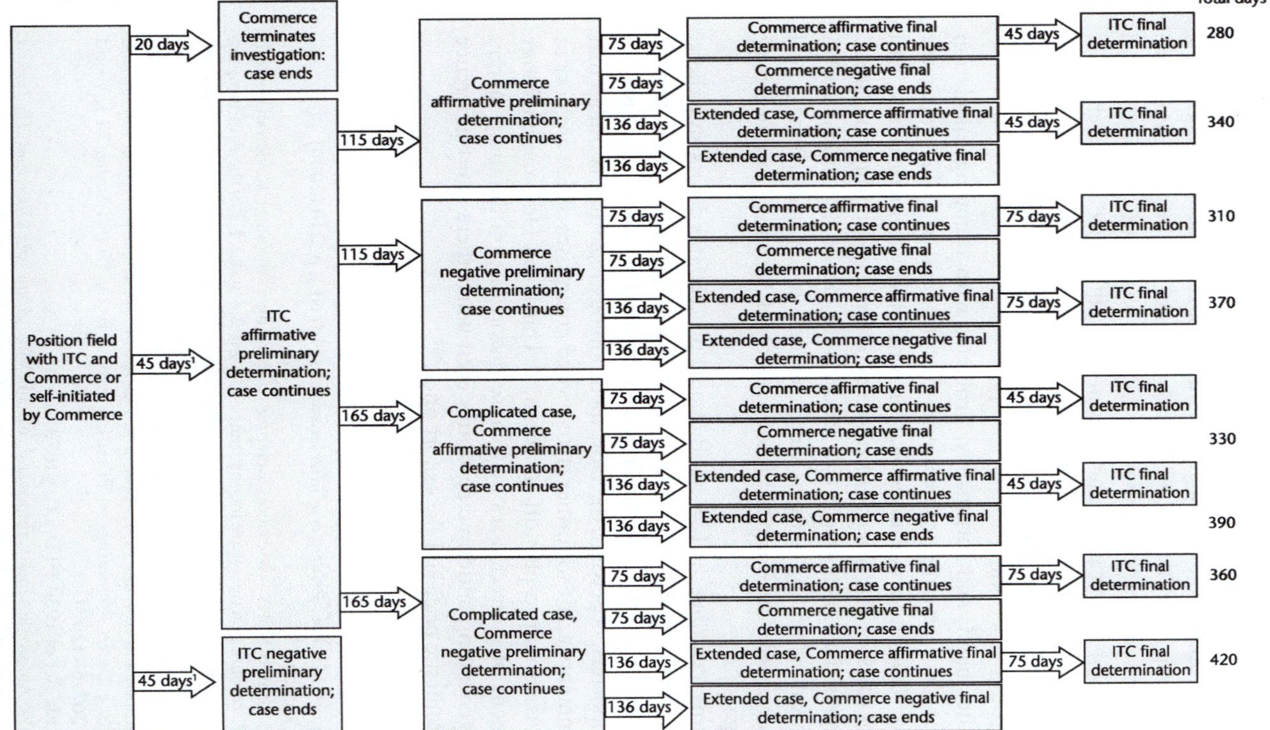

¹ Normal case. ITA may extend the time allowed for it to intiate an investigation from 20 days to up to 40 days after a position is filed if the extra time is needed to determine industry support for the position. In the event of such an extension, the deadline for the ITC 's preliminary determination and all following dates would be increased by the amount of the extension.

FIGURE 16 Statutory timetables for antidumping and countervailing duties investigations[125]

125 See U.S. International Trade Commission, www.usitc.gov/trade_remedy/731_ad_701_cvd/TIMETABL.PDF (last visit, April 30, 2017).

market (a closed home market for a foreign producer) is weak, at best; (iii) indirect selling expenses are fully deducted from U.S. prices in Constructed Export Price (CEP) transactions, but not from the home-market prices to which they are compared; and (iv) CEP profit is also deducted from U.S. prices in these situations but no corresponding deduction is made on the home-market side.

There is also a bias toward finding dumping regarding the definition of the products being compared. The existence or nonexistence of dumping margins can turn on unavoidably arbitrary definitions of the products being compared. Thus, comparisons of non-identical products, even with difference in merchandise adjustments, can easily produce dumping margins that reflect nothing more than different commercial values, which are common in markets whose main feature is the monopolistic competition.[126]

On the other hand, and fortunately, problems with dumping calculation no longer exist since zeroing practices were discontinued in 2012[127] after the Appellate Body held in several cases that such method was inconsistent with the WTO legal rules.[128] The practice of zeroing consisted of ignoring "negative" dumping margins (i.e., cases where U.S. prices were higher than home-market prices); as a result, dumping margins were routinely much higher than actual difference in net-price levels (which take into account both "positive" and "negative" dumping margins).

The problems regarding the U.S. antidumping proceedings do not stop there. First, the ITC uses a cumulative analysis, instead of an individual study of imports per country, which biases the results in favor of plaintiffs (i.e., domestic industries), and against importers.[129] Second, the DoC methodology regarding subsidies that foreign governments grant to former state-owned enterprises which are now in private hands is also a pro-plaintiff approach.[130] Third, the DoC methodology for the treatment of indirect taxes may cause distortions on dumping margin calculations, generating antidumping duties even when there is no difference between the domestic price and the export price.[131]

126 See N. Gregory Mankiw, *Principles of Microeconomics* (4th ed.), p. 210 (2006).

127 See URAA Section 123.

128 See DS322, United States – Measures Relating to Zeroing and Sunset Reviews (holding that the U.S. zeroing practices were inconsistent with Arts 2.4 and 2.4.2 of the Antidumping Agreement. For other similar cases, see DS-294, United States – Laws, Regulations and Methodology for Calculating Dumping Margins (Zeroing), and DS-402, United States – Use of Zeroing in Antidumping Measures Involving Products from Korea. See also Aluisio de Lima-Campos and Adriana Vito, *Abuse and Discretion: The Impact of Antidumping and Countervailing Duties Proceedings on Brazilian Exports in the United States*, 38 J. World Trade 239, 267–68 (2004).

129 See U.S. Trade Act of 1930 19 U.S.C. §1673.

130 See *id.* See also Aluisio de Lima-Campos and Adriana Vito, *Abuse and Discretion: The Impact of Antidumping and Countervailing Duties Proceedings on Brazilian Exports in the United States*, 38 J. World Trade 239, 271–74 (2004).

131 See U.S. Trade Act of 1930 19 U.S.C. §1673, and Aluisio de Lima-Campos and Adriana Vito, *Abuse and Discretion: The Impact of Antidumping and Countervailing Duties*

This section turns now to the analysis of antidumping proceedings in the European Union. Any plaintiff considering that dumped imports from non-E.U. countries are causing material injury (or threat thereof) and representing at least 25 percent of the total E.U. production of the good in question may submit a complaint to the European Commission, either directly or through its national government.[132] The Commission has 45 days to examine the complaint, to consult the E.U. Member States, and to decide whether or not there is enough evidence to start a formal investigation.[133] If such evidence is lacking, the case is rejected.[134] If the evidence exists, the Commission analyzes (i) whether or not dumping is taking place and (ii) whether or not it is causing material injury (or threat thereof) to the relevant E.U.'s industry.[135]

To ensure the compliance with transparency standards, E.U. Member States must be consulted while producers, importers, users, and consumers are able to present their views.[136] Once these proceedings are completed, the Commission may, within 60 days to nine months, impose provisional duties.[137] The Council of Ministers, and not the Commission, is the body entitled to impose definitive duties, which are valid for five years.[138] Notwithstanding, if E.U. producers demonstrate that removal of the duties is likely to lead to renewed dumping, the Commission may reopen the investigation.[139] Interested parties may challenge any decision imposing antidumping duties before the European Court of First Instance.[140]

Having discussed the antidumping proceedings both in the United States and in the European Union, this section turns to the analysis of dumping investigations in non-market economies, which have special features.[141] WTO members

Proceedings on Brazilian Exports in the United States, 38 J. World Trade 239, 271–74 (2004).

132 See Regulation (EU) 2016/1036 of the European Parliament and of the Council of 8 June 2016 on protection against dumped imports from countries not members of the European Union (substituting Council Regulation (EC) No 1225/2009).

133 See *id.*

134 See *id.*

135 See *id.*

136 See *id.*

137 See *id.*

138 See *id.*

139 See *id.*

140 See *id.*

141 The United Nations Conference on Trade and Development (UNCTAD) defines a market economy as "[a] national economy of a country that relies heavily upon market forces to determine levels of production, consumption, investment and savings without government intervention." UNCTAD's Glossary of Customs Terms is available at www.asycuda.org/cuglossa.asp?term=market+economy (last visit, April 30, 2017). This organization also defines a non-market economy as:

> [a] national economy in which the government seeks to determine economic activity largely through a mechanism of central planning, as in the former Soviet Union, in contrast to a market economy which depends heavily upon market forces to allocate productive resources. In a 'non-market' economy, production targets, prices, costs, investment allocations, raw

are allowed to use particular methodologies to calculate dumping values related to imports coming from non-market economies, China being the primary example.[142] Thus, in such cases, the investigating authorities have a broad margin to choose creative and usually protectionist methodologies in order to estimate, or even increase, dumping margins.[143] Likewise, an injury test and the use of prices in third-countries as an indicator of normal values are not mandatory.[144] As a consequence, the imposition of antidumping duties in cases of non-market economies is almost always guaranteed.[145] The only question is the amount of the duty.[146]

Before ending this section, it is worth mentioning the main antidumping issues in other WTO members.[147] The first one is related to the non-disclosure of confidential information. The WTO legal rules deprive interested parties of a meaningful way to make their cases because a significant percentage of the relevant information is usually regarded as confidential.[148] Examples of confidential information are reports from the administering authorities as well as information that some interested parties have submitted and which is not widely circulated. There are also problems regarding the preliminary phase of the investigation.[149] First, the initial procedures are usually very time-consuming.[150] Second, relations between the domestic industry and the government are too close, triggering frequent conflicts of interest (for instance, the speaker of the industry might have

materials, labor, international trade and most other economic aggregates are manipulated within a national economic plan drawn up by a central planning authority; hence, the public sector makes the major decisions affecting demand and supply within the national economy. See *id.*

142 WTO, Report of the Working Party on the Accession of China, WT/ACC/CHN/49, October 2001, para. 4. In such protocol, China accepted that other countries could apply special antidumping methodologies for a 15-year term, which has elapsed. See *id.* In any event, it is debatable whether China is still a non-market economy. For a famous case about antidumping duties levied on using a special methodology, see United States – Definitive Antidumping and Countervailing Duties on Certain Products from China, WT/DS379/AB/R, March 11, 2011.

143 See generally Vera Thorstensen et al., *WTO – Market and Non-Market Economies: The Hybrid Case of China*, 1(2) Latin Am. J. Int'l Trade L. 765 (2003).

144 See *id.*

145 See *id.*

146 See *id.*

147 This analysis is based on Gary N. Horlick and Edwin Vermulst, *The 10 Major Problems with the Antidumping Instrument: An Attempt at Synthesis*, 39(1) J. World Trade 67 (2005). In spite of the fact that this paper was written more than ten years ago, the issues described there still persist.

148 See AD Agreement Art. 6.1.2. See also Gary N. Horlick and Edwin Vermulst, *The 10 Major Problems with the Antidumping Instrument: An Attempt at Synthesis*, 39(1) J. World Trade 67 (2005).

149 See Gary N. Horlick and Edwin Vermulst, *The 10 Major Problems with the Antidumping Instrument: An Attempt at Synthesis*, 39(1) J. World Trade 67 (2005).

150 See *id.*

been a recent high government official or vice versa).[151] Third, the application of the rule providing that at least 25 percent of the industry must support the petition requesting the beginning of the investigation is non-consistent and unclear.[152]

Antidumping issues do not only arise during the early stages of the proceedings but also during the final steps. The so-called sunset review procedures are not working well.[153] The drafting of ADA Art. 13, which is a too open-ended provision (the duties may be extended when "expiry of the duty would be likely to lead to continuation or recurrence of dumping and injury"), allows countries to keep antidumping duties indefinitely or at least for too long periods.[154] Some criticisms also exist regarding the administrative and judicial reviews since the proceedings are too slow and local courts are usually unwilling to double-check and to annul administrative determinations.[155]

As two final comments, the Constructed Normal Value (CNV) calculation tends to be too artificial, discretionary and usually biased against importers and international trade,[156] and there is too much administrative discretion in the determination of injury, causation, and injury margins.[157]

11.3 Subsidies and countervailing measures

The Subsidies and Countervailing Measures Agreement (SCM Agreement or SCMA) defines a subsidy as (i) a financial contribution, (ii) by a government or any public body within the territory of a member, (iii) which confers a benefit.[158] These three elements are explained below.

Regarding the financial contribution, a subsidy requires a charge on a public account.[159] The SCM Agreement contains a non-exhaustive list of measures that represent a financial contribution, such as grants, loans, equity infusions, loan guarantees, fiscal incentives, the provision of goods or services, and the purchase of goods.[160]

151 See *id.*

152 See Gary N. Horlick and Edwin Vermulst, *The 10 Major Problems with the Antidumping Instrument: An Attempt at Synthesis*, 39(1) J. World Trade 67 (2005). See also Aluisio de Lima-Campos, *Nineteen Proposals to Curb Abuse in Antidumping and Countervailing Duties Proceedings* 39(2) J. World Trade 239, 250 (2005).

153 See *id.*

154 See *id.*

155 See *id.*

156 See Aluisio de Lima-Campos, *Nineteen Proposals to Curb Abuse in Antidumping and Countervailing Duties Proceedings* 39(2) J. World Trade 239, 274–76 (2005).

157 See Aluisio de Lima-Campos, *Nineteen Proposals to Curb Abuse in Antidumping and Countervailing Duties Proceedings* 39(2) J. World Trade 239, 249–50 (2005).

158 See SCMA Art. 1.

159 See SCMA Art. 1.1.

160 See *id.*

The financial contribution must be granted "by or at the direction of a government or any public body within the territory of a Member."[161] Thus, the SCM Agreement is applicable not only to national government's measures but also to measures of sub-national governments and public bodies such as state-owned enterprises.[162]

Lastly, a financial contribution by a government is not a subsidy unless it confers a benefit to a domestic industry.[163] In many cases, the existence of a benefit is clear-cut while in other more interesting cases it may be not so clear. The AB has held that the existence of a benefit must be determined based on the amount that the recipient could have received in the market vis-a-vis the amount received from the government.[164]

Even if a measure is regarded as a subsidy within the context of the SCM Agreement, it is against the WTO legal rules if it has been provided to an enterprise or industry or group of enterprises or industries (this is the requirement of specificity).[165] There are four types of specificity within the meaning of the SCM Agreement:[166] (i) enterprise-specificity, when the subsidy is granted to a particular company or group of companies; (ii) industry-specificity, happening when the subsidy targets a particular sector or sectors; (iii) regional-specificity, arising when the subsidy is given to producers in specified parts of the territory; and (iv) prohibited subsidies (which are always regarded as specific subsidies), targeting export goods or goods using domestic inputs. This last kind of subsidies are always prohibited[167] because, by giving a boost to exports not based on competitiveness, they alter the equilibrium of international trade favoring less efficient companies and punishing most efficient ones in other countries.

Agriculture is one of the hot topics in the WTO rules and, because of that, such sector has a special agreement, the Agreement on Agriculture. Art. 13 of such agreement provides some rules regarding subsidies for agricultural products during the implementation period.[168] Thus, the SCM Agreement did not prohibit export subsidies which were in full conformity with the Agreement on Agriculture; however, they remain countervailable.[169] A similar legal rule exists regarding domestic support measures which were in full conformity with the Agreement on Agriculture: they could be subject to countervailable duties but they are non-actionable subsidies.[170] Finally, domestic support measures within

161 See SCMA Art. 1.1(a)(1).

162 See Appellate Body Report, Canada – Measures Affecting the Export of Civilian Aircraft, WT/DS70/AB/R (adopted 20 August, 1999), para. 157.

163 See SCMA Art. 1.1(b).

164 See *id.*

165 See SCMA Art. 2.

166 See SCMA Art. 2.

167 See SCMA Art. 3.1(a).

168 See WTO Agreement on Agriculture Art. 13.

169 See SCMA Art. 10.

170 See SCMA Art. 8.

the so-called "green box" of the Agriculture Agreement were neither actionable on a multilateral level nor subject to countervailable measures.[171]

Subsidies may be classified in three categories: (i) general subsidies, which are granted to all enterprises or industries, without exceptions; thereby, they are not actionable; (ii) specific subsidies, granted to a particular company or group of companies, or to a particular industry, or group of industries; they are actionable (this is the most common situation); and (iii) prohibited subsidies, which are conditioned, *de jure* or *de facto*, on the exports or on the use of domestic inputs (in detriment of imported inputs); they are subject to countervailing duties.[172] The SCM Agreement also places limitations on the use of undertakings to settle countervailing duties investigations in exchange for a price increase of the subject imports or a quantitative limitation of such imports.[173] These types of undertaking, also known as suspension agreements in the U.S., are Voluntary Restraint Agreements (VRA). VRAs, not unusual during the second half of the last decade, were essentially "agreements not to compete" of the following kind: companies from country A yielded its right to export goods X to country B in exchange for companies in country B doing the same in respect of goods Y.[174] Needless to say, such kind of conduct, which domestically might have amounted to a violation of antitrust legal rules,[175] was very harmful to international trade.[176]

To be countervailable, subsides must also cause adverse effects to a WTO member.[177] Generally speaking, there are three types of adverse effects.[178] First, injury that subsidized imports cause to a domestic industry of a WTO member.[179] This is the sole basis for countervailing action.[180] Second, serious prejudice, which usually arises as a result of adverse effects such as export displacement in the market of the subsidizing WTO member or in a third country market.[181] For instance, and because of a subsidy that the government of country A granted to its domestic companies, the output and sales of these enterprises grew while exports from country B decreased. Similarly, exports from country A might displace exports from country B to country X. Unlike injury, serious prejudice can serve as the

171 See *id.*
172 See SCMA Art. 2 and 3.
173 See SCMA Art. 18. See also SGA Art. 11.1(b).
174 See Sabina Nüesch, *Voluntary Export Restraints in WTO and EU Law: Consumers, Trade Regulation and Competition Policy* p. 1(2010); and Ken Jones, *The Political Economy of Voluntary Export Restraint Agreements* 37(1) Kyklos Int'l Rev. Social Sciences 82 (1984).
175 See generally Andrew I. Gavil, William E. Kovacic and Jonathan B. Baker, *Antitrust Law in Perspective: Cases, Concepts and Problems in Competition Policy* (2002).
176 See Sabina Nüesch, *Voluntary Export Restraints in WTO and EU Law: Consumers, Trade Regulation and Competition Policy* p. 1(2010); and Ken Jones, *The Political Economy of Voluntary Export Restraint Agreements* 37(1) Kyklos Int'l Rev. Social Sciences 82 (1984).
177 See SCMA Art. 5.
178 See *id.*
179 See SCMA Art. 5 and 15.
180 See SCMA Art. 5 and 15.
181 See SCMA Art. 5 and 6.

basis for a complaint related to harm to a WTO member's exports.[182] Third, subsidies may cause the nullification or impairment of benefits under GATT 1994.[183] In such a case, the affected WTO member may challenge the subsidy before a WTO Panel.[184]

After describing the legal rules that are applicable to subsidies, this section turns now to the analysis of countervailing duties. A country intending to impose such kind of duties, besides consulting with other WTO members which might be affected by such measure,[185] must comply with the following three-pronged test: (i) evidence of a subsidy that another WTO member has granted,[186] (ii) evidence of material injury or threat thereof to a domestic industry,[187] and, the most difficult part, (iii) a causal link between the subsidy and the injury.[188]

Besides such requirements, there are some other legal rules governing the proceedings to impose countervailing duties. Similar to antidumping duties, at least the 25 percent of a domestic industry must sign a petition to start an investigation intended to impose a countervailing duty.[189] After receiving such petition, a preliminary investigation is conducted, which may or may not impose preliminary duties.[190] Later on, definitive duties may be imposed.[191] Sunset reviews are also applicable here: the SCMA requires that a countervailing measure be terminated after five years unless it is determined that expiration of the duty would likely to lead to continuation or recurrence of subsidization and injury[192] (so, the rule is identical to the one in the ADA).[193] The SCM Agreement also provides that WTO members shall maintain an independent tribunal to review the consistency of the domestic investigating authority's determinations with the applicable laws.[194]

To comply with transparency standards,[195] WTO members must notify all specific subsidies, at all levels of government and covering all kind of goods, including agriculture, to the WTO Committee on Subsidies and Countervailing Measures.[196] Likewise, all WTO members shall notify their countervailing duties laws and regulations[197] as well as all preliminary and final actions taken with respect

182 See SCMA Arts 5 and 6.
183 See SCMA Art. 5 and GATT Art. XXIII.
184 See DSU Art. 3.8.
185 See SCMA Art. 13.
186 See SCMA Part I.
187 See SCMA Part V.
188 See SCMA Part V.
189 See SCMA Art. 11.4.
190 See SCMA Art. 11.
191 See SCMA Art. 19.1
192 See SCMA Art. 21.3.
193 See *supra* Section 11.2.
194 See SCMA Art. 23.
195 See generally GATT Art. X.
196 See SCMA Art. 25 and GATT Art. XVI para. 1.
197 See SCMA Art. 32.6.

to countervailing duties to the Committee on Subsidies and Countervailing Measures.[198] WTO members shall also submit, on a semi-annual basis, reports on any countervailing duty actions taken within the preceding six months.[199]

Many cases have discussed the legal rules on subsidies and countervailing duties. One of the most relevant of them is the so-called the "Desiccated Coconut Case," which is summarized below.[200] Brazil applied countervailing duties to imports of desiccated coconut from the Philippines after contending that the applicable law was the Code of the Tokyo Round because the investigation was initiated prior to the date that the WTO Agreement on Subsidies and Countervailing Measures came into effect for Brazil (i.e., January 1, 1995).[201] In 1995, the Philippines requested consultations with Brazil claiming that the countervailing duties were not in compliance with GATT and WTO rules.[202] The United States, Canada, the European Union, Indonesia, Malaysia, and Sri Lanka were third parties.[203] In 1996, the Philippines requested the establishment of a Panel, being such request deferred in the first try but was successful after a second request.[204] As Brazil had argued, the Panel held that GATT Arts I, II, and VI did not apply to the Brazilian countervailing duty at issue because it was based on an investigation initiated prior to January 1, 1995.[205] The AB upheld the Panel report[206] and the DSB adopted the AB report in March, 1997.[207] This legal dispute is relevant because it was the only countervailing duty case discussing the issue of whether the GATT rules could be applied independently of the ASCM Agreement.

In spite of the existence of WTO legal rules, the proceedings to impose countervailing duties are also based on domestic rules and, as a result, differ among countries. In the United States, and similar to antidumping proceedings, industries may file a petition before the ITC and the DoC to initiate the proceedings, whose first step consists of consultations with affected foreign countries.[208] If the DoC finds that an imported product is subsidized and the ITC finds that an U.S. industry manufacturing a like product is materially injured or threatened with material injury, a countervailing duty is imposed to offset the subsidy.[209]

198 See SCMA Art. 25.11.
199 See *id.*
200 See DS22, Brazil – Measures Affecting Desiccated Coconut.
201 See *id.*
202 See *id.*
203 See *id.*
204 See *id.*
205 See *id.*
206 See *id.*
207 See *id.*
208 See Tariff Act of 1930 Title VII.
209 See *id.* Notice that the countervailing duty transfers the financial contribution that the foreign government originally granted to some of its enterprises or industries to the country conducting the investigation (or to the affected companies or industries located there). Assume that the amount of the subsidy is S, the original price of imports from the country granting the subsidy was P and that the new price is P – S. The countervailing duty (CD)

When a countervailing duty is imposed, the DoC instructs the Bureau of Customs and Border Protection to levy this duty on imports of the relevant product into the United States from the subsidizing country.[210] The collected countervailing duties are distributed to affected domestic producers for qualifying expenditures incurred during the process.[211] Thus, and following the imposition of a countervailing duty order, the ITC provides the Bureau of Customs and Border Protection with a list of the affected domestic producers (i.e., those who publicly expressed support for the petition during the investigation).[212] These producers could then submit certifications to the Bureau of Customs and Border Protection of qualifying expenditures in order to receive a pro rata share of the annual distribution of the duties that were collected.[213]

The ITC and the DoC are responsible for conducting countervailing duty investigations and five year reviews (the so-called sunset reviews).[214] In these sunset reviews, the ITC and the DoC determine whether revocation of the order would be likely to lead to continuation or recurrence of material injury and subsidies, respectively, within a reasonable foreseeable time.[215] If both agencies make affirmative determinations, the order is renewed for another five years; otherwise, the order is revoked.[216] The rest of the process is exactly the same used for antidumping investigations.[217]

As to the European Union, the terms of the SCMA are incorporated in the regulation on protection against subsidized imports.[218] Notice that such regulation only concerns imports from outside the European Union and not from one E.U. member to another, i.e., this regulation provides for imposition of countervailing duties on goods that non-E.U. countries subsidize and whose imports into the European Union cause or threatens to cause injury to E.U. producers of a like product.[219]

will be equal to S, which will be paid to the importing country. Thus, the new importing price will be P – S + CD = P – S + S = P. The company exporting the goods will receive a subsidy S but will pay the extra duty CD, with a zero-net effect. The foreign government will pay S and the importing country will receive CD = Such amount might be partially or totally transferred to the harmed domestic producers.

210 See Tariff Act of 1930 Title VII.

211 See *id.*

212 See *id.*

213 See *id.*

214 See *id.*

215 See *id.*

216 See *id.*

217 See *supra* Section 11.2.

218 See Regulation (EU) 2016/1037 of the European Parliament and of the Council of 8 June 2016 on protection against subsidized imports from countries not members of the European Union.

219 See *id.* Something similar occurs regarding the E.U. antidumping regulation. See *supra* Section 11.2.

Three conditions must be met before countervailing duties may be imposed in the European Union.[220] The first two requirements are the same as those provided in the WTO rules (i.e., the SCM Agreement) but the third one is different.[221] First, the subsidy must be specific, i.e., it must be an export subsidy, or a subsidy limited to a company, an industry or a group of companies or industries.[222] In any event, some types of subsidies are not subject to countervailing measures in spite of being specific.[223] Some examples are certain state aid for research activities, subsidies for disadvantaged regions, or subsidies granted to help companies to adapt to new environmental rules.[224] Second, the subsidy must cause material injury or threat thereof to an E.U. industry.[225] As a third and original requirement, the costs for the European Union of imposing a counter-vailing duty must not be disproportionate to its benefits.[226] On top of that, and pursuant not only to the SCMA Art. 2 but also to the E.U. Anti-Subsidy Regulation, there must be a financial contribution from the government of the exporting country, and also a benefit for the recipient company.[227]

As with antidumping actions, the European Commission conducts the investigation and imposes provisional measures.[228] It is, however, the Council of Ministers (likewise regarding antidumping duties) which imposes definitive measures.[229] The complaint and investigation procedures are similar to those governing antidumping duties.[230] Figure 22, reproduced in the section on antidumping duties,[231] summarizes such proceedings.

On a global scale, the issues affecting countervailing duty proceedings are similar to those mentioned in respect of antidumping investigations.[232] To begin with, and given the tremendous impact of countervailing duties investigations, even if exporters are cleared of charges and duties are not imposed, the screening of petitions is arguably the most important problem to solve.[233] While the SCM Agreement establishes a 25 percent threshold, how such percentage is determined

220 See *id.*
221 See *id.*
222 See *id.*
223 See *id.*
224 See *id.*
225 See *id.*
226 See *id.*
227 See SCMA Art. 1.1. and Regulation (EU) 2016/1037 of the European Parliament and of the Council of 8 June 2016 on protection against subsidized imports from countries not members of the European Union.
228 Regulation (EU) 2016/1037 of the European Parliament and of the Council of 8 June 2016 on protection against subsidized imports from countries not members of the European Union.
229 See *id.*
230 See *supra* Section 9.2.
231 See Section 11.2.
232 See *supra* Section 9.2.
233 See SCMA Art. 11.4.

is unclear; therefore, it is here where the degree of discretion that the SCMA Agreement grants is the highest and its resulting consequences to exporters the worst.[234] Second, the establishment of an automatic review after five years is in conformity with the SCM Agreement;[235] however, such agreement does not establish rules or specific criteria for the proceedings, leaving basically all to the discretion of investigating authorities.[236] Thus, not surprisingly, and similar to what happens regarding antidumping duties,[237] countervailing duties are rarely revoked, at least in the United States and in the European Union.[238]

Third, and pursuant to the SCM Agreement, determinations may be made based on the best facts available in case interested parties refuse to provide the information to the investigating authorities.[239] Unfortunately, the agreement lacks a basic framework on how these determinations should be made, which gives wide or even excessive discretion to investigating authorities. Fourth, the SCM Agreement provides that "[t]here shall be immediate termination in cases where the amount of a subsidy is *de minimis*, or where the volume of subsidized imports, actual or potential, or the injury, is negligible."[240] These cases should include both investigations and reviews and not only investigations, as the U.S. Trade Act provides.[241] Fifth, both GATT Art. VI and the SCM Agreement provide that a WTO member cannot impose countervailing duties to a similar product from another WTO member without determination of injury or threat of injury to the domestic industry and of a subsidy with regard to the imports.[242] The U.S. Trade Act, however, establishes that the DoC can expand the scope of a countervailing duty in some cases.[243]

Sixth, the SCM Agreement provides that a countervailing duty shall be levied "in the appropriate amounts in each case,"[244] on imports of such product found to be subsidized and causing injury to the importing country's industry.[245] In this sense, while the U.S. Trade Act establishes the general preference for individual margins of subsidy for each producer and exporter under investigation, an average

234 See SCMA Art. 11.4. See also *supra* Section 11.2.
235 See SCMA Art. 21.3.
236 See *supra* Section 11.2.
237 See *supra* Section 11.2.
238 See Laura Rovegno and Hylke Vandenbussche, 'A Comparative Analysis of EU Antidumping Rules and Application', in *Liberalizing Trade in the EU and the WTO: Comparative Perspectives* (Sanford Gaines, Birgitte Egelund Olsen and Karsten Engsig Sørensen Eds), p. 1 (2011); and Peter A. Dohlman, *Determinations of Adequacy in Sunset Reviews of Antidumping Orders in the United States* 14(5) Am. Univ. Int'l L. Rev. 1281 (1999).
239 See SCMA Art. 12.7.
240 SCMA Art. 11.9.
241 See U.S. Trade Act 1930.
242 See GATT Art. VI and SCMA Arts 1, 2 and 15.
243 See U.S. Trade Act 1930.
244 SCMA Art. 19.3.
245 See *id*.

subsidy margin is established in cases involving a large number of producers and exporters.[246]

Finally, the SCM Agreement sets forth that subsidies shall not be countervailed when they are granted within and directly linked to a privatization program of a developing WTO member, provided that both the program and the subsidy are granted for a limited period and that such measure is duly notified to the WTO.[247] Notwithstanding, the U.S. Trade Act provides that a partial or a total transfer of a company's property or productive assets does not require determination from the DoC that the countervailable subsidies received before the transfer of ownership are no longer countervailable after the transaction.[248]

246 See U.S. Trade Act 1930.
247 See SCMA Art. 27.13.
248 See U.S. Trade Act 1930.

12
CURRENCY MANIPULATION AND TRADE

12.1 Introduction

Chapter 12 discusses currency manipulation, the grand new topic in international trade, and its economic, legal and policy ramifications. For that purpose, Section 12.2 describes the macroeconomic effects of undervalued currencies. Section 12.3, in turn, explains the legal effects of currency manipulation. Finally, Section 12.4 summarizes some solutions that have been proposed to deal with the issue of currency manipulation.[1]

12.2 The economics of currency manipulation

To begin with, notice that the debate about the relationship between devaluations and trade is not new. John Maynard Keynes addressed this topic in the early 1940s and proposed a mechanism to deal with devaluations. His proposal was to combine a fixed but adjustable exchange rate system with a mechanism demanding from creditor nations, those with a persistently positive balance of trade, the initiative to eliminate this imbalance while "maintaining enough discipline in the debtor countries to prevent them from exploiting the advantages coming from

1 To be clear, the authors of these books, and particularly Professor Aluisio de Lima-Campos, have written elsewhere making the case for considering currency manipulations and, specifically, predatory and persistent currency misalignment as harmful measures for international trade that might be counterweighted by multilateral, plurilateral, bilateral or even unilateral decisions. Notwithstanding, and since this is a textbook mainly intended for graduate students, this chapter is intentionally written with a neutral approach. For the texts mentioned above, see, e.g., Aluisio de Lima-Campos and Juan Antonio Gaviria, *A Case for Currency Misalignments as Countervailable Subsidies*, 16(5) J. World Trade 1019 (2012).

a persistently negative balance."[2] Dexter White, Keynes's counterpart in the Bretton Woods negotiations, successfully replied with a plan that included the establishment of the gold standard and the creation of the International Monetary Fund (IMF), an international organization empowered with the mission of providing short-term loans to countries running negative balances of trade.[3]

The gold standard prevented currency manipulation by fixing exchange rates against a certain value of gold. Since all currencies were fixed against gold, they were also fixed against one another.[4]

If an IMF member wanted to change that parity (i.e., its currency's exchange rate against gold), it would have to obtain approval from the IMF or to take the chances of losing access to the Fund's resources. The IMF would only approve such a change if it was necessary to correct a "fundamental disequilibrium" or, in other words, unexpected macroeconomic conditions. The gold standard also allowed the IMF to closely monitor if any country was deviating from the standard and, if so, to take corrective actions.[5] Thus, deviations from the norm could be clearly identified and dealt with.

Since the end of the gold standard in the 1970s and until now, currencies have been allowed to fluctuate; i.e., member states have been free to choose their exchange arrangements, including floating. As a result of it and, particularly, with currency values fluctuating according to market forces and other factors, devaluations have become commonplace.[6]

Under free floating exchange rates, competitive devaluations returned. Also labeled "currency wars,"[7] competitive devaluations entail that countries indifferently allow their currencies to plunge vis à vis the U.S. dollar or take explicit monetary measures to achieve such an outcome.[8]

In any event, not all devaluations and not even all competitive devaluations entail currency manipulations. To make clear the difference between these notions, it is worth describing first the economic effects of devaluations. On the one hand, an undervalued currency grants increased protection to domestically produced goods because imports become more expensive. On the other hand, a devaluation, *ceteris paribus*, increases the price competitiveness of exports by allowing the seller to reduce the price of domestic goods in foreign currencies or, if the price

2 'Post War Currency Policy', reprinted in Donald E. Moggridge (Ed.), *The Collected Writings of John Maynard Keynes*, 30 (1980).

3 See *id.*

4 Joseph Gold, *Legal and Institutional Aspects of the International Monetary System: Selected Essays* 20 (1979).

5 See *supra* Chapter 1.

6 See *id.*

7 See *The Global Economy, How to Stop a Currency War*, The Economist (October 14, 2010), www.economist.com/node/17251850 (last visit, April 30, 2017) This article refers to a declaration on September 27, 2010 from Brazil's Finance Minister, Guido Mantega, according to which an international currency war had broken out.

8 Surjit S. Bhalla, *Devaluing to Prosperity: Misaligned Currencies and their Growth Consequences,* p. 1 (2012).

remains unchanged because it is determined by global markets, by giving exporters a higher amount in local currency at the time of exchanging the foreign currency resulting from the sales abroad.

The scenario in countries whose currencies are overvalued is the opposite. There, exports lose competitiveness while local producers are harmed due to a lower level of protection against imports.[9] Thus, and although the nominal level of actual and bound tariffs remains unchanged, the real level is lower or even negative. The negative consequences of an overvalued currency might be even worse for countries which cannot devalue on an individual basis because of their membership of a monetary union, such as the Eurozone. Specifically, these countries are not allowed to raise tariffs above the levels agreed to in their schedule of concessions, grant subsidies that are in breach of the ASCM, or devalue their currency without a collective action through their monetary union. Consequently, they may suffer the harm that devaluations of other WTO members' currencies cause without receiving trade concessions in exchange.

The following example is useful for a better understanding of the economic effects of undervalued and over-valued currencies. Suppose a world with only two countries, A and B, that have a one-to-one currency exchange rate, such that one unit of currency A (1a) is equal to one unit of currency B (1b). Assume also that domestic prices of goods are the same in both countries, that there is no inflation in either of these two countries and that all else remains the same. If 1b devalues by 20 percent, citizens of A will now be able to afford 1.2 units of B goods for each 1a, which is the equivalent of reducing the export price of B goods or lowering import tariffs in A. In country B, the effect is the reverse. Citizens of B will now have to pay 1.2b for each 1a, which is the same effect resulting from raising the import price of A goods for B citizens or increasing import tariffs in B. In other words, the devaluation in B is akin to a simultaneous reduction in import tariffs in A and to an export subsidy in B.[10] This happens because exports from B become cheaper for A consumers after 1b devalues (and exports from B increase), but imports from A become more expensive to B consumers (and imports from A fall), resulting in a trade surplus for B. In an extreme but not implausible scenario, exports from country A to country B may plummet while imports may surge with the subsequent problems in the balance of payments. Even worse, some devaluations might wipe off the protection effectiveness of import tariffs as well as all trade remedy duties in place.

Moving from hypothetical illustrations to real ones, Professors Vera Thorstensen, Emerson Marçal and Lucas Ferraz measured the impact of devaluations on the

9 Pursuant to GATT Art. II(1)(b), WTO Members have to keep their applied tariffs in equal or lower levels than their bound tariffs.

10 Professors Robert Staiger and Alan Sykes disagree. They contend that "in the long run, currency devaluation does not alter export volumes, and in the short run, its effects depend on firms' invoicing decisions." See Robert Staiger and Alan Sykes, *Currency "Manipulation" and World Trade: A Caution*, http://voxeu.org/article/currency-manipulation-and-world-trade-three-reasons-caution (last visit, May 5, 2017). However, the long run may be too far down the road to wait while the negative impacts of currency manipulation take hold.

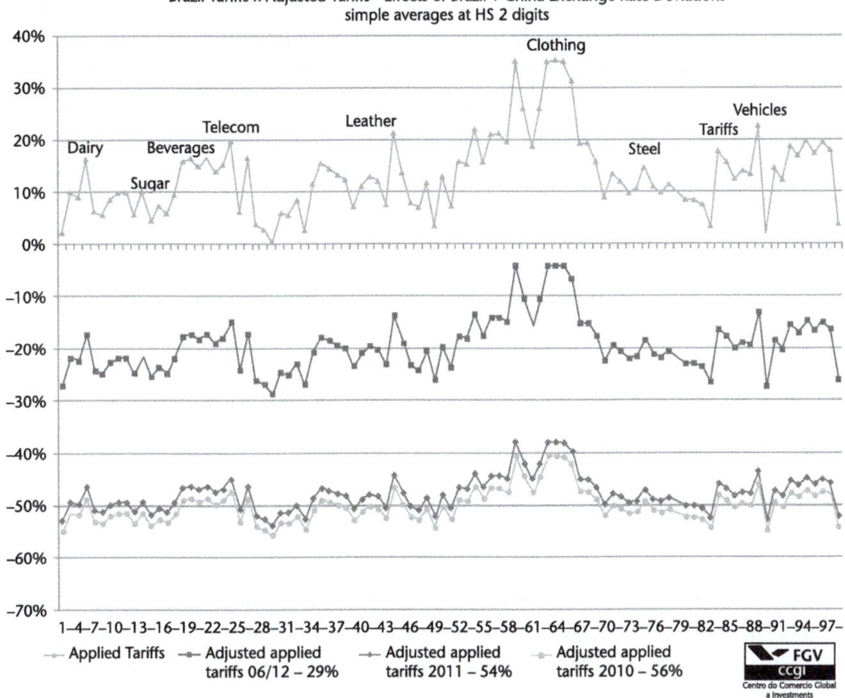

FIGURE 17 Impact of exchange rate misalignments on Brazil tariff profile[11]

tariff schedules of several countries.[12] For instance, Thorstensen, Marçal and Ferraz calculate that a 10 percent devaluation of the U.S. dollar may decrease Brazil's bound rates from their actual levels (12 percent to 50 percent) to a range from 0 percent to 35 percent.[13] As another illustration, a 20 percent devaluation of the Chinese yuan might reduce the Brazilian bound tariff rates to a range from –10 percent to 19 percent.[14] Figure 17 shows the impact of Chinese devaluations on Brazilian tariffs.

In another study, Professors Mattoo, Mishra and Subramanian analyze the so-called "spillover effect," i.e. the effect of devaluations on exports and imports.[15] On average, a 10 percent appreciation of China's real exchange rate boosts a

11 See Vera Thorstensen, Emerson Marçal and Lucas Ferraz, *Impacts of Exchange Rates on International Trade Policy Instruments: The Case of Tariffs*, São Paulo School of Economics (EESP), Fundação Getulio Vargas (2011).

12 Vera Thorstensen, Emerson Marçal and Lucas Ferraz, *Exchange Rate Misalignments and Trade Policy: Impacts on Tariffs* 46(3) J. World Trade 597 (2012).

13 See *id.*, at 597.

14 See *id.*, at 597. If the real bound rate is negative, it might be a subsidy to imports.

15 Aaditya Mattoo, Prachi Mishra and Arvind Subramanian, *Spillover Effects of Exchange Rates: A Study of the Renminbi*, IMF Working Paper (2012).

developing country's exports of a typical four-digit Harmonized System (HS) product category to third markets by about 1.5 to 2 percent.[16]

The effects of devaluations would be offset in the long-run if prices in the devaluing country adjust upwards as a result of the increase in demand of goods while prices in other countries adjust downwards due to the opposite reason.[17] These adjustments, however, only take place if markets work in perfect competition and, additionally, if prices were fully flexible. Imperfect competition, however, is more the rule than the exception while, in some markets, prices are sticky. Others contend, with respect to China as the primal example of a devaluing country, that "in the short run, its effects depend on firms' invoicing decisions,"[18] i.e. on the decisions of companies about the prices that they charge. However, there is no evidence that the examples of invoicing decisions used are so widespread to the point of having a different impact on trade than the norm. In any case, and assuming that the effect of devaluations will disappear in the long-term, WTO members may still suffer significant harm in the meantime. As John Maynard Keynes smartly put it when he was still alive: "In the long-run, we are all dead."[19]

As mentioned earlier, not all devaluations are the same or, in other words, not all types of misalignments are considered harmful from an economic point of view. Generally speaking, currency misalignments may have one of the following four causes: (i) market fluctuations and other factors that normally influence markets (legitimate devaluations), (ii) government intervention in order to correct macroeconomic imbalances (legitimate devaluations), (iii) government intervention in order to obtain a trade advantage over other countries (possibly illegitimate devaluation), or (iv) a combination of two or three of the previous causes, a scenario where it is very difficult to establish whether the devaluation is legitimate or not.

Most of the time, misalignments pertaining to categories (i) or (ii) are temporary. Put it another way, they should go away once the macroeconomic problems that triggered them disappear. On the other hand, misalignments exclusively used to generate trade surpluses may, in addition to not being economically justified, last for longer periods, i.e., be persistent. The term "persistent" might mean, for instance, any devaluation standing for at least one year,

16 See *id.*

17 See Robert W. Staiger and Alan O. Sykes, 'Currency "Manipulation" and World Trade: A Caution', in *The US-Sino Currency Dispute: New Insights from Economics, Politics and Law* (Simon Evenett Ed.), p. 110 (2010).

18 Robert W. Staiger and Alan O. Sykes, *Currency Manipulation and World Trade*, SSRN Working Paper (2008), http://voxeu.org/article/currency-manipulation-and-world-trade-three-reasons-caution (last visit, May 15, 2017).

19 John Maynard Keynes, *A Tract on Monetary Reform* p. 65 (1924). Rationally, this argument is not completely sound, as our descendants will not be dead in the long-run. The economist Joseph Schumpeter said, in a Keynes obituary, that Keynes was disposed to such a view because he did not have children. See Joseph A. Schumpeter, *John Maynard Keynes 1883–1946* 36(4) Am. Econ. Rev. 495 (1946).

if we use injury requirements in trade remedies investigations as a guideline.[20] Misalignments might also be slight or significant. The term "significant," in turn, might mean that the currency misalignment must be greater than either a given absolute percentage (5 percent, for example) or a percentage of a benchmark (for example, 20 percent of the country's trade weighted average import tariff rate).

Generally speaking, misalignments whose only causes are market factors are as normal events as market-based price fluctuations in a stock market. The concern regarding international trade is with deviations from that norm, like when there is significant and persistent government intervention in a given market to counter the effects of market forces (similar to when a powerful participant is altering the normal price fluctuations in a stock market). To be clear, not all interventions are wrongful, though. If the intervention is intended to correct economic imbalances (e.g., a negative GDP growth), such a policy is fine as long as it stops once the objective is reached (e.g., once the GDP growth is positive). Thus, and generally speaking, it is normally accepted that these types of corrective economic policies are legitimate sovereign choices that every government may resort to. Indeed, and since a long time ago, the IMF has prescribed devaluation policies as medicine for countries with balance of payments issues and other economic illnesses.

Thus, and in contrast with temporary measures, persistent government intervention raises some concerns since they might be used to sustain a non-negligible long-term undervaluation without economic justification. In such a case, a government, most likely, will have been manipulating its currency to generate more reserves and obtain an unfair advantage over trade partners. To put it differently, if all pertinent economic indicators in a particular country are favorable, this country's currency, under normal market conditions, would most likely tend to appreciate overtime and not to stay undervalued for a long period. Under this scenario, a governmental intervention might improve the country's balance of trade (BOT) through currency manipulation, as a result of creating an artificial advantage for its exports and, at the same time, increasing its tariff barriers to imports. This kind of intervention might be coined as predatory currency misalignment.

Persistent and significant misalignments, indeed, might be predatory taking into account the damage that they might cause to competitors in other countries. In such cases, the countries altering their exchange rates have been called currency manipulators, a term that some are suggesting to change because of its derogatory connotation.[21] Joseph E. Gagnon, from the PIIE, defines manipulators as countries complying with the following three-pronged test: (i) their foreign exchange

20 In injury examinations, a minimum requirement in national trade regulations of one to three years of data is not uncommon.

21 C. Fred Bergsten, *The Dollar and the Renminbi*, Statement before the Hearing on US Economic Relations with China: Strategies and Options on Exchange Rates and Market Access, Subcommittee on Security and International Trade and Finance, Committee on Banking, Housing and Urban Affairs, United States Senate (May 23, 2007), https://piie.com/commentary/testimonies/dollar-and-renminbi (last visit, April 30, 2017).

reserves are greater than the value of six months of goods and services imports; (ii) their average current account balance, measured as a percent of GDP, over the last ten years is greater than zero; and (iii) they have increased their reserve stocks relative to their GDP over the past ten years.[22]. As a second approach, Vera Thorstensen, from FGV, has suggested a minimum and maximum percent variation of exchange rates (a "snake-in-the-tunnel" method), where exchange rate fluctuations beyond the maximum and minimum borders would entail that the currency is being manipulated.[23]

In order to understand the difference between "legitimate" and "possibly illegitimate devaluations," it is necessary to define the notion of currency misalignments. Generally speaking, and according to the IMF, which is the official authoritative source on the subject, currency misalignments are the difference between an actual or observed exchange rate and its estimated or theoretical equilibrium rate, which is the one that would be consistent with the economic fundamentals and desirable policies of such country.[24]

In more technical terms, William R. Cline and John Williamson from the PIIE, define the Fundamental Equilibrium Exchange Rate (FEER) as

> the currency exchange rate which is expected to generate a current account surplus or deficit that matches the country's underlying capital flow over the cycle, assuming that the country is pursuing internal balance as well as it can and that it is not restricting trade for balance-of-payments reasons.[25]

In other words, the FEER is the exchange rate that is expected to be indefinitely sustainable on the basis of existing monetary and fiscal policies.[26]

The IMF has been publishing data on currency misalignments, on a regular basis, since 2012.[27] Take into account that the IMF measurements are the most

22 Joseph E. Gagnon, *Combating Widespread Currency Manipulation*, PIIE Policy Brief (2012).

23 Vera Thorstensen, *Normalized PPP – Trade Weighted World Basket*, Powerpoint Presentation (2013), www.youtube.com/watch?v=7A6qprQi9JU&feature=player_embedded (last visit, May 15, 2017).

24 IMF, Pilot External Sector Report (2014) available at: www.imf.org/external/np/pp/eng/2014/062614.pdf (last visit, May 15, 2017).

25 William R. Cline and John Williamson, *Updated Estimates of Fundamental Equilibrium Exchange Rates*, Peterson Institute for International Economics (2012).

26 See William R. Cline, *Estimating Consistent Fundamental Equilibrium Exchange Rates*, Working Paper 08-6, Peterson Institute for International Economics (2008), available at: https://piie.com/sites/default/files/publications/wp/wp08-6.pdf (last visit, April 30, 2017). For an updated version of FEER calculations, see William R. Cline, *Estimates of Fundamental Equilibrium Exchange Rates*, Policy Brief, Peterson Institute for International Economics (2016) (last visit, April 30, 2017). See also John Williamson, *The Exchange Rate System*, Policy Analyses in International Economics, Peterson Institute for International Economics (1983).

27 IMF, Pilot External Sector Report (2014), www.imf.org/external/np/pp/eng/2014/062614.pdf (last visit, May 15, 2017).

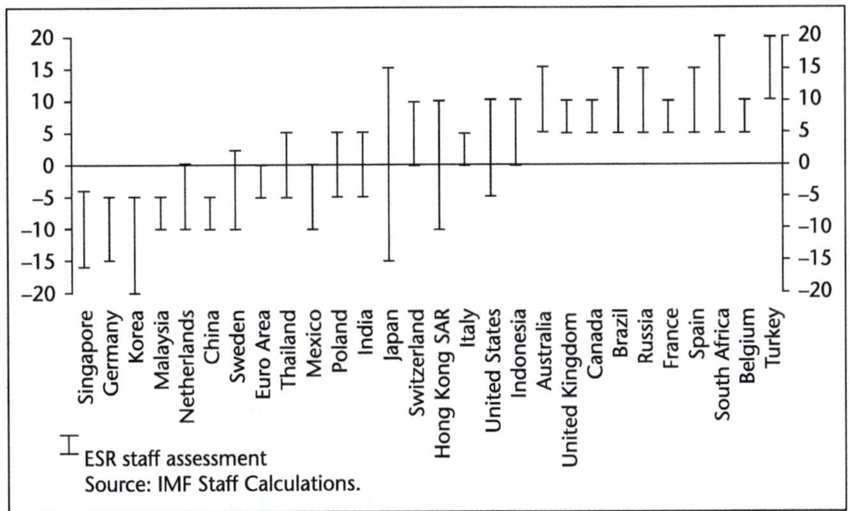

FIGURE 18 IMF estimates of exchange rate misalignments[28]

conservative when compared to other models mentioned here, which means that all other available misalignment estimates are higher. Figure 18 reports the data from the IMF for 2014.

Not only the IMF but also experts from academia, think tanks and financial markets have monitored and measured currency misalignments. Emerson Marçal,[29] from Fundação Getulio Vargas (FGV) at São Paulo, Brazil, has calculated currency misalignments as a variable dependent on the net foreign assets and other fundamentals of a country. Figure 19 shows data from this research.

The model of the Peterson Institute of International Economics, in turn, estimates the "ideal" exchange rate of any country vis-à-vis the U.S. dollar.[30] This model also compares this "ideal" exchange rate with the current exchange rate.[31] Since the dollar is used as the basis of the calculation, the model assumes that the U.S. currency is not misaligned.[32] Table 35 shows the results of the FEER model.

28 IMF, Pilot External Sector Report (2014), www.imf.org/external/np/pp/eng/2014/062614.pdf (last visit, May 15, 2017). See also Vera Thorstensen, Emerson Marçal and Lucas Ferraz, *Trade Rules and Exchange Rate Misalignments: In Search for a WTO Solution* 34(3) Rev. Econ. Pol. 1 (2014).

29 Vera Thorstensen, Emerson Marçal and Lucas Ferraz, *Exchange Rate Misalignments and Trade Policy: Impacts on Tariffs* 46(3) J. World Trade 597 (2012).

30 See William R. Cline, *Estimates of Fundamental Equilibrium Exchange Rates*, May 2016, Policy Brief, Peterson Institute for International Economics, https://piie.com/publications/policy-briefs/estimates-fundamental-equilibrium-exchange-rates-may-2016 (last visit, April 30, 2017).

31 See *id.*

32 Since the U.S. dollar itself might be misaligned, this, of course, is not always a right assumption.

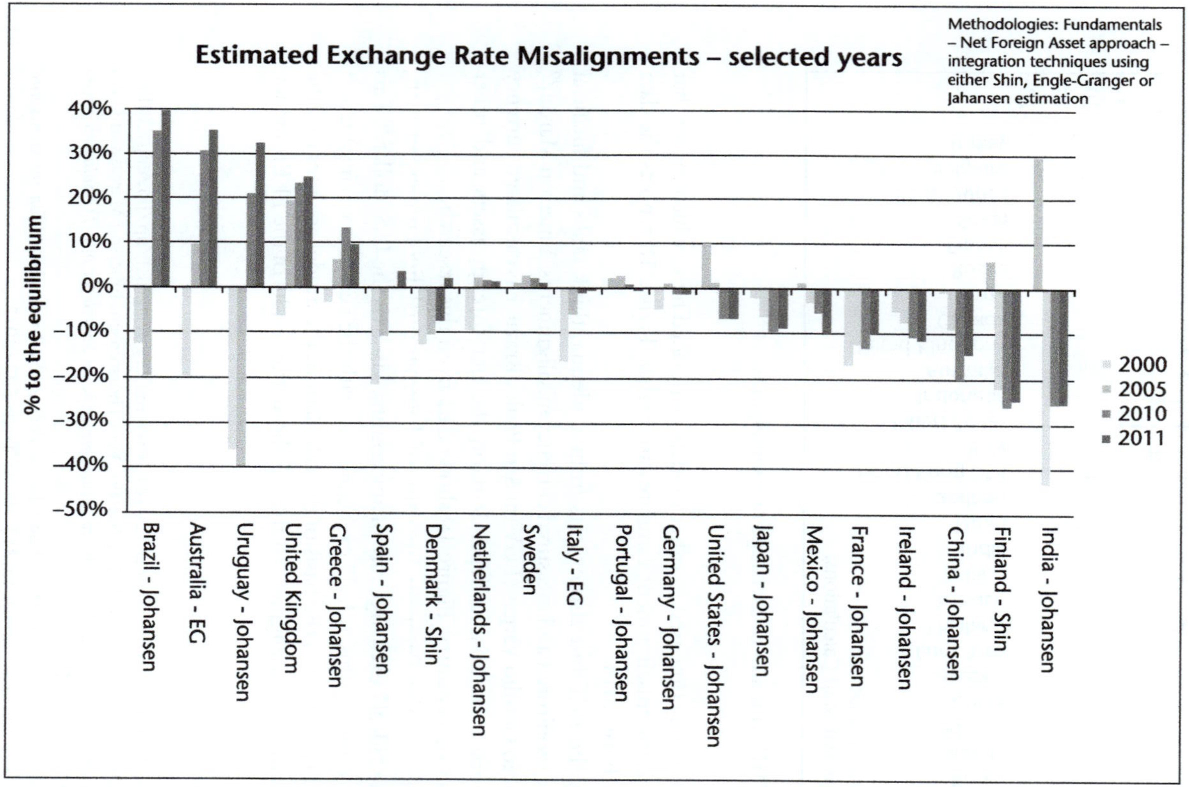

FIGURE 19 Exchange rate misalignments (FGV)[33]

33 See Fundação Getulio Vargas, Observatory on Exchange Rates, http://ccgi.fgv.br/en/observatory-exchange-rates (last visit, April 30, 2017).

Finally, Professor Surjit Bhalla has made its own calculations. Professor Surjit Bhalla calculates currency misalignments using an "exponential model," which results in an S-shaped evolution of real exchange rates with respect to income.[34]

12.3 The legal effects of currency manipulation

After having explained the economic effects of devaluations, this chapter turns to the legal side. As mentioned in the previous section, a WTO member devaluing its currency might produce the same effect as pushing tariffs higher and even perhaps beyond the currency's bound limits at the WTO. Under some circumstances, such action might be in breach of a member's commitments before the WTO.[35] At the same time, devaluations might have the same effect as reducing import tariffs in other WTO members. Sometimes, indeed, negotiated levels of tariff protection of affected countries might be wiped out while any trade remedies that such WTO members had in place might no longer have any effect on dumped or subsidized imports.[36] In short, WTO members' rights to apply permitted levels of tariff protection as well as their rights under the Antidumping, Subsidies and Countervailing Measures, and Safeguards Agreements might be violated or nullified as a result of some currency manipulations. On top of that, and pursuant to the SCM Agreement, a predatory currency devaluation could arguably be viewed as a prohibited subsidy. This section will explain in more detail the previous statements.

TABLE 35 The FEER model[37]

Region	*Country*	*Changes in FEER (%)*		*Dollar exchange rate*		*FEER consistent dollar rate*
		Target change	*Change in simulation*	*2012*	*% change*	
Oceania	Australia	–9.4	–10.6	1.03	–6.8	0.96
	New Zealand	–14.1	–15.2	0.82	–13.4	0.71
Asia	China	4.2	3.1	6.26	5.9	5.91
	Hong Kong	8.2	7.6	7.75	12.9	6.86
	India	–0.4	–1.3	53.1	1.4	52.4
	Indonesia	0.0	–1.1	9593	4.7	9160

(continued)

34 See Surjit S. Bhalla, *Devaluing to Prosperity: Misaligned Currencies and their Growth Consequences,* p. 25 (2012).

35 See Vera Thorstensen, Vera, Emerson Marçal and Lucas Ferraz, *Impacts of Exchange Rates on International Trade Policy Instruments: The Case of Tariffs*, São Paulo School of Economics (EESP), FGV (2011).

36 See *id.*

37 See *id.*

TABLE 35 The FEER model *(continued)*

Region	*Country*	*Changes in FEER (%)*		*Dollar exchange rate*		*FEER consistent dollar rate*
		Target change	*Change in simulation*	*2012*	*% change*	
	Japan	0.0	–1.1	79	2.4	77
	Korea	0.0	–1.0	1106	2.4	1080
	Malaysia	5.2	4.1	3.05	10.2	2.77
	Philippines	0.0	–1.0	41.4	4.5	39.6
	Singapore	25.7	24.5	1.22	28.5	0.95
	Taiwan	9.4	8.5	29.3	13.3	25.8
	Thailand	0.0	–1.1	30.7	3.0	29.8
Middle East; Africa	Israel	0.0	–0.7	3.86	0.8	3.83
	S. Arabia	0.0	–0.8	3.75	2.2	3.67
	S. Africa	–5.2	–5.9	8.65	–3.8	8.99
Europe	Czech R.	0.0	–0.5	19.2	0.4	19.2
	Euro Area	0.0	–0.9	1.30	0.4	1.30
	Hungary	0.0	–0.5	217	0.3	217
	Norway	0.0	–0.7	5.71	1.5	5.63
	Poland	–1.6	–2.2	3.17	–1.4	3.21
	Russia	0.0	–0.5	31.1	0.4	31.0
	Sweden	14.4	13.7	6.64	14.4	5.81
	Switzerland	4.8	4.3	0.93	5.5	0.88
	Turkey	–22.5	–23.2	1.80	–21.9	2.31
	U.K.	0.0	–0.8	1.61	0.5	1.62
Western Hemisphere	Argentina	0.0	–1.2	4.73	–0.2	4.74
	Brazil	–1.0	–2.3	2.03	–0.4	2.04
	Canada	0.0	–0.5	0.99	0.4	0.98
	Chile	0.0	–1.1	476	0.8	472
	Colombia	0.0	–0.9	1806	0.1	1804
	Mexico	0.0	–0.5	12.9	0.5	12.8
	U.S.	–0.6	–2.2	1.00	0.0	1.00
	Venezuela	0.0	–0.7	4.29	1.0	4.25

Before doing so, an important and often forgotten legal rule of the IMF Agreement will be first reminded. Section 1 of Art. IV of the IMF Agreement provides (the underlined text is not part of the original):

> Recognizing that the essential purpose of the international monetary system is to provide a framework that facilitates the exchange of goods, services, and capital among countries, and that sustains sound economic growth, and that a principal objective is the continuing development of the orderly underlying conditions that are necessary for financial and economic stability, each member undertakes to collaborate with the Fund and other members to assure orderly exchange arrangements and to promote a stable system of exchange rates. In particular, each member shall:

(i) endeavor to direct its economic and financial policies toward the objective of fostering orderly economic growth with reasonable price stability, with due regard to its circumstances;
(ii) seek to promote stability by fostering orderly underlying economic and financial conditions and a monetary system that does not tend to produce erratic disruptions;
(iii) avoid manipulating exchange rates or the international monetary system in order to prevent effective balance of payments adjustment or to gain an unfair competitive advantage over other members; and
(iv) follow exchange policies compatible with the undertakings under this Section.

The plain meaning of this legal rule indicates that IMF members should not manipulate exchange rates in order to obtain trade advantages. GATT Art. XV (4) confirms this understanding by providing that (underlined text is not part of the original):

> Contracting parties shall not, by exchange action, frustrate the intent of the provisions of this Agreement, nor, by trade action, the intent of the provisions of the Articles of the Agreement of the International Monetary Fund.

The footnote to this legal rule, in turn, states that:

> [t]he word frustrate is intended to indicate, for example, that infringements of the letter of any Article of this Agreement by exchange action shall not be regarded as a violation of that Article if, in practice, there is no appreciable departure from the intent of the Article.

Predatory currency misalignments might frustrate the intent of GATT because they alter the equilibrium of rights and obligations among WTO members, giving unfair trade advantages to one country by: (i) artificially increasing the competitiveness of manipulators' products in other markets; (ii) artificially increasing their domestic market protection from imports and even creating the effect of higher bound tariffs in breach of WTO commitments, and (iii) reducing tariff protection of their trade partners.[38]

In particular, misaligned currencies might be in breach of GATT Art. II(1)(b), according to which a WTO member cannot impose duties or charges in excess of its bound tariffs. Since no WTO member has committed to a specific currency regime in its schedule of concessions, an artificially undervalued currency, acting as a duty on top of the applied rates, is not a *de jure* violation. Nonetheless, it may be a *de facto* violation. On top of that, a misaligned currency might give rise to a non-violation nullification or impairment claim in accordance with GATT Art. XXIII:1(b). Take into account, in any event, that the Appellate Body has said that

38 See Vera Thorstensen, Emerson Marçal and Lucas Ferraz, *Impacts of Exchange Rates on International Trade Policy Instruments: The Case of Tariffs*, São Paulo School of Economics (EESP), Fundação Getulio Vargas (2011).

a non-violation claim is an exceptional cause of action which should be used with caution and only if the following four elements are proved: (1) A WTO member has applied a measure (e.g., it has artificially undervalued its currency); (2) another WTO member has a benefit accruing under a WTO agreement (e.g., the bound tariffs agreed in the schedule of concessions); (3) the expectations of a benefit are legitimate (e.g., they are in accordance with GATT 1994 and other WTO rules); and (4) there is a nullification or impairment of the benefit as a result of the application of the measure (e.g., the bound rates are ineffective as a trade protection against imports coming from a country whose currency is misaligned).[39]

On the other hand, and as indicated before, a devaluation has the same economic effect that a uniform tariff on imports plus a subsidy on exports. Based not only on this economic understanding but also on a legal analysis of the SCM Agreement, some authors contend that predatory currency manipulations entail an illegal and countervailable subsidy.[40]

A WTO member that intends to challenge a misaligned currency as a subsidy has two different but not exclusive options. The first and offensive option is to challenge the subsidy before the WTO.[41] The second and defensive option is to impose countervailing duties on the products from the devaluing country. The country whose misaligned currency led to this action might, in turn, challenge those countervailing duties before the WTO.

A WTO member that chooses the route of imposing countervailing duties shall determine not only that a currency is misaligned but also that it amounts to a subsidy from a legal point of view.[42] Recall from Chapter 11 that GATT Art. XVI and the ASCM Art. 1. GATT Art. XVI defines subsidies as "measures that directly or indirectly result in the sale of an exported product for less than the price for buyers on the comparable domestic market."

Thus, the country imposing countervailing duties must prove that a misaligned currency meets the definition of subsidy under ASCM Art. 1. Again, recall from Chapter 11 that a subsidy shall be deemed to exist if: (1) there is a financial contribution[43] or any form of income or price support[44]; and (2) a benefit is

39 See Panel Report, *Japan-Measures Affecting Consumer Photographic Film and Paper*, WT/DS44/$ (adopted March 31, 1998), paras 10.41 and 10.76.

40 See Aluisio de Lima-Campos and Juan Gaviria, *A Case for Misaligned Currencies as Countervailable Subsidies*, 46(5) J. World Trade 1017 (2012).

41 See Gregory Hudson, Pedro Bento de Faria and Tobias Peyerl, *The Legality of Exchange Rate Undervaluation Under WTO Law*, CTEI Working Paper, Centre for Trade and Economic Integration at the Graduate Institute of International and Development Studies (IHEID) 1 (2011). See also Benjamin Blase Caryl, *Is China Currency Regime a Countervailable Subsidy? A Legal Analysis Under the World Trade Organization's SCM Agreement* 45(1) J. World Trade 187 (2011).

42 See generally *infra* Chapter 11.

43 ASCM Art. 1.1(a)(1).

44 ASCM Art. 1.1(a)(2).

conferred.[45] Also, a WTO member can only impose countervailing measures against (3) subsidies that are deemed specific.[46] Each of these three requirements are analyzed below.

ASCM Art. 1.1(a) mentions four types of financial contributions. While this issue is hotly debated, misaligned currencies may fit at least the first – "A government practice involving a direct transfer of funds or potential direct transfer of funds or liabilities" – and fourth categories:

> A government makes payments to a funding mechanism, or entrust or directs a private body to carry out one or more of the type of functions illustrated in (i) to (iii) above which would normally be vested in the government and the practice, in no real sense, differs from practices normally followed by governments.[47]

Regarding the first category, governmental measures that keep a currency at an artificially low level may generate a transfer of funds because the amount in local currency that exporters receive in exchange for their proceeds in any foreign currency is higher than the units that they would have obtained if the exchange rate were not misaligned. Put more simply, the government is paying the exporters an extra price or a bonus for the international reserves that they are exchanging into local currency. The more the local currency is undervalued, the more extra money exporters receive and the government gives away (and perhaps, print, adding to the cost of inflation).[48] Still, the transfer of funds must be direct. It will be so when the laws or regulations require exporters and other holders of foreign currencies to exchange them for local currency at levels not based on market considerations. Similarly, measures imposing a dual foreign exchange regime, with a preferential exchange rate for exporters and a general exchange rate for other holders of foreign currency, might amount to a direct transfer of funds.[49]

45 ASCM Art. 1.1(b).

46 ASCM Arts 1.2, 2 and Part. V.

47 See Benjamin Blase Caryl, *Is China Currency Regime a Countervailable Subsidy? A Legal Analysis Under the World Trade Organization's SCM Agreement* 45(1) J. World Trade 187, 200 (2011) (affirming that the first category – a direct transfer of funds – has the best chances to succeed as a financial contribution before a panel).

48 See Gregory Hudson, Pedro Bento de Faria and Tobias Peyerl, *The Legality of Exchange Rate Undervaluation Under WTO Law*, CTEI Working Paper, Centre for Trade and Economic Integration at the Graduate Institute of International and Development Studies (IHEID) 1, 9, 46 (2011) (affirming that as long as exporters receive an extra amount of domestic currency, the requirement of financial contribution is fulfilled).

49 The Chinese regime that was in legal force between 1988 and 1993 is an example of a dual exchange rate system. This regime ended on January 1, 1994, when the official rate (at this time, 5.8 yuan per U.S. dollar) and the market rate (at this time, 8.7 yuan per U.S. dollar) were unified. Under this regime, some companies, such as exporters, exchanged their foreign currencies at the market rate in the so-called swap markets, which accounted for up to 80 percent of the transactions in foreign exchange. See Tao Wang, *China: Sources of Real*

With regard to the fourth paragraph, this might be applicable when a government has made a financial contribution (e.g., a direct transfer of funds) through one or more private entities, such as banks that, acting as governmental agents without any real autonomy, exchange any foreign currency for the domestic currency at the rate that the government has fixed.[50]

As a second requirement, the currency misalignment shall entail a benefit. The notion of benefit encompasses some form of advantage.[51] More specifically, a benefit exists when a governmental measure "makes the recipient 'better off' than it would otherwise have been, absent that contribution."[52] In the case of currencies, governmental measures intended to keep them at artificially low levels might make exporters better off in comparison with a scenario in which the exchange rate is close to its equilibrium value.

The precise nature and extent of the benefit depends on the type of financial contribution.[53] If the financial contribution is a governmental service allowing exporters to obtain protection against market fluctuations, the benefit would be the value of the hedging service in the financial markets. In the more plausible scenario in which the financial contribution is a direct transfer of funds (or if there is any form of income or price support), the benefit would be twofold. On the one hand, the units of the local currency that exporters receive for each unit of foreign currency that is exchanged outweighs the units that they would have received if the exchange rate were close to its equilibrium value. On the other hand, an undervalued currency would allow exporters to reduce the price of their exports in foreign currencies and, consequently, increase the number of goods sold in foreign markets.

The benefit is the least controversial element among scholars regarding misaligned currencies.[54] This is not to say that this matter is completely settled. For instance, Robert W. Staiger and Alan O. Sykes contend that any benefit may not

Exchange Rate Fluctuations, IMF Working Paper WP/04/18, Asian and Pacific Department 1 (2004). See also Yi Gang, *Renminbi Exchange Rates and Relevant Institutional Factors* 28(2) Cato J.187 (2008).

50 See Gregory Hudson, Pedro Bento de Faria and Tobias Peyerl, *The Legality of Exchange Rate Undervaluation Under WTO Law*, CTEI Working Paper, Centre for Trade and Economic Integration at the Graduate Institute of International and Development Studies (IHEID) 1, 45–46 (2011), and Benjamin Blase Caryl, *Is China Currency Regime a Countervailable Subsidy? A Legal Analysis Under the World Trade Organization's SCM Agreement* 45(1) J. World Trade 187, 197–98 (2011).

51 Panel Report, *Canada – Measures Affecting the Export of Civilian Aircraft*, as modified by Appellate Body Report WT/DS70/AB/R WT/DS70/R (adopted 20 August, 1999), para. 9.112.

52 Appellate Body Report, *Canada – Measures Affecting the Export of Civilian Aircraft*, WT/DS70/AB/R (adopted 20 August, 1999), para. 157. See also Benjamin Blase Caryl, *supra* note 50, at 201.

53 See Benjamin Blase Caryl, *Is China Currency Regime a Countervailable Subsidy? A Legal Analysis Under the World Trade Organization's SCM Agreement* 45(1) J. World Trade 187, 201 (2011).

54 E.g., Nathan Fudge, *Walter Mitty and the Dragon: An Analysis of the Possibility for WTO or IMF Action against China's Manipulation of the Yuan* 45 (2) J. World Trade 352 (2011) (stating that finding a benefit is not an issue).

be readily conferred if prices rise because inflation and other economic variables may counterweigh such a price increase.[55] Yet, as indicated before, this adjustment will only occur in perfect markets and in the long term. In the interim, exporters might have accrued huge profits and caused material injury to local manufacturers in one or several WTO members. It is also argued that exporters using their sales proceeds to buy inputs abroad or to invest in financial instruments denominated in foreign currencies do not receive any benefit.[56] While this is true, other exporters, those exchanging their profits in foreign currencies for local currency, do receive a benefit. Furthermore, a highly-undervalued currency makes it more profitable to convert foreign currencies into domestic currency than to keep the money abroad provided that domestic inflation and taxes, but not real interest rates, are relatively low.

Assuming that a benefit exists in the case of misaligned currencies, one question remains: how to quantify the benefit? Quantification, of course, is required to set the amount of the countervailing duties. As a general answer, the benefit per unit of foreign currency amounts to the difference between the undervalued exchange rate and the equilibrium exchange rate. Unfortunately, this answer raises another question: which should be the equilibrium rate? Most of the time, neither a domestic nor an international comparison is possible because an artificially undervalued currency that is fixed or pegged to another currency has the same exchange rate everywhere. The alternative is to compare the undervalued exchange rate with an estimated equilibrium rate.[57]

55 See Robert W. Staiger and Alan O. Sykes, Currency Manipulation and World Trade, SSRN Working Paper (2008), http://voxeu.org/article/currency-manipulation-and-world-trade-three-reasons-caution (last visit, May 15, 2017). See also Dukgeun Ahn, "Is the Chinese Exchange-rate Regime 'WTO-legal'?", in *The US-Sino Currency Dispute: New Insights from Economics, Politics and Law* (Simon Evenett Ed.), p. 142 (2010) (stating that a benefit may not occur if market prices tend to adjust to exchange rate regimes).

56 See Robert W. Staiger and Alan O. Sykes, *Currency Manipulation and World Trade*, SSRN Working Paper, June 13, 2008. See also Dukgeun Ahn, "Is the Chinese Exchange-rate Regime 'WTO-legal'?", in *The US-Sino Currency Dispute: New Insights from Economics, Politics and Law* (Simon Evenett Ed.), p. 142 (2010) (stating that a benefit may not occur if market prices tend to adjust to exchange rate regimes).

57 WTO case law has approved the use of constructed or proxy market rates. In U.S.-Softwood Lumber IV, the Appellate Body said that, in order to measure a benefit, WTO Members have "the possibility to select any method that is in conformity with the 'guidelines' set out in Art. 14 [of the ASCM]." See Appellate Body Report, *United States – Final Countervailing Duty Determination with Respect to Certain Softwood Lumber from Canada (US – Softwood Lumber IV)*, WT/DS257/AB/R (adopted February 17, 2004) para. 91. See also Benjamin Blase Caryl, *Is China Currency Regime a Countervailable Subsidy? A Legal Analysis Under the World Trade Organization's SCM Agreement* 45(1) J. World Trade 187, 203–04 (2011). In turn, in *U.S. – Definitive Antidumping and Countervailing Duties on Certain Products from China*, the U.S. Department of Commerce estimated the benefit resulting from loans that state-owned commercial banks made to some Chinese enterprises using a proxy interest rate instead of Chinese actual interest rates. On the assumption that an inverse relationship existed between income levels and lending rates, the proxy interest was estimated through a regression analysis of inflation-adjusted interest rates in thirty lower-middle-income countries. Panel Report, *U.S. – Definitive Antidumping and Countervailing Duties on Certain Products from China*, WT/DS379/R (adopted October 22, 2010), para. 10.193.

Third, a currency misalignment is only countervailable if it is specific. This is the most hotly debated issue regarding currency manipulations. Generally speaking, whether or not a subsidy is specific depends on if it is either actionable under ASCM Art. 2.1 or prohibited under ASCM Art. 3.1. Actionable subsides are specific when they are granted to an enterprise or industry or a group of enterprises or industries. If an exchange rate is market-based and general for all entities, a misaligned currency would unlikely amount to an actionable subsidy because the criteria governing the access to the undervalued exchange rate would be objective and not exclusive for exporters. However, a subsidy might be actionable if some or all exporters may exchange foreign currencies at a preferential rate.

On the other hand, and pursuant to ASCM Arts. 2.3 and 3.1, all prohibited subsides shall be deemed to be specific. A subsidy is prohibited when it is contingent upon export performance. Unless legislators or regulators are too naïve or obliged to enact a legal rule providing that exports are a condition to exchange foreign currency for local currency, an artificially undervalued currency will not be expressly contingent in law upon export performance.[58]

More likely, a currency that is kept at an artificially low level might be a subsidy contingent in fact upon export performance since companies will only obtain the benefit of extra units of local currency in exchange for any foreign currency if they export.[59] The Appellate Body has held that:

> satisfaction of the standard for determining de facto export contingency ... requires proof of three different substantive elements: first, the 'granting of a subsidy'; second, 'is ... tied to ...'; and, third, 'actual or anticipated exportation or export earnings.'[60]

A misaligned currency might comply with those three conditions and pass this test.

A relevant question is whether the fact that exporters are usually a group of enterprises comprising a diverse range of activities does not exclude specificity.[61] An additional question is whether the fact that an undervalued currency benefits not only exporters but also other groups such as tourists, foreign investors, and

58 While it will be a rare event, a subsidy may be *de jure* export contingent without express words in the law if the connection between the exports and the subsidy is implied in the legal text. Appellate Body Report, *Canada – Measures Affecting the Export of Civilian Aircraft*, WT/DS70/AB/R (adopted 20 August, 1999), para. 100. See also Benjamin Blase Caryl, *Is China Currency Regime a Countervailable Subsidy? A Legal Analysis Under the World Trade Organization's SCM Agreement* 45(1) J. World Trade 187, 209 (2011).

59 Appellate Body Report, *Canada – Measures Affecting the Export of Civilian Aircraft*, WT/DS70/AB/R, para. 169.

60 *Id.*, para. 169.

61 Panel Report, *U.S. – Definitive Antidumping and Countervailing Duties on Certain Products from China*, WT/DS379/R paras 9, 38–40, "[W]e do not consider that the sheer diversity of economic activities supported by a given subsidy is sufficient by itself to preclude that subsidy from being specific." An exception to this diversity of economic activities will be a country in which a single product accounts for most of its exports.

currency speculators eliminate its nature as a subsidy contingent in fact upon export performance.[62] According to the WTO case law, the fact that subsidies granted in a second set of circumstances (e.g., tourism or foreign investment) are not export contingent does not dissolve the export contingency arising in a first set of circumstances (e.g., exports).[63] In other words, the existence of export contingency must be determined for each category on its own (e.g., exports, tourism, foreign investment, etc.).

For the category of exporters, specificity might exist if the national authority of a WTO member proves that an undervalued currency is tied to an increase in exports.[64] This, of course, is an uphill task. Notwithstanding, econometric studies showing that the artificially low value of a currency, or the money that a government has spent to reduce such value, is correlated to an increase in the volume or price of exports might indicate the existence of this link. Of course, if the econometric study shows that the devaluation of a currency is not only correlated to but also causing a rise in exports, the evidence, and the case for specificity, would be stronger.

On the other hand, the issue of whether dispute regarding countervailing measures levied to offset the effects of misaligned currencies is in accordance with WTO legal rules will raise another issue: whether a panel is obliged to consult the IMF and, if so, whether it shall accept any factual or legal determination from this international organization.[65] Some might argue that it is, based on Arts XV (2) and XV (9), which obligates the Contracting Parties to consult with the IMF.[66] In any event, and in such a case, some questions will remain. For instance, who in the IMF gives the advice to the WTO (the board or the staff?), whether a DSB panel is obligated or not to follow that advice, or whether the IMF might choose, if it does not have a clear answer, not to respond.

GATT Art. XV (2), the applicable legal rule to the issue mentioned above, reads (emphasis added):

> In all cases in which the CONTRACTING PARTIES are called upon to consider or deal with problems concerning monetary reserves, balances

62 See Catharina E. Koops, *Manipulating the WTO? The Possibilities for Challenging Undervalued Currencies Under WTO Rules*, 2010 Research Paper Series, Amsterdam Center for International Law 3 (2010), http://papers.ssrn.com/sol3/papers.cfm?abstract_id=1564093 (last visit, May 15, 2017).

63 Appellate Body Report, *United States – Tax Treatment for Foreign Sales Corporations*, Resource to Art. 21.5 of the DSU by the European Communities, WT/DS108/AB/RW (adopted 14 January 2002), para. 119. While this case concerned tax issues, its rationale may be applicable to artificially undervalued currencies. See Nathan Fudge, *supra* note 54, at 358 and Benjamin Blase Caryl, *supra* note 41, at 209.

64 See Appellate Body Report, *Canada – Measures Affecting the Export of Civilian Aircraft*, WT/DS70/AB/R, para. 169 (holding that de facto export contingency requires evidence of the granting of a subsidy that is tied to actual or anticipated exportation or export earnings).

65 See Deborah Siegel, *Legal Aspects of the IMF/WTO Relationship: The Fund's Articles of Agreement and the WTO Agreements* 96 Am. J. Int'l L. 561, 595 (2002).

66 See *id.*

> of payments or foreign exchange arrangements, they shall consult fully with the International Monetary Fund. In such consultations, the CONTRACTING PARTIES shall accept all findings of statistical and other facts presented by the Fund relating to foreign exchange, monetary reserves and balances of payments, and shall accept the determination of the Fund as to whether action by a contracting party in exchange matters is in accordance with the Articles of Agreement of the International Monetary Fund, or with the terms of a special exchange.

Based on this legal rule, some authors contend that a panel is not obliged either to consult or to follow any determination that the IMF makes regarding undervalued currencies.[67] In accordance to this view, the parties, but not a panel, are the entities who shall consult the IMF in matters concerning monetary reserves, balances of payments or foreign exchange arrangements.

Pursuant to this view, the fact that the parties shall accept the factual findings of the IMF does not mean that such findings are irrefutable but just that they must be received as evidence and weighed against other documents, such as the reports from other experts. Under this rationale, GATT Art. XV (2) provides that the parties shall accept the IMF's determination as to whether the country's measures that have kept an exchange rate at an artificially low level are in breach of the Articles of Agreement of this institution. Thus, the IMF would be the competent authority to hold whether a country is in breach of its own rules. Yet, the IMF is not allowed to hold whether a currency misalignment violates WTO rules or, specifically, the ASCM.

Besides GATT Art. XV (2), other two WTO legal rules are relevant to establish whether or not panels have the duty to consult the IMF as an expert organization in cases concerning the categorization of misaligned currencies as subsidies.[68] First, DSU Art. 11 requires a panel to make an objective assessment. The authors of this book have contended elsewhere that if the opinion of the IMF were dispositive, a panel would not be able to make an objective assessment of the

67 See Aluisio de Lima-Campos and Juan Gaviria, *A Case for Misaligned Currencies as Countervailable Subsidies,* 46(5) J. World Trade 1017 (2012). But see Catharina E. Koops, *Manipulating the WTO? The Possibilities for Challenging Undervalued Currencies Under WTO Rules,* 2010 Research Paper Series, Amsterdam Center for International Law 3, 9 (2010), http://papers.ssrn.com/sol3/papers.cfm?abstract_id=1564093 (last visit, May 15, 2017).

68 The same is true for the IMF, which has the right, but not the legal duty, to consult the WTO in cases that, while decided in accordance with the Articles of Agreement, have trade effects. If one entity (e.g., the WTO) has the legal duty to consult the other entity (e.g., the IMF), and to follow its factual and legal findings, it will be against reciprocity that this second entity (the IMF) does not have the obligation to consult and follow the determinations from the first entity (the WTO). As no rule requiring the IMF to consult the WTO is in legal force, reciprocity suggests that there must not be any rule requiring the WTO to consult the IMF. See Deborah Siegel, *supra* note 65, at 572 (stating that GATT Art. XV is one-sided because no correspondence requirement is mandatory on the IMF).

matter in dispute.[69] The second legal rule is DSU Art. 13, pursuant to which a panel has the right to seek information and technical advice from any individual or body which it deems appropriate – appropriate being the key word here (e.g., the IMF but also other institutions).[70]

In practice, panels have not felt bound to consult the IMF. In India – Quantitative Restrictions on Imports of Agricultural, Textile and Industrial Products, which concerned rules allowing a WTO member to impose trade restrictions to safeguard its balance of payments, the panel sought the IMF opinion, not because any rule requiring it to do so was in legal force, but just under its authority to seek information from outside experts.[71] Once received, the IMF opinion was critically assessed and compared with information that other entities, such as the Reserve Bank of India, provided.[72] Thus, the panel treated consultations and IMF's findings as discretionary and not dispositive. Furthermore, the panel in India – Quantitative Restrictions on Imports of Agricultural, Textile and Industrial Products gave the same weight to the part of the IMF's opinion concerning the matters that GATT Art. XV (2) addresses and to other parts of this opinion regarding financial matters that GATT Art. XV (2) does not mention.[73]

In another case, Dominican Republic – Measures Affecting the Importation and Internal Sale of Cigarettes, the Panel considered that it needed to consult with the IMF whether a foreign exchange measure was an exchange restriction.[74] The panel, however, did not acknowledged that it was obliged to either consult with the IMF or to accept its opinion.

In a third case, Argentina – Measures Affecting Imports of Footwear, Textiles, Apparel and Other Items, Argentina unsuccessfully claimed that the panel failed to make an objective assessment of the matter before it, as DSU Art. 11 requires, by not consulting with the IMF whether this organization had requested Argentina to levy a tax on imports in order to finance statistical services to importers, exporters and the general public.[75] The Appellate Body found that while consultation in this case might have been useful, the decision of not seeking advice

69 See Aluisio de Lima-Campos and Juan Gaviria, *A Case for Misaligned Currencies as Countervailable Subsidies,* 46(5) J. World Trade 1017 (2012).

70 See *id.*

71 Panel Report, *India – Quantitative Restrictions on Imports of Agricultural, Textile and Industrial Products,* DS90/R (adopted September 22, 1999), paras 5.11–13.

72 See Deborah Siegel, *supra* note 65, at 594.

73 See Deborah Siegel, *supra* note __, at 592–93 note 96.

74 Panel Report, *Dominican Republic – Measures Affecting the Importation and Internal Sale of Cigarettes,* DS302/R (adopted May 19, 2005) para. 7.139, "The Panel considered during the proceedings that it needed to seek more information on the precise legal nature and status of the foreign exchange fee measure in the stand-by arrangement between the IMF and the Dominican Republic."

75 See Appellate Body Report, *Argentina - Measures Affecting Imports of Footwear, Textiles, Apparel and Other Items,* WT/DS/56/AB/R (adopted April 22, 1998), paras 75, 82–83.

from the IMF was within the panel's discretion.[76] This discretion allows panels to decide not only whether to consult with an expert but also to choose the expert.[77]

Lastly, the dispute United States – Import Prohibition of Certain Shrimp and Shrimp Products is also relevant even though it was not related to financial issues. In this case, the Appellate Body confirmed the right and discretion that panels have to seek and accept information.[78]

12.4 How to deal with the issue of currency misalignments

Under the hotly debated view that predatory currency manipulations are harmful and against WTO legal rules, the next question is how to deal with such issue. A first route is to keep the status quo or, perhaps, just to apply IMF Agreement Section 1 of Art. IV (providing that countries should not manipulate exchange rates) coupled with GATT Art. XV (providing that countries should not frustrate the intent of its rules).

This path has some drawbacks. Any reference to the IMF's Articles of Agreement may open the door to political pressures, in the first place. Decisions to label a country as "currency manipulator" are very political in the IMF because they would require authorization from the board and, even if such authorization is given, there is no effective enforcement mechanism. After all, the IMF can do "close monitoring" but cannot force a member country to change its exchange rate. Thus, and also taking into account that the rules to declare a country as a currency manipulator require a 70 percent majority of votes, it is not surprising that no member country has been accused of currency manipulation by the IMF. Moreover, such rules do not provide material sanctions that would offer some sort of compensation to other members negatively affected by manipulators.[79] On top of that, and as mentioned before, many things remain unclear regarding the IMF role.

As another disadvantage of this approach, IMF Agreement Art. IV, Section 1 requires that members "avoid manipulating exchange rates or the international monetary system in order to prevent effective balance of payments adjustment or to gain an unfair competitive advantage."[80] This legal rule, by using the term

76 See *id.* para. 86.

77 See *id.* para. 84, "Pursuant to Article 13.2 of the DSU, a panel may seek information from any relevant source and may consult experts to obtain their opinions on certain aspects of the matter at issue. This is a grant of discretionary authority: a panel is not duty-bound to seek information in each and every case or to consult particular experts under this provision."

78 Panel Report, *United States – Import Prohibition of Certain Shrimp and Shrimp Products*, WT/DS58/R (adopted 15 May 1998) para. 7.8, "Pursuant to Article 13 of the DSU, the initiative to seek information and to select the source of information rests with the Panel."

79 See IMF Agreement Art. XXVI, Section 2.

80 For a complete discussion of Art. IV changes see "Article IV of the Fund's Articles of Agreement: An Overview of the Legal Framework," IMF Legal Department, June 28, 2006, www.imf.org/external/np/pp/eng/2006/062806.pdf.

"avoid," seems to make proof of intent a requirement. This, of course, is very difficult to demonstrate.

Another route to solving the issues triggered by currency manipulations is to amend the present legal rules through unilateral, bilateral or plurilateral approaches. Unilateral approaches are not consistent with the rule of law that has existed at least since the WTO was established as a result of the Uruguay Round. This is not to say that unilateral approaches have not been undertaken or that they will not be in the future. To take an illustration, Section 3004 of the Omnibus Trade and Competitiveness Act of 1988 requires the U.S. Treasury to determine if any country with global current account and significant bilateral trade surpluses with the United States is manipulating the exchange rate between their currency and the U.S. dollar for the purposes of preventing effective balance of payments adjustments or gaining unfair competitive advantage in international trade. If the U.S. Treasury concludes in the affirmative, expedited negotiations, through the IMF or bilaterally, are to be initiated. The U.S. Treasury, for political or other reasons, has never decided on the affirmative.

In turn, countries lacking a specific mechanism in their laws or regulations to deal with currency manipulations are either trying to enact new laws and regulations or defending against the effects of currency misalignments either through capital controls, increases in tariff and new specific regulations, while their most affected industries have requested an increased use of trade remedies, especially antidumping. Some of these measures, such as tariff increases within the bound limits and antidumping duties, are WTO legal, but other restrictive measures in use such as import prohibitions, export restrictions, domestic content requirements, among others, might be not.

More importantly, some of the affected countries have also unilaterally resorted to competitive currency devaluations (currency wars).[81] Thus, and in response to the persistent misalignment of some currencies, particularly in China and Southeast Asia, developed and developing countries in Europe and the Americas have been pursuing policies that directly or indirectly devalue their currencies.[82] As these countries' counter action continues and others join, the risks resulting from the currency wars to the world's economies, as well illustrated by the Great Depression of the 1930s,[83] increase.

Bilateral approaches, in turn, have the advantage of being easier to reach; i.e., their transaction costs are lower than under the multilateral approach. The main disadvantage regarding bilateral agreements is that they intend to solve a problem that is global. Thus, bilateral treaties might deal with the issue of currency misalignments within their two-country world but will not do the same elsewhere,

81 See generally Surjit S. Bhalla, *Devaluing to Prosperity: Misaligned Currencies and Their Growth Consequences*, p. 1 (2012).

82 See *id.*

83 See Liaquat Ahamed, *The Bankers Who Broke the World*, p. 1 (2009).

i.e., they are limited to putting some patches in the quilt of international trade. Unless, under the building block theory, other countries follow suit and eventually this solution reaches a multilateral stage. In any case, this is likely to be an endless process.

Since the issue of currency misalignments is global, the ideal approach would be a multilateral one. The problem here is that transactions costs, i.e., the hurdles that must be surpassed in order to have all WTO members reaching an agreement on this issue, are very high. Thus, as the Doha Development Round of negotiations' difficulties have made clear, any consensus on a negotiated solution in the WTO is bound to be a long-term proposition. Indeed, the WTO initiated discussions on this topic in 2011 without any solution in sight until now. This does not mean that the multilateral approach is impossible but indicates that it is not going to happen overnight.

Another issue regarding multilateral solutions is that countries reaping benefits from currency manipulations lack an incentive to negotiate amendments to the present legal rules. In other words, they have nothing to lose and everything to gain by keeping the status quo.

In any event, negotiations under a multilateral approach should involve both the IMF, since predatory currency manipulations are a financial issue, but also the WTO since negative effects of such manipulations on trade rules are a WTO responsibility. After all, if the intention is to protect and compensate member countries against frustration of WTO rights and obligations, and to provide an enforcement mechanism against currency manipulations, both institutions need to be involved because any resolution will probably require clarifications and/or changes in their existing agreements, specifically in the IMF's Art. IV and in WTO's Art. XV.

Unfortunately, cooperation between the IMF and the WTO in the process of amending the current legal rule does not seem easy. As former Federal Reserve Director Paul Volcker said, the negotiators of the Bretton Woods agreements should not have placed the IMF and the World Bank in the same city (a block away from each other), but instead the IMF and the WTO in order to encourage cooperation between these two organizations.

Also, and to avoid that negotiations advance at a crawling pace, one or some influential WTO members should take the lead of multilateral initiatives. Put it differently, only large economies might speed up a solution at the multilateral level. Thus, a first step toward reaching a multilateral solution might be discussing the issue of currency manipulation and reaching a common understanding among the largest economies, which regularly meet under the name of G20. While some declarations have been made, not significant agreement has been reached there. For instance, Paragraph 17 of the G20's Leaders Declaration regarding the agreement at the Saint Petersburg meeting on September 2013 reads:

> We reiterate our commitments to move more rapidly toward more market-determined exchange rate systems and exchange rate flexibility to reflect

> underlying fundamentals, and avoid persistent exchange rate misalignments. We will refrain from competitive devaluation and will not target our exchange rates for competitive purposes. We will resist all forms of protectionism and keep our markets open.[84]

While having this declaration is better than lacking it, there is no guarantee that the G20 countries will comply with their statement and, if they don't, no penalties or compensation are provided.

Other solutions have also been proposed. For instance, and in the course of several discussions with members of the IMF staff, think-tanks and academia, there have been suggestions about the IMF having a dispute resolution system like the WTO's. Alternatively, C. Fred Bergsten, from PIIE, has proposed that the IMF allows countries to do countervailing currency intervention (CCI). Under CCI,

> [C]ountries in whose currencies intervention took place, if their requests to stop the objectionable practice were unsuccessful, would buy the currencies of would-be manipulators in sufficient amounts to offset the impact on their own exchange rates. Such a measure would parallel the well-established WTO rule under which countries can apply countervailing duties against prohibited export subsidies. If the indicted manipulators felt they were being treated unjustly, they could protest to the Fund and the counter-interveners would have to desist if it found against them.[85]

This is a novel proposal that might improve the present mechanism and partially solve the problem for other injured countries since it would lead to an appreciation of the currency of the manipulator country vis-à-vis the U.S. dollar, which is the key reference currency. However, not all currencies are freely negotiated in foreign exchange markets, which could limit the ability of CCI actions to counter currency manipulations globally. In addition, few injured countries would be able to implement this policy successfully since it requires huge amounts of foreign reserves. There is also the possibility that a certain country may decide, for political reasons, not to act against a manipulator. In this case, other injured countries would be left in a bind.

Summing up, currency misalignments are a big financial and trade issue nowadays whose economic and legal solution remains unclear and, without close cooperation between the IMF and the WTO, unresolved.

84 See Russia G20's Leaders Declaration, September 2013, http://en.g20russia.ru/load/782795034 (last visit, May 20, 2017).

85 C. Fred Bergsten, *Currency Wars, The Economy of the United States and Reform of the International Monetary System,* Stavros Niarchos Foundation Lecture, PIIE (2013).

13

REGULATORY MEASURES

13.1 Introduction

When GATT 1947 was enacted, tariff barriers were the main issue affecting international trade. Indeed, such barriers might have been one of the causes of the great recession two decades earlier.[1] Today, while tariff barriers already exist, WTO rules limit them to bound tariffs and, more generally, they are no longer a big issue. Nowadays, the so-called non-tariff barriers are the main restrictions to international trade.[2] Technical barriers to trade, and sanitary and phytosanitary measures are the most relevant non-tariff barriers. They are necessary to ensure that goods comply with certain standards and that they are not harmful for consumers, animals and plants. Some countries, however, might use such measures to unfairly protect their domestic industries. Besides sanitary and phytosanitary measures and technical barriers to trade, Chapter 13 will also discuss rules of origin.

GATT Art. XX, titled "General Exceptions," allows WTO members to restrict international trade in order to protect human, animal or plant life or health, provided that such measures are neither discriminatory nor a disguised protectionism.[3] This legal rule's chapeau provides:

> Subject to the requirement that such measures are not applied in a manner which would constitute a means of arbitrary or unjustifiable discrimination between countries where the same conditions prevail, or a disguised

1 See Liaquat Ahamed, *The Bankers Who Broke the World*, p. 1 (2009).

2 See generally OECD, *Looking Beyond Tariffs: The Role of Non-Tariff Barriers in World Trade* (OECD Trade Policy Studies, 2006).

3 See GATT Art. XX.

> restriction on international trade, nothing in this Agreement shall be construed to prevent the adoption or enforcement by any contracting party of measures.[4]

Other relevant parts of this legal rule, paragraphs b) and d), respectively state:

> b) "necessary to protect human, animal or plant life or health;" and d) "necessary to secure compliance with laws or regulations which are not inconsistent with the provision of this Agreement, including those relating to customs enforcement, the enforcement of monopolies operated under paragraph 4 of Article II and Article XVII, the protection of patents, trade marks and copyrights, and the prevention of deceptive practices;"

There are two specific WTO agreements dealing with each one of these paragraphs. On the one hand, the Agreement on the Application of Sanitary and Phytosanitary Measures (ASPS or just the SPS Agreement), intended to protect food safety and animal and plant health and safety and, on the other hand, the Agreement on Technical Barriers to Trade (ATBT or just the TBT Agreement). Both agreements share the feature of providing the standards that WTO members shall comply with when they enact and apply legal rules related to sanitary and phytosanitary measures or to technical barriers to trade. As a general rule, domestic measures intended to protect the health of human beings, animals and plants or to comply with some standards that are based on international standards are less likely to be successfully challenged before the WTO than if such measures are based on local or endemic standards.[5] After this introduction, this chapter will describe the main rules of the SPS Agreement and then, in the next section, the main features of the TBT Agreement.

13.2 Sanitary and phytosanitary measures

The SPS Agreement sets out the basic rules to ensure that the goods that consumers in the WTO members buy are safe and in accordance with the appropriate standards and the knowledge frontier at the time of such consumption.[6] This agreement also guarantees that a country enacting and enforcing strict health and safety regulations does not use them as an excuse for protecting domestic industries.[7]

Pursuant to the SPS Agreement, countries are allowed to set their own standards to protect health and safe consumption if the following three-pronged test is

4 *Id.*
5 See SPS Agreement Art. 5.1 and TBT Agreement Art. 2.4.
6 See SPS Agreement Art. 1.1 and Annex A para. 1.
7 See SPS Agreement Art. 2.3. *Cfr.* GATT Art. XX.

complied with: (i) regulations must be based on scientific evidence[8]; (ii) regulations shall be applied only to the extent necessary to protect human, animal or plant life or health; and last but not least,[9] (iii) regulations should not arbitrarily or unjustifiably discriminate among countries where identical or similar conditions prevail.[10]

As indicated above, the SPS Agreement encourages countries to use international standards, guidelines and recommendations (provided that they exist).[11] If the measures follow these guidelines, it is highly unlikely that they can be successfully challenged before a WTO panel.[12] In any event, the recommendation to adopt international standards does not amount to a prohibition to use local measures.[13] WTO members may use measures resulting in higher standards if there is scientific evidence justifying such rules.[14] Thus, a WTO member pondering whether to enact any rule that might be categorized as an SPS measure must ponder the pros and cons of either using an international standard that will probably not be challenged or adopting a more stringent standard that might be more useful to protect consumption and health but that, at the same time, might end up being challenged before a WTO panel.[15] A kind of middle and safe road is the so-called precautionary principle: WTO members, to some extent, may apply this principle and enact temporary protective measures whenever there is scientific uncertainty about the effect of the rules.[16]

Regarding other provisions, the SPS Agreement allows countries to use different standards and methods to inspect goods.[17] Nonetheless, if an exporting country can demonstrate that the measure it applies to its exports achieve the same level of health protection as in the importing country, the latter is expected to accept the exporting country's standards and methods as equivalent.[18] The SPS Agreement also includes provisions on control, inspection and approval procedures.[19] Finally,

8 See SPS Agreement Arts 2.2 and 5.2.
9 See SPS Agreement Art. 2.2.
10 See SPS Agreement Art. 2.3.
11 See SPS Agreement Arts 3.1 and 5.1.
12 See SPS Agreement Arts 3.1 and 5.1.
13 See SPS Agreement Art. 5.
14 See SPS Agreement Arts 3.3 and 5.
15 See SPS Agreement Art. 11.
16 See SPS Agreement Art. 5.7, which reads: "In cases where relevant scientific evidence is insufficient, a Member may provisionally adopt sanitary or phytosanitary measures on the basis of available pertinent information, including that from the relevant international organizations as well as from sanitary or phytosanitary measures applied by other Members. In such circumstances, Members shall seek to obtain the additional information necessary for a more objective assessment of risk and review the sanitary or phytosanitary measure accordingly within a reasonable period of time."
17 See SPS Agreement Art. 4.1.
18 See SPS Agreement Art. 4.1.
19 See SPS Agreement Art. 8.

and in order to comply with transparency standards,[20] governments shall provide advance notice of new or modified sanitary and phytosanitary regulations, and establish a national enquiry point to provide information.[21]

Before finishing this section, it is worth summarizing the most important case law regarding the SPS Agreement. Three cases will be mentioned here: European Communities – Measures Affecting Asbestos and Products Containing Asbestos,[22] Brazil – Measures Affecting Imports of Retreaded Tyres,[23] and European Communities – Measures Concerning Meat and Meat Products (Hormones).[24]

European Communities – Measures Affecting Asbestos and Products Containing Asbestos was about a French ban on the manufacture, process, sale, and transfer of all varieties of asbestos fibers in order to prevent cancer.[25] France argued that it was applying the health exception under GATT Art. XX paragraph b, "Nothing in this Agreement shall be construed to prevent the adoption or enforcement by any contracting party of measures: … (b) necessary to protect human, animal or plant life or health."[26] The AB sanctioned the French measure applying such exception in a case that is also relevant because it was the first one when such a thing happened.[27] Indeed, the prevailing view before this case was that the word "necessary" meant that WTO members should apply the least restrictive measure and that any alternative measure might be regarded as an unreasonable restriction on trade.[28]

The AB changed this case law by stating not only that all WTO members have the right to choose the level of protection even if it is the highest but also that a reasonable alternative is any one allowing the importing country to achieve the level of desired protection.[29] Thus, an alternative is not reasonable when it is merely theoretical in nature; for instance, when it is impossible to apply it or when such application means prohibitive costs, undue burdens, or substantial technical difficulties.[30] In any case, the AB makes it clear that it is the country enacting and applying the challenged measure which must submit evidence proving *prima facie* that the measure is necessary.[31] Likewise, if the complainant indicates a WTO

20 See generally GATT Art. X.

21 See SPS Agreement Art. 7.

22 See DS135, European Communities – Measures Affecting Asbestos and Products Containing Asbestos.

23 See DS332, Brazil – Measures Affecting Imports of Retreaded Tyres.

24 See DS26, European Communities – Measures Concerning Meat and Meat Products (Hormones).

25 See DS135, European Communities – Measures Affecting Asbestos and Products Containing Asbestos.

26 GATT Art. XX para. b).

27 See DS135, European Communities – Measures Affecting Asbestos and Products Containing Asbestos.

28 See *id.*

29 See *id.*

30 See *id.*

31 See *id.*

consistent and less trade restrictive alternative, the respondent is required to show that such alternative is not reasonable.[32]

The test of necessity under GATT Art. XX paragraph b) was again tested in Brazil – Measures Affecting Imports of Retreaded Tyres.[33] The Brazilian Government contended that its measure had a legitimate objective: the maximum reduction of the risk derived of waste tire accumulation.[34] Similar to European Communities – Measures Affecting Asbestos and Products Containing Asbestos,[35] the AB held that the complainant must prove the existence of a reasonable alternative; i.e., a less restrictive and reasonably available measure preserving the WTO member's right to achieve the desired level of protection.[36] The AB also held that complimentary measures are not reasonable alternatives and that balancing between trade restrictions and the objective of the measure does not require quantification of the contribution of the alternatives.[37] In this particular case, however, and pursuant to the chapeau of GATT Art. XX, the AB held that Brazil applied the import ban in a manner that was unjustifiably discriminatory.[38]

Finally, European Communities – Measures Concerning Meat and Meat Products (Hormones) was a legal fight between heavy contenders: the E.U. Members on the defending side (then, the European Communities), and the United States and Canada on the other side.[39] The challenged measure was a ban on meat and meat products coming from cattle that had been treated with natural and synthetic hormones for growth promotion purposes.[40] A WTO panel, in a decision that the AB affirmed,[41] held that the measure was inconsistent with both GATT Art. XX and the SPS Agreement.[42]

In particular, the AB reminded that a country may impose a measure when the risk that it is deterring is possible even if the likelihood of its occurrence is not

32 See *id.*

33 See DS332, Brazil – Measures Affecting Imports of Retreaded Tyres.

34 See *id.*

35 See DS135, European Communities – Measures Affecting Asbestos and Products Containing Asbestos.

36 See DS332, Brazil – Measures Affecting Imports of Retreaded Tyres.

37 See *id.*

38 See GATT Art. XX, chapeau ("Subject to the requirement that such measures are not applied in a manner which would constitute a means of arbitrary or unjustifiable discrimination between countries where the same conditions prevail, or a disguised restriction on international trade."). See also DS332, Brazil – Measures Affecting Imports of Retreaded Tyres. The AB also dismissed the Brazilian claim according to which the import volume from other countries belonging to Mercosur, which were excepted from the restriction, did not undermine the import ban, since such a measure lacked support on GATT Art. XX. See DS332, Brazil – Measures Affecting Imports of Retreaded Tyres.

39 See DS26, European Communities – Measures Concerning Meat and Meat Products (Hormones).

40 See *id.*

41 See *id.*

42 See *id.*

high.[43] The AB also noted that the list of factors to take into account in a risk assessment, pursuant to the SPS Agreement Art. 5.3, is not closed (i.e., this list is not exhaustive). Thus, the requirement in this, the SPS Agreement Art. 5.1 –

> Members shall ensure that their sanitary or phytosanitary measures are based on an assessment, as appropriate to the circumstances, of the risks to human, animal or plant life or health, taking into account risk assessment techniques developed by the relevant international organizations

– implies that there must be a rational relationship between the measure and the risk assessment but does not mean that it has to be based on the majority of the scientific evidence (i.e., the measure must be based on evidence supported by a minority of scientists).[44]

In this case, and according to both the panel and the AB, there was evidence through general studies about the relationship between hormones and cancer.[45] However, there was also evidence that hormones for growth promotion are safe in good use (i.e., not abusive use) and the European Communities did not prove such abusive use of hormones and did not submit evidence "sufficiently specific" indicating that meat from cattle treated with hormones for growth purposes increases the risk of cancer to humans.[46]

13.3 Technical barriers to trade

The TBT Agreement intends to ensure that regulations, standards, testing and certification procedures do neither create unnecessary obstacles to trade nor discriminate among WTO members.[47] This agreement, however, also recognizes the countries' rights to adopt the standards they consider appropriate.[48] Summing up, the TBT Agreement aims to find a delicate balance between the countries' right to set domestic standards and to apply international ones and the importance for the sake of international trade of avoiding that such rights might be used (or abused) to obtain unfair trade advantages.

The TBT Agreement sets out a code of good practices for both governments and non-governmental or industry bodies intending to prepare, adopt and apply voluntary standards.[49] Nowadays, over 200 standards-setting bodies apply such

43 See *id.* See also SPS Agreement.

44 See DS26, European Communities – Measures Concerning Meat and Meat Products (Hormones). See also SPS Agreement.

45 See *id.*

46 See *id.*

47 See TBT Agreement Art. 2.2.

48 See TBT Agreement Preamble.

49 See TBT Agreement Art. 4.

code.[50] The TBT Agreement also states that the procedures used to decide whether a product conforms with relevant standards shall be fair and equitable, thus discouraging any methods that would give domestically produced goods an unfair advantage.[51] This Agreement also encourages countries to recognize each other's procedures for assessing whether a product conforms with regulations, standards, and testing and certification procedures.[52] Finally, regarding the transparency principle,[53] and to ensure that information about regulations, standards and procedures is public knowledge (i.e., available to all interested parties such as other countries, manufacturers and exporters), all WTO members shall establish national enquiry points and keep each other informed through the WTO.[54] Under this legal rule, around 900 new or modified regulations are notified each year.[55]

Among several cases related to TBT measures,[56] the most relevant are European Communities – Trade Description of Sardines,[57] European Communities – Selected Customs Matters,[58] and Australia – Certain Measures Concerning Trademarks and Other Plain Packaging Requirements Applicable to Tobacco Products and Packaging.[59]

In European Communities – Trade Description of Sardines, a E.C. regulation stated that only one kind of sardine, "*sardines pilchardus*" can be marketed in its territory as "preserved sardines."[60] Peru, the claimant and also an exporter of another kind of sardine ("*sardinops sagax*"), argued that such regulation was against TBT Agreement Art. 2.4,[61] which states:

> Where technical regulations are required and relevant international standards exist or their completion is imminent, Members shall use them, or the relevant part of them, as a basis for their technical regulations except when

50 Committee on Technical Barriers to Trade, WTO, *Twenty-first Annual Review of Implementation and Operation of the TBT Agreement* (March 24, 2016), www.wto.org/english/tratop_e/tbt_e/tbt_e.htm (last visit, April 30, 2017).

51 See TBT Agreement Art. 5.

52 See TBT Agreement Art. 6.

53 See generally GATT Art. X.

54 See TBT Agreement Art. 10.

55 Committee on Technical Barriers to Trade, WTO, *Twenty-first Annual Review of Implementation and Operation of the TBT Agreement* (March 24, 2016), www.wto.org/english/tratop_e/tbt_e/tbt_e.htm (last visit, April 30, 2017).

56 At least 52 cases cite the TBT Agreement in its request for consultations. See WTO, *Dispute Settlement: The Disputes, Disputes by Agreement*, www.wto.org/english/tratop_e/dispu_e/dispu_agreements_index_e.htm?id=A22# (last visit, April 30, 2017).

57 See DS321, European Communities – Trade Description of Sardines.

58 See DS315, European Communities – Selected Customs Matters.

59 See DS434, Australia – Certain Measures Concerning Trademarks and Other Plain Packaging Requirements Applicable to Tobacco Products and Packaging.

60 DS321, European Communities – Trade Description of Sardines.

61 *See id.*

> such international standards or relevant parts would be an ineffective or inappropriate means for the fulfillment of the legitimate objectives pursued, for instance because of fundamental climatic or geographical factors or fundamental technological problems.

Thus, the issue in this case was whether or not the E.C.'s measure was based on an international standard.

The European Communities contended that the Codex Stan 94 was a set of rules ineffective or inappropriate for the fulfilment of the legitimate objectives that they pursued,[62] that the measure was a "naming rule" and not a labeling requirement (thus, not subject to the TBT Agreement), and that the regulation did not affect the imports of *sardinops sagax*.[63] A WTO panel found the measure inconsistent with TBT Art. 2.4.[64] The AB affirmed the decision holding that Codex Stan 94 is a relevant international standard under the TBT Agreement Art. 2.4, which the European Communities did not use as a basis for the regulation.[65] The AB, however, reversed the panel's holding that the European Communities had the burden of proving that Codex Stan 94 was an ineffective or inappropriate standard to fulfill the regulation's goals.[66] In any event, the AB found that Peru met this burden of proof.[67]

In a second case, European Communities – Selected Customs Matters, the challenged measure was related to the enforcement of customs laws.[68] According to the United States, the complainant, the European Communities, by applying this measure in a non-uniform basis (depending on the importing country), had breached GATT Art. X:3(a).[69] According to a WTO Panel and to the AB, the European Communities violated GATT Art. X:3 in three cases involving tariff classification and customs valuation, had not violated the same legal rules in five cases related to tariff classification, customs valuation and customs procedures and, finally, the United States had not proved that the European Communities had violated Art. X:3(a) in one case in the areas of tariff classification, customs valuation and customs procedures.[70] The AB also held that not only substantial but also procedural rules, such as the one that was discussed in this case, can be challenged proving that they lead to a lack of uniform, impartial or reasonable administration.[71]

62 See generally Codex Alimentarius, International Food Standards, www.fao.org/fao-who-codexalimentarius/standards/list-standards/ (last visit, July 31, 2016).
63 See DS321, European Communities – Trade Description of Sardines.
64 See *id.*
65 See DS321, European Communities – Trade Description of Sardines.
66 See *id.*
67 See *id.*
68 See DS315, European Communities – Selected Customs Matters.
69 See *id.*
70 See *id.*
71 See *id.*

Another interesting case is Australia – Certain Measures Concerning Trademarks and Other Plain Packaging Requirements Applicable to Tobacco Products and Packaging,[72] which was already mentioned in the chapter about the Australian trade policy system.[73] The challenged measures are the Australia's Tobacco Plain Packaging Act 2011 and its implementing regulations, the Trade Marks Amendment (Tobacco Plain Packaging) Act 2011; and any other amendments, extensions, related instruments or practices that Australia have adopted to enforce the former two measures.[74] Honduras, the claimant, contends that the Australian measures limit the rights of tobacco distributors to completely show their trademarks on the packages of their products and, therefore, that such legal rules are inconsistent with TBT Arts 2.1 and 2.2 and with some rules of GATT 1994 and of TRIPS Agreement as well.[75] On 30 May, 2016, pursuant to Article 12.12 of the DSU, the panel's jurisdiction lapsed.[76]

13.4 Private standards

After perusing the previous sections, the reader might think that WTO members have the legal monopoly to enact rules regarding sanitary, phytosanitary and technical standards. This is not completely true, though. A recent and growing trend, whose effect on the global rules about standards is still unclear, consists of some large multinational enterprises, and particularly retailers such as Walmart and Carrefour, establishing their own standards for the purchase of goods.[77] These are the so-called "Private Standards," a term referring to "any requirements that are established by non-governmental entities, including wholesale or retail stores, national producer associations, civil society groups, or combinations of them"[78] and addressing "concerns related to food safety,

72 See DS434, Australia – Certain Measures Concerning Trademarks and Other Plain Packaging Requirements Applicable to Tobacco Products and Packaging.

73 See *supra* Section 9.3.

74 See DS434, Australia – Certain Measures Concerning Trademarks and Other Plain Packaging Requirements Applicable to Tobacco Products and Packaging.

75 See *id.*

76 See *id.*

77 See generally Vera Thorstensen, Reinhard Weissinger and Xinhua Sun, *Private Standards—Implications for Trade, Development, and Governance, E15 Initiative.* Geneva, International Centre for Trade and Sustainable Development (ICTSD) and World Economic Forum, http://e15initiative.org/wp-content/uploads/2015/07/E15-Regulatory-Thorstensen-et-al.-final.pdf (last visit, May 15, 2017). See also Alessandra Arcuri, 'The TBT Agreement and Private Standards', in *Research Handbook on the WTO and Technical Barriers to Trade* (Tracey Epps and Michael J. Trebilcock Eds), p. 485 (2013).

78 See generally Vera Thorstensen, Reinhard Weissinger and Xinhua Sun, *Private Standards—Implications for Trade, Development, and Governance, E15 Initiative.* Geneva, International Centre for Trade and Sustainable Development (ICTSD) and World Economic Forum, http://e15initiative.org/wp-content/uploads/2015/07/E15-Regulatory-Thorstensen-et-al. final.pdf (last visit, May 15, 2017).

environmental protection, animal welfare, fair trade, labor conditions, and human rights issues."[79]

At first sight, this surge of private standards does not seem either surprising or problematic. It is not surprising taking into account the rising influence of multinational enterprises and the emergence of the so-called global value chains.[80] On the other hand, private standards might improve manufacturing procedures in exporting countries giving them, in the long-run, a competitive advantage.[81] As a second advantage, private standards allow large corporations and retailers, which manage global value chains accounting for around 80 percent of global trade,[82] to ensure coherence among its suppliers.[83] Private standards might also be in fashion because of a "lack of public confidence in regulatory agencies, the legal requirements on companies to demonstrate 'due diligence' in the prevention of food safety risks, a growing focus on 'corporate social responsibility' and the global expansion of food service companies."[84]

Private standards would not have negative side-effects if they were carefully drafted in order to fill gaps that WTO legal rules or other global rules have left.[85] The issue, however, is that most private standards may conflict with either the TBT or the SPS Agreement and even with domestic standards. For instance, some private standards give an advantage to products or schemes that are allegedly favorable for the environment but whose beneficial effects lack scientific evidence, in contradiction with SPS Agreement Art. 5.[86] On top of that, too stringent private standards might preclude access to markets in developed countries of exporters located in developing countries lacking the required capital and technical expertise to comply with them.[87] As a result, some multinational corporations with significant market power might use private standards to wield their market power in order to exclude potential competitors from some markets.[88] This is not only a

79 See generally *id.*

80 See generally *id.*

81 See generally *id.*

82 UNCTAD's World Investment Report (2013: XXII).

83 See generally Vera Thorstensen, Reinhard Weissinger and Xinhua Sun, *Private Standards—Implications for Trade, Development, and Governance, E15 Initiative.* Geneva, International Centre for Trade and Sustainable Development (ICTSD) and World Economic Forum, http://e15initiative.org/wp-content/uploads/2015/07/E15-Regulatory-Thorstensen-et-al.-final.pdf (last visit, May 15, 2017).

84 Makane Moïse Mbengue, *Private Standards and WTO Law* 5(1) Biores, Int'l Centre Trade & Sustainable Dev. (2011), www.ictsd.org/bridges-news/biores/news/private-standards-and-wto-law (last visit, May 15, 2017).

85 See generally Vera Thorstensen, Reinhard Weissinger and Xinhua Sun, *Private Standards—Implications for Trade, Development, and Governance, E15 Initiative.* Geneva, International Centre for Trade and Sustainable Development (ICTSD) and World Economic Forum, http://e15initiative.org/wp-content/uploads/2015/07/E15-Regulatory-Thorstensen-et-al.-final.pdf (last visit, May 15, 2017).

86 See generally *id.*

87 See generally *id.*

88 See *id.*

theoretical concern. To take an illustration, Saint Vincent and the Grenadines, a tiny WTO member, recently expressed its concern before the SPS Committee about a private standard blocking its export of bananas into some European markets.[89]

As Professor Alessandra Acuri put it: "transnational private standards have contributed to enhancing the process of economic globalization. Today, however, questions are raised as to whether the burgeoning phenomenon of (transnational) private regulation is working as an impediment to free trade."[90]

A final and not less relevant concern regarding private standards is that, most of the time, they are not widely known; thereby, they are not in sync with the transparency principle, which is so important under WTO rules.[91]

Professor Makane Moïse Mbengue summarizes the concerns mentioned above about private standards:

> Critics stress that private voluntary standards may exclude small producers in developing countries from markets; strong opponents emphasize that such standards are much more rigid than public-sector standards, and without scientific justification. In other words, private standards may not be based on science or risk analysis, and their adoption is neither democratic nor transparent.[92]

As a result of this new round of competition between public and private international law, the applicable rules regarding standards might exponentially grow in a situation resembling the spaghetti bowl that will be mentioned later on regarding the conflict between WTO and PTA rules. After all, and nowadays, the numbers of private standards might be unmanageable. It is estimated that only the International Organization for Standardization (ISO) has enacted more than 19,000 standards, which are in addition to an overabundance of private regulation.[93]

Such uncontrolled expansion of rules might not only trigger uncertainty among sellers and buyers about the applicable standards but also might exponentially increase the cost of international transactions in goods. In the words of Professors Thorstensen, Weissinger and Sun:

89 See Makane Moïse Mbengue, *Private Standards and WTO Law* 5(1) Biores, Int'l Centre Trade & Sustainable Dev. (2011), www.ictsd.org/bridges-news/biores/news/private-standards-and-wto-law (last visit, May 15, 2017).

90 Alessandra Arcuri, 'The TBT Agreement and Private Standards', in *Research Handbook on the WTO and Technical Barriers to Trade* (Tracey Epps and Michael J. Trebilcock Eds), p. 485 (2013).

91 *See* Makane Moïse Mbengue, Private Standards and WTO Law 5(1) Biores, Int'l Centre Trade & Sustainable Dev. (2011), www.ictsd.org/bridges-news/biores/news/private-standards-and-wto-law (last visit, May 15, 2017).

92 *Id.*

93 *See* Alessandra Arcuri, 'The TBT Agreement and Private Standards', in *Research Handbook on the WTO and Technical Barriers to Trade* (Tracey Epps and Michael J. Trebilcock Eds), p. 485 (2013).

> [P]roliferating private standards can result in competition, duplication, and even conflicts among private standards and between private standards and standards developed through the formal standardisation system. Particularly, private standards have the potential to weaken the roles of governments and international standards-setting bodies and may, under certain conditions, even render their work irrelevant. This causes inefficiency in achieving public policy objectives; it can create confusion for producers and consumers, and raises questions about the legitimacy of the market-driven private initiatives.

Recognizing that private standards generate not only benefits but also threats to the multilateral trade system, the WTO has led some discussions and proposed possible legal amendments to the current legal rules. So far, the results are disappointing.[94] To begin with, it is not even clear whether WTO rules govern private standards.[95] The rationale that such rules do not cover private standards is that TBT and SPS agreements usually deal with standards set by international bodies but not by private organizations. On the opposite side, it might be argued that WTO rules are applicable to private standards because both TBT and SPS agreements provide rules forcing members to avoid that non-governmental entities within their territories act inconsistently with such legal rules.[96]

Another pressing question regarding private standards is whether they could or should be imported into the WTO legal system or, on the alternative, whether WTO rules should rather be exported to private standards.[97] Importing private standards would allow WTO members to develop national standards based on private standards as well as to allow imports complying with them. As the reader might have anticipated, this approach assumes that private rules might be more efficient than public rules.

The drawback of this proposal is that private standards, as mentioned earlier, often go beyond international standards and, as a result, might exclude small competitors from international markets.[98] This is an economic constraint to the import of private standards into WTO law. Legal restrictions also exist since

94 See Vera Thorstensen, Reinhard Weissinger and Xinhua Sun, *Private Standards—Implications for Trade, Development, and Governance, E15 Initiative*. Geneva, International Centre for Trade and Sustainable Development (ICTSD) and World Economic Forum, http://e15initiative.org/wp-content/uploads/2015/07/E15-Regulatory-Thorstensen-et-al.-final.pdf (last visit, May 15, 2017).

95 See *id.*

96 See SPS Agreement Art. 13 and TBT Agreement Arts 4 and 8.

97 See Makane Moïse Mbengue, Private Standards and WTO Law 5(1) Biores, Int'l Centre Trade & Sustainable Dev. (2011), www.ictsd.org/bridges-news/biores/news/private-standards-and-wto-law (last visit, May 15, 2017).

98 See *id.*

current WTO legal rules might not allow such import of legal standards.[99] This is not a lesser concern taking into account that amending WTO legal rules requires unanimity.[100]

The alternative, in an approach considering that public rules might be more efficient than private rules, is to export WTO legal rules into the private standards realm. In simpler terms, such approach would consist of the SPS Committee, the TBT Committee or other WTO Committee supervising the development of private standards and determining whether they, in a case-by-case basis, constitute restrictions to trade disguised as measures intended to protect labor, environmental, consumer, human or other rights.[101] Naturally, the task of monitoring and evaluating the conformity of all private standards with WTO rules might go well beyond the current administrative capacity of the WTO.

Pursuant to Art. 13 of the SPS Agreement,

> Members shall take such reasonable measures as may be available to them to ensure that non-governmental entities within their territories, as well as regional bodies in which relevant entities within their territories are members, comply with the relevant provisions of this Agreement.

This legal rule might be another option to export SPS rules to the private world because it provides that WTO members are responsible for the standards set by their private sectors.[102] Regarding the TBT Agreement, another path to export the WTO rules to the private sector might be a legal rule compelling private standard-setting bodies to adhere to the basic principles of the TBT Code of Good Practice.[103]

Some other approaches have been proposed to deal with the legal, economic and technical issues resulting from the emergence of private standards and to generate coherence between them and international standards.[104] Some of these proposals are encouraging information exchange between international organizations and private standardization bodies, strengthening the role of standard bodies such as the ISO, negotiating a Code of Conduct for Standards Development and Implementation, starting multilateral negotiations among all parties interested in or affected by private standards, and clarifying and strengthening WTO legal rules on these matters.[105]

99 See *id.*

100 1994 WTO Agreement.

101 See Makane Moïse Mbengue, *Private Standards and WTO Law* 5(1) Biores, Int'l Centre Trade and Sustainable Dev. (2011), www.ictsd.org/bridges-news/biores/news/private-standards-and-wto-law (last visit, May 15, 2017).

102 See *id.*

103 See *id.*

104 See *id.*

105 See generally Vera Thorstensen, Reinhard Weissinger and Xinhua Sun, *Private Standards—Implications for Trade, Development, and Governance, E15 Initiative.* Geneva, International

In sum, private standards are a trend that triggers many benefits but that, at the same time, might hinder the advance of international trade by blocking access to some markets and by increasing the number and complexity of the applicable rules. The solutions, needless to say, are neither prohibiting private standards nor allowing them without any restriction. By contrast, the challenge for the international trade system is to make private standards more clear, predictable and transparent and, as a result, finding an efficient balance between them and international standards (i.e., finding the point where the marginal benefit of private standards equals its marginal cost).

13.5 Rules of origin

Rules of origin, in short, are the criteria used to define where a product was made.[106] Needless to say, rules of origin are an essential part of trade rules since WTO members need to know the country where a given product comes from in order to know whether or not it is subject to general tariffs, tariffs according to a preferential trade agreement, antidumping and countervailing duties, application of SPS and TBT measures, quotas, etc. Rules of origin are also useful to compile trade statistics (e.g., exports classified by countries) as well as for "made in..." labels that are attached to goods, especially in the case of apparel.

Nowadays, when economic globalization is not even a novelty and when global value chains (products that are processed in several countries before they are ready to be exported) are more the rule than the exception,[107] determining the origin of some goods is a complex task. On top of that, some producers may be tempted to do some treaty shopping by making any change to the goods, even if it is marginal, and claiming that they come from a country with some preferential treatment (e.g., the country is a member of a customs union) and not from the original country.[108]

Fortunately, there are some criteria to solve this issue. First, if the products were manufactured in only one country; this WTO member is, of course, the origin of the goods. If, by contrast, the goods were made in several countries, they

Centre for Trade and Sustainable Development (ICTSD) and World Economic Forum, http://e15initiative.org/wp-content/uploads/2015/07/E15-Regulatory-Thorstensen-et-al.-final.pdf (last visit, May 15, 2017); and Makane Moïse Mbengue, Private standards and WTO law 5(1) Biores, Int'l Centre Trade and Sustainable Dev. (2011), www.ictsd.org/bridges-news/biores/news/private-standards-and-wto-law (last visit, May 15, 2017).

106 See Agreement on Rules of Origin Art. 1.1, whose relevant text reads: "[R]ules of origin shall be defined as those laws, regulations and administrative determinations of general application applied by any Member to determine the country of origin of goods."

107 See generally WTO, *Global Value Chains in a Changing World* (2013), and Jeffrey Neilson, Bill Pritchard and Henry Yeung Wai-Chung (Eds), *Global Value Chains and Global Production Networks: Changes in the International Political Economy* (2015).

108 See generally Olivier Cadot, Antoni Estavadeoral, Akiko Suwa Eisenmann and Thierry Verdier (Eds), *The Origin of Goods: Rules of Origin in Regional Trade Agreements*, Centre for Economic Policy Research (2006).

have the origin of the goods where they were manufactured provided that they have not suffered a "substantial transformation in another country."[109] This rule does not solve the issue but just asks another question in each case: whether any transformation is substantial. This is another difficult question whose answer is not in the Agreement on Rules of Origin. Pursuant to the WTO legal rules,[110] the criteria to determine whether or not a transformation is substantial must be agreed upon in each Preferential Trade Agreement provided that at least the following factors are taken into account: (i) change of classification of the goods in the harmonized system; (ii) percentage of domestic content or added value; (iii) criterion of production, manufacturing and elaboration.

In spite of delegating the task of determining whether a transformation is substantial, the Agreement on Rules of Origin provides some important provisions. Generally speaking, this agreement aims at a long-term harmonization of rules of origin.[111] This agreement also intends to ensure that such rules do not themselves create unnecessary obstacles to trade.[112]

Pursuant to the Agreement on Rules of Origin, the contracting parties are expected to ensure that: (i) the rules of origin are transparent[113]; (ii) they do not have restricting, distorting or disruptive effects on international trade[114]; (iii) they are administered in a consistent, uniform, impartial and reasonable manner[115]; and (iv) they are based on a positive standard or, in other words, such rules state what does confer origin rather than what does not.[116]

The Agreement on Rules of Origin also established a harmonization program, which was initiated shortly after the end of the Uruguay Round (in 1995) and which, theoretically, should have concluded within the following three years.[117] The harmonization program was based upon a set of principles, including making rules of origin objective, understandable and predictable.[118]

While a lot of work was done and substantial progress was achieved during the three years following the approval of the Agreement on Rules of Origin, the harmonization program could not be completed during this term mainly due to the complexities of the issues and, in particular, the fact that harmonization of rules of origin was, for many countries, incompatible with trade defense.[119]

109 See Agreement on Rules of Origin Arts 2(a) and 9.2(c).
110 See Rules of the WTO Committee on Rules of Origin (CRO) in Geneva and of the WCO Technical Committee (TCRO).
111 See Agreement on Rules of Origin Art. 3.
112 See *id.*
113 See Agreement on Rules of Origin Art. 2(a).
114 Agreement on Rules of Origin Art. 2(c).
115 *Id.*
116 Agreement on Rules of Origin Art. 2(f).
117 See Agreement on Rules of Origin, Art. 9.2.
118 See Agreement on Rules of Origin Art. 9.
119 See generally World Customs Organization, Harmonization Work Program, www.wcoomd.org/en/topics/origin/activities-and-programmes/nonpreferencial-origin/harmonization-work-

Thus, more than two decades after the end of the Uruguay Round, the harmonization program is still in process and this situation might continue unchanged in the long-term.[120] Indeed, rules of origin are one of the more complex topics in international trade nowadays.[121] After all, recall that the Agreement on Rules of Origin defers on Preferential Trade Agreements the criteria to determine whether a transformation is substantial and that there are currently hundreds of those types of agreements, forming the so-called "spaghetti bowl" effect,[122] i.e., a tangled mess of criteria which are anything but harmonized.[123]

programme.aspx (last visit, April 30, 2017). See also John J. Barceló III, *Harmonizing Preferential Rules of Origin in the WTO System*, Cornell Law Faculty Publications. Paper 72 (2006), http://scholarship.law.cornell.edu/lsrp_papers/72 (last visit, April 30, 2017).

120 See *id.*

121 See *id.*

122 See Jagdish Bhagwati, *Termites in the Trading System: How Preferential Agreements Undermine Free Trade*, p. 1 (2008).

123 See *infra* Chapter 15.

14
DISPUTE SETTLEMENT

14.1 Generalities of the Dispute Settlement Understanding

The purpose of this chapter is to discuss how WTO members may settle their disputes arising out of international trade and in accordance with the WTO rules.

Reaching multilateral agreements is, of course, a step on the process of liberalizing international trade. This step, however, is not enough if WTO members may breach such rules without any punishment or, in other words, if they are not enforceable. Even though economic globalization and, to a lesser degree, legal globalization, are no longer a novelty, a global court in charge of enforcing international trade agreements does not exist. Notwithstanding, some rules exist to settle disputes about the construction and enforcement of international trade rules and about the bodies that have the jurisdiction to lead these processes as well. This is the goal of the Dispute Settlement Understanding (DSU), one of the WTO's most important agreements, so important that it had been called the "jewel of the crown."[1]

Pursuant to the DSU, WTO members have agreed that if they believe fellow members are breaching WTO rules, they will use the multilateral system to settle the dispute instead of taking unilateral measures (i.e., instead of retaliating).[2] In particular, a trade dispute arises whenever a WTO member adopts a trade policy measure or takes some other action that at least another WTO member considers to be in breach of one or more of the WTO agreements, or to

1 Pascal Lamy, former WTO Director-General, was the one that first used the words "jewel of the crown" to refer to the DSU. See *WTO disputes reach 400 mark*, WTO, Press Release, November 6, 2009, www.wto.org (last visit, April 30, 2017).

2 See DSU Art. 1.1.

be a failure to live up to its obligation (i.e., the breaching country's measure nullify a trade benefit).[3]

The number of disputes since GATT 1947 rules were adopted and, especially, since the WTO was established in 1995, have been considerable and growing.[4] More than 100 panel reports were adopted within the framework of GATT 1947[5] while over 500 disputes have settled since the WTO was established more than 20 years ago.[6] These figures allow their readers to see the glass either half empty or half full. In the former case, the figures would be indicating that countries breach the WTO rules very often. The most prevalent view, however, is the opposite – a big number of cases signal that the DSU is working well and that countries prefer to settle their disputes through this legal mechanism and not through trade retaliation or through other measures, such as political retaliation or, as happened until the nineteenth or even the earlier twentieth centuries, through military force.[7]

Table 36 indicates the number of cases and per country. Not surprisingly, the United States and the European Union, given their economic power and the available resources for trade litigation, are the main contenders in WTO litigation. China numbers are lower taking into account that this country has only been a WTO member since 2001.

The litigation expenses of a WTO dispute might be up to $10.000.000[8]. Top-notch law firms may charge more than $1,000 per hour[9]. The famous cotton litigation between Brazil and the United States is one example of a dispute whose costs were on the seven figures[10]. To put these expenses in perspective, consider that the exports of some WTO Members, such as Djibouti and Dominica, are under one million dollars[11]. Take also into account that the DSU follows the

3 See DSU Arts 1.1, 3.8 and 6.2.

4 See WTO Dispute Settlement, www.wto.org/english/tratop_e/dispu_e/dispu_e.htm (last visit, April 30, 2017).

5 See WTO Dispute Settlement, GATT Report List, Adopted Panel Reports Within the Framework of GATT 1947, www.wto.org/english/tratop_e/dispu_e/gt47ds_e.htm (last visit, April 30, 2017).

6 See WTO Dispute Settlement, The Disputes, Chronological List of Disputed Cases, www.wto.org/english/tratop_e/dispu_e/dispu_status_e.htm (last visit, April 30, 2017).

7 See *supra* note 947.

8 See James C. Hartigan, *Trade Disputes and the Dispute Settlement Understanding of the WTO: An Interdisciplinary Assessment*, p. 222 (2009).

9 See *id.* See also Gregory Shaffer, *How to Make the WTO Dispute Settlement System Work for Developing Countries: Some Proactive Developing Country Strategies*, ICTSD Resource Paper No 5, Geneva (2003); and Chad P. Bown and Bernard M. Hoekman, *WTO Dispute Settlement and the Missing Developing Country Cases: Engaging the Private Sector* 8(4) 861 J. Int'l Econ. L. (2005).

10 See DS267, United States – Subsidies on Upland Cotton. See also Luiz Eduardo Salles, 'Procedures for the Design and Implementation of Trade Retaliation in Brazil', in *The Law, Economics and Politics of Retaliation in WTO Dispute Settlement* (Chad P. Bown and Joost Pauwelyn Eds), p. 297 (2014).

11 See World Bank Data, http://data.worldbank.org/indicator/NE.EXP.GNFS.ZS (last visit, April 30, 2017).

so-called American legal rule, by which each country, regardless of whether it wins or lose the case, pays its own expenses. The high costs of legal proceedings might be one of the reasons why the most common complainants and respondents are the United States, the European Union, China, and other developed WTO Members[12]. While the United States and the European Union are, by far, the main users of the DSU (they are a party in around the 80% of the cases), its joint participation in global trade is only around 40%[13].

Some history about the settlement of international trade disputes is warranted. Before 1947, both substantial and procedural multilateral rules were absent, and, therefore, many disputes were settled by military force (or the threat thereof). This changed when a procedure for settling trade disputes was established under GATT in 1947. These proceedings, however, were ineffective since adopting the decision of a panel required positive consensus or unanimity (including the vote

TABLE 36 Disputes by WTO member as either complainant or respondent[14]

Country	*Complainant*	*Respondent*	*Total*
United States	111	128	239
European Union	97	82	179
Canada	35	18	53
China	13	37	50
Brazil	30	16	46
India	23	23	46
Argentina	20	22	42
Japan	22	15	37
Mexico	23	14	37
Korea	17	16	33
Indonesia	10	14	24
Chile	10	13	23
Australia	7	15	22
Thailand	13	4	17
Other countries	111	114	225
Total	*542*	*531*	*1,073*

12 See WTO Disputes by Country/Territory, www.wto.org/english/tratop_e/dispu_e/dispu_by_country_e.htm (last visit, April 30, 2017).

13 See World Bank Data, available at: http://data.worldbank.org/indicator/NE.EXP.GNFS.ZS (last visit, April 30, 2017).

14 See WTO Dispute Settlement, The Disputes, Disputes by Country/Territory, www.wto.org/english/tratop_e/dispu_e/dispu_by_country_e.htm (last visit, April 30, 2017). Recall, in any event, that WTO Members may also declare that they have an interest in the case and enjoy some procedural rights as third parties. See DSU Art. 10. Countries are individually shown in this table when they have been at least ten times complainants or at least ten times respondents.

of the losing country).[15] As a result, many rulings were easier to block while others did not even reach a panel decision, dragging on as ghosts for a long time.

A better system was approved during the Uruguay Round. Indeed, the DSU is regarded as a quantum leap.[16] It introduced a more structured process, with clearly defined stages and penalties for non-compliance as well.[17] The DSU also introduced greater discipline for the maximum time a case should take to be settled, with flexible deadlines set in various stages of the procedure.[18] More importantly, the DSU, by requiring negative consensus to avoid the adoption of a ruling (including the vote of the winning party) made it impossible for the losing country to block an unfavorable decision.[19] In other words, a ruling is automatically adopted unless there is a consensus to reject it.[20]

The Dispute Settlement Body or DSB, composed of all WTO members, is the body in charge of settling trade disputes.[21] In such capacity, the DSB has the sole authority to establish "panels" of experts to consider the case, to accept or reject the panels' findings or do the same regarding the findings of the Appellate Body (AB) if the losing party appealed the report.[22] The DSB also monitors the implementation of the rulings and recommendations, having the power to authorize retaliation when a country does not comply with a ruling.[23]

14.2 Stages of the dispute settlement process

After having explained the generalities of the DSU, this section now turns to the description of the main stages of the dispute settlement process. The first stage is

15 See GATT 1947. See also Petko D. Kantchevski, *The Differences Between the Panel Procedures of the GATT and the WTO: The Role of GATT and WTO Panels in Trade Dispute Settlement* 3(1) Brigham Young U. Int'l L. & Mgmt. Rev. 82 (2007) ("The adoption of panel reports by positive consensus of all GATT Parties appears contestable, because from a legal perspective, GATT Art. XXV:4 provides, 'except as otherwise provided for in this Agreement, decisions of the CONTRACTING PARTIES shall be taken by a majority of the votes cast.' The agreement does not prescribe any exceptions to this Art.; therefore, in the early years of the GATT, adoption of panel reports required a majority vote. However, in the 1950s, it became a customary practice for Contracting Parties to adopt panel reports by consensus. The Ministerial Declaration of 1982 clarified this procedure, stating that 'PARTIES reaffirmed that consensus will continue to be the traditional method of resolving disputes.'"). Ministerial Decision on Dispute Settlement of 29 November 1982, L/5424, GATT B.I.S.D. (29th Supp.) at 13, (x) (1983).

16 See Judith H. Bello, *Some Practical Observations About WTO Settlement of Intellectual Property Disputes* 37 Va. J. Int'l L. 357–58 (1996–1997).

17 See *id.*

18 See DSU Arts 4 to 20. In particular, see DSU Art. 20, "Unless otherwise agreed to by the parties to the dispute, the period from the date of establishment of the panel by the DSB until the date the DSB considers the panel or appellate report for adoption shall as a general rule not exceed nine months where the panel report is not appealed or 12 months where the report is appealed."

19 See DSU Arts 2.4 and 16.4.

20 See *id.*

21 See DSU Art. 2.1.

22 See *id.*

23 See *id.*

consultations.[24] Before taking any other action, the countries in dispute have to talk to each other to see if they can settle their differences by themselves.[25] This stage may last up to 60 days.[26] If the consultations stage fails, the complaining country may request the establishment of a panel.[27] The DSB has up to 45 days to establish the panel and the appointed experts have up to six months to make their findings (this time is extendable).[28]

The losing party (or both parties if they are dissatisfied with the findings) may appeal the panel's report before the AB.[29] The AB, which can only review possible legal errors but not factual errors, has between 60 and 90 days to make its decision.[30] The DSB, in turn, has other 30 days to adopt the report.[31]

The panel stage is in itself composed of many sub-stages that are worth mentioning in further detail. The first one is the establishment of the panel.[32] Panels are composed of three experts unless the parties to the dispute agree, within ten days from the establishment of the panel, to a panel composed of five panelists.[33] The WTO Secretariat, based on an indicative list of names of governmental and non-governmental individuals,[34] proposes nominations for the panel to the parties to the dispute.[35] Needless to say, potential candidates must meet certain requirements in terms of expertise and independence.[36]

Once the panel has been established, each side submits its case in writing.[37] Then, the first hearing in Geneva is scheduled, when the complaining country, the respondent party, and those countries that have announced that they have an interest in the dispute as third parties, make their cases.[38] Later on, at the panel's second meeting, the parties may submit written rebuttals and present oral arguments.[39] On top of that, if one party raises scientific or other technical matters, the panel may consult experts or appoint an expert review group in order to prepare an advisory report.[40]

After such stages have finished, the panel submits the descriptive sections of its report, containing the factual and argumentative sections, to the two sides, giving them two weeks to make their comments.[41] This report does not include either

24 See DSU Art. 4.
25 See *id.*
26 See *id.*
27 See DSU Art. 6.
28 See *id.*
29 See DSU Art. 16.4.
30 See DSU Art. 17.
31 See *id.*
32 See DSU Art. 5.
33 See DSU Art. 8.5.
34 See DSU Art. 8.4. Since the list is only indicative, other names may be proposed.
35 See DSU Art. 8.6.
36 See DSU Arts 8.1 and 8.2.
37 See DSU Annex 3 Art. 4.
38 See DSU Annex 3 Arts 5–6.
39 See DSU Annex 3 Art. 7.
40 See DSU Annex 3 Art. 13.2.
41 See DSU Art. 15.1

findings or conclusions.[42] After receiving the parties' comments, the panel submits the so-called interim report, which includes findings and conclusions.[43] The parties may ask for a review of such report.[44] During the review period, the panel may hold additional meetings with the two sides.[45] Then, a final report is submitted to the parties and, 3 weeks later, it is circulated to all WTO members.[46] If the panel found that the disputed trade measure does break a WTO agreement or any other obligation, it recommends that the measure be made to conform with the WTO rules (indicating how this could be done).[47] Finally, the panel's report becomes the DSB's ruling or recommendation within 60 days unless a consensus reject it (it has never happened since the WTO was established) or, more likely, any party appeals it.[48]

Appeals have to be based on points of law such as legal construction; i.e., they cannot reexamine existing evidence or examine new issues.[49] The AB may uphold, modify or reverse any of the appealed panel's legal findings and conclusions.[50] Each appeal is heard by three members of a permanent seven-member AB that the DSB sets up and who broadly represent the range of WTO membership.[51] Members of the AB, which have four-year terms,[52] shall be individuals with recognized standing in the field of law and international trade and not affiliated with any government.[53]

If the respondent country loses, it must follow either the panel's or the AB's recommendations, which are usually to abrogate or at least to modify the challenged measure.[54] The losing country shall state its intention to comply with the ruling at a DSB meeting held within 30 days of the report's adoption.[55] If, however, immediate compliance with the recommendation proves impractical, the WTO losing member will be given a "reasonable period of time" to do so.[56] In any event, if the losing party fails to comply with the DSB's recommendations during this grace period, it shall enter into negotiations with the complaining country in order to determine, in a term no longer than 20 days, a mutually acceptable compensation such as tariff reductions in areas of particular interest to the complaining side.[57] If no satisfactory compensation is agreed on, the complaining party may ask the DSB permission to impose limited trade sanctions

42 See *id.*
43 See DSU Art. 15.2.
44 See *id.*
45 See *id.*
46 See DSU Annex 3 Art. 12(k).
47 See DSU Art. 19.
48 See DSU Art. 16.
49 See DSU Art. 17.6.
50 See DSU Art. 17.13.
51 See DSU Art. 17.1.
52 See DSU Art. 17.2.
53 See DSU Art. 17.3.
54 See DSU Art. 19.1.
55 See DSU Art. 21.3.
56 See *id.*
57 See DSU Art. 22.2.

(i.e., to suspend concessions or obligations) against the other side.[58] The DSB must grant this authorization within 30 days of the expiry of the "reasonable period of time" unless there is a consensus against the request.[59]

In principle, trade sanctions should be in the same sector that gave rise to the dispute.[60] If, however, this is not practical or effective (i.e., the imports of other goods from the complaining country in the same sectors are very low), the sanctions may be imposed in a different sector of the same agreement (i.e., GATT, GATS or TRIPS).[61] If, again, this is not practicable or effective, and if the circumstances are serious enough, the action can be taken under any other agreement, under what is known as cross-retaliation.[62] In any event, the DSB monitors how adopted rulings are implemented and any outstanding case remains on its agenda until the issue is resolved.[63] Figure 20 summarizes the dispute settlement process that was described in the previous paragraphs.

14.3 The ups and downs of the DSU

Generally speaking, the DSU has been considered successful; indeed, as already mentioned, it has been referred to as the jewel of the crown (the WTO being, naturally, the crown).[64] The main indicator of this success is the fact that, in most cases, the losing country complies with either the panel or the AB report without additional procedures.[65] In the first ten years of the WTO, for instance, the compliance rate was estimated at 83 percent.[66] During recent years such compliance rate has been even higher, around 90 percent.[67] Indeed,

> WTO dispute settlement experience to date does not suggest that responding members have a manifestly worse record of compliance with DSB rulings in cases where the complaining member was a small or developing country than in cases where the complaining member was another developed country.[68]

58 See DSU Art. 22.2. See generally Chad P. Bown and Joost Pauwelyn, *The Law, Economics and Politics of Retaliation in WTO Dispute Settlement* (2014).

59 See DSU Art. 22.2.

60 See DSU Art. 22.3(a).

61 See DSU Art. 22.3(b).

62 See DSU Art. 22.3(c).

63 See DSU Art. 21.6.

64 See *supra* note 59. See also Peter Van Den Bossche, *The Law and Policy of the World Trade Organization* (2nd ed.) p. 308 (Cambridge University Press, 2010) (reminding that the DSU has been successful).

65 William J. Davey, *The WTO Dispute Settlement System: The First Ten Years*, 8 J. Int'l Econ. L. 17, 46–48 (2005).

66 See *id.*

67 See Hunter Nottage, 'Evaluating the Criticism that WTO Retaliation Rules Undermine the Utility of WTO Dispute Settlement for Developing Countries', in *The Law, Economics and Politics of Retaliation in WTO Dispute Settlement* (Chad P. Bown and Joost Pauwelyn Eds) p. 320 (2014).

68 See *id.* at 327.

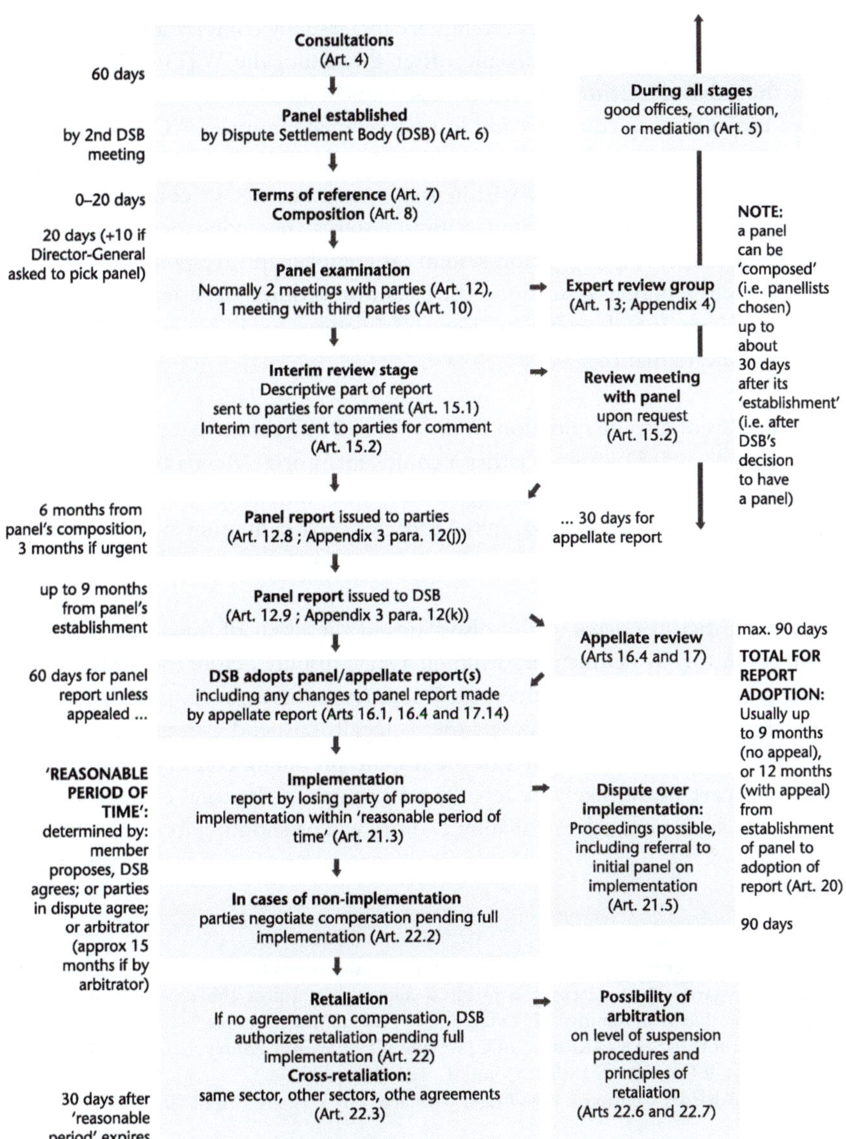

FIGURE 20 The dispute settlement process[69]

There are, however, some criticisms of the DSU. The main criticism is related to the hurdles that the DSU imposes to developing and least-developed countries.[70]

69 Figure made by the authors.

70 See Andrea Ewart, *Small Developing State in the WTO: A Procedural Approach to Special and Differential Treatment Through Reforms to Dispute Settlement* 35 Syracuse J. Int'l L. & Commerce 27 (2007), "Paradoxically, the move toward a more judicial system of dispute

Such hurdles exist because proceedings are increasingly complex and, as a result, ever more expensive.[71] To partially offset this issue, the WTO established in 2001 the Advisory Centre on WTO Law,[72] whose main purpose is to give legal advice to developing countries and least developed countries.[73] On top of that, developing countries, and particularly least-developed countries, have a reduced human and technical capital within their governments in comparison with developed countries.[74] A related criticism states that countries that do not participate in the WTO litigation system (as complainants, respondents or third parties) face a bigger cost since they cannot acquire experience regarding the proceedings (i.e., learning by doing).[75] In this regard, Professors Davis and Bermeo indicate that the

> analysis of dispute initiation from 1975 to 2003 shows that past experience in trade adjudication, as either a complainant or a defendant, increases the likelihood that a developing country will initiate disputes. As weaker countries overcome these initial capacity constraints they will increasingly benefit from the international legal structures they have joined.[76]

A second criticism relates to the disparities in the levels of trade among WTO members. A tiny WTO member winning a legal dispute before the DSU, whose losing party (suppose it is a developed country) refuses to voluntarily comply, might face big challenges finding how to legally suspend concessions (i.e., to retaliate).[77] After all, the imports of the dispute-prevailing country coming from its counterpart would likely be less than 1 percent of the total exports of such country. In such a case, the retaliating country will be shooting its own foot since

settlement under the WTO has heightened the disadvantages the developing countries face in this regard. Most patently, a juridical approach requires the use of professionals knowledgeable in substantive WTO law and WTO/DSM procedures."

71 See *supra* note 9. See also Kristin Bohl, *Problems of Developing Country Access to WTO Dispute Settlement*, 9 Chi-Kent J. Int'l & Comp. L. 131, 146 (2009).

72 See The Advisory Centre on WTO Law, www.acwl.ch/ (last visit, April 30, 2017).

73 See *id.*

74 For instance, the USTR has about thirty senior officers, plus a significant quantity of other employees. See The USTR, https://ustr.gov/about-us/biographies-key-officials (last visit, April 30, 2017).

75 See Kristin Bohl, *Problems of Developing Country Access to WTO Dispute Settlement*, 9 Chi-Kent J. Int'l & Comp. L. 131, 146 (2009).

76 Christina L. Davis and Sarah B. Bermeo, *Who Files? Developing Country Participation in GATT/WTO Adjudication* 71(3) J. Politics 1033 (2009).

77 See generally Hunter Nottage, 'Evaluating the Criticism that WTO Retaliation Rules Undermine the Utility of WTO Dispute Settlement for Developing Countries', in *The Law, Economics and Politics of Retaliation in WTO Dispute Settlement* (Chad P. Bown and Joost Pauwelyn Eds), p. 320 (2014). In any event, retaliation is rare. Nottage found that, out of sixty cases where retaliation was possible, it was requested only in seventeen cases and authorized by the DSB only in nine cases. See *id.*

the suspension of concessions will be harmful for it but insignificant for its counterpart.[78] This might have happened in the famous gambling case United States – Measures Affecting the Cross-Border Supply of Gambling and Betting Services, the poster case of least developed countries.[79] In such a case, Antigua and Barbuda requested the establishment of a panel contending that some U.S. measures affect the cross-border supply of gambling and betting services and were against the GATS agreement.[80] The AB affirmed the panel's finding that the United States acted inconsistently with some GATS provisions by enacting certain restrictions on market access not specified in its schedule.[81] When the DSB granted Antigua and Barbuda to suspend concessions,[82] this tiny country found that

> [c]easing all trade whatsoever with the United States (approximately US$180 million annually, or less than 0.02 percent of all exports from the United States) would have virtually no impact on the economy of the United States, which could easily shift such a relatively small volume of trade elsewhere.[83]

Another illustration of the issues that some developing countries that prevail in WTO litigation might have at the time of securing compliance with a panel's report by suspending concessions is the case European Communities – Regime for the Importation, Sale and Distribution of Bananas,[84] where the arbitrator in charge of the compliance recourse recognized that

> given the fact that Ecuador, as a small developing country, only accounts for a negligible proportion of the EC's exports of these products, the suspension of concessions is unlikely to have any significant effect on demand for these EC exports.[85]

78 See Hunter Nottage, 'Evaluating the Criticism that WTO Retaliation Rules Undermine the Utility of WTO Dispute Settlement for Developing Countries', in *The Law, Economics and Politics of Retaliation in WTO Dispute Settlement* (Chad P. Bown and Joost Pauwelyn Eds), p. 320 (2014).

79 See DS285, United States – Measures Affecting the Cross-Border Supply of Gambling and Betting Services. See *infra* Chapter 16.

80 See *id.*

81 See *id.*

82 See *id.*

83 See Hunter Nottage, 'Evaluating the Criticism that WTO Retaliation Rules Undermine the Utility of WTO Dispute Settlement for Developing Countries', in *The Law, Economics and Politics of Retaliation in WTO Dispute Settlement* (Chad P. Bown and Joost Pauwelyn Eds), p. 320 (2014).

84 See DS27, European Communities – Regime for the Importation, Sale and Distribution of Bananas.

85 DS285, United States – Measures Affecting the Cross-Border Supply of Gambling and Betting Services. See also Robert E. Hudec, 'The Adequacy of WTO Dispute Settlement

A third criticism contends that the system is incomplete since either the panel or the AB recommends to the losing country to derogate the challenged measure but it is not compelled to reimburse the damages that such measure caused to other countries while it was in legal force (i.e., the only legal remedy under the DSU is the abrogation of the measure – an injunction or an equivalent to a cease and desist order, and there are no monetary damages).[86] On top of that there is no specific performance, i.e., the losing country might choose between complying with the panel or AB report or accepting the suspension of concessions.[87] While this criticism might be valid, it is worth remembering that international treaties, as the product of complex political, legal and economic negotiations, are not intended to be perfect but just to include feasible solutions. Thus, the current regime is preferable, albeit incomplete, to the previous one when the approval of any decision required positive consensus or the regime existing before GATT 1997, which was based on political and military power.

Two famous cases illustrate the dispute settlement process and, in particular, the fact that the proceedings can be very time consuming: (i) United States – Standards for Reformulated and Conventional Gasoline (the gasoline case),[88] and (ii) United States – Subsidies on Upland Cotton (the cotton case).[89] In the gasoline case, Venezuela requested the establishment of a panel arguing that some U.S. gasoline regulations were in breach of GATT Arts I and III and the TBT Agreement Art. 2. In the cotton case, in turn, Brazil contended that some subsidies that the United States granted to producers, users and/or exporters of upland cotton, as well as the legal rules providing such subsidies, were inconsistent with some provisions of GATT, the SCM Agreement and the Agreement on Agriculture.

In any event, the purpose of this part of the text is not to analyze in detail such cases but to show how some disputes under the DSU might be very protracted and complex. For that purpose, Table 37 summarizes the timeline of the gasoline case while Table 38 does the same in respect of the cotton case.

Remedies: A Developing Country Perspective', in *Development, Trade and the WTO* (Bernard Hoekman, Aaditya Mattoo and Philip English Eds), Washington, D.C., World Bank.

86 See Alan O. Sykes, 'Optimal Sanctions in the WTO: The Case for Decoupling (and the Uneasy Case for the Status Quo)', in *The Law, Economics and Politics of Retaliation in WTO Dispute Settlement* (Chad P. Bown and Joost Pauwelyn Eds), p. 339 (2014).

87 Pascal Lamy, former WTO Director, stated, when he was Commissioner for Trade at the European Commission, that "[a]s long as you pay the penalties, you can go on." See Marco C.E. J. Bronckers, *More Power to the WTO?* 4(41) J. Int'l Econ. L. 60 (2001).

88 See DS2, United States – Standards for Reformulated and Conventional Gasoline.

89 See DS267, United States – Subsidies on Upland Cotton.

TABLE 37 Timetable of the gasoline case

Time (0 = start of the case)	*Target / actual period*	*Date*	*Action*
–5 years		1990	U.S. Clean Air Act amended
–4 months		September 1994	The U.S. restricts gasoline imports under Clean Air Act
0	60 days	January 23, 1993	Venezuela complains to DSB and asks for consultations
+1 month		February 24, 1995	Consultations take place and fail
+2 months		March 25, 1995	Venezuela asks DSB to establish a panel
+2 ½ months	30 days	April 10, 1995	DSB agrees to appoint a panel. U.S. does not block it. Brazil starts complaint and request consultations with the U.S.
+3 months		April 28, 1995	Panel appointed. Panel was assigned to Brazil on May 31, 1995
+6 months	9 months (target is 6–9 months)	July 10–12 and July 13–15, 1995	Panel meets
+11 months		December 11, 1995	Panel gives interim report to the parties for comments
+1 year		January 29, 1996	Panel circulates final report to DSB
+1 year, 1 month		February 21, 1996	U.S. appeals
+1 year, 3 months	60 days	April 29, 1996	AB submits report
+1 year, 4 months	30 days	May 20, 1996	DSB adopts panel and appeal's report
+1 year, 10 ½ months		December 3, 1996	The U.S. and Venezuela agree on what the U.S. should do
+1 year, 11 ½ months		January 9, 1997	The U.S. makes first of monthly reports to DSB on status of implementation
2 years 7 months		August 19–20, 1997	The U.S. and Venezuela signs new regulation. End of agreed implementation period

TABLE 38 Timetable of the cotton case

Time (0 = start of the case)	*Date*	*Action*
0	September 27, 2002	Brazil complains to DSB and asks for consultations
+4 months	February 6, 2003	Brazil requests the DSB the establishment of a panel
+6 months	March 18, 2003	DSB agrees to appoint a panel
+8 months	May 19, 2003	Panel appointed
+2 years	September 8, 2004	Panel circulates the report to WTO members
+2 years, 1 month	October 18, 2004	The U.S. appeals
+2 years, 4 months	March 3, 2005	AB submits report
+2 years, 5 months	March 21, 2005	DSB adopts panel and appeal's reports
+2 years, 7 months	April 20, 2005	The U.S. states its intention to comply with the recommendations
+2 years, 9 months	July 4, 2005	Brazil requests authorization to suspend concessions in respect of the prohibited subsidies
+2 years, 9 ½ months	July 14, 2005	The U.S. submits its objection to the Brazilian requests for authorization
+2 years, 9 ½ months	July 15, 2005	DSB refers the matter to arbitration
+2 years, 10 months	August 17, 2005	Brazil and the U.S. requests suspension of the arbitration proceedings
+3 years	October 6, 2005	Brazil requests authorization to suspend concessions in respect of the actionable subsidies
+3 years, 1/2 month	October 17, 2005	The U.S. submits its objections to the Brazilian request for authorization
+3 years, 1/2 month	October 18, 2005	DSB refers the matter to arbitration
+3 years, 2 months	November 21, 2005	Brazil and the U.S. requests suspension of the arbitration proceedings
+3 years, 10 ½ months	August 18, 2006	Brazil requests the establishment of a compliance panel
+3 years, 11 months	September 1, 2006	DSB defers the establishment of a compliance panel
+4 years	September 28, 2006	DSB agrees, if possible, to refer the matter to the original panel
+4 years, 1 month	October 25, 2006	Compliance panel appointed
+4 years, 10 ½ months	July 27, 2007	Panel gives interim report to the U.S. and Brazil
+4 years, 11 months	October 15, 2007	Compliance panel confidentially releases the official version of its ruling
+5 years, 5 months	February 12, 2008	The U.S. notifies its intention to appeal the reports
+5 years, 5 months	February 25, 2008	Brazil notifies its intention to appeal the report
+5 years, 9 months	June 2, 2008	Panel circulates the final reports
+7 years, 2 months	August 25, 2010	Brazil and the U.S. agree on framework for a mutually agreed solution
Total = 11+ years	October 1, 2014	Brazil and the U.S. reach an agreement

14.4 The settlement of disputes under PTAs

The Dispute Settlement Understanding (DSU), the jewel in the crown of the multilateral trade system,[90] is not the only path to settle international trade disputes since most preferential trade agreements include provisions on such topic. Currently, there are three systems to settle disputes under PTAs.[91] The first one is the settlement of disputes through diplomatic or political channels.[92] This system, very common in PTAs that the European Union negotiated during most of the twentieth century, is very unusual nowadays.[93] A second system, sometimes used in customs unions, consists of a permanent tribunal in charge of settling both trade and non-trade disputes, such as the European Court of Justice[94] or the MERCOSUR dispute settlement system.[95] The third and most common system, NAFTA and CAFTA-DR being two illustrations, allows the establishment of panels governed by rules that are similar to those applicable under the DSU.[96]

Nowadays, this third system faces two salient issues. On the one hand, and in spite of few recent disputes settled under some trade agreements, such as the so-called CAFTA-DR,[97] dispute settlement rules under PTAs have not often been resorted to.

On the other hand, and more often than it is desirable, this third system allows a PTA member, or more precisely, the complainant party, to choose between the rules that such agreement provides regarding the settlement of disputes and the WTO rules (i.e., the DSU).[98] For instance, NAFTA provides that disputes

90 Pascal Lamy, former WTO Director-General, was the first individual to use the words "jewel of the crown" to refer to the DSU. See *WTO Disputes Reach 400 Mark*, WTO, Press Release, 6 November 2009, www.wto.org (last visit, February 20, 2017).

91 See Amelia Porges, 'Dispute Settlement', in *Preferential Trade Agreements, Policies for Development, A Handbook* (Jean-Pierre Chauffour and Jean-Christophe Maur Eds), p. 467.

92 See *id.*

93 See *id.*

94 See John Jackson, William Davey and Alan O. Sykes, *Legal Problems of International Economic Relations* p. 150 (2013). Indeed, EU Members shall litigate their disputes before this court. See Tomer Broude, 'From Pax Mercatoria to Pax Europea: How Trade Dispute Procedures Serve the EC's Regional Hegemony', in *Economics of European Union Law* (Paul B. Stephan Ed.) p. 319 (2007), also available at Bepress Legal Series Working Paper 650 (http://law.bepress.com/expresso/eps/650 (last visit, February 20, 2017).

95 See ECLAC, *Dispute Settlement Within the Southern Common Market (MERCOSUR)* https://idatd.cepal.org/soluciones/iTemplate-MERCOSUR-explicacion.pdf (last visit, May 9, 2017).

96 See Porges, *supra* note 91, at 475.

97 See (i) Costa Rica – Tariffs on Tires, Juices and Canned Tuna (2014); and (ii) In the Matter of Guatemala – Issues Relating to the Obligations Under Art. 16.2.1(a) of the CAFTA-DR (2015).

98 See John Jackson, William Davey and Alan O. Sykes, *Legal Problems of International Economic Relations,* p. 516 (2013).

arising out of this treaty and also out of the WTO rules might be settled under any of these two fora, whichever the complainant party prefers.[99] Naturally, this choice requires that all parties to the dispute are members of both the respective PTA and the WTO and that both kinds of legal rules govern the disputed topic.[100]

That a complaining party may choose the forum has some drawbacks. To begin with, such choice prevents the unification of the case law since very similar disputes might be settled by different tribunals governed by different substantive and procedural rules.[101] Second, this choice gives the complainant party an unjustified advantage since it can select the more favorable forum. Indeed, there are significant differences between the WTO rules and PTA's rules in topics such as panelist's rosters, the requirement that they shall comply (e.g., expertise, nationality, code of conduct, etc.), the proceedings to follow when one of the parties does not appoint a panelist, the third-parties' participation, and rules on transparency.[102]

Third, the existence of two fora triggers the risk of a complainant litigating a dispute in one forum, for example, the PTA forum, and, later on, the loser making a claim before the other forum (e.g., the WTO forum, recalling that this is, pursuant to DSU Art. 23, a mandatory forum).[103] This is not an unlikely possibility considering that there is no legal rule prohibiting a panel or the Appellate Body from holding that it does have jurisdiction to hear a case that a PTA's arbitral

99 See NAFTA Arts 2005.6 and 2005.7. There are, however, some exceptions. For instance, if the dispute is about environmental issues, the settlement cannot be before a WTO Panel. See NAFTA Arts 104 and 2005(3). Other treaties allowing to choose the forum are, among others, the U.S. trade agreements with Colombia (Art. 21.3) and with Chile (Art. 22.3). *Cfr.* PTA between Chile and the European Union Art. 189.4 (providing that if a dispute arises out of the non-compliance of a legal obligation under the treaty that is substantially equivalent to an obligation under the WTO, the only legal forum is the DSU). See also DSU Art. 23 (providing that the WTO is the mandatory forum for disputes arising out of the interpretation and performance of WTO legal rules). See generally Porges, *supra* note 91, at 477; and Ignacio García Bercero, 'Dispute Settlement in European Union Free Trade Agreements: Lessons Learned?' in *Regional Trade Agreements and the WTO Legal System* (Lorand Bartels and Federico Ortino Eds) (2006).

100 See Fernando Piérola and Gary Horlick, *WTO Dispute Settlement and Dispute Settlement in the "North-South" Agreements of the Americas: Considerations for Choice of Forum* 41 J. World Trade 883, 893 (2007).

101 See Porges, *supra* note 91, at 477.

102 See *id.* Generally speaking, the procedural rules providing for more expedited proceedings might be more favorable for the complaining party. See *id.*

103 See DSU Art. 23. The opposite case is more unlikely since most PTAs give complaining parties the choice of forum but, once such a choice is made, going to the other forum is not allowed. See Piérola and Horlick, *supra* note 100, at 898; and Jean-Pierre Chauffour and Jean-Christophe Maur, 'Overview', in *Preferential Trade Agreements, Policies for Development, A Handbook* (Jean-Pierre Chauffour and Jean-Christophe Maur Eds), p. 16.

tribunal has already settled.[104] Such possibility, of course, increases not only the already very high costs of litigating trade disputes but also the time that some governments' officials might spend on such cases. Regarding the costs of litigating a WTO case, they might be up to $10,000,000.[105] In respect of the wasted time, such resource is of critical importance for all countries but, in particular, for some developing and least-developed countries whose trade offices are short-staffed for either budget reasons or a shortage of well-trained human capital.

Indeed, the double litigation indicated above has already happened. In the most famous case, Brazil challenged an Argentinian measure restricting its poultry exports before a Mercosur tribunal.[106] This tribunal held that Mercosur rules did not govern the challenged measure and, therefore, it was not inconsistent with Argentinian legal obligations under this customs union.[107] Brazil, unhappy with such an outcome, successfully requested the establishment of a panel under the WTO rules, which concluded that the measure was in breach of the WTO antidumping agreement.[108]

In a similar case, Brazil successfully challenged an Argentinian safeguard measure before a Mercosur tribunal without Argentina immediately complying with the award. The case was only settled after Brazil started legal proceedings before the WTO.[109] In a third case, involving other WTO members, Mexico levied taxes on some kinds of beverages coming from the United States, who claimed that such measure was imposed as retaliation for the U.S. refusing to integrate a panel under NAFTA rules in a dispute related to exports of Mexican sugar.[110] The United States successfully challenged such measure before the WTO claiming that the principle of national treatment had been breached.[111] A fourth case was a dispute between the United States and Canada about trade in lumber where a

104 Nonetheless, some PTA expressly prohibits litigating twice the same case (e.g., the trade agreements that the United States has entered into after NAFTA). See Porges, *supra* note 91, at 477.

105 See James C. Hartigan, *Trade Disputes and the Dispute Settlement Understanding of the WTO: An Interdisciplinary Assessment,* p. 222 (2009).

106 See Arbitral Award on the dispute between Brazil and Argentine on the application of antidumping measures against the export of poultry coming from Brazil (Res. 574/2000 of the Argentinian Ministry of Finance dated on May 21, 2001).

107 See *id.*

108 See Panel Report Argentina – Definitive Antidumping Duties on Poultry from Brazil – WT/DS241R adopted on May 19, 2003. See also Porges, *supra* note 91, at 477. The Protocol of Olivos of 2002 solved this issue by prohibiting Mercosur Members from re-litigating a case before the WTO. See *id.*, p. 477.

109 See *id.*, p. 477.

110 See William J. Davey and André Sapir, *The Soft Drinks Case: The WTO and the Regional Agreements* 8 World Trade Rev. 5, 21 note 78 (2009).

111 See GATT Art. III. See also Mexico – Tax Measures on Soft Drinks and Other Beverages WT/AB/R DS-308 (report adopted on March 24, 2006). See also Michael Trebilcock and Robert Howse, *The Regulation of International Trade* (4th ed.) p. 125 (2012), and Davey and Sapir, *supra* note 110, at 16–17.

tribunal under NAFTA and the Appellate Body under the WTO rules reached opposing conclusions.[112]

Some statistics indicate that countries belonging to a PTA prefer to settle a significant percentage of their disputes through the WTO forum and not through their respective trade agreement. NAFTA is a clear illustration of such trend. Before such agreement entered into legal force, some experts had predicted that its members would prefer the WTO forum.[113] So far, such prediction has proved right: only three disputes have been solved under NAFTA tribunals while, at the same time, its members have settled more than 35 regional disputes (i.e., among them) before the DSU.[114]

A similar situation occurs regarding other geographical zones.[115] Professor Yan Luo indicates that since 1996, when the ASEAN dispute settlement procedures were enacted, and until at least 2005, not a single case had been solved under this forum.[116] Indeed, and at least until 2011, the seven-member appellate body of such organization, in accordance with the protocol establishing such dispute settlement system, had not yet been appointed.[117] Likewise, Professor Junji Nakagawa, after analyzing dispute settlement among Southeastern Asian countries, successfully predicted in 2007 that the majority of disputes among them would be litigated before the WTO.[118] The outlook is similar in Latin America, where, according to Professor Sebastián Sáez, countries prefer to use the WTO settlement proceedings and not their PTA's procedural rules.[119]

112 See United States – Final Countervailing Duty Determination with respect to certain Softwood Lumber from Canada WT/AB/R/257 (adopted on February 17 2004). See also Piérola and Horlick, WTO, p. 891.

113 See William Davey, *Pine & Swine: Canada – United States Trade Dispute Settlement, the FTA Experience and NAFTA Prospects*, Ottawa, Centre for Trade Policy and Law (1996).

114 See Davey and Sapir, *supra* note 110, at 21. See also WTO Dispute Settlement: The Disputes, Chronological List of Disputed Cases, www.wto.org/english/tratop_e/dispu_e/dispu_status_e.htm (last visit, February 20, 2017). At least two of these disputes arose out the PTA between the United States and Canada before the establishment of the WTO in 1994. That under the original GATT 1947 a positive consensus was required to adopt a report might have influenced the regional and not the multilateral settlement of such cases. They would likely had been litigated before the WTO should they had happened after 1995, where the rule of negative consensus was enacted. See Porges, *supra* note 91, at 492; and Davey and Sapir, *supra* note 110, at 21.

115 See Yan Luo, *Dispute Settlement in the Proposed East Asian Free Trade Agreement: What We Can Learn from the EU and the NAFTA*. Presentation made in the ILA British Branch Spring 2005 Conference, Edinburgh, Scotland (available at: www.hss.ed.ac.uk/ila/Day2.htm) (last visit, February 20, 2017).

116 See *id.*

117 See Porges, *supra* note 91, at 481.

118 See Junji Nakagawa, *No More Negotiated Deals? Settlement of Trade and Investment Disputes in East Asia*, 10 (4) J. Int'l Econ. L. 837 (2007).

119 See Sebastián Sáez, *The Countries of Latin America and the Caribbean and Trade Disputes: An Analysis.* Bulletin FAL 249 (2007). As an exception, take into account that an important number of cases have been solved under the Mercosur and CAN rules. Indeed, CAN

Members both of the WTO and of at least a PTA prefer to settle their disputes before the DSU and not before the respective PTA panel on several grounds. First, the large WTO case law, of over 500 cases and going back almost 70 years if proceedings under GATT 1947 are taken into account, generates predictability about the possible outcome of a dispute.[120] In particular and in spite of the fact that there is no *stare decisis* under the DSU, the role of the Appellate Body in the WTO,[121] contributes to a positive role of the case law.[122] By contrast, not only the case law under PTAs is very scarce but also courts of appeals are a rarity.[123] As a result, the outcome of a given case under this forum is more unpredictable.[124]

As a second reason, the third-parties' participation, allowed under the WTO rules but restricted or even prohibited under most PTAs, makes the WTO forum more favorable in this regard (although it might be more expensive and lengthy vis-à-vis the same litigation under a regional forum). After all, such participation facilitates coalitions during the proceedings, which is particularly useful for countries with small trade disputes against major players, such as the United States, the European Union or China.[125] On top of that, this third-party participation may increase the economic and political pressure for amicably settling the dispute (i.e., reaching an agreement) or, after one of the parties have been defeated, for complying without major delay with either the panel or the Appellate Body report.[126]

Third, it is easier to secure the participation of neutral panelists under a WTO forum than under a PTA forum, where the lists are usually restricted to individuals from PTA members. This is a complex issue when the number of PTA members

Members have never settled any dispute among them before the WTO. See Piérola and Horlick, *supra* note 100, at 903, and Andrew L. Stoler, 'TBT and SPS Measures in Practice', in *Preferential Trade Agreements, Policies for Development, A Handbook* (Jean-Pierre Chauffour and Jean-Christophe Maur Eds), The World Bank, Washington, D.C., 2011, pp. 230–31.

120 See Peter Drahos, *The Bilateral Web of Trade Dispute Settlement*, Paper for the workshop on WTO Dispute Settlement and Developing Countries: Use, Implications, Strategies, Reforms, University of Wisconsin at Madison, 20-1, 2005, p. 11.

121 See DSU Art. 17. See also United States – Definitive Antidumping and Countervailing Duties on Certain Products from China, WT/DS379/AB/R, p. 325.

122 See Piérola and Horlick, *supra* note 100, at 891.

123 See Chauffour and Maur, *supra* note 119, at 16.

124 See Piérola and Horlick, *supra* note 100, at 891, 899.

125 See Michael Trebilcock and Robert Howse, *The Regulation of International Trade* (4th ed.) 189–90 (2012). Participation of third parties may be so relevant that some experts have proposed, in order to improve transparency standards, that they may be part of disputes under a PTA forum. See Davey and Sapir, *supra* note 110, at 23. Such proposal, however, seems unfeasible because it would not make sense that third parties may be part of a process discussing legal rules that do not affect them.

126 See Piérola and Horlick, *supra* note 100, at 889–90. But see Davey and Sapir, *supra* note 100, at 19 (contending that third party participation increases the litigation cost, reduces the likelihood of a negotiated solution, and lengthen the litigation time).

is just two or three.[127] On a related note, a country using delaying tactics might have a higher likelihood of blocking the establishment of a panel under a PTA[128] than under the WTO.[129] Under the latter forum, a panel is established unless there is consensus for not doing that; since such consensus requires the vote of the complainant, it never happens.[130] Fourth, in disputes under the WTO, countries may have access to legal assistance, such support is non-existent or minimum under the PTA (with the possible exception of NAFTA).[131]

Taking into account the issues described above, and in particular, the problems arising out of the possibilities that complainant parties have to choose one forum over another, one of the authors of this book has proposed, given the success of the DSU, that the WTO multilateral system has mandatory jurisdiction over disputes arising out of the interpretation or the performance of PTA's provisions.[132]

On the alternative, if this proposal is not politically feasible in the short-term, and as a second-best solution, this author has proposed elsewhere that dispute settlement procedures under PTAs should be subject to at least two amendments. First, and once a forum (either the DSU or a panel under the respective PTA) has been chosen, the issue shall not be re-litigated under the other forum. Second, and without prejudice of both the due process and the transparency principles, the procedures should be streamlined, restricting the number of issues, the length of briefs and the participation of *amicus curiae* in order to make PTA's procedures more competitive vis-à-vis litigation under the DSU and, consequently, to increase the pressure on the latter system to adopt more efficient procedures in accordance with some recent proposals such as the so-called DDG Brauner's Informal "DS Efficiency Process"[133] as well as Canada's DSB Proposal for an Informal Framework

127 See Trebilcock and Howse, *supra* note 125, at 187.

128 For NAFTA cases where such strategy paid off, see USA-98-2008-1 (about some U.S. legal rules preventing Mexican-owned trucking firms for operating in U.S. border states), CDA-95-1904-04 (about some antidumping duties that Canada levied on sugar imports coming from the United States), and MEX-98-1904-01 (about some antidumping duties that Mexico levied on some syrup coming from the United States). See also Piérola and Horlick, *supra* note 100, at 883, 893 n. 49; and Davey and Sapir, *supra* note 110, at 5.

129 See DSU Art. 6.1. See also Piérola and Horlick, *supra* note 100, at 883, 893 n. 49.

130 See *id.*

131 See Piérola and Horlick, *supra* note 100, at 898.

132 See Juan Antonio Gaviria, *Una Propuesta de Expansión del Sistema de Solución de Controversias de la OMC como Contrapeso a la Tendencia Creciente de los Tratados de Comercio Preferencial* [*A Case for Expanding the WTO Dispute Settlement System as a Counterweight to the Growing Trend of Preferential Trade Agreements*], 4 Rev. D. Econ. Int'l 1 (2013).

133 See WTO Dispute Settlement Body, Minutes of meeting held in the Centre William Rappard on August 31, 2015, "[T]o some extent, when more Members burdened the Secretariat and the panelists with bigger briefs, covering more issues, requiring more time and attention, there was an inevitable domino effect that led to the unavailability of resources for later cases in the line-up. That had triggered some discussion, as was mentioned among the major

for Procedural DSU Innovation.[134] Thus, and under the incentive of competition, both systems for the settlement of international trade disputes might converge to procedural rules more suitable for the salient issues and trends that nowadays affect trade among nations.

users, regarding whether Members themselves could do something to help to contribute to a more streamlined process. This could be either voluntarily between the parties or by agreement on best practices or potentially procedurally, and ultimately, referred to the DSU negotiations for consideration.

134 See WTO Dispute Settlement Body, Minutes of meeting held in the Centre William Rappard on June 22, 2016, "[I]n response to both the workload challenges that were causing delays, and taking into account the deadlock in efforts to modify formally the DSU, Canada was, at the present meeting, proposing a different approach to developing new practices and procedures in the conduct of WTO disputes. Canada's approach was to create an informal framework for the development of procedural innovation that could take place both outside the bilateral context of specific disputes, and outside the multilateral context of discussions of changes to the DSU that would be binding on all Members. Using this framework, groups of Members would commit to trying out new ideas only with other Members who were also prepared to try them out. By agreeing to these changes outside of specific disputes, the pressure and opportunity to seek litigation advantage in a specific dispute was minimized. Anything these willing Members agreed to do in disputes with each other would not be binding on Members who were not yet comfortable trying the new approaches. If certain practices did not work, or were not as beneficial as originally envisaged, they could simply be abandoned by those who had proposed and had experimented with them. On the other hand, if they did work, in the longer run it would build confidence in their feasibility, could be expanded to other Members, and could eventually facilitate the codification in the DSU, once agreed by all Members."

15

TRADE AGREEMENTS

Chapter 15 discusses the preferential trade agreements (PTAs) or, in short, the agreements, that countries negotiate in order to maximize the gains from international trade.[1] As an introductory note, take into account that the correct term is preferential trade agreements and not free trade agreements since complete free trade (i.e., international trade without any tariff or any other barriers) still does not exist, while trade preferences do.

This chapter will first analyze the various types of trade agreements, such as bilateral trade agreements, regional trade agreements, plurilateral trade agreements and multilateral trade agreements. In sequence, the chapter will discuss regionalism vis-à-vis multilateralism, using the cases that the building block and the stumbling block theories make.

15.1 Why countries seek trade agreements

The first question is what are the reasons that lead countries to negotiate trade agreements. As mentioned at the beginning of this book,[2] and in accordance with the theory of competitive advantage, trade is a win-win situation for countries since they can focus on manufacturing the goods in which they are more efficient and import from other countries the remaining goods, that can be more efficiently produced abroad than at home. Of course, trade agreements are not good for everybody in the country signing a trade agreement. After all, some sectors (e.g., the industrial one) might benefit from the agreement while other sectors (e.g., the agricultural one) might suffer. Thus, a trade agreement is

1 See *supra* Chapter 1.

2 See *supra* Chapter 1.

not Pareto efficient.[3] This is why there is usually fierce opposition from some sectors to some trade agreements.[4]

Nonetheless, and after a trade agreement has been negotiated, the sectors that obtain gains from it might transfer part of them to the government (e.g., via taxes), which, in turn, will transfer such money to the harmed sectors (e.g., via subsidies). If the gains are higher than the losses and if such transfer is possible, the trade agreement will be efficient from the so-called Kaldor-Hicks perspective.[5]

If trade agreements are efficient, a second question arises: why are not all trade agreements negotiated at the multilateral level? Indeed, and nowadays, the trend is to negotiate trade agreements at the bilateral, regional or plurilateral level and not at the multilateral level, where only one agreement has been signed (the TFA Agreement) since the end of the Uruguay Round. The answer is not so difficult and is related to an economic term: transaction costs. These costs are the expenses, not only in money but also in time or measured as a political cost, of negotiating, executing, performing and enforcing agreements.[6] Needless to say, it is far easier to reach an agreement when the parties are very few (e.g., two) than when the parties are 164 members, as in the WTO.[7] The next section explains in detail the kinds of trade agreements and their main features.

15.2 International trade agreements

Preferential trade agreements might be of four kinds: (i) multilateral, (ii) plurilateral, (iii) regional, and (iv) bilateral. Multilateral agreements are those negotiated in the WTO Forum. Plurilateral trade agreements, as its name suggests, are those negotiated and executed among many (at least more than two) non-neighboring countries. One of the most relevant illustrations, nowadays, is the Trans-Pacific Partnership or TPP, a trade agreement among 12 countries from the Pacific Rim whose negotiations officially ended in New Zealand on February 4, 2016 but whose ratification by the competent bodies (usually, the Legislative) in the country

3 A change is said to be Pareto efficient when it makes *everybody* better off (or at least not worse off) than it was before. Of course, it is very difficult to find any treaty, or more generally, any law or regulation that is Pareto efficient. Because of that, Pareto efficiency has been called the nirvana criterion and it is not the usual goal of legal amendments. The so-called Kaldor-Hicks efficiency is a better criterium. See Richard A. Posner, *Economic Analysis of Law* (9th ed.), pp. 12–13 (2014).

4 For example, the TPP.

5 See Richard A. Posner, *Economic Analysis of Law* (9th ed.), pp. 12–13 (2014). In a strict sense, it is not necessary that the redistribution of wealth occurs. It is only necessary that such redistribution is possible. See *id.*

6 Nobel Laureate Oliver E. Williamson defines transaction costs as "[t]he ex ante costs of drafting, negotiating, and safeguarding an agreement." Oliver E. Williamson, The Mechanisms of Governance, pp. 373, 379 (1996).

7 See Chapter 14 for an advanced analysis of the complexities of trade negotiations. Afghanistan was the 164th member. See WTO, www.wto.org/english/news_e/news16_e/acc_afg_29jul16_e.htm (last visit, August 1, 2016).

members is still pending.[8] A second illustration is the Transatlantic Trade and Investment Partnership or TTIP, a proposed trade agreement between the European Union and the United States that is still in an early negotiation stage.[9] A third example is the Regional Comprehensive Economic Partnership (RCEP), a trade agreement under negotiation among some countries from Oceania and Asia (including China, which is not a member of the TPP).[10]

In a strict sense, regional trade agreements are also plurilateral since their members are usually more than two. The difference, as its name suggests, is that in regional trade agreements its members are located in the same geographical zone or are even neighbors. The best illustration of this kind of agreements is the North American Free Trade Agreement or NAFTA, whose members are Canada, the United States of America and Mexico, and that will be discussed in further detail below.

Finally, bilateral trade agreements, which obviously have two parties, are the most common type of trade agreements. Nowadays, the number of these kinds of agreements is around 300.[11] Take into account that, nowadays, bilateral, regional and plurilateral trade agreements do not exclusively deal with trade matters but with other topics as well such as foreign investment, labor rights, environmental rights, etc.[12]

In any event, there are also many bilateral treaties that, while dealing with some economic matters, do not include provisions related to the lowering of either tariff or non-tariff barriers. Such agreements are usually of two kinds: (i) treaties to avoid double taxation or DTT Treaties and (ii) Bilateral Investment Treaties or BIT. The main purpose of the first kind, as its name indicates, is to establish, regarding international transactions, which signing country has the authority to levy an income tax.[13] Treaties to avoid double taxation are very useful to incentivize foreign investment and international business transactions since, if such treaties were not in legal force and unless a country has some domestic rules accepting taxes paid abroad as an allowance at home, a single transaction would trigger taxes in two or more countries and, as a result, will no longer be profitable.

8 See The USTR, https://ustr.gov/tpp/ (last visit, April 30, 2017).

9 See The USTR, https://ustr.gov/ttip (last visit, April 30, 2017) and European Commission, http://ec.europa.eu/trade/policy/in-focus/ttip/ (last visit, April 30, 2017).

10 See Department of Foreign Affairs and Trade, http://dfat.gov.au/trade/agreements/rcep/pages/regional-comprehensive-economic-partnership.aspx (last visit, April 30, 2017).

11 See WTO, *the Regional Trade Agreements Information System*, http://rtais.wto.org/ (last visit, April 30, 2017). See also Jean-Pierre Chauffour and Jean-Christophe Maur, 'Overview', in *Preferential Trade Agreements, Policies for Development, A Handbook* (Jean-Pierre Chauffour and Jean-Christophe Maur Eds), p. 1; and Acharya et al., 'Landscape', in *Preferential Trade Agreements, Policies for Development, A Handbook* (Jean-Pierre Chauffour and Jean-Christophe Maur Eds), p. 37.

12 See, e.g. the TPP, The USTR, https://ustr.gov/tpp/ (last visit, April 30, 2017).

13 See, e.g., European Commission, Taxation and Customs Union, https://ec.europa.eu/taxation_customs/individuals/personal-taxation/treaties-avoidance-double-taxation-concluded-member-states_en (last visit, April 30, 2017), listing the treaties for the avoidance of double taxation that EU Members have concluded.

BITs, in turn, are treaties providing rules intended to foster foreign investment by restricting the cases where a country may directly or indirectly expropriate foreign assets; determining the prompt, adequate and effective compensation to be paid to the investor in such cases; and providing that an international arbitral tribunal, usually the International Center for Settlement of Investment Disputes (ICSID),[14] has jurisdiction to settle any dispute between the foreign investor and the national government.[15] BITs are easier to negotiate than PTAs and, as a result, the number of the former (over 3,000) is about ten times the number of the latter.[16]

After having mentioned and described the main kinds of trade agreements, this section turns to the description of two trade agreements: NAFTA and Mercosur. NAFTA whose members are Canada, the United States of America and Mexico was signed on December 7, 1992 and came into effect on January 1, 1994. [17]

NAFTA eliminated the majority of tariffs between goods traded among its members and gradually phased out other tariffs over a 15-year period that, of course, has already elapsed. Restrictions were removed from many categories, including motor vehicles, computers, textiles, and agriculture. The agreement is trilateral in nature since their terms apply equally to all countries in all areas except agriculture, a very sensitive topic, and in which tariff reductions, phase-out terms, and protection of selected industries were negotiated on a bilateral basis.

This treaty was a turning point in the negotiation of trade agreements because it was the first major one that not only included provisions about purely trade topics but also about other matters.[18] For instance, NAFTA protects intellectual property rights such as patents, trademarks and copyrights and outlines the removal of investment restrictions among the three countries.[19] NAFTA also provides some legal rules on investment, services and related matters.[20] As a third illustration, the North American Agreement on Environmental Cooperation (NAAEC) and the North American Agreement on Labor Cooperation (NAALC),

14 See ICSID, https://icsid.worldbank.org/apps/ICSIDWEB/Pages/default.aspx

15 See Rudolf Dolzer and Christoph Schreuer, *Principles of International Investment Law* (2nd ed.), p. 1 (2012).

16 According to the UNCTAD, there are 2,959 BIT, of which 2,326 are in legal force. See UNCTAD, Investment Policy Hub, http://investmentpolicyhub.unctad.org/IIA (last visit, April 30, 2017). For a database of BIT, showing the treaties that each country has signed, see ICSID, https://icsid.worldbank.org/apps/ICSIDWEB/resources/Pages/Bilateral-Investment-Treaties-Database.aspx (last visit, April 30, 2017).

17 See NAFTA Now, www.naftanow.org/ (last visit, April 30, 2017). See also NAFTA Secretariat, www.nafta-sec-alena.org/Home/Welcome (last visit, April 30, 2017).

18 See NAFTA Secretariat, Legal Texts, www.nafta-sec-alena.org/Home/Legal-Texts (last visit, April 30, 2017).

19 See North American Free Trade Agreement, Part VI – Chapter 17 (Intellectual Property).

20 See North American Free Trade Agreement, Part V – Chapters 11 to 16 (Investment, Services and Related Matters).

which is a supplemental agreement of NAFTA, includes provisions on worker and environmental protections.[21]

Although the issue of whether NAFTA has been favorable for its members is hotly debated,[22] it is generally admitted that trade has increased dramatically among the three members of NAFTA since this treaty came into effect. Thus, and from 1993 (the year preceding NAFTA) to 2008, trade among NAFTA countries had more than tripled, increasing from US$304 billion to US$946 billion in 2008.[23] In particular, trade between the United States and Canada has almost tripled while trade between the United States and Mexico has more than quadrupled.[24] On top of that, and since NAFTA came into effect and until 2008, the combined GDP for its three members has more than doubled, going from US$7.6 trillion in 2003 to over US$17 trillion in 2008.[25] Last but not least, around 40 million jobs have been created in North America between 1993 and 2008.[26] While NAFTA is not, of course, the only cause of these trends, it seems to be one of its main drivers.[27]

In addition to the classification of trade agreements in accordance with their number of members, another categorization is important. Some trade agreements, on top of reducing tariff and non-tariff barriers and providing some rules on related topics such as foreign investment, intellectual property rights, and labor and environmental rights, also provide a common external tariff applicable to the imports coming from any country not belonging to the agreement. This kind of agreement is called a customs union.[28]

Mercosur is one example of a customs union.[29] Its founding members are Argentina, Brazil, Paraguay and Uruguay. Venezuela has been a full member

21 See NAALC, www.naalc.org/index.cfm?page=137 (last visit, April 30, 2017).

22 See, e.g., James McBride and Mohammed Aly Sergie, *NAFTA's Economic Impact*, Council on Foreign Relations, www.cfr.org/trade/naftas-economic-impact/p15790 (last visit, April 30, 2017).

23 See NAFTA Now, Results: North Americans Are Better Off After 15 Years of NAFTA, www.naftanow.org/results/default_en.asp (last visit, April 30, 2017).

24 See *id.*

25 See *id.*

26 See *id.*

27 See, e.g., James McBride and Mohammed Aly Sergie, *NAFTA's Economic Impact*, Council on Foreign Relations, www.cfr.org/trade/naftas-economic-impact/p15790 (last visit, April 30, 2017).

28 See generally GATT 1947 para. 2, "For the purposes of this Agreement a customs territory shall be understood to mean any territory with respect to which separate tariffs or other regulations of commerce are maintained for a substantial part of the trade of such territory with other territories." An even deeper form of integration occurs when, on top of a common external tariff, the treaty provides the establishment of some supranational bodies in charge of enacting some legal rules and public policies. The European Union is the typical and, perhaps, only example of this advanced form of integration.

29 See Mercosur, www.mercosur.int/ (last visit, April 30, 2017).

since 2006,[30] although its membership was suspended recently for not incorporating some Mercosur resolutions in its domestic legislation, and more significantly, because of the recent controversial Constitutional Assembly elections in Venezuela that may result in the country becoming a dictatorship.[31] Bolivia signed a Protocol of Adhesion in 2015 and will be a new member once the Legislatives of the member states ratifies it.[32] In turn, Chile, Colombia, Ecuador, Guyana, Peru and Suriname are associate members.[33] Mercosur comprises a population of almost 300 million people while the combined Gross Domestic Product of its members is in excess of US$2.42 trillion,[34] a figure that makes Mercosur the fifth largest economy in the world.[35]

This customs union, whose purpose is of course the promotion of trade among its members as well and the fluid movement of goods, people and currencies, was established in 1991 through the Treaty of Asunción (the Paraguayan capital),[36] which was amended and updated in 1994 by the Treaty of Ouro Preto (a Brazilian town, whose name means Black Gold).[37] While Mercosur officially started in 1991, its negotiation process goes back to the 1960s when the Latin American Free Trade Association (Asociación Latino Americana de Libre Comercio) was established[38] and, then, to the 1980s, when the Latin American Association of Integration – ALADI (Asociación Latino Americana de Integración) superseded this first organization.[39] Likewise, the integration process between Argentina and Brazil had begun with the signature in 1986 of the Act for Argentine-Brazilian Integration (Acta para la Integración Argentino Brasileña).[40]

30 See Mercosur, www.mercosur.int/innovaportal/v/7823/2/innova.front/paises-del-mercosur (last visit, April 30, 2017).

31 See Mercosur, www.mercosur.int/ (last visit, April 30, 2017).

32 See Mercosur, www.mercosur.int/innovaportal/v/7823/2/innova.front/paises-del-mercosur (last visit, April 30, 2017).

33 See *id.*

34 See Institute for Latin American and Caribbean Integration, Inter-American Development Bank, Mercosur Report No 20, https://publications.iadb.org/bitstream/handle/11319/7280/Informe_MERCOSUR_N_20_2014_2015_Segundo_Semestre_2014_Primer_Semestre_2015.pdf?sequence=1 (last visit, April 30, 2017), pp. 12–28.

35 See Mercosur, *En Pocas Palabras* (*In Few Words*), www.mercosur.int/innovaportal/v/3862/2/innova.front/en-pocas-palabras (last visit, April 30, 2017).

36 See Treaty of Asunción, www.mercosur.int/innovaportal/file/719/1/CMC_1991_TRATADO_ES_Asuncion.pdf (last visit, April 30, 2017).

37 See Additional Protocol to the Treaty of Asunción on the Institutional Structure of Mercosur, www.mercosur.int/innovaportal/file/721/1/1994_protocoloouropreto_es.pdf (last visit, April 30, 2017).

38 See ALADI, www.aladi.org/nsfaladi/preguntasfrecuentes.nsf/fd7fc5dc8b0352c1032567bb004f8e78/13f6e7196eff45a2032574be0043f187?OpenDocument (last visit, April 30, 2017).

39 See ALADI, www.aladi.org/sitioAladi/index.html (last visit, April 30, 2017).

40 See María Victoria Daract, Mercosur, 'Antecedentes Históricos' ['Mercosur, Historical Background'], in *Estudios sobre el Mercosur* [*Studies on Mercosur*] (Juan F. Armagnague, Silvia Barón et al. Eds), p. 135 (2007).

The Ouro Preto Protocol, which sets forth the institutional framework of Mercosur, recognizes the legal existence of the bloc under international law, ascribing it with the legal authority to negotiate, on its own behalf, agreements with third-party countries, groups of countries or international organizations.[41] For instance, Mercosur entered into a Complementation Economic Agreement (Acuerdo de Complementación Económica) with the Andean Community trade block (CAN) in 2004, which paves the way for future negotiations towards South American integration.[42]

Some of Mercosur's goals are the free transit of production goods, services and factors among the member states with, *inter alia*, the elimination of customs rights and also the non-tariff restrictions on the transit of goods through internal borders.[43] Since Mercosur is a customs union, these are not the only goals: the rules also fix a common external tariff for every good and encourage the adoption of a common trade policy regarding non-member states or groups of states and the coordination of positions in regional and international trade and economic meetings.[44] In order to ensure free competition among companies established in member states, coordination is also important regarding other matters, such as member states' macroeconomic and sectorial policies of member states related to foreign trade, agriculture, industry, tax system, monetary system, foreign exchange, services, customs, transport and communications, and other matters that may be agreed on.[45] For such purposes, member states have committed to make the necessary adjustments to their laws in pertinent areas to allow for the strengthening of the integration process.[46]

A comparison between the two trade agreements discussed in this section is relevant. As a customs union, the Mercosur structure goes beyond the trade liberalization measures of NAFTA since its goal is not only the reduction of tariff and non-tariff barriers and the agreement on trade-related matters such as investment measures and intellectual property rights but also the application of a common external tariff and the harmonization of certain political and economic

41 See Additional Protocol to the Treaty of Asunción on the Institutional Structure of Mercosur, www.mercosur.int/innovaportal/file/721/1/1994_protocoloouropreto_es.pdf (last visit, April 30, 2017).

42 See Comunidad Andina de Naciones (Andean Nations Community), www.comunidadandina.org/Seccion.aspx?id=111&tipo=TE&title=mercosur (last visit, April 30, 2017).

43 See Mercosur, *En Pocas Palabras* [*In Few Words*], www.mercosur.int/innovaportal/v/3862/4/innova.front/en-pocas-palabras (last visit, April 30, 2017).

44 See Mercosur, *Régimen de Origen y Arancel Externo Común* [*Rules of Origin and Common External Tariff*], www.mercosur.int/innovaportal/v/6630/2/innova.front/regimen-de-origen-y-arancel-externo-comun (last visit, April 30, 2017).

45 See Additional Protocol to the Treaty of Asunción on the Institutional Structure of Mercosur, www.mercosur.int/innovaportal/file/721/1/1994_protocoloouropreto_es.pdf (last visit, April 30, 2017).

46 See *id.*

activities of the member states, especially those related to trade negotiating positions.

The next degree of deepened integration in trade agreements is an economic union. This is basically a customs union with one or more common economic policies, like the European Union.[47]

15.3 The debate of regionalism vs. multilateralism

Theoretically, multilateral agreements are preferable than bilateral, regional or plurilateral ones since the former involve all WTO members and therefore, make a greater contribution to the unification of international trade law. In practice, however, negotiation of bilateral and regional agreements is much easier than reaching an agreement among all WTO members. As a result, it is not surprising that not only the number of PTAs is very high, over 300,[48] but also that this number is still growing since there are many agreements under negotiations while the progress of multilateral trade deals, with the exception of the recent TFA Agreement, is almost completely stalled. Not only is the number of PTAs growing but also their scope.[49] The times when PTAs were limited to reducing or eliminating tariffs or even non-tariff barriers are long gone.[50] Since NAFTA, PTAs usually include provisions not only on purely international trade matters but also on related topics such as intellectual property rights, foreign investment, environmental protection, and labor and human rights.[51]

The proliferation of bilateral and trade agreements has given rise to two kinds of theories: one stating that such agreements are good for trade and the other one contending the opposite. The defenders of bilateral and regional trade agreements contend that while multilateral agreements would be the ideal path, they

47 For a discussion of this topic, see *supra* Chapter 3.

48 Indeed, almost all WTO members are also members of at least one PTA (Mongolia is one of the few exemptions). See Acharya et al., 'Landscape', in *Preferential Trade Agreements, Policies for Development, A Handbook* (Jean-Pierre Chauffour and Jean-Christophe Maur Eds), p. 37. To this amount of over 300 trade agreements, it is necessary to add around other 100 agreements that are in legal force but that have not been notified to the WTO plus a non-negligent number of PTAs which are still under negotiation and that might be in legal force soon. See *id.*, p. 42.

49 See Jean-Pierre Chauffour and Jean-Christophe Maur, 'Beyond Market Access', in *Preferential Trade Agreements, Policies for Development, A Handbook* (Jean-Pierre Chauffour and Jean-Christophe Maur Eds), p. 17; and Acharya et al., 'Landscape', in *Preferential Trade Agreements, Policies for Development, A Handbook* (Jean-Pierre Chauffour and Jean-Christophe Maur Eds), p. 37.

50 See Bernard Hoekman, 'North-South Preferential Trade Agreements', in *Preferential Trade Agreements, Policies for Development, A Handbook* (Jean-Pierre Chauffour and Jean-Christophe Maur Eds), p. 99. See also Jean-Christophe Maur and Ben Shepherd, 'Product Standards', in *Preferential Trade Agreements, Policies for Development, A Handbook* (Jean-Pierre Chauffour and Jean-Christophe Maur Eds), p. 197.

51 See *id.*

are almost impossible feats in practice due to the negotiation hurdles.[52] More importantly, these scholars also argue that bilateral and regional trade agreements among a few countries give an incentive to other countries to also liberalize their economies under the rationale that if they do not follow suit, their companies will lose their market share in other countries.[53] Thus, trade agreements that enter in legal force incentivize a race to sign other trade agreements triggering a snow ball effect that might end up with a much more liberalized world.[54] On top of that, defenders of this view contend that bilateral and regional trade agreements are "building blocks" to multilateralism or, in other words, a first step in the process of trade liberalization that will facilitate negotiations at the multilateral stage.[55]

Not all trade economists agree with this view.[56] On the contrary, they contend that bilateral and regional trade agreements are not "building blocks" but "stumbling blocks" to multilateralism.[57] The most famous defender of this view is Jagdish N. Bhagwati, an Indian economist and Tenured Professor at Columbia University.[58] Professor Bhagwati argues that PTAs create pockets of trade exclusion and not of trade inclusion since they divide the world in few trade blocks that benefit its members but that, at the same time, isolate other countries.[59] In other words, bilateral and regional trade agreements demolish the internal walls among members but build higher external walls making it more difficult for other countries to export their goods there.

According to Bhagwati, this is not the only problem that bilateral and regional trade agreements trigger.[60] The number of trade agreements are currently so high that the result is an entanglement of multiple and varied trade rules (some of them applicable to three countries, others applicable to another two countries, and so on) that will be very hard to harmonize later on.[61] Indeed, the argument goes, the proliferation of trade agreements triggers a fragmentation of the applicable

52 See C. Fred Bergsten, *Globalizing Free Trade: The Ascent of Regionalism*, 75(3) Foreign Affairs 105 (1996). See also Jeffrey J. Schott (Ed.), *Free Trade Agreements: U.S. Strategies and Priorities*, Institute for International Economics, Special Report, 2004; and Jean-Pierre Chauffour and Jean-Christoph Maur, 'Overview', in *Preferential Trade Agreements, Policies for Development, A Handbook* (Jean-Pierre Chauffour and Jean-Christophe Maur Eds), p. 93.

53 See *id.*

54 See *id.*

55 See *id.*

56 Jagdish Bhagwati, *Termites in the Trading System: How Preferential Agreements Undermine Free Trade* (2008); and Bernard Hoekman, 'North-South Preferential Trade Agreements', in *Preferential Trade Agreements, Policies for Development, A Handbook* (Jean-Pierre Chauffour and Jean-Christophe Maur Eds), p. 107.

57 See *id.*

58 See Columbia University, Professor Jagdish N. Bhagwati, www.columbia.edu/~jb38/ (last visit, April 30, 2017).

59 See Jagdish Bhagwati, *Termites in the Trading System: How Preferential Agreements Undermine Free Trade* (2008).

60 See *id.*

61 See *id.*

legal rules to international trade, which goes not only against the goal of having the same rules and standards all around the world but also makes it very complex and expensive for individuals and companies to understand which the applicable trade rules in a given country are.[62] This is the so-called "spaghetti bowl" effect.[63]

On top of that, it is said that PTAs divert efficient trade from the countries that are not a party to the treaty to the more inefficient countries that do belong to it.[64] For instance, the exporters' costs in the latter country might be higher than the exporters' costs in the displaced country (e.g., the manufacturing costs in the country outside the PTA are $20 but they are subject to a tariff amounting to 50%, for a total of $30, while the costs in the country within the PTA are $25). Such trade diversion, some experts contend, might be against the MFN principle, a staple of the WTO agreements.[65] For instance, assume that 130 out of 164 WTO members have signed among them a PTA reducing tariffs below the MFN tariff for a given product. Under this scenario, the MFN tariff would only be applicable to a reduced group of 29 countries, less than 20 percent of the WTO members. In such a case, a more appropriate name for this principle would be Less Favored Nation and not Most Favored Nation. Of course, the example is hypothetical since no trade agreement has such a high number of members (yet).

The GATT drafters, foreseeing the issue described above, included a legal rule on trade agreements. In this sense, GATT Art. XXIV allows PTAs as an exception to the MFN principle as long as the agreement under analysis covers a substantial part of the trade existing under the participating countries, does not increase tariffs for third countries, and be duly notified to the WTO. Because of the reasons mentioned above, some prestigious trade economists propose to amend GATT Art. XXIV in order to restrict the number and scope of PTAs and keep the WTO Negotiation Rounds as the only available road to increase trade.[66]

However, it is important to keep in mind that there are currently two routes for the legal progress of international trade: one is through PTAs, which is likely to continue growing, and the other is through the multilateral system (WTO), which except for the minor advances achieved in the Ninth Ministerial Conference

62 See *id.*

63 See *id.* See also Michael Trebilcock and Robert Howse, *The Regulation of International Trade* (4th ed.) (2012). Notwithstanding, the trade diversion that some PTAs trigger might be less harmful than some people believe.

64 See *id.* See Richard Baldwin and Caroline Freund, 'Preferential Trade Agreements and Multilateral Liberalization', in *Preferential Trade Agreements, Policies for Development, A Handbook* (Jean-Pierre Chauffour and Jean-Christophe Maur Eds), pp. 134–37.

65 See Bernard Hoekman, 'North-South Preferential Trade Agreements', in *Preferential Trade Agreements, Policies for Development, A Handbook* (Jean-Pierre Chauffour and Jean-Christophe Maur Eds), p. 101.

66 See Bernard Hoekman, 'North-South Preferential Trade Agreements';, in *Preferential Trade Agreements, Policies for Development, A Handbook* (Jean-Pierre Chauffour and Jean-Christophe Maur Eds), p. 107; and Jagdish Bhagwati, *Termites in the Trading System: How Preferential Agreements Undermine Free Trade*, p. 1 (2008).

in Bali, Indonesia, has been stagnant since the Doha Round in 2008.[67] It seems that when a path to a more liberalized trade world is not working well the solution is to adjust it and not mutilate or close it by closing the other route that is working well.

Another option, which is becoming more common, is to advance negotiations through a plurilateral approach. Plurilateral agreements are those that are not all WTO members subscribe to and which, as a logical consequence, are easier to conclude than multilateral agreements. One key difference is that reservations to plurilateral treaties are not allowed without the consent of all other parties to the treaty. This principle is codified in international law by Art. 20(2) of the Vienna Convention on the Law of Treaties. At the WTO and under the MFN principle, plurilateral agreements must extend their benefits to signatories and non-signatories alike, but not their obligations, unless an MFN waiver is obtained pursuant to GATT 1994 Art. IX:3. There are currently two MFN plurilateral agreements in legal force: the Agreement on Trade in Civil Aircraft and the Agreement on Government Procurement, and none with an MFN waiver.[68] Other plurilateral agreements are currently under negotiation such as the Information Technology Agreement (ITA) and the Trade in Services Agreement (TiSA). Proposals for a more extensive use of plurilateral agreements as an option to multilateral agreements have also been published.[69]

67 See Acharya et al., 'Landscape', in *Preferential Trade Agreements, Policies for Development, A Handbook* (Jean-Pierre Chauffour and Jean-Christophe Maur Eds), p. 37. See also Richard Baldwin and Caroline Freund, 'Preferential Trade Agreements and Multilateral Liberalization', in *Preferential Trade Agreements, Policies for Development, A Handbook* (Jean-Pierre Chauffour and Jean-Christophe Maur Eds), The World Bank, Washington, D.C., 2011, pp. 134–37, arguing that while the future of multilateral negotiations is dark, the PTAs will continue growing.

68 In order to resolve the impasse over agriculture negotiations in the Doha Round, academics have proposed plurilateral agreements as a solution. For a MFN plurilateral proposal, see Peter Gallagher and Andrew Stoler, *Viability of a Critical Mass Framework for Agricultural Trade Negotiations*, p. 1 (2010). For a plurilateral proposal with a MFN waiver, see Aluisio de Lima-Campos, 'In Agriculture, it is Time to Act with Plurilaterals', in *Tackling Agriculture in the Post-Bali Context* (Ricardo Meléndez-Ortiz, Christophe Bellmann and Jonathan Hepburn Eds) (2014).

69 See Gary C. Hufbauer and Jeffrey J. Schott, *Will the World Trade Organization Enjoy a Bright Future?*, Policy Brief 12-11, PIIE (2012), https://piie.com/publications/policy-briefs/will-world-trade-organization-enjoy-bright-future (last visit, May 15, 2017).

16

ADVANCED ANALYSIS OF INTERNATIONAL TRADE AGREEMENTS

The purpose of Chapter 16 is, on the one hand, to introduce the reader to the basic techniques and topics regarding trade negotiations, and, on the other hand, to describe the methods and results of all GATT and WTO rounds as well as trade agreements negotiations.

16.1 Basics of negotiation

In any trade negotiation, the interested parties debate the following four basic questions: (i) what issues and sectors should be included in the agreement? (ii) How deep should the trade agreement be? (iii) How will any decisions be enforced? And (iv) should all signatories be treated equally – in particular – how should developing countries be treated?

The answers to these policy questions are made in a political context through negotiations between the Executive (i.e., the government), the Legislative (the Congress), the Private Sector, and the Public Sector on the domestic side; and governments, private corporations, NGOs, and other interested groups, on the international side.

The first question is about the coverage of trade agreements. On the one hand, some individuals, companies and trade policy formulators believe that the scope of trade agreements should be narrow; i.e., limited only to policies that are directly related to trade and to those aspects of domestic policy that explicitly discriminate against foreign goods.[1] The rationale of this view's proponents is that having too

1 See generally Leonardo Baccini and Andreas Dur, *The New Regionalism and Policy Interdependence* 42 Brit. J. Pol. Sci. 57 (2012); and Henrik Horn, Petros C. Mavroidis and André Sapir, *Beyond the WTO? An Anatomy of EU and US Preferential Trade Agreements*

many targets may prevent any negotiation from being closed and, thus, any goal from being attained.[2]

On the other hand, others believe that the trading system requires rules on a broad range of issues, not limited to issues directly related to trade but including, among others, investment rules facilitating economic integration, competition rules ensuring that international markets are contestable (i.e., that anticompetitive or monopolistic behavior affecting international trade is blocked), and rules on labor, environmental and human rights.[3] After all, this view's defenders argue, trade rules encourage or discourage investment, affect workers by displacing jobs from some places to others, have an impact, either positive or negative, on global warming, and are also related to the enforcement of human rights.[4] Nowadays, most preferential trade agreements are wide in scope.[5] The next paragraphs will explain not only this trend but its antecedents in more detail.

In the years following the Second World War, trade agreements covered mainly border barriers such as tariffs and quotas.[6] Indeed, multilateral trade negotiations happening between 1947 and 1967 focused on reducing these tariffs.[7] Once this goal was achieved, and during the Tokyo Round, the GATT's purview was extended to non-tariff barriers.[8] Changes did not stop there.[9] On the one hand, the Uruguay Round liberalized the flow of services, agricultural goods and investment.[10] On the other hand, the scope of trade agreements was dramatically broadened in numerous bilateral, regional and multilateral negotiations during the 1980s.[11] In the following decade, NAFTA was a turning point by including side agreements on labor and the environment.[12]

From the bilateral and plurilateral perspective, the PTAs negotiated during the current century have been very broad in scope, including not only the already mentioned topics but also rules on intellectual property rights, foreign investment, human rights, dispute resolution, etc.[13] The TPP is one illustration from the

33(11) World Econ. 1565 (2010). See also Leslie Johns and Lauren Peritz, 'The Design of Trade Agreements', in *The Oxford Handbook of the Political Economy of International Trade* (Lisa L. Martin Ed.) (2015).

2 See *id.*

3 See *id.*

4 See *id.*

5 See *id.*

6 See Andreas F. Lowenfeld, *International Economic Law* (2nd ed.) p. 23 (2008) and Joanne Gowa, 'Explaining the GATT/WTO: Origins and Effects', in *The Oxford Handbook of the Political Economy of International Trade* (Lisa L. Martin Ed.) (2015).

7 See *id.*

8 See *id.*

9 See *id.*

10 See *id.*

11 See *id.*

12 See *id.*

13 See Jean-Pierre Chauffour and Jean-Christophe Maur, 'Overview', in *Preferential Trade Agreements, Policies for Development, A Handbook* (Jean-Pierre Chauffour and Jean-Christophe Maur Eds), p. 1.

plurilateral side[14] while the PTA between the United States and Colombia is an example on the bilateral side.[15] From the multilateral perspective (i.e., the WTO arena), it is not so clear and the question of which issues should be included in trade agreements remains controversial and unlikely to be solved anytime soon.[16] While a new negotiation round was launched in Doha, Qatar, in 2001, negotiations on the so-called Singapore issues (competition, trade facilitation, and investment and transparency in government procurement) were postponed.[17] Later on, and due to the fundamental international conflicts on these issues, only trade facilitation remained on the Doha agenda. Finally, an agreement on trade facilitation was reached on the Ninth WTO Ministerial Conference held in Bali, Indonesia (the so-called Bali Package).[18]

The second question is about the depth of an international trade agreement. The simplest agreement just requires that governments operate without discrimination and transparently; i.e., countries only shall engage in reciprocal reductions of border barriers, treat all GATT Contracting Parties equally (the MFN principle), and treat foreign and domestic goods in the same way (the National Treatment Principle). At the other side of the spectrum, trade agreements may seek, in addition to trade liberalization, full policy harmonization. An intermediate approach, in turn, sets minimum standards that all signatories must adhere to.

Unsurprisingly, early trade agreements did not have much depth.[19] This characteristic, however, began to change with the Tokyo Round, by which GATT Contracting Parties were subject to more constraints such as the Code of Technical Barriers to Trade, that encouraged countries to adopt international standards and allowed them to use local standards as long as they were applied transparently, were not discriminatory, and did not create unnecessary obstacles to trade.[20]

The third question is about the enforcement of trade agreements. To begin with, some agreements are not binding.[21] That is, countries proclaim their intention to abide by their rules but suffer no legal consequences if they fail to

14 See The USTR, https://ustr.gov/tpp/ (last visit, April 30, 2017).

15 See The USTR, https://ustr.gov/trade-agreements/free-trade-agreements/colombia-fta/final-text (last visit, April 30, 2017).

16 See generally Ronder Wilkinson and James Scott (Eds), *Trade, Poverty, Development: Getting Beyond the WTO's Doha Deadlock* (2012).

17 See *id.*

18 See *infra* Section 9.3.

19 See Andreas F. Lowenfeld, *International Economic Law* (2nd ed.), p. 23 (2008) and Joanne Gowa, 'Explaining the GATT/WTO: Origins and Effects', in *The Oxford Handbook of the Political Economy of International Trade* (Lisa L. Martin Ed.) (2015).

20 See Andreas F. Lowenfeld, *International Economic Law* (2nd ed.) p. 23 (2008) and Joanne Gowa, 'Explaining the GATT/WTO: Origins and Effects', in *The Oxford Handbook of the Political Economy of International Trade* (Lisa L. Martin Ed.) (2015).

21 See generally Amelia Porges, 'Dispute Settlement', in *Preferential Trade Agreements, Policies for Development, A Handbook* (Jean-Pierre Chauffour and Jean-Christophe Maur Eds), p. 467.

follow through (thus, they are gentlemen's agreements).[22] A second and more developed kind of trade agreement consists of those that are theoretically binding but that lack a formal enforcement mechanism.[23] In a third group, the primary enforcers of binding agreements are domestic courts but international or foreign participants (e.g., governments) may withdraw concessions (i.e., retaliate) in cases of non-compliance.[24] In the fourth and next stage, non-compliance may result in fines or penalties.[25] Finally, in a fifth type, countries may actually turn over to an international body their ability to determine or to regulate certain policies.[26] To take one illustration, countries within the European Union have ceded sovereignty on this to a supranational institution in trade and other matters.[27]

The fourth and last question is whether all signatories of a trade agreement should be treated equally.[28] One view does not see any need to give favorable treatment to developing or least developed countries on at least three grounds: (i) the results of favorable treatments have not always been positive; (ii) developing and, in particular, least developed countries have limited means and, as a result, are often unable to enforce the commitments undertaken in trade agreements; and (iii) an increase in imports can significantly contribute to a country's economic development.[29] This is, however, the minority view.[30] The majority view, by contrast, considers that some countries need favorable treatment taking into account not only that they need special and preferential rules to face international competition in their domestic markets and to conquer foreign markets but also that international trade and, more generally, liberalization in poor countries, will be in the interest of developed countries.[31] After all, higher economic growth triggered by special treatment to developing and least-developed countries will entail more trade opportunities for companies in developed countries.[32]

The majority view prevailed. Since GATT 1947, developing countries were granted differential and special treatment. For example, the so-called Enabling

22 See *id.* The best definition of a gentlemen's agreement is the following one: "A gentleman's agreement is an agreement which is not an agreement, made between two persons neither of whom is a gentleman, whereby each expects the other to be strictly bound without himself being bound at all." *Chemco Leasing S.p.a. v. Rediffusion plc* [1983] (Engl. Q.B. Comm'l Ct.) (unreported) (Mr. Justice Vaisey) (citing Sir Robert Edgar Megarry): *aff'd* [1987] 1FTLR 201.

23 See *id.*

24 See *id.*

25 See *id.*

26 See *id.*

27 See Court of Justice of the European Union, https://europa.eu/european-union/about-eu/institutions-bodies/court-justice_en (last visit, April 30, 2017).

28 See generally Amrita Narlikar, *International Trade and Developing Countries: Bargaining Coalitions in GATT and WTO* (2005); and Robert E. Hudec and J. Michael Finger, *Developing Countries in the GATT Legal System* (2014).

29 See *id.*

30 See *id.*

31 See *id.*

32 See *id.*

Clause adopted in the Tokyo Round made permanent a set of waivers originally adopted in 1971 that allowed, but did not require, developed countries to provide developing countries with better than MFN treatment through the Generalized System of Preferences.[33] On top of that, and while all countries are expected to meet the same obligations in some areas, developing countries continue to enjoy more lenient treatment in other areas. For instance, the TRIPS agreement enforces the same regime on both developed and developing countries, although the latter are given more time to adjust.[34]

16.2 The GATT and WTO rounds of negotiation

The structure of any trade negotiation may be analyzed through four dimensions: issues, parties, levels and linkages.[35] The simplest negotiation involves just two monolithic parties negotiating over a single issue.[36] In this case, the goal of both parties is simply to claim value.[37] On the opposite side of the spectrum, the most complex and usual negotiations involve multiple issues, parties, levels and linkages of issues.[38] As a result, these kind of deals involve many rounds of ongoing negotiations.[39] Figure 21 depicts the bargaining range in the simplest negotiation.

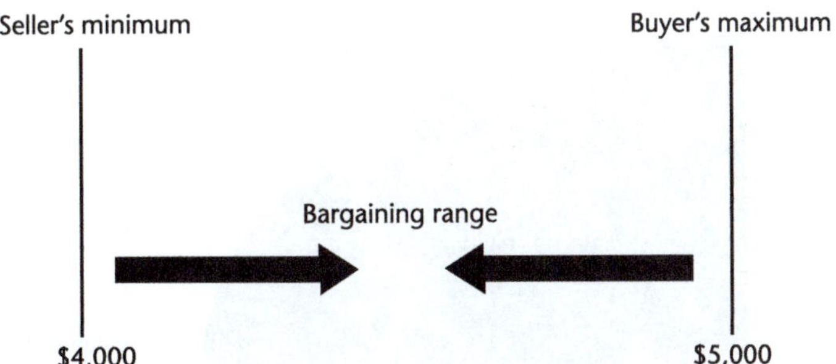

FIGURE 21 Bargaining range in a distributed negotiation[40]

33 See Decision on Differential and More Favourable Treatment, Reciprocity and Fuller Participation of Developing Countries, Decision of 28 November 1979 (L/4903), para. 1, "Notwithstanding the provisions of Art. I of the General Agreement, contracting parties may accord differential and more favourable treatment to developing countries, without according such treatment to other contracting parties."

34 See TRIPS Agreement Art. 66. See also, e.g., TFA Section II.

35 See generally Geza Feketekuty, *Policy Development and Negotiations in International Trade: A Practical Guide to Effective Commercial Diplomacy* (2013).

36 See *id.*

37 See *id.*

38 See *id.*

39 See *id.*

40 Figure made by the authors.

The move from negotiating one issue to dealing with multiple issues, as happens in real trade negotiations, dramatically changes the nature of the process since it gives the parties opportunities to create value and to claim value as well. The quantity of value than can be created or claimed in trade negotiations depends on, among other factors, how the issue agenda is constructed. Thus, if the agenda is too narrow, the parties might lack enough bargaining chips (i.e., enough topics to give and take) and, as a result, might have serious difficulties creating enough value to make a deal possible. To take an illustration, a narrow agenda was a key factor in the failed Organization for Economic Cooperation and Development negotiations over a Multilateral Agreement on Investment.[41] Having a too broad agenda is not good either: in such a case, the process might become unmanageable unless it is divided in smaller sub-negotiations or chunks. However, such division is only feasible if each cluster contains a range of issues sufficiently broad to enable value to be created and claimed. Figure 22 shows the bargaining range in an interactive negotiation.

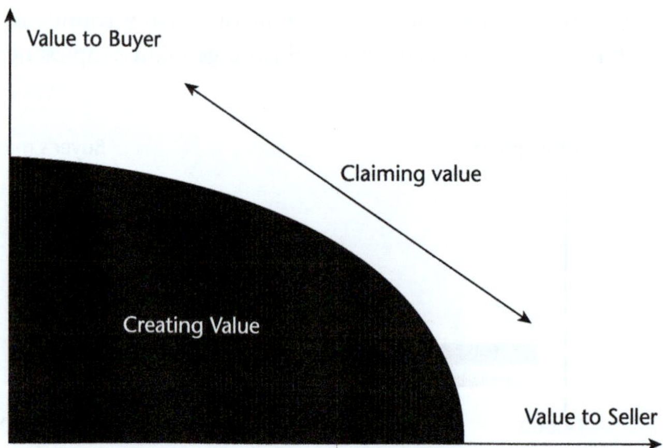

FIGURE 22 Bargaining range in an interactive negotiation[42]

Not only the number of issues may grow but also the number of countries or parties to the negotiation. As such number rises, so too does the challenge of reaching a mutually acceptable agreement, especially if a consensus is required for

41 "Negotiations on a proposed multilateral agreement on investment (MAI) were launched by governments at the Annual Meeting of the OECD Council at Ministerial level in May 1995. The objective was to provide a broad multilateral framework for international investment with high standards for the liberalisation of investment regimes and investment protection and with effective dispute settlement procedures, open to non-OECD countries. Negotiations were discontinued in April 1998 and will not be resumed." OECD, Multilateral Agreement on Investment, www.oecd.org/investment/internationalinvestmentagreements/multilateralagreementoninvestment.htm (last visit, April 30, 2017).

42 Figure made by the authors.

a decision (as happens in relation or amendments to the WTO Agreements).[43] In such a case, a single determined spoiler has the power to halt the process if it does not receive some concessions (i.e., it has a veto power). This was, for instance, what happened in the recent process of ratification of the Trade Facilitation Agreement when India momentarily held this agreement hostage by refusing to approve it unless other WTO Members accepted that some subsidies that this country grants to its farmers were accepted as consistent with the WTO legal rules.[44]

Naturally, negotiations that take place among groups, organizations and nations simultaneously occur within the parties that belong to a determined party or country. For instance, a government may negotiate the position of its country with the Legislative, the Private Sector and the Public Interest before making public its position on a given issue in the trade negotiations. Synchronizing internal and external negotiations involves a delicate balancing act since their interactions may restrict tactical flexibility. To take one illustration, exhibiting unyielding behavior in the external talks may make a leader appear as a tough negotiator and, as a consequence, bolster internal political support; but it may also lock such leader into untenable positions with outside counterparts.

On the other hand, trade policy is usually shaped through multiple rounds of negotiations involving the same parties, a pattern that influences the negotiating process in several important ways. In particular, prior relationships may strongly shape the outcomes of negotiations. For instance, the perception among developing countries that they were stiffed in the Uruguay Round powerfully influenced their approach to negotiations once a new round of multilateral trade talks started in Doha, Qatar.[45] The asymmetry in negotiations is another important factor to take into account. Many times negotiations are among, on the one hand, developed countries with access to an army of negotiators and experts in several legal, economic and policy topics and which might exert political pressures and, on the other hand, developing countries, which do not have such abundance of human capital and that are less important from a geopolitical standpoint.[46] In such cases, of course, the strategy of developing countries needs to take into account how to negotiate with more powerful counterparts.

43 See Marrakesh Agreement Establishing the World Trade Organization. Art. X.

44 See Section 9.3.

45 See, e.g., J. Michael Finger, *The Doha Agenda and Development: A View from the Uruguay Round*, 31 ERD Working Paper No 21 Economics and Research Department, Asian Development Bank (2002), www.adb.org/sites/default/files/publication/28316/wp021.pdf (last visit, April 30, 2017); and Sonia E. Rolland, *From the Uruguay Round to the Doha Round: Changing Dynamics in Developing Countries' Participation*, Oxford Scholarship Online (2012), www.oxfordscholarship.com/view/10.1093/acprof:oso/9780199600885.001.0001/acprof-9780199600885-chapter-6 (last visit, April 30, 2017).

46 See, e.g., CAFTA, the PTA between the United States and Costa Rica, El Salvador, Guatemala, Honduras, Nicaragua and the Dominican Republic. See The USTR, https://ustr.gov/trade-agreements/free-trade-agreements/cafta-dr-dominican-republic-central-america-fta (last visit, April 30, 2017).

Before ending this chapter, it is worth making reference to the design of negotiation strategies. First, solid and stable institutions need to be created or amended, staffed, funded and directed in ways that adequately influence the trade negotiation process. Second, not all forums are equal in order to achieve the goals of trade negotiations. The most promising forum in which to pursue one's objectives must be selected, ensuring that negotiations take place there. For instance, a place where there are many hostilities against globalization or international trade might not be the most appropriate venue.[47] Third, the agenda must be efficiently shaped. Thus, a large agenda should be divided into modules for parallel negotiations while some high-level principles that will govern the negotiating process must be defined. Fourth, a party should identify potential winning and blocking allies in order to devise plans for building supportive coalitions and breaking or forestalling opposing ones. Fifth, some complex issues might be de-linked (separating them to make an agreement easier) while simpler ones might be linked with others in order to create or claim value. Sixth, the issues and the options to deal with them must be clearly crafted and framed. Seventh, momentum should be created; i.e., the flow of negotiations must be channeled in promising directions by establishing appropriate stages to demarcate the process, as well as by instigating or taking advantage of action-forcing events.

47 For instance, Seattle, United States, where many people protested against globalization and international trade during the Third WTO Ministerial Conference in 1999. See Hanna Murphy, *The Making of International Trade Policy: NGOs, Agenda-Setting and the WTO* 88–90 (2010). See also WTO, The Third WTO Ministerial Conference, www.wto.org/english/thewto_e/minist_e/min99_e/min99_e.htm (last visit, April 30, 2017).

SECTION III
GATS and TRIPS agreements

This short section discusses the legal rule of two important WTO Agreements. On the one hand, GATS, related to trade in services, a topic very important nowadays when services usually account for a large portion of most economies. On the other hand, TRIPS, which is about the rules governing issues both related to international trade and to intellectual property.

17

GENERAL AGREEMENT ON TRADE AND SERVICES (GATS)

17.1 Introduction

International trade is naturally not only about goods but also about services. Indeed, as the preamble of GATS recognized more than 20 years ago,[1] and also due to the progress of the technologies of information and communications, trade in services is a significant and increasing percentage of global trade.[2] According to the WTO, the world exports of commercial services went from US$1,179 billion in 1995 to US$2,516 billion in 2005 and to US$4,872 billion in 2014.[3] To put these figures in perspective, and for the same years, the world exports of goods were US$5,168, US$10,509, and US$19,002 billion.[4] Some other figures confirm the importance of the services sector in the world economy. The services sector accounts for around 70 percent of global GDP and it is also the world's largest employer[5]; for instance, such sector provides around 80 percent of jobs in the United States.[6] Thus, this growing importance of the services sector in the

1 See GATS Preamble.

2 See J. Bradford Jensen, *Global Trade in Services: Fear, Facts, and Offshoring*, Peterson Institute of International Economics (2011) (providing some facts about the service sector and service trade). See also European Commission, http://ec.europa.eu/trade/policy/in-focus/tisa/ (last visit, April 30, 2017) (reminding that the importance of services in the global economy is growing).

3 See WTO, International Trade Statistics 2015, www.wto.org/english/res_e/statis_e/its2015_e/its2015_e.pdf (last visit, April 30, 2017).

4 See *id.*

5 See The USTR, https://ustr.gov/TiSA (last visit, April 30, 2017). See also Coalition of Services Industries, http://servicescoalition.org/negotiations/trade-in-services-agreement (last visit, April 30, 2017).

6 See *id.*

world economy entails that any trade agreement restricted to international trade in goods would be incomplete.[7]

This is what happened shortly after the end of the Second World War. GATT 1947 only referred to trade in goods; i.e., trade in services was not part of this agreement. This is not surprising taking account not only that reaching a first multinational trade agreement was already an uphill task, but also that the services sector is linked to sensible topics such as labor migration, visas and domestic regulation. Subsequent rounds of negotiations attempted to reach a deal regarding trade of services but the current agreement, GATS, was only approved at the end of the Uruguay Round in 1994.[8]

17.2 GATS overview

GATS Art. I provides four modes of supplying services across national borders. Mode 1 is a service rendered "from the territory of one WTO Member into the territory of another Member"[9]; for instance, the legal advice that an individual from his/her headquarters in the United States provides to one of his/her customers in France. Mode 2 refers to any service rendered "in the territory of one Member to the service consumer of any other Member."[10] In this case, the consumer goes to the place where the provider of the service is. Tourism is the most common example of this kind of service. Mode 3 is any service rendered by the supplier of a WTO member to a customer in another WTO member through commercial presence in the latter country.[11] This mode usually entails that the provider of the service incorporates either a subsidiary or a branch in a foreign country, a topic related to foreign investment issues and regulated in many BITs.[12] Finally, Mode 4 applies when the provider of the service sends individuals to perform some tasks in the country where the beneficiary is located[13]; e.g., when an engineer from Germany travels to Mexico in order to give technical assistance related to some machinery. The WTO estimates that "Mode 4 remains a very small component of overall trade in services, accounting for between 1 and 2 per cent of the total."[14]

7 See generally J. Bradford Jensen, *Global Trade in Services: Fear, Facts, and Offshoring*, Peterson Institute of International Economics (2011).

8 Joanne Gowa, 'Explaining the GATT/WTO: Origins and Effects', in *The Oxford Handbook of the Political Economy of International Trade* (Lisa L. Martin Ed.) (2015).

9 See GATS Art. I.

10 See *id.*

11 See *id.*

12 Recall that the WTO Agreement on Trade-Related Investment Measures, pursuant to its Art. 1, only applies to investment measures related trade in goods.

13 See *id.*

14 See WTO Services: Sector by Sector, Movement of Natural Persons, www.wto.org/english/tratop_e/serv_e/mouvement_persons_e/mouvement_persons_e.htm (last visit, April 30, 2017).

The main principles of GATT, the MFN clause, the national treatment and the transparency principle, are also a staple of the GATS agreement. GATS Art. II para. 1 provides the MFN treatment by stating that (underlines are not part of the legal text): "With respect to any measure covered by this Agreement, each Member shall accord immediately and unconditionally to services and service suppliers of any other Member treatment no less favourable than that it accords to like service suppliers of any other country."[15]

Unfortunately for international trade in services, the scope of the MFN clause is more restricted in comparison with trade in goods.[16] This is not surprising, taking into account that trade in services is a more sensitive topic that trade in goods since the former may affect the regulatory powers of countries, on the one hand, and the employment of qualified personnel, on the other hand.[17] Thus, GATS Art. II para. 2 provides that, regarding measures listed in Annex on Art. II, a WTO member "may maintain a measure inconsistent with paragraph 1."[18]

The national treatment principle, in turn, is incorporated in GATS Art. XVII para. 1, which reads:

> In the sectors inscribed in its Schedule, and subject to any conditions and qualifications set out therein, each Member shall accord to services and service suppliers of any other Member, in respect of all measures affecting the supply of services, treatment no less favourable than that it accords to its own like services and service suppliers."[19]

As the reading of this legal rule indicates, the national treatment principle, likewise the MFN principle, is more limited in trade in services in comparison with trade in goods since, in the former, the national treatment is only applicable to a positive list composed of the sectors that each country inscribed in its schedule.[20]

Third, GATS Art. III is about the transparency principle. This legal rule provides that, save emergency situations, each WTO member shall publish promptly "all relevant measures of general application which pertain to or affect the operation of this Agreement."[21]

Besides the legal rules on the MFN, the national treatment and the transparency principle, there are other articles in the GATS agreement that are worth mentioning here. First, GATS Art. V provides that being part of the GATS

15 See GATS Art. II para. 1. *Cfr.* GATT Art. I.

16 GATS Art. II para. 2.

17 The Preamble of GATS recognizes this particularity by acknowledging the existence of asymmetries regarding the degree of development of service regulations across countries.

18 GATS Art. II para. 2.

19 *Cfr.* GATT Art. III.

20 See GATS Art. XVII para. 1

21 GATS Art. III para. 1.

agreement does not prevent a WTO member from being a party to a preferential trade agreement provided that such agreement has substantial sector coverage and provides for the absence or elimination of substantially all discrimination among the parties in accordance with the national treatment principle. This legal rule is similar to GATT Art. XXIV.

Second, GATS Art. VI reminds WTO members that, "in sectors where specific commitments are undertaken," they shall ensure that "all measures of general application affecting trade in services are administered in a reasonable, objective and impartial manner."

Third, GATS Art. II (MFN), XVI (Market Access), and XVII (National Treatment) are not applicable to laws, regulations or requirements related to services purchased for governmental purposes. Recall that this topic is governed by the Agreement on Government Procurement, a WTO plurilateral agreement, whose parties are some but not all WTO members.

Fourth, and like GATT Art. XX, GATS Art. XIV provides some general exceptions to the application of its legal rules. Thus, and

> [s]ubject to the requirement that such measures are not applied in a manner which would constitute a means of arbitrary or unjustifiable between countries where like conditions prevail, or a disguised restriction on trade in services, nothing in this Agreement shall be construed to prevent the adoption or enforcement by any Member of measures" (a) "necessary to protect public morals or to maintain public order"; (b) "necessary to protect human, animal or plant life or health"; (c) necessary to secure compliance with laws or regulations which are not inconsistent with the provisions of this Agreement"; (d) "inconsistent with Article XVII [national treatment], provided that the difference in treatment is aimed at ensuring the equitable or effective imposition or collection of direct taxes in respect of services or service suppliers of other Members; and (e) "inconsistent with Article II [MFN treatment], provided that the difference in treatment is the result of an agreement on the avoidance of double taxation or provisions on the avoidance of double taxation in any other international agreement or arrangement by which the Member is bound.

Fifth, GATS Art. XVI, which is about market access, provides in its para. 2 that WTO members shall not maintain or adopt, in sectors where commitments are undertaken, "measures which restrict or require specific types of legal entity or joint venture through which a service supplier may supply a service;" or limitations on the number of service suppliers, on the total value of service transactions or assets, on the total number of service operations or on the total quantity of service output, on the total number of natural persons that may be employed in a particular sector or that a service supplier may employ, and on the participation of foreign capital in terms of maximum percentage limit on foreign shareholding or the total value of individual or aggregate foreign investment.[22] This legal rule also provides that such restricted limitations might be in the form of quotas, monopolies, the requirement of exclusive service suppliers, and the requirements of an economic needs test (i.e., a test that conditions market access upon the fulfilment of certain economic criteria).[23]

Sixth, GATS Art. XXII provides that any WTO member considering that any other member has breached its obligations under this Agreement is entitled to request consultations and, if this stage fails, to request the establishment of a panel in accordance with the legal rules of the DSU.

Seventh, and finally, the GATS Agreement includes eight annexes, to wit: Annex on Art. II exemptions, Annex on movement of natural persons supplying services under the agreement; Annex on air transport services; Annex on financial services (including insurance services); a second Annex on financial services; Annex on negotiations on maritime transport services; Annex on telecommunications; and Annex on negotiations on basic telecommunications.

17.3 Other agreements on trade in services

As already mentioned, reaching an agreement on trade in services is a more complex task than reaching a deal on trade in goods.[24] As a result, it is not surprising that GATS has a more limited scope that the GATT. Notwithstanding and taking into account the technological advances that have dramatically changed the ways that services are rendered across borders in the last two decades, there have been some efforts to complement and update the legal rules on GATS in order to further lower the barriers to trade in services and, consequently, to increase the volume of such trade.[25] Some of such barriers include but are not limited to monopoly practices and unfair competition, restrictions on cross-border data flows, processes to obtain licenses and permits, and regulation of services.[26]

Such efforts have been mainly channeled through two ways: preferential trade agreements, and the negotiation of the Trade in Services Agreement (TISA). As mentioned in a previous chapter,[27] PTAs used to be limited to lowering trade barriers.[28] Since the approval and ratification of NAFTA in the early 1990s, however, the scope of PTAs was increased and, therefore, such treaties usually

22 See GATS Art. XVI para. 2.

23 See *id.*

24 See *supra* Section 17.1.

25 See The USTR, https://ustr.gov/TiSA (last visit, April 30, 2017). See generally J. Bradford Jensen, *Global Trade in Services: Fear, Facts, and Offshoring*, p. 1(2011).

26 See *id.*

27 See *supra* Chapter 13.

28 See *id.*

provide rules not only in services,[29] but also in other related topics such as labor mobility,[30] investment,[31] competition policy,[32] government procurement,[33] environmental protection[34] and labor rights.[35] Taking into account the snail pace of the Doha Round and meanwhile, if the plurilateral negotiations of TISA do not end successfully, the PTAs would likely be the legal instruments through which trade in services will be liberalized in the short- and mid-term.[36] Indeed, this has been also the trend in the recent past: the coverage of sectors in PTAs regarding modes 1 (services rendered from one WTO member to an individual or a company in another WTO member) and 3 (services rendered through commercial presence in another WTO country)[37] is at least twice the scope of GATS.[38]

On the other hand, TISA is a plurilateral trade agreement that 23 WTO members (including the United States and the European Union but not China),[39] accounting for around 70 percent of the global services economy,[40] have been negotiating since 2012 and whose main purpose is to improve and expand trade across the full spectrum of service sectors.[41] Should TISA negotiations end up in a multilateral agreement, international trade in services might thrive. While the overall effects might be positive (e.g., consumers of services would benefit from lower prices while workers would be able to work almost anywhere without previously doing too much paperwork in order to obtain licenses and permits), some countries, especially those not being part of this agreement, might experience

29 See Aaditya Matoo and Pierre Sauvé, 'Services', in *Preferential Trade Agreement Policies for Development* (Jean-Pierre Chauffour and Jean-Christophe Maur Eds) (2011).

30 See Sherry Stephenson and Gary Hufbauer, 'Labor Mobility', in *Preferential Trade Agreement Policies for Development.*

31 See Sébastien Miroudout, 'Investment', in *Preferential Trade Agreement Policies for Development.*

32 See Kamala Dawar and Peter Holmes, 'Competition Policy', in *Preferential Trade Agreement Policies for Development.*

33 See Kamala Dawar and Simon J. Evenett, government Procurement, in *Preferential Trade Agreement Policies for Development.*

34 See Anuradha R.V., 'Environment', in *Preferential Trade Agreement Policies for Development* (2011).

35 See Kimberly Ann Elliott, 'Labor Rights', in *Preferential Trade Agreement Policies for Development* (2011).

36 See generally Aaditya Matoo and Pierre Sauvé, 'Services', in *Preferential Trade Agreement Policies for Development* (2011).

37 See Aaditya Matoo and Pierre Sauvé, 'Services', in *Preferential Trade Agreement Policies for Development* (2011). See also GATS Art. I para. 2.

38 See Martin Roy et al., *Services Liberalization in the New Generation of Preferential Trade Agreements: How Much Further than GATS?* WTO Staff Working Paper ERSD 2006–07, World Trade Organization, Geneva (2006).

39 Although this country has asked to join the negotiations. See European Commission, http://ec.europa.eu/trade/policy/in-focus/tisa/ (last visit, April 30, 2017).

40 See European Commission, http://ec.europa.eu/trade/policy/in-focus/tisa/ (last visit, April 30, 2017).

41 See *id.* See also The USTR, https://ustr.gov/TiSA (last visit, April 30, 2017).

detrimental effects.[42] In particular, since TISA would "freeze" the rules applying to many services, at least until such treaty is amended in the future, the states' regulatory powers would be considerably reduced, something that might impede the enactment of public policies intended to help some disadvantaged sectors (e.g., a sector facing a systemic crisis) or individuals, and, even worse, many jobs might be displaced.[43] On a related note, TISA negotiations have also been criticized for not being open to the public, since the documents are only available to the negotiating countries.[44]

17.4 Case law on trade in services

Taking into account that the scope of GATS is lower than the scope of GATT, it is not surprising that the number of disputes in the former agreement (24)[45] has been lower than in the latter one (414).[46] Perhaps the most famous case, since it resembled the David v. Goliath story, has been United States – Measures Affecting the Cross-Border Supply of Gambling and Betting Services (DS285).[47] Antigua and Barbuda, an archipelago of tiny islands in the Antilles and, therefore, one of the smallest WTO members, requested in 2003 the establishment of a panel regarding several U.S. measures that, according to the complainant, prevented the supply of gambling and betting services from another WTO member to the United States on a cross-border basis.[48] The panel found that: (i) the GATS schedule of the United States included specific commitments for gambling and betting services under the sub-sector "Other Recreational Services;" (ii) some U.S. federal laws and state laws prohibited some cross-border services included in Mode 1 of GATS, which was in breach of GATS Art. XVI (Market Access); and (iii) that the United States failed to successfully prove that the challenged measures were necessary under GATS Art. XIV (a) and (c) and also consistent with the chapeau of the same legal rule.[49] After both WTO members appealed certain issues of law and legal interpretations of the panel report, the AB upheld most parts of the panel report.[50] Notwithstanding, and since the United States failed to comply with some DSB's recommendations and rulings, Antigua and Barbuda requested

42 See generally J. Bradford Jensen, *Global Trade in Services: Fear, Facts, and Offshoring* (2011).

43 See generally J. Bradford Jensen, *Global Trade in Services: Fear, Facts, and Offshoring* (2011).

44 See European Commission, http://ec.europa.eu/trade/policy/in-focus/tisa/ (last visit, April 30, 2017).

45 See WTO www.wto.org/english/tratop_e/dispu_e/dispu_agreements_index_e.htm?id=A8# (last visit, April 30, 2017).

46 See WTO www.wto.org/english/tratop_e/dispu_e/dispu_agreements_index_e.htm?id=A9# (last visit, April 30, 2017).

47 See DS285, United States – Measures Affecting the Cross-Border Supply of Gambling and Betting Services.

48 See *id.*

49 See *id.*

50 See *id.*

and was granted authorization to suspend the application to the United States of concessions under the GATS and the TRIPS Agreement.[51] As the reader might have anticipated, and given the disparity between the economic size of both contenders, such retaliation was not very harmful for the United States.[52]

51 See *id.*

52 See Mark E. Mendel, 'Retaliation in the WTO: The Experience of Antigua and Barbuda in US – Gambling', in *The Law, Economics and Politics of Retaliation in WTO Dispute Settlement* (Chad P. Bown and Joost Pauwelyn Eds) (2014).

18

THE TRIPS AGREEMENT

18.1 Introduction

The four main WTO agreements are GATT, including (i) the Annex 1A to the Marrakesh Agreement Establishing the WTO on Multilateral Agreements on Trade in Goods, (ii) GATS (Annex 1B), (iii) the Understanding on Rules and Procedures Governing the Settlement of Disputes (the DSU, Annex 2), and (iv) the Agreement on Trade-Related Aspects of Intellectual Property Rights (TRIPS, Annex 1C). Having already mentioned or explained the other three agreements, the purpose of the present chapter is the analysis of the TRIPS agreement. Besides the preamble, this agreement is divided into the following seven parts: (i) General Provisions and Basic Principles; (ii) Standards Concerning the Availability, Scope and Use of Intellectual Property Rights; (iii) Enforcement of Intellectual Property Rights; (iv) Acquisition and Maintenance of Intellectual Property Rights and Related Inter-Partes Procedures; (v) Dispute Prevention and Settlement (vi) Transitional Arrangements; and (vii) Institutional Arrangements and Final Provisions.

In spite of having seven sections, take into account that the TRIPS agreement does not contain all the international rules governing intellectual property rights. Other legal instruments in this regard are: (i) some international treaties, such as the Paris Convention for the Protection of Industrial Property; the Berne Convention for the Protection of Literary and Artistic Works; the Rome Convention for the Protection of Performers, Producers of Phonograms and Broadcasting Organizations; the Washington Treaty on Intellectual Property in Respect of Integrated Circuits; and the Madrid Agreement Concerning the International Registration of Marks; (ii) many recent PTAs which usually include chapters providing rules on intellectual property rights, being sometimes more stringent than the WTO rules and, therefore, called TRIPS+ (one illustration are the PTAs where the United States is a party)[1]; and (iii) domestic rules taking into account that WTO members "may implement in their law more extensive protection than is required by this Agreement, provided that such protection does not contravene the provisions of this Agreement."[2] On top of that, it is WIPO and not the WTO who is the main international organization regarding intellectual property rights.[3]

Even though it is limited in scope, the approval of the TRIPS agreement during the Round of Uruguay was a significant achievement, taking into account that the issue of whether or not to protect intellectual property rights is even more sensible than the issue of whether or not to liberalize services and, of course, clearly more complicated than the issue of whether or not to lower both tariff and non-tariff barriers to trade in goods. After all, and regarding intellectual property rights, two different views collide.[4] On the one hand, developed countries, with the support of big multinational enterprises, contend that intellectual property rights should be clearly defined in the legal rules and strictly enforced.[5] On the other hand, developing countries and least developed ones argue that intellectual property rights cannot avoid the access of the poorest population to basic goods and services, such as medications and health procedures.[6] The Preamble to the TRIPS agreement, being aware of this dilemma, takes "into account the need to promote effective and adequate protection of intellectual property rights, and to ensure that measures and procedures to enforce intellectual property rights do not themselves become barriers to legitimate trade."[7]

18.2 TRIPS overview

Like GATT and GATS, the TRIPS agreement is based on the MFN and National Treatment Principle. Regarding the former, the chapeau of TRIPS Art. 4 provides that: "With regard to the protection of intellectual property, any advantage, favour, privilege or immunity granted by a Member to the nationals of any other country shall be accorded immediately and unconditionally to the nationals of all other Members."[8] Paragraphs (a) to (d) of this legal rule provides some limited exceptions to this principle.

1 See generally Carsten Fink, 'Intellectual Property Rights', in *Preferential Trade Agreement Policies for Development* (Jean-Pierre Chauffour and Jean-Christophe Maur Eds) (2011).

2 See TRIPS Art. 1 para. 1.

3 See WIPO, www.wipo.int/portal/en/index.html (last visit, April 30, 2017).

4 See Carsten Fink, 'Intellectual Property Rights', in *Preferential Trade Agreement Policies for Development*.

5 See, e.g., the so-called Special 301 Report, by which the United States verifies that other countries have enforced intellectual property rights. See The USTR, https://ustr.gov/issue-areas/intellectual-property/Special-301 (last visit, April 30, 2017). See generally Carsten Fink, 'Intellectual Property Rights', in *Preferential Trade Agreement Policies for Development*.

6 See generally Carsten Fink, 'Intellectual Property Rights', in *Preferential Trade Agreement Policies for Development*.

7 TRIPS Preamble.

8 *Cfr.* GATT Art. I.

TRIPS Art. 3, in turn, provides the National Treatment principle by stating that

> Each Member shall accord to the nationals of other Members treatment no less favourable than that it accords to its own nationals with regard to the protection of intellectual property, subject to the exceptions already provided in, respectively, the Paris Convention (1967), the Berne Convention (1971), the Rome Convention or the Treaty on Intellectual Property in Respect of Integrated Circuits.[9]

The transparency principle is also part of the TRIPS Agreement, whose relevant part of Art. 63 para. 1 reads:

> Laws and regulations, and final judicial decisions and administrative rulings of general application, made effective by a Member pertaining to the subject matter of this Agreement (the availability, scope, acquisition, enforcement and prevention of the abuse of intellectual property rights) shall be published, or where such publication is not practicable made publicly available, in a national language, in such a manner as to enable governments and right holders to become acquainted with them.[10]

Regarding other legal rules of the TRIPS Agreement, Art. 61 provides that WTO "Members shall provide for criminal procedures and penalties to be applied at least in cases of willful trademark counterfeiting or copyright piracy on a commercial scale." Developed countries were the ones proposing this legal rule in order to give legal teeth to the enforcement of intellectual property rights. Art. 64, in turn, provides that the provisions of GATT Arts XXII and XXIII, "as elaborated and applied by the Dispute Settlement Understanding shall apply to consultations and the settlement of disputes under this Agreement."[11] Last but not least, the TRIPS agreement lacks a legal rule similar to GATT Art. XXIV or to GATS Art. V; i.e., a legal rule allowing WTO members to enter into PTAs without infringing the MFN principle.[12] Such omission might indicate that rules on PTAs regarding intellectual property are either prohibited (since there is no multilateral rule allowing them) or permitted (under the rationale that everything that is not expressly restricted is allowed). In any event, this omission has not been an impediment for most recent PTAs including provisions on intellectual property rights.[13]

9 *Cfr.* GATT Art. III.
10 *Cfr.* GATT Art. X.
11 *Cfr.* GATS Art. XXIII.
12 See Fink, *supra* note 1, pp. 388–89.
13 See *supra* Chapter 13.

SECTION IV
Trade policy simulations

Section IV, covering Chapters 19 to 22, consists of simulation exercises based on specific trade policy cases and involving trade policy decision-making and trade agreement negotiations in a bilateral, plurilateral and multilateral setting.

19

SIMULATION EXERCISE

Trade policy decision-making process

Chapter 19 consists of a simulation of a hypothetical case on trade policy decision-making process. In particular, it is a role-playing exercise designed to reproduce as close as possible the realities of what happens behind the scenes as far as trade policy is concerned. The objective is to provide students with a practical experience through which they can learn and appreciate the often-complicated dynamics of trade policy making. In this exercise, they will have an opportunity to apply all the knowledge acquired in prior chapters.

A typical simulation like this can be done in two three-hour sessions. Ideally, with enough time between sessions to allow for further analysis and to prepare to rebut arguments and negotiating positions for the second session.

19.1 Preparation

Preparation should be done days in advance in order to give enough time for students to research and study their respective roles. In preparing for this exercise the following steps should be taken:

- Divide your class in four groups: Executive, Legislative, Private Sector and Public Interest. The ideal size is five students per group. Not too big, so as to be manageable, and not too small to accommodate differing positions within each group.
- Choose a policy objective to be pursued by the Private Sector: for example, a set of protectionist policies, such as tariff increases, more aggressive use of trade remedies, voluntary restraint agreements, or changes in trade agreements.
- Choose the Private Sector industry: try to pick a sector, for instance, that would be likely to request protection and that has plenty of statistical data publicly available, so that students can work with real data. For example, the steel industry in the United States or the agricultural sector in Europe would be good options.

- Choose the trade PFS (policy formulation system) under which the exercise will be conducted: for example, if the U.S. steel industry is chosen, then the trade PFS should be the American, with the Legislative being the U.S. House of Representatives and the U.S. Senate, and the Executive main agencies being the Department of Commerce, USTR and the Office of Trade and Manufacturing Policy.
- Divide responsibilities within each group: If the U.S. steel industry is chosen, then the Private Sector can play the role of that industry's association, say, for instance, the National Steel Association. The five students in this group should decide who should be the leading advocate, the persons in charge of legal arguments, economic arguments, statistical information, public interest arguments (labor, environment, health, etc.). It is important that the question of who would do what within the group be left to the discretion of the group, so as to encourage team work. They should circulate to all the groups in advance a list of actions that they intend to pursue (for example, increase in tariffs, change in trade remedies law, government infrastructure support, etc.). This will enable the other groups to prepare. The Executive should be divided among the main government agencies involved in trade policy formulation (Department of Commerce, USTR, OTMP, etc.). Try to include agencies that could oppose the idea (such as Treasury, in order to create discussion). The students in this group are encouraged to study their respective roles by learning the agency's responsibilities and policies so as to position themselves accordingly during the simulation. The Legislative should be carefully chosen, in order to reflect the realities of the trade PFS in question. If the American PFS is being used, the students in the group should be divided into three republicans and two democrats. The states represented by these senators should include producing as well as consuming states. Students are encouraged to study their role by researching the respective senators' positions and all pertinent information (economic, social, etc.) from his state. The Public Interest should include NGOs that are likely to oppose the policy (steel consumers, environmental concerns) as well as those that may support (labor, energy, national security).
- Coaching by experts during the sessions is an option. Otherwise the instructor will also play that role by helping with preparation and negotiations during the exercise.
- Monitoring should be done with regard to time keeping and making sure students are playing their designated roles as close to reality as possible. If one student is supposed to play the role of a conservative politician, he or she must think and react as such even if his/her thinking in real life is more in sync with that of an extreme liberal.

19.2 First session (three hours)

- The first round of meetings (one hour): the Private Sector will have introductory meetings with each of the other three groups, starting with

Congress, followed by the Executive and the Public Interest. These meetings must be separate, meaning that the groups outside the meeting cannot hear what is going on. Around 15 minutes should be allocated for each meeting. The purpose here is to allow the private sector to advocate their positions to each group, which they would have specifically targeted in their arguments. They should deliver to each group a written statement, with their requests and respective initial arguments, and do a ten-minute oral presentation, followed by questions from their interlocutors. If there is no time to answer all questions, they may provide them later in subsequent rounds. The coach should instruct the Private Sector to tailor their arguments to their audience. For example, senators are interested in the welfare of their constituents without the support of whom he or she cannot be reelected. In this case, the arguments should focus on benefits to their respective states. The Executive, on the other hand, requires more technical data and national focus. All students should be encouraged to take notes during the meetings so as to help them prepare for the following meetings.

- The second round of meetings (one hour): at this point all groups know what the Private Sector is after and may have additional questions or require answers to previous questions. On the other hand, the Legislative group may want to meet with other groups to learn of their reaction to the Private Sector proposals and so may the other groups too. So, here is where additional separate bilateral meetings of around 15 minutes each should take place until all groups have met with each other. This round can start with Congress meeting with the Executive, while separately the Public Interest meets with the Private Sector and so on.
- The third round of meetings (one hour): in this round, groups should be allowed to meet with any group or individual(s) within a group they desire. It is a chance for groups and individuals within groups to convert opposing views and garner support for their own. These meetings must be conducted bilaterally and separately.

19.3 Second session (three hours)

- The fourth round of meetings (one hour): time should be spent lobbying the opposition and giving the final touches to their statements for the public hearing that will follow.
- A public hearing (part 1) is convened by Congress (one and a half hours): the senators select a hearing chairperson, take their respective places in front of the class and the chairperson calls the hearing to order. A total of 15 minutes is allocated to each of the three presenting groups for oral statements. Written statements must be submitted before the hearing starts. The Private Sector speaks first. The Executive and the Public Interest will follow and will have the option to divide the 15 minutes among the other group members so as to accommodate differing views within the groups (in the Public Interest

group, an environmental NGO may not be in agreement with a consumer rights NGO, for example). Congress may use an additional five minutes for any questions it may have. At this point, Congress should thank all participants and call a recess. The remaining 30 minutes should be used to lobby Congress and remaining opposing parties in other groups and address any additional questions Congress people might have.

- The public hearing (part 2) reconvenes (half hour): senators express their final position with regard to the private sector proposal. They should not take more than three minutes each.
- Evaluation: the professor should review what was finally accomplished by the Private Sector in comparison to its initial proposal. Comment on compromises reached and ask the class if the exercise gave them a better understanding and new appreciation for what goes on behind the trade policies adopted by governments. This understanding will serve well those that either seek to promote or oppose trade policies in the future, in their own countries.

20

SIMULATION EXERCISE

Bilateral trade agreement negotiations

Chapter 20 consists of a simulation of a hypothetical case on trade agreement negotiations. In particular, the bilateral trade agreement simulation is, like the previous simulation, a role-playing exercise designed to reproduce as close as possible the realities of what happens behind the scenes and during negotiations of an international trade agreement. The objective is to provide students with a practical experience through which they can learn and appreciate the often-unknown dynamics of trade negotiations. In this exercise, students will have an opportunity to apply what they learned in previous chapters with regard to trade agreements, trade negotiations and all other components that make up the substance of these agreements.

A typical simulation like this can be done in two three-hour sessions. Ideally, with enough time between sessions to allow for further analysis and prepare to rebut arguments and negotiating positions for the second session.

20.1 Preparation

Preparation should be done days in advance in order to give enough time for students to research and study their respective roles. In preparing for this exercise the following steps should be taken:

- Divide your class in two groups: a developing country and a developed country. The ideal size is ten students per group, but it can be adapted to fit smaller or bigger numbers. Each group should be divided in two sub-groups: one with seven students to represent domestic interests and the other with three students to represent the negotiators.
- Choose two countries: try to choose countries that are not perfectly complementary in their trade, so as to provide grounds for harder negotiations

in certain items. Also, pick real countries with readily accessible statistics so that students can work with real data.

- Set up the sub-groups: the domestic interests sub-group should include representatives of the Executive (2), Legislative (2), Private Sector (2) and Public Interest (1). The remaining three students form the negotiators group, which will choose the head of delegation for the negotiations.
- Divide responsibilities within each group: the Executive group (2) should include one representative of the trade authority and one representative from another relevant agency (if agriculture is an important item, for example, it should be this agency). The Legislative group (2) should have two politicians with different views about trade. The Private Sector (2), if agriculture is the important item, should include one from agricultural business and one, for example, from manufacturing. The Public Interest (1), if agriculture is the main item, could be someone representing environmental and labor NGOs.
- Coaching by experts during the sessions is an option. Otherwise the instructor will also play that role by helping with preparation and negotiations during the exercise.
- Monitoring should be done with regard to time keeping and making sure students are playing their designated roles as close to reality as possible. If one student is supposed to play the role of a conservative politician, he or she must think and react as such even if he or she is an extreme liberal.

20.2 First session (three hours)

- The first round (one and a half hours): the sub-groups of domestic interests and negotiators in each country meet to discuss negotiating objectives (depth, coverage, differentiated treatment, compliance, remedies, dispute resolution, etc.). Here, at the discretion of the professor, the number of topics to be negotiated can be limited to a manageable number. Meetings must be done separately, ideally each country in a different room. The result of these meetings will be the instructions that negotiators must follow. If later negotiators believe changes are needed, they must consult with domestic interests and absolutely not continue the negotiation in violation of instructions. Negotiators must also have a negotiating strategy, i.e., how they should conduct the negotiations in order to fulfill their instructions.
- The second round of meetings (one and a half hours): the negotiators convene in one room and sit across a table, with the remaining members of each country taking seats away and behind their negotiators. The head of delegation on each side introduces the members of his/her negotiating team and subsequently each reads an opening statement spelling out in general terms what they are looking for in this agreement negotiation (30 minutes). Following that, the negotiation itself starts with the negotiators following their instructions and the strategy they put together (one hour).

- Heads of delegation must instruct the team with regard to who would be speaking at the negotiating table. Usually, in real life, others in the team can only speak if the head of delegation so wishes.

20.3 Second session (three hours)

- In the third round (two and a half hours) negotiations proceed until an agreement is reached or not. Students must be encouraged to negotiate and compromise if the resulting agreement brings a net positive result for their country. Otherwise, they must conclude that the deal is not worth pursuing and bring negotiations to an end.
- Evaluation (30 minutes): the professor should review what was accomplished by both delegations, where they faulted and where they excelled, if possible with examples from real negotiations. They should also comment on creative solutions, compromises reached and ask the class if the exercise gave them a better understanding and new appreciation for what goes on behind the scenes during trade agreement negotiations. This understanding will serve well those that either seek to pursue a trade career in academia, government and Private Sector, or to analyze trade agreements for the perspective of press or media in general.

21

SIMULATION EXERCISE

Plurilateral trade agreement negotiations

The plurilateral trade agreement simulation is, like the previous simulation, a role-playing exercise designed to reproduce as close as possible the realities of what happens behind the scenes and during negotiations of a plurilateral trade agreement at the WTO. The objective is to provide students with a practical experience through which they can learn and appreciate the often-unknown dynamics of different trade negotiations. In this exercise, they will have an opportunity to apply what they learned in previous chapters with regard to trade agreements, trade negotiations and all other components that make up the substance of these agreements.

A typical simulation like this can be done in two three-hour sessions. Ideally, with enough time between sessions to allow for further analysis and prepare to rebut arguments and negotiating positions for the second session.

21.1 Preparation

Preparation should be done days in advance in order to give enough time for students to research and study their respective roles. In preparing for this exercise the following steps should be taken:

- Divide your class in four groups: two developing countries and two developed countries. The ideal size is five students per country, but it can be adapted to fit smaller or bigger numbers. Each group should be divided in two sub-groups: one negotiator and four to represent domestic interests. The domestic interests sub-group should include representatives of the Executive (1), Legislative (1), Private Sector (1) and Public Interest (1).
- Choose countries and topic: usually plurilateral agreements are negotiated among like-minded countries, so the countries must be chosen having in

mind their common purpose but not necessarily a common level of ambition. Pick real countries with readily accessible information and statistics so that students can work with real data and information. Plurilaterals also usually cover one topic like trade in civil aircraft, government procurement, or services, so pick a topic that can be researched in all countries and that students have time to study.

- Coaching by experts during the sessions is an option. Otherwise the instructor will also play that role by helping with preparation and negotiations during the exercise.
- Monitoring should be done with regard to time keeping and making sure students are playing their designated roles as close to reality as possible. If one student is supposed to play the role of a conservative politician, he or she must think and react as such even if he or she is an extreme liberal in real life.

21.2 First session (three hours)

- The first round (one and a half hours). The sub-groups of domestic interests and negotiator in each country meet to discuss negotiating objectives (coverage, differentiated treatment, compliance, remedies, dispute resolution, etc.). Meetings must be done separately, ideally each country in a different room. The result of these meetings will be the instructions that negotiators must follow. If later negotiators believe changes are needed, they must consult with domestic interests and absolutely not continue the negotiation in violation of instructions. Negotiators must also have a negotiating strategy, i.e., how they should conduct the negotiations in order to fulfill their instructions.
- The second round of meetings (one and a half hours): the negotiators convene in one room and sit around a table, with the remaining members of each country taking seats away and behind their negotiators. The head of delegation on each side introduces the members of his/her negotiating team and subsequently each reads an opening statement spelling out in general terms what they are looking for in this agreement negotiation (30 minutes). Following that, the negotiation itself starts with the negotiators following their instructions and strategy they put together (one hour).
- Heads of delegation must instruct the team with regard to who will be speaking at the negotiating table. Usually, in real life, others in the team can only speak if the head of delegation so wishes.

21.3 Second session (three hours)

- In the third round (two and a half hours) negotiations proceed until an agreement is reached or not. Students must be encouraged to negotiate and compromise if the resulting agreement brings a net positive result for their country. Otherwise, they must conclude that the deal is not worth pursuing and withdraw from negotiations.

- Evaluation (30 minutes): The professor should review what was accomplished by both delegations, where they faulted and where they excelled, if possible with examples from real negotiations. They should also comment on creative solutions, compromises reached and ask the class if the exercise gave them a better understanding and new appreciation for what goes on behind the scenes and during a plurilateral trade agreement negotiation. This understanding will serve well those that either seek to pursue a trade career in academia, government and Private Sector, or to analyze trade agreements from the perspective of the press or media in general.

22

SIMULATION EXERCISE

Multilateral trade agreement negotiations

This simulation exercise is very similar to the previous one save two key differences: (i) all and not only most WTO members participate in multilateral negotiations, and (ii) multilateral negotiations usually cover more issues, not only in number but also in complexity, than plurilateral negotiations.

Thus, this role-playing exercise is designed to reproduce as close as possible the realities of what happens behind the scenes and during negotiations of a multilateral trade agreement at the WTO. The goal is to provide students with a practical experience through which they can learn and appreciate the often-unknown dynamics of different trade negotiations and observe the differences between multilateral negotiations and other kinds of trade deals.

A typical simulation like this can be done in two three-hour sessions. Ideally, with enough time between sessions to allow for further analysis and prepare to rebut arguments and negotiating positions for the second session.

21.1 Preparation

Preparation should be done days in advance in order to give enough time for students to research and study their respective roles. In preparing for this exercise the following steps should be taken:

- Divide your class in four groups: two developing countries and two developed or even least-developed countries. The ideal size is five students per country, but it can be adapted to fit smaller or bigger numbers. Each group should be divided in two sub-groups: one negotiator and four to represent domestic interests. The domestic interests sub-group should include representatives of the Executive (1), Legislative (1), Private Sector (1) and Public Interest (1).

- Choose countries and topic: unlike plurilaterals, multilateral agreements are usually negotiations among countries with different views and stances about international trade. In order to make the simulation more challenging and realistic, the countries must be chosen having in mind their diversity of purposes. Pick real countries with readily accessible information and statistics so that students can work with real data and information. Also unlike plurilaterals, multilateral agreements usually cover several topics, which, of course, make their negotiation more complex. Nonetheless, and in order to keep the simulation manageable, pick only very few topics that can be researched in all countries and that students have time to study.
- Coaching by experts during the sessions is an option. Otherwise the instructor will also play that role by helping with preparation and negotiations during the exercise.
- Monitoring should be done with regard to time keeping and making sure students are playing their designated roles as close to reality as possible. If one student is supposed to play the role of a conservative politician, he or she must think and react as such even if he or she is an extreme liberal in real life.

21.2 First session (three hours)

- The first round (one and a half hours). The sub-groups of domestic interests and negotiator in each country meet to discuss negotiating objectives (coverage, differentiated treatment, compliance, remedies, dispute resolution, etc.). Meetings must be done separately, ideally each country in a different room. The result of these meetings will be the instructions that negotiators must follow. If later negotiators believe changes are needed, they must consult with domestic interests and absolutely not continue the negotiation in violation of instructions. Negotiators must also have a negotiating strategy, i.e., how they should conduct the negotiations in order to fulfill their instructions.
- The second round of meetings (one and a half hours): The negotiators convene in one room and sit around a table, with the remaining members of each country taking seats away and behind their negotiators. The head of delegation on each side introduces the members of his/her negotiating team and subsequently each reads an opening statement spelling out in general terms what they are looking for in this agreement negotiation (30 minutes). Following that, the negotiation itself starts with the negotiators following their instructions and strategy they put together (one hour).
- Heads of delegation must instruct the team with regard to who will be speaking at the negotiating table. Usually, in real life, others in the team can only speak if the head of delegation so wishes.

21.3 Second session (three hours)

- In the third round (two and a half hours) negotiations proceed until an agreement is reached or not. Students must be encouraged to negotiate, seek coalitions in topics, and compromise if the resulting agreement brings a net positive result for their country. Otherwise, they must conclude that the deal is not worth pursuing and withdraw from negotiations.

- Evaluation (30 minutes): the professor should review what was accomplished by both delegations, where they faulted and where they excelled, if possible with examples from real negotiations. They should also comment on creative solutions, compromises reached and ask the class if the exercise gave them a better understanding and new appreciation for what goes on behind the scenes and during a multilateral trade agreement negotiation. This understanding will serve well those that either seek to pursue a trade career in academia, government and private sector, or to analyze trade agreements from the perspective of the press or media in general.

EPILOGUE

Trade under attack

These are not favorable times for international trade. As previous chapters indicated, the Doha Round has been stalled since 2001 and, as a result and besides the recent ratification of the WTO Trade Facilitation Agreement,[1] no single amendment to the WTO agreements has been approved since the WTO itself was established on January 1, 1995. Things are even worse in the financial arena, where IMF members recently issued a statement indicating that they would "promote a level playing field in international trade," but did not reiterate a previous commitment to "resist all forms of protectionism."[2] In any event, it is the WTO and not the IMF which is the international organization in charge of international trade matters.

Regarding the multilateral trade level, the issue is that international trade is not making any substantial progress. Perhaps for this reason, some trade economists have proposed to focus on plurilateral agreements.[3] On the regional level, as Chapter 3 described in further detail,[4] Brexit was a step back regarding integration. Notwithstanding, this does not entail that the European Union is condemned to its disintegration, especially taking into account the presidential election in France in May 2017, where a candidate pro integration (Emmanuel

1 See *supra* Chapter 10.

2 See Financial Times, *G20 Drops Vow to Resist all Forms of Protectionism*, www.ft.com/content/241cdf2a-0be9-11e7-a88c-50ba212dce4d (last visit, May 14, 2017). See also *Global Prospects and Policy Challenges*, available at: www.imf.org/external/np/g20/pdf/2017/031417.pdf (last visit, May 14, 2017). Such new approach might indicate the influence of the new U.S. administration on international organizations in trade matters.

3 See *supra* Chapter 15.

4 See *supra* Chapter 3.

Macron) defeated, among others, candidates who defended the exit of France from the European Union.

However, the trade policies that the U.S. President elected for the term 2017–2021 has announced seems clearly protectionist.[5] In particular, such policies are intended to renegotiate or, if this is not possible, to denounce some international trade agreements which the United States is a party to, to promote domestic production, to discourage national companies from relocating plants abroad, and to force or at least encourage American companies to buy local products. As a recent WTO report put it:

> The role of trade in the global economy is at a critical juncture. Increased trade integration helped to drive economic growth in advanced and developing economies in the latter part of the 20th century. Since the early 2000s, however, a slowdown in the pace of trade reform, a post-crisis uptick in protectionism, and risk of further reversals have been a drag on trade, productivity, and income growth. At the same time, trade is leaving too many individuals and communities behind, notably also in advanced economies. To be sure, job losses in certain sectors or regions in advanced economies have resulted to a large extent from technological changes rather than from trade. But adjustment to trade can bring a human and economic downside that is frequently concentrated, sometimes harsh, and has too often become prolonged.[6]

For all the reasons mentioned above, this epilogue is titled "Trade under attack." In any event, and to be clear, protests against international trade are not new. For instance, mercantilism, mainly consisting of discouraging imports via prohibitive tariffs, was the predominant view during the sixteenth century.[7] Much more recently, some protests were held in Seattle during the Third WTO Ministerial Conference in 1999.[8] Notwithstanding, and while trade has been always under attack during recent decades, the current forces against it had not been so strong since the time elapsed between the two world wars.[9] During such years, many

5 See President Donald J. Trump's inaugural speech (January 20, 2017), which considers business partners as enemies and protectionism as a generator of progress. *The Inaugural Address*, The White House, www.whitehouse.gov/inaugural-address (last visit, April 20, 2017).

6 WTO, *Making Trade an Engine of Growth for All, The Case for Trade and for Policies to Facilitate Adjustment*, 3, www.wto.org/english/news_e/news17_e/wto_imf_report_07042017.pdf (last visit, April 20, 2017).

7 See Dani Rodrik, The Globalization Paradox 1 (2012). See also the Sugar Act and the Navigation Acts.

8 See WTO, www.wto.org/english/thewto_e/minist_e/min99_e/min99_e.htm (last visit, April 30, 2017).

9 See Liaquat Ahamed, *The Bankers Who Broke the World*, p. 1 (2009). Likewise, technological progress is also under attack, although perhaps, the attack is not so strong as in the case of

developed countries resorted to protectionism under the wrong view that such trade policy was the best path to avoid another Great Depression.[10]

Two other differences between the current time and other difficult times for trade are noticeable. First, while it has been always the rule rather than the exception that many people have not gotten the case for free trade,[11] such trend might be accentuating. This is particularly true regarding people without any legal or economic studies. Thus, while many economists are in favor of international trade,[12] many lay people are in favor of limiting imports.[13] For instance, a global survey made in the late 1990s found that nearly 70 percent of the respondents were in favor of limiting imports.[14] In the words of Professor and economist Dani Rodrik:

> It is easy to pooh-pooh many anti-trade arguments because they make little sense upon scrutiny. Yet among the general public, skepticism about trade is too widespread to dismiss so easily. Survey after survey finds that a distinct majority of people support restrictions on imports to "protect" jobs and the economy.[15]

As a second difference, some politicians holding views against international trade are now wielding important political positions. The most noticeable example is the current U.S. President.[16] Since the policies of this new U.S. government are, nowadays, the main force against international trade, it is worth describing them in further detail.

Since the U.S. President was a candidate, he had promised that protectionism would make America great again by bringing back facilities and jobs that have

the forces against international trade. Many politicians are nowadays worried about the impact that technology might have in jobs. See generally Martin Ford, *Rise of the Robots: Technology and the Threat of a Jobless Future* (2016). Similar to the trends against trade, the concerns about the impact of technology are not new. Recall, for instance, the Luddites on the eve of the nineteenth century, who were strongly against the industrial revolution. See *id*. On the other hand, take into account that the current development of the U.S. technology and the higher levels of labor prices might make it impossible to bring many jobs back from Mexico or other countries. Indeed, bringing a factory from Mexico into the United States would not create the same amount of jobs, simply because there would be more automation in the United States. Generally speaking, one of the ways to compete with a low-income country is through automation (the other way is by outsourcing and producing overseas).

10 See Liaquat Ahamed, *The Bankers Who Broke the World*, p. 1 (2009).

11 See Dani Rodrik, *The Globalization Paradox*, p. 1 (2012).

12 See, e.g, many of the authors cited in this book.

13 See Dani Rodrik, *The Globalization Paradox*, p. 1 (2012).

14 See World Values Survey online database, available at: http://worldvaluessurvey.org (last visit, April 20, 2017). See also Dani Rodrik, *The Globalization Paradox*, p. 51 (2012).

15 See *id*, at 51.

16 In other cases, politicians against international trade have failed in their purpose to be elected, as recently happened in the French presidential election.

moved to other countries such as China and Mexico and, more generally, by shielding the United States from the alleged ravages of foreign competition.[17]

The trade team that this president appointed to chair the three most important U.S. agencies regarding trade (Department of Trade, Office of Trade and Manufacturing Policy and USTR) confirms that its protectionist policies were not only a campaign promise in order to clear the way to the White House, but that they will be implemented and strictly enforced.[18]

To begin with, the Secretary of Commerce[19] is a millionaire with investments in industries such as steel and coal, which might benefit from the new protectionist policies.[20] In turn, the leader of the freshly minted Office of Trade and Manufacturing Policy is a Harvard educated Doctor of Economics[21] whose stance seems to be against international trade as his most famous book, *Death by China*, indicates.[22] In this book, he makes the case for protectionist measures as a counterweight to Chinese measures such as huge subsidies to domestic companies and alleged currency manipulation.[23] He has also stated that one of the trade priorities will be the unwinding and repatriation of international supply chains on which many U.S. multinational companies rely.[24] In his words:

> It does the American economy no long-term good to only keep the big box factories where we are now assembling "American" products that are composed primarily of foreign components.... We need to manufacture those components in a robust domestic supply chain that will spur job and wage growth.[25]

The new U.S. Trade Representative[26] is the third member of this U.S. trade "troika."[27] He is an attorney that has represented the domestic steel industry for many years in trade remedy cases. More importantly, he was the deputy USTR in the 1980s, who led the negotiations of the unprecedented Voluntary Restraint

17 See www.donaldjtrump.com/ (last visit, April 20, 2017).

18 Aluisio de Lima-Campos, *A Política Comercial de Donald Trump* 130 Rev. Brasileira de Comércio Exterior 6 (2017).

19 Wilbur Ross.

20 Aluisio de Lima-Campos, *A Política Comercial de Donald Trump* 130 Rev. Brasileira de Comércio Exterior 6 (2017).

21 Peter Navarro.

22 Peter Navarro and Greg Autry, *Death by China. Confronting the Dragon – A Global Call to Action*, p. 1 (2011).

23 See *id.*

24 See James Pethokoukis, *Does Trump Want to Somehow get rid of Global Supply Chains?* AEIdeas, January 31th, 2017, www.aei.org/publication/does-trump-want-to-somehow-get-rid-of-global-supply-chains/ (last visit, April 20, 2017).

25 See *id.*

26 Robert Lighthizer.

27 Russian term meaning a collaboration of three (individuals or animals).

Agreements (VRAs) on steel products. Under VRAs, some countries exporting goods to the United States were compelled to quantitatively limit their sales to this country in exchange for the repeal of all anti-dumping and anti-subsidy duties in legal force.[28] The return of VRAs in the U.S. is now a possibility. If so, that might be imitated by other WTO members.

As put forth by the new Administration, the staples of the new U.S. trade policy are the following ones. First, the United States will attempt to renegotiate or, if it is not possible, to withdraw from some Preferential Trade Agreements which it is a party to, such as NAFTA. In particular, the United States would like to include new provisions in such agreements (i) protecting against currency manipulation, (ii) allowing withdrawals from treaties with 30 days' notice, and (iii) making changes in the procedures to settle disputes between a foreign investor and a host state.

Second, the U.S. Government has re-launched the "Buy American" campaign. The word "re-launched" is used because an original program under the same name had been launched during the previous U.S. administration as part of the economic program that was designed and implemented to fasten the recovery of the U.S. economy from the 2008–2009 economic crisis. Notwithstanding, the "Buy American" program was not forcefully implemented by that administration.

As its name suggests, the goal of "Buy American" is to encourage or even force individuals, companies and public entities to purchase domestic and not foreign products. In any event, to successfully implement this policy might be an uphill task since the United States does not manufacture enough goods for domestic consumption in many industries. On the other hand, and taking into account that a lot of pressure might be expected on states and localities to enforce the "Buy American" policy in combination with it becoming a requirement for federal government purchases, the impact of such policy on infrastructure projects such as oil pipelines and highways might be considerable. Indeed, such impact is estimated between US$150 billion and US$1 trillion during the next ten years.[29]

Nonetheless, this possible benefit would perhaps not outweigh the cost for American companies, localities and states resulting from not purchasing the least expensive or most technologically-advanced goods from foreign countries. On top of that, this new policy might negatively affect all those countries, such as Mexico, which are highly export dependent on the United States. As a consequence, WTO members might attempt to reduce their dependence on the United States and diversify their trade markets by pursuing trade agreements with countries that they have overlooked for years, such as Brazil in the Mexican case.[30]

28 See *supra* Chapter 11 for a detailed explanation of VRAs.

29 Aluisio de Lima-Campos, *A Política Comercial de Donald Trump* 130 Rev. Brasileira de Comércio Exterior 6 (2017).

30 See *U.S. New Trade Policy: Opportunities and Challenges for Brazil*, Brazil Monitor, April 13, 2017, www.brazilmonitor.com/index.php/2017/04/13/u-s-new-trade-policy-opportunities-and-challenges-for-brazil/ (last visit, April 30, 2017).

Third, the U.S. Government plans to protect the domestic industry by increasing the number and scope of trade remedies and other commercial defenses and by strictly and effectively enforcing U.S. trade laws. Put it differently, an intensification of activities on trade remedies, and on the use of Section 301 of 1974 as leverage,[31] is expected in the short-term, probably with a growing number of anti-dumping and anti-subsidy petitions, more rigorous investigations and enforcement and, perhaps, a greater bias in favor of the domestic industry.

Fourth, the current U.S. administration is promoting a tax reform, which includes a drastic reduction in individual and corporate taxes (from 35/40 percent to 15/20 percent), a lower tax (10 percent) for the repatriation of capital that companies keep abroad (estimated at $2.5 trillion) and some sort of Border Adjustment Tax (BAT). BAT, a tax levied on goods being imported to the United States from any other country, has the economic purpose of offsetting the disadvantaged position that the United States has in international trade as a result of it being one of the very few countries in the world that does not impose a Value-Added Tax (VAT).[32] Since the proposed BAT is intended to offset the trade advantage that producers from other countries have as a result of the VAT reimbursement, it might be argued that BAT would not be against the National Treatment Principle or, more generally speaking, against the WTO legal rules. Under this rationale, it is VAT and not BAT the tax that might be very distortive regarding trade between a country having the former tax and a country lacking it. On the other hand, some may view potential violations of Art. III:2 of GATT 94 (for favoring domestic production over imports) and Art. 3.1 of the ASCM (if shown to be a subsidy conditional upon the use of domestic products or a direct tax break for exports).

Regardless of its conformity with WTO legal rules, BAT will increase the cost of all U.S. imports in an amount equivalent to the rate of the new tax. The effect on all other countries will not be the same, though. It is anticipated that BAT will have a stronger effect on countries that are largely dependent on exports to the United States. However, a lesser impact is expected on exporters of products where the U.S. market share is not so large as well as in cases where the U.S. industry is not as competitive as the exporting one or where such domestic industry does not have enough capacity to satisfy all the demand for a given product provided that the price elasticity is low.

Nonetheless, not all the odds are in favor of a return to blatant protectionism in the United States. There are checks and balances ingrained in the U.S. Constitution and laws and there is also the specter of possible retaliation measures

31 This legal rule authorizes the USTR to take "appropriate measures" in response to actions that violate international trade agreements or that are unjustifiable, unreasonable, discriminatory and that adversely affect U.S. trade. See *supra* Chapter 2.

32 See generally Caroline Freund and Joseph Gagnon, *Consumption Taxes, Real Exchange Rates, and Trade Balances, Border Tax and Corporate Tax Reform*, PIIE Briefing (Adam Posen and Chad Bown Eds) 1 (2017).

from other countries. It might happen that not all protectionist trade policies that the U.S. President has mentioned since he was a candidate would be implemented. Under such scenario, the U.S. administration might realize that trade wars resulting from the implementation of protectionist policies are not good for the U.S. economy and, in particular, that they might affect positive results in growth and jobs. In addition, many of the proposed trade policies depend upon Congressional approval and some in Congress might object to the new measures. To take one illustration, it is difficult to imagine a considerable escalation of U.S. tariffs.

Moving from the U.S. trade particularities to a more global analysis, and also as closing remarks, the main trade risk looming over the global economy is that other countries or regions, such as the European Union or China, follow the new U.S. protectionist trade policies, either by a belief that they are the best economic policy or by retaliation. Under this scenario, the perspectives for an integrated world through trade does not look reassuring.

A lesser but not negligible risk consists of the WTO choosing to be very careful regarding decisions against the United States in order to avoid that the U.S. administration uses any panel or AB's decision against it to pull the United States out of the Organization. This might be a non-negligible concern since the U.S. Trade Policy Agenda clearly states:

> Even if a WTO dispute settlement panel – or the WTO Appellate Body – rules against the United States, such a ruling does not automatically lead to a change in U.S. law or practice. Consistent with these important protections and applicable U.S. law, the Trump Administration will aggressively defend American sovereignty over matters of trade policy.[33]

Of course, withdrawing the United States from the WTO is a decision under the scope of Congress and not of the Executive, being predictable that such an attempt will face tremendous opposition in Capitol Hill. In any event, more negotiations before panels reach conclusions are anticipated. Perhaps, for this reason, China has shown some restraint by requesting consultations with the European Union and the United States regarding its "market economy status" under the WTO, but requesting the establishment of a panel only in the E.U.'s case.[34]

33 *Id.*

34 See generally Gary C. Hufbauer, *As President, Trump Can Shackle Trade. But Will He?*, January 5, 2017, Peterson Institute for International Economics (Trade and Investment Policy Watch), https://piie.com/blogs/trade-investment-policy-watch/president-trump-can-shackle-trade-will-he (last visit, April 30, 2017). See also Gary C. Hufbauer, *Trump on Trade: A Few Cautions*, November 30, 2016, Peterson Institute for International Economics (Trade and Investment Policy Watch), https://piie.com/blogs/trade-investment-policy-watch/trump-trade-few-cautions (last visit, April 30, 2017).

In spite of the title of this Epilogue and of some recent trade trends, there are reasons to remain optimistic and to believe that international trade would emerge stronger from the current quandary. Making an analogy with economic growth and recessions, the current situation might be a recession in international trade, a non-negligible one, but, in the long run, both trade and economic integration might continue their expansion, similar to what happened to the world economy after previous crises, such as the Great Depression of 1929 or, more recently, the financial crisis of 2008–2009. The big question is how the global economy will surpass the current predicament: either with international trade and integration suffering minor bruises or with major effects that will take a longer time to be reversed.

REFERENCES

Papers and presentations

Arnaud Costinot and Dave Donaldson, *Ricardo's Theory of Comparative Advantage: Old Idea, New Evidence*, National Bureau of Economic Research, Working Paper 17969 (2012), available at: www.nber.org/papers/w17969.pdf

Arndt Wonka et al., *Measuring the Size and Scope of the EU Interest Group Population* (2011), European Union Politics, available at: http://eup.sagepub.com/content/11/3/463

Bülent Ulaşan, *Openness to International Trade and Economic Growth: A Cross-Country Empirical Investigation* Discussion Paper No 2012-25, Economics, the Open-Access, Open-Assessment E-Journal, available at: www.economics-ejournal.org/economics/discussionpapers/2012-25

C. Fred Bergsten, *Currency Wars, The Economy of the United States and Reform of the International Monetary System*, Stavros Niarchos Foundation Lecture, PIIE (2013), available at: https://piie.com/publications/papers/bergsten201305.pdf

C. Fred Bergsten, *The Dollar and the Renminbi*, Statement before the Hearing on US Economic Relations with China: Strategies and Options on Exchange Rates and Market Access, Subcommittee on Security and International Trade and Finance, Committee on Banking, Housing and Urban Affairs, United States Senate (May 23, 2007), https://piie.com/commentary/testimonies/dollar-and-renminbi

C. Fred Bergsten and Joseph E. Gagnon, *Currency Manipulation, the US Economy, and the Global Economic Order*, Policy Brief 12-25, Peterson Institute for International Economics (2012), available at: https://piie.com/publications/pb/pb12-25.pdf

Catharina E. Koops, *Manipulating the WTO? The Possibilities for Challenging Undervalued Currencies Under WTO Rules*, 2010 Research Paper Series, Amsterdam Center for International Law 3 (2010), available at: http://papers.ssrn.com/sol3/papers.cfm?abstract_id=1564093

Christoph Martin Lieb, *The Environmental Kuznets Curve – A Survey of the Empirical Evidence and of Possible Causes*, Discussion Paper Series No 391, Department of Economics, University of Heideberg, available at: www.uni-heidelberg.de/md/awi/forschung/dp391.pdf

Cynthia J. Arnson, *Mercosur and the Pacific Alliance: Whither the Relationship*, Wilson Center Home, available at: www.wilsoncenter.org/article/mercosur-and-the-pacific-alliance-whither-the-relationship

David Kupfer, *Case Studies of Successful and Unsuccessful Industrial Policies: The Case of Brazil*, Powerpoint Presentation at International Economic Association (IEA) – World Bank Roundtable May 22–23, Washington, D.C.: World Bank (2012), available at: www.powershow.com/view4/5a27b8-Y2U3N/Case_Studies_of_Successful_and_Unsuccessful_Industrial_Policies_The_Case_of_Brazil_David_Kupfer_UFRJ_and_BNDES_powerpoint_ppt_presentation

David W. Skully, *Economics of Tariff-Rate Quota Administrations*, Market and Trade Economics Division, Economic Research Service, U.S. Department of Agriculture. Technical Bulletin No 1893 (2001) available at: www.ers.usda.gov/webdocs/publications/tb1893/31998_tb1893_002.pdf

Department of Business, Energy and Industrial Strategy of the United Kingdom, *Green Paper on Trade Defense Instruments*, available at: http://webarchive.nationalarchives.gov.uk/20090609003228/www.berr.gov.uk/files/file38283.pdf

Francisco Rodríguez and Dani Rodrik, *Trade Policy and Economic Growth: A Skeptic's Guide to the Cross-National Literature*. Cambridge, MA: National Bureau of Economic Research. NBER Working Paper 7081 (1999), available at: www.nber.org/chapters/c11058.pdf

Gary C. Hufbauer, *The Evolving US View on TPP*, Working Paper No 484, Center for International Development of Stanford University (2013), available at: http://ycsg.yale.edu/sites/default/files/files/hufbauer_TPP.pdf

Gary C. Hufbauer, *As President, Trump Can Shackle Trade. But Will He?*, January 5, 2017, Peterson Institute for International Economics (Trade and Investment Policy Watch), available at: https://piie.com/blogs/trade-investment-policy-watch/president-trump-can-shackle-trade-will-he

Gary C. Hufbauer, *Trump on Trade: A Few Cautions*, November 30, 2016, Peterson Institute for International Economics (Trade and Investment Policy Watch), available at: https://piie.com/blogs/trade-investment-policy-watch/trump-trade-few-cautions

Gary C. Hufbauer and Jeffrey J. Schott, *Will the World Trade Organization Enjoy a Bright Future?*, Policy Brief 12-11, PIIE (2012), available at: https://piie.com/publications/policy-briefs/will-world-trade-organization-enjoy-bright-future

Gene M. Grossman and Alan B. Krueger, *Environmental Impacts of a North American Free Trade Agreement*. National Bureau of Economic Research Working Paper 3914, NBER, Cambridge (1991), available at: www.nber.org/papers/w3914

Graeme Douglas and Shannon Kindornay, *Development and the Private Sector: Canada's Approach*, Research Report, The North-South Institute (2013), available at: www.nsi-ins.ca/wp-content/uploads/2013/10/Development-and-the-Private-Sector-Canada%E2%80%99s-Approach-updated.pdf

Gregory Shaffer, *How to Make the WTO Dispute Settlement System Work for Developing Countries: Some Proactive Developing Country Strategies*, ICTSD Resource Paper No 5, Geneva (2003), available at: https://peacepalacelibrary.nl/ebooks/files/ICTSD_Shaffer_How-to-Make.pdf

Hongliang Zheng and Yang Yang, *Chinese Private Sector Development in the Past 30 Years: Retrospect and Prospect*, Discussion Paper 45, China Policy Institute, the University of Nottingham (2009), available at: www.nottingham.ac.uk/cpi/documents/discussion-papers/discussion-paper-45-hongliang-zheng-chinese-private-sector.pdf

Iain Begg and Fabian Mushövel, *The Economic Impact of Brexit: Jobs, Growth and the Public Finances*, European Institute, London School of Economics, available at: www.lse.

ac.uk/europeanInstitute/LSE-Commission/Hearing-11---The-impact-of-Brexit-on-jobs-and-economic-growth-sumary.pdf

Institute for Latin American and Caribbean Integration, Inter-American Development Bank, *Mercosur Report No 20*, available at: https://publications.iadb.org/bitstream/handle/11319/7280/Informe_MERCOSUR_N_20_2014_2015_Segundo_Semestre_2014_Primer_Semestre_2015.pdf?sequence=1

Iyabo Masha et al., *The Common Monetary Area in Southern Africa: Shocks, Adjustment, and Policy Challenges*, WP/07/158, IMF Working Paper (2007), available at: www.imf.org/external/pubs/ft/wp/2007/wp07158.pdf

J. Michael Finger, *The Doha Agenda and Development: A View from the Uruguay Round*, 31 ERD Working Paper No 21 Economics and Research Department, Asian Development Bank (2002), available at: www.adb.org/sites/default/files/publication/28316/wp021.pdf

James McBride and Mohammed Aly Sergie, *NAFTA's Economic Impact*, Council on Foreign Relations, available at: www.cfr.org/trade/naftas-economic-impact/p15790

Jayanta Roy, Pritam Banerjee and Ankur Mahanta, *The Evolution of Indian Trade Policy: State Intervention and Political Economy of Interest Groups. Historical Development of Indian Trade Policy and the Impact of Institutional Choices on Present Time*, International Institute for Sustainable Development (2012), available at: www.ipekpp.com/admin/upload_files/Report_3_54_The_2552084041.pdf

Jennifer Hillman and David Kleinman, *Trading Places: The New Dynamics of EU Trade Policy Under the Treaty of Lisbon*, Economic Policy Paper Series (2010), available at: www.gem.sciences-po.fr/content/publications/pdf/Hillman_Kleiman_TradingPlaces_Oct10.pdf

Jim O'Neill, *Building Better Global Economic BRICs*, Goldman Sachs, Economics Research from the GS Financial Workbench (2001), available at: www.goldmansachs.com/our-thinking/archive/archive-pdfs/build-better-brics.pdf

John J. Barceló III, *Harmonizing Preferential Rules of Origin in the WTO System*, Cornell Law Faculty Publications. Paper 72 (2006), available at: http://scholarship.law.cornell.edu/lsrp_papers/72

John Schaus, *Private Sector Development in India's Foreign Policy*, Centre for Strategic and International Studies (2015), available at: https://csis-prod.s3.amazonaws.com/s3fs-public/legacy_files/files/publication/150504_Schaus_PrivateSecDevelIndia_Web.pdf

John Springford and Simon Tilford, *The Great British Trade-Off. The Impact of Leaving the EU on the UK's Trade and Investment*, Centre for European Reform (2014), available at: www.cer.org.uk/sites/default/files/publications/attachments/pdf/2014/pb_britishtrade_16jan14-8285.pdf

Joseph E. Gagnon, *Combating Widespread Currency Manipulation*, PIIE Policy Brief (2012), https://piie.com/publications/pb/pb12-19.pdf

Joseph E. Stiglitz, *Towards a New Paradigm for Development: Strategies, Policies, and Processes*, Prebisch Lecture, UNCTAD, Geneva (1998), available at: http://siteresources.worldbank.org/NEWS/Resources/prebisch98.pdfJulian Birkinshaw, *Three Bureaucracy Busting Lessons from Brexit*, Forbes (2016), available at: www.forbes.com/sites/lbsbusinessstrategyreview/2016/07/07/three-bureaucracy-busting-lessons-from-brexit/#31146cde445f

Martin Roy et al., *Services Liberalization in the New Generation of Preferential Trade Agreements: How Much Further than GATS?* WTO Staff Working Paper ERSD 2006-07, World Trade Organization, Geneva (2006), available at: www.wto.org/english/res_e/reser_e/ersd200607_e.pdf

Nemat Shafik and Sushenjit Bandyopadhyay, *Economic Growth and Environmental Quality: Time Series and Cross-Country Evidence*, Background Paper for the World Development Report 1992, The World Bank, Washington, D.C. (1992), available at: http://documents.worldbank.org/curated/en/833431468739515725/Economic-growth-and-environmental-quality-time-series-and-cross-country-evidence

Osvaldo Rosales and Sebastián Herreros, *Mega-Regional Trade Negotiations: What is at Stake for Latin America?* The Inter-American Dialogue, available at: http://archive.thedialogue.org/tradepp

Peter Drahos, *The Bilateral Web of Trade Dispute Settlement*, Paper for the workshop on WTO Dispute Settlement and Developing Countries: Use, Implications, Strategies, Reforms, University of Wisconsin at Madison (2005) available at: www.twn.my/.../DisputeResolution/TheBilateralWebOfTradeDisp

Rafal Kierzenkowskil, Nigel Pain, Elena Rusticelli and Sanne Zwart, *The Economic Consequences of Brexit, A Taxing Decision* (2016), available at: www.oecd-ilibrary.org/economics/the-economic-consequences-of-brexit_5jm0lsvdkf6k-en

Robert Staiger and Alan Sykes, *Currency Manipulation and World Trade: A Caution*, available at: http://voxeu.org/article/currency-manipulation-and-world-trade-three-reasons-caution.

Roman Stöllinger and Mario Holzner, *State Aid and Export Competitiveness in the EU*, Working Paper 106, The Vienna Institute for International Economics Studies (2013), available at: https://wiiw.ac.at/state-aid-and-export-competitiveness-in-the-eu-dlp-3092.pdf

Renato Baumann, Josefina Rivero and Yohana Zavattiero, *Tariffs and the Plano Real in Brazil*, CEPAL Document (1998), available at: www.cepal.org/en/publications/10671-tariffs-and-plano-real-brazil

Sebastián Sáez, *The Countries of Latin America and the Caribbean and Trade Disputes: An Analysis.* Boletín FAL 249 (2007).

Sonia E. Rolland, *From the Uruguay Round to the Doha Round: Changing Dynamics in Developing Countries' Participation*, Oxford Scholarship Online (2012), available at: www.oxfordscholarship.com/view/10.1093/acprof:oso/9780199600885.001.0001/acprof-9780199600885-chapter-6

Swati Dhingra and Thomas Sampson, *Life after BREXIT: What are the UK's Options Outside the European Union?* Centre for Economic Performance, London School of Economics (2016), available at: http://cep.lse.ac.uk/pubs/download/brexit01.pdf

Todd Allee, *Developing Countries and the Initiation of GATT/WTO Disputes*, paper presented at the annual meeting of the American Political Science Association (2008), available at: http://wp.peio.me/wp-content/uploads/2014/04/Conf1_Allee_Developing.Countries.WTO_.Disputes.pdf

Vera Thorstensen, *Normalized PPP – Trade Weighted World Basket*, Powerpoint Presentation (2013), video available at: www.youtube.com/watch?v=7A6qprQi9JU&feature=player_embedded

Vera Thorstensen, Emerson Marçal and Lucas Ferraz, *Impacts of Exchange Rates on International Trade Policy Instruments: The Case of Tariffs*, São Paulo School of Economics (EESP), FGV (2011), available at: http://bibliotecadigital.fgv.br/dspace/bitstream/handle/10438/15781/Exchange%20rate%20misalignments%20and%20international%20trade%20policy%20-%20impacts%20on%20tariffs.pdf?sequence=1&isAllowed=y

Vera Thorstensen, Reinhard Weissinger and Xinhua Sun, *Private Standards—Implications for Trade, Development, and Governance, E15 Initiative*, Geneva, International Centre for Trade and Sustainable Development (ICTSD) and World Economic Forum, available at: http://e15initiative.org/wp-content/uploads/2015/07/E15-Regulatory-Thorstensen-et-al.-final.pdf

William R. Cline, *Estimating Consistent Fundamental Equilibrium Exchange Rates*, Working Paper 08-6, the Peterson Institute for International Economics (2008), available at: https://piie.com/sites/default/files/publications/wp/wp08-6.pdf

William R. Cline, *Estimates of Fundamental Equilibrium Exchange Rates*, Policy Brief, Peterson Institute for International Economics (2016), available at: https://piie.com/publications/policy-briefs/estimates-fundamental-equilibrium-exchange-rates-may-2016

William Davey, *Pine and Swine: Canada – United States Trade Dispute Settlement, the FTA Experience and NAFTA Prospects*, Ottawa, Centre for Trade Policy and Law (1996), available at: meiguyba.ru/mynogaqy.pdf

Yan Luo, *Dispute Settlement in the Proposed East Asian Free Trade Agreement: What We Can Learn from the EU and the NAFTA*, presentation made in the ILA British Branch Spring 2005 Conference, Edinburgh, Scotland: available at: www.hss.ed.ac.uk/ila/Day2.htm

Articles in journals

Aaditya Mattoo, Prachi Mishra and Arvind Subramanian, *Spillover Effects of Exchange Rates: A Study of the Renminbi*, IMF Working Paper (2012).

Alan O. Sykes, *The Persistent Puzzles of Safeguards* 7(3) J. Int'l Econ. L. 523 (2004).

Aluisio de Lima-Campos, *Dumping e Subsidies: Impacto para e Brasil da Nova Legislação dos Estados Unidos* Rev. Brasileira de Comércio Exterior (1995).

Aluisio de Lima-Campos, *Causas e Consequências da Crise Internacional de Preços do Algodão* 73 Rev. Brasileira de Comércio Exterior, 73, 25 (2002).

Aluisio de Lima-Campos, *Nineteen Proposals to Curb Abuse in Anti-dumping and Countervailing Duties Proceedings* 39(2) J. World Trade 239, 250 (2005).

Aluisio de Lima-Campos, *Acordos Preferenciais de Comércio* Comércio e Negociações Internacionais para Jornalistas, Centro Brasileiro de Relações Internacionais – CEBRI (2009).

Aluisio de Lima-Campos, *A Nova Realidade das Politicas Comerciais e Seus Efeitos sobre o Multilateralismo* 19(3) Rev. Pol. Externa 1(2010).

Aluisio de Lima-Campos, *Brazil and Predatory Currency Misalignments* 2(10) CEBRI Dossiê, Edição Especial: O Brasil e a Agenda Global 1(2012).

Aluisio de Lima-Campos, *A Política Comercial de Donald Trump* 130 Rev. Brasileira de Comércio Exterior 6 (2017).

Aluisio de Lima-Campos and Adriana Vito, *Abuse and Discretion: The Impact of Antidumping and Countervailing Duties Proceedings on Brazilian Exports in the United States* 38 J. World Trade 34 (2004).

Aluisio de Lima-Campos and Cynthia Kramer, *Criação de Varas Especializadas em Defesa Comercial: uma necessidade para o comercio exterior brasileiro* 19–22 Rev. do IBRAC (2012).

Aluisio de Lima-Campos and Juan Gaviria, *A Case for Misaligned Currencies as Countervailable Subsidies* 46(5) J. World Trade 1017 (2012).

Andrea Ewart, *Small Developing State in the WTO: A Procedural Approach to Special and Differential Treatment Through Reforms to Dispute Settlement* 35 Syracuse J. Int'l L. & Com. 27, 27 (2007).

Anne O. Krueger, *Why Trade Liberalization is Good for Growth* 108 Econ. J.1513 (1998).

Ardnt Wonka et al., *Measuring the Size and Scope of the EU Interest Group Population* 11(3) Eur. Union Pol. 463 (2010).

Benjamin Blase Caryl, *Is China Currency Regime a Countervailable Subsidy? A Legal Analysis Under the World Trade Organization's SCM Agreement* 45(1) J. World Trade 187 (2011).

Brink Lindsey and Daniel J. Benson, *Reforming the Antidumping Agreement: A Real Map for WTO Negotiations* 21 Trade Pol. Anal. (2002).

C. Fred Bergsten, *Globalizing Free Trade: The Ascent of Regionalism* 75(3) Foreign Affairs 105 (1996).

Chad P. Bown and Bernard M. Hoekman, *WTO Dispute Settlement and the Missing Developing Country Cases: Engaging the Private Sector* 8(4) 861 J. Int'l Econ. L. (2005).

Christina L. Davis and Sarah B. Bermeo, *Who Files? Developing Country Participation in GATT/WTO Adjudication* 71(3) J. Pol. 1033 (2009).

Deborah Siegel, *Legal Aspects of the IMF/WTO Relationship: The Fund's Articles of Agreement and the WTO Agreements* 96 Am. J. Int'l L. 561, 595 (2002).

ECLAC, *Dispute Settlement Within the Southern Common Market (MERCOSUR)*, available at: https://idatd.cepal.org/soluciones/iTemplate-MERCOSUR-explicacion.pdf.

Eli Heckscher, *The Effect of Foreign Trade on the Distribution of Income* Ekonomisk Tidskrift 497 (1919).

Fernando Piérola and Gary Horlick, *WTO Dispute Settlement and Dispute Settlement in the "North-South" Agreements of the Americas: Considerations for Choice of Forum* 41 J. World Trade 883, 893 (2007).

Gary N. Horlick and Edwin Vermulst, *The 10 Major Problems with the Antidumping Instrument: An Attempt at Synthesis* 39(1) J. World Trade 67 (2005).

Gregory Hudson, Pedro Bento de Faria and Tobias Peyerl, *The Legality of Exchange Rate Undervaluation Under WTO Law*, CTEI Working Paper, Centre for Trade and Economic Integration at the Graduate Institute of International and Development Studies (IHEID) 1 (2011).

Henrik Horn, Petros C. Mavroidis and André Sapir, *Beyond the WTO? An Anatomy of EU and US Preferential Trade Agreements* 33(11) World Econ. 1565 (2010).

Jeffrey A. Frankel and David Romer, *Does Trade Cause Growth?* 89(3) Am. Econ. Rev. 379 (1999).

John Williamson, *The Exchange Rate System*, Policy Analyses in International Economics, Peterson Institute for International Economics (1983).

Joseph A. Schumpeter, *John Maynard Keynes 1883–1946* 36(4) Am. Econ. Rev. 495 (1946).

Juan Antonio Gaviria, *Una Propuesta de Expansión del Sistema de Solución de Controversias de la OMC como Contrapeso a la Tendencia Creciente de los Tratados de Comercio Preferencial* [*A Case for Expanding the WTO Dispute Settlement System as a Counterweight to the Growing Trend of Preferential Trade Agreements*] 4 Rev. D. Econ. Int'l (2013).

Judith H. Bello, *Some Practical Observations About WTO Settlement of Intellectual Property Disputes* 37 Va. J. Int'l L. 357 (1996–1997).

Junji Nakagawa, *No More Negotiated Deals? Settlement of Trade and Investment Disputes in East Asia* 10 (4) J. Int'l Econ. L. 837 (2007).

K. S. Vataliya and Bhanupen N. Parmar, *An Article on Foreign Capital and Foreign Investment (Foreign Direct Investment)* 1(3) Int'l J. Advance Res. Computer Sci. & Mgmt. Stud. 1 (2013).

Ken Jones, *The Political Economy of Voluntary Export Restraint Agreements* 37(1) Kyklos Int'l Rev. Soc. Sci. 82 (1984).

Kristin Bohl, *Problems of Developing Country Access to WTO Dispute Settlement* 9 Chi-Kent J. Int'l & Comp. L. 131, 146 (2009).

Leonardo Baccini and Andreas Dur, *The New Regionalism and Policy Interdependence* 42 Brit. J. Pol. Sci. 57 (2012).

Makane Moïse Mbengue, *Private Standards and WTO Law* 5(1) Biores, Int'l Centre Trade & Sustainable Dev. (2011), available at: www.ictsd.org/bridges-news/biores/news/private-standards-and-wto-law.

Marco C. E. J. Bronckers, *More Power to the WTO?* 4(41) J. Int'l Econ. L. 60 (2001).

Matthew Cole, Anthony J. Rayner and John M. Bates, *The Environmental Kuznets Curve: An Empirical Analysis* 2(4) Env't & Dev. Econ. 401 (1997).

Nathan Fudge, *Walter Mitty and the Dragon: An Analysis of the Possibility for WTO or IMF Action against China's Manipulation of the Yuan* 45 (2) J. World Trade 352 (2011).

Peter A. Dohlman, *Determinations of Adequacy in Sunset Reviews of Antidumping Orders in the United States* 14(5) Am. Univ. Int'l L. Rev. 1281 (1999).

Peter Iadicola, *Globalization and Empire* 1(2) Int'l J. Soc. Inquiry 1 (2008).

Petko D. Kantchevski, *The Differences Between the Panel Procedures of the GATT and the WTO: The Role of GATT and WTO Panels in Trade Dispute Settlement* 3(1) Brigham Young U. Int'l L. & Mgmt. Rev. 82 (2007)

Raymond Vernon, *International Investment and International Trade in the Product Cycle* LXXX Q. J. Econ. 190 (1966).

Richard T. Carson, *The Environmental Kuznets Curve: Seeking Empirical Regularity and Theoretical Structure* 4(1) Rev. Env't Econ. & Pol. 3 (2010).

Sergei Kirsanov and Evgeny Safonov, *The Consequences of Russia's Accession to WTO: Conclusions and Recommendations* 10(16) Eur. Sci. J. 195 (2014).

Simon Kuznets, *Economic Growth and Income Inequality* 45(1) Am. Econ. Rev. 1 (1955).

Tao Wang, *China: Sources of Real Exchange Rate Fluctuations*, IMF Working Paper WP/04/18, Asian and Pacific Department 1 (2004).

Todd Landman and Marco Larizza, *Inequality and Human Rights: Who Controls What, When, and How?* 53(3) Int'l Stud. Q. 715 (2009).

Uwe Becker and Alexandra Vasileva, *Russia's Political Economy Re-conceptualized: A Changing Hybrid of Liberalism, Statism and Patrimonialism* J. Eurasian Stud. (2016).

Vera Thorstensen, Emerson Marçal and Lucas Ferraz, *Impacts of Exchange Rates on International Trade Policy Instruments: The Case of Tariffs*, São Paulo School of Economics (EESP), Fundação Getulio Vargas (2011).

Vera Thorstensen, Emerson Marçal and Lucas Ferraz, *Exchange Rate Misalignments and Trade Policy: Impacts on Tariffs* 46(3) J. World Trade 597 (2012).

Vera Thorstensen, Emerson Marçal and Lucas Ferraz, *Trade Rules and Exchange Rate Misalignments: In Search for a WTO Solution* 34(3) Rev. Econ. Pol. 1 (2014).

Vera Thorstensen et al., *WTO – Market and Non-Market Economies: The Hybrid Case of China* 1(2) Latin Am. J. Int'l Trade L. 765 (2003).

William J. Davey, *The WTO Dispute Settlement System: The First Ten Years* 8 J. Int'l Econ. L. 17, 46-48 (2005).

William J. Davey and André Sapir, *The Soft Drinks Case: The WTO and the Regional Agreements* 8 World Trade Rev. 5, 21 n. 78 (2009).

William R. Cline, *Estimates of Fundamental Equilibrium Exchange Rates*, Policy Brief, Peterson Institute for International Economics (2016).

William R. Cline and John Williamson, *Updated Estimates of Fundamental Equilibrium Exchange Rates*, Peterson Institute for International Economics (2012).

Wolfang Stolper and Paul Samuelson, *Protection and Real Wages* 9(1) Rev. Econ. Stud. 58 (1941).

Xavier Sala-I-Martin, *I Just Ran Two Million Regressions* 87(2) Am. Econ. Rev. 178 (1997).

Yi Gang, *Renminbi Exchange Rates and Relevant Institutional Factors* 28(2) Cato J.187 (2008).

Books

Adam Smith, *The Wealth of Nations* (London, Bantam Classics, 2014[1776]).

Amrita Narlikar, *International Trade and Developing Countries: Bargaining Coalitions in GATT and WTO* (London, Routledge, 2005).

Arthur E. Appleton and Michael G. Plummer, *The World Trade Organization: Legal, Economic and Political Analysis* (Berlin, Springer Science and Business Media, 2007).

Asian Development Bank, *Trade Policy, Industrial Performance, and Private Sector Development in India* (London, Oxford University Press, 2008).

Bertil Ohlin, *Interregional and International Trade* (2nd. ed.) (Cambridge, Harvard University Press, 1933).

Andrea C. Bianculli and Andrea Ribeiro (Eds), *Regional Organizations and Social Policy in Europe and Latin America: A Space for Social Citizenship?* p. 405 (New York, Palgrave Macmillan, 2015).

Andreas F. Lowenfeld, *International Economic Law* (2nd ed.) p. 23 (London, Oxford University Press, 2008).

Andrew I. Gavil, William E. Kovacic and Jonathan B. Baker, *Antitrust Law in Perspective: Cases, Concepts and Problems in Competition Policy* (New York, American Casebook Series, 2002).

Benn Steil, *The Battle of Bretton Woods* p. 223 (New York, Princeton University Press, 2014).

Bill Browder, *Red Notice: A True Story of High Finance, Murder, and One Man's Fight for Justice* (New York, Simon and Schuster, 2015).

Chad P. Bown and Joost Pauwelyn, *The Law, Economics and Politics of Retaliation in WTO Dispute Settlement* (Cambridge, Cambridge University Press, 2014).

Charles Adams, *Those Dirty Rotten Taxes: The Tax Revolts that Built America* (New York, The Free Press, 1998).

Dan Jones, Magna Carta: The Birth of Liberty (New York, Penguin Books, 2015).

Dani Rodrik, *The Globalization Paradox* (New York, W. W. Norton and Company, 2012).

David Ricardo, *On the Principles of Political Economy and Taxation* (London, Dover Publications, 2014).

Drew Fudenberg and Jean Tirole, *Game Theory* (Cambridge, The MIT Press, 1991).

Donald E. Moggridge (Ed.), *The Collected Writings of John Maynard Keynes* (London, Macmillan, 1980).

Edward A. Leamer, *The Craft of Economics: Lessons from the Heckscher-Ohlin Framework* (Cambridge, The MIT Press, 2012).

Encyclopedia of Chicago, available at: www.encyclopedia.chicagohistory.org/pages/326.html.

Enrique Krauze, *La Presidencia Imperial* [*The Imperial Presidency*] (Mexico, Tusquets, 2014).

Gary C. Hufbauer, *Synthetic Materials and the Theory of International Trade* (Cambridge, Harvard University Press, 1966).

Geza Feketekuty, *Policy Development and Negotiations in International Trade: A Practical Guide to Effective Commercial Diplomacy* (New York, Create Space Independent Publishing Platform, 2013).

Greg Mastel, *Antidumping Laws and the U.S. Economy* p. 123 (London, Routledge 1998).

Hal R. Varian, *Intermediate Microeconomics: A Modern Approach* (9th ed.) (New York, W.W. Norton and Company, 2014).

Hannah Murphy, *The Making of International Trade Policy: NGOs, Agenda-Setting and the WTO* (New York, Edward Elgar Publishing, 2010).

Harry Harding, *China's Second Revolution: Reform after Mao* (Washington, D.C., Brookings Institution Press, 2010).

Homer, *The Odyssey* (Robert Fagles, Translator) (New York, Penguin Classics, 1997).

IBP USA, *South African Customs Union (Sacu) Business Law Handbook 1* (New York, International Business Publications, 2009).

I. M. Destler, *American Trade Politics* (4th ed.) (Washington, D.C., Peterson Institute for International Economics, 2005).

J. Bradford Jensen, *Global Trade in Services: Fear, Facts, and Offshoring* (Washington, D.C., Peterson Institute of International Economics, 2011).

Jagdish Bhagwati, *Termites in the Trading System: How Preferential Agreements Undermine Free Trade* (New York, Oxford University Press, 2008).

James C. Hartigan, *Trade Disputes and the Dispute Settlement Understanding of the WTO: An Interdisciplinary Assessment* p. 222 (New York, Emerald Group Publishing, 2009)

Jeffrey J. Schott (Ed.), *Free Trade Agreements: U.S. Strategies and Priorities* (Washington, D.C., Peterson Institute for International Economics, 2004).

Jeffrey Neilson, Bill Pritchard and Henry Yeung Wai-Chung (Eds), *Global Value Chains and Global Production Networks: Changes in the International Political Economy* (London, Routledge, 2015).

Jennifer A. Hillman and Gary Horlick, *Legal Aspects of Brexit: Implications of the United Kingdom's Decision to Withdraw from the European Union* (New York, Institute of International Economic Law, 2017).

Jennifer Bair, Doug Miller and Marsha Dickson (Eds), *Workers' Rights and Labor Compliance in Global Supply Chains: Is a Social Label the Answer?* (London, Routledge, 2016).

John H. Jackson et al., *Legal Problems of International Economic Relations* (6th ed.) (New York, West Academic Publishing, 2013).

John Muthyala, *Dwelling in American: Dissent, Empire, and Globalization* p. 1 (New York, Darmouth, 2012).

John Maynard Keynes, *A Tract on Monetary Reform* p. 65 (London, Macmillan, 1924).

John Williamson, *The Exchange Rate System. Policy Analyses in International Economics* (Washington, D.C., Peterson Institute for International Economics, 1983).

Jorge I. Domínguez et al. (Eds), *Mexico's Evolving Democracy: A Comparative Study of the 2012 Elections* (Washington, D.C., John Hopkins University Press, 2014).

Joseph Gold, *Legal and Institutional Aspects of the International Monetary System: Selected Essays* (Washington, D.C., International Monetary Fund, 1979).

Joseph E. Stiglitz and Andrew Charlton, *Fair Trade for All: How Trade can Promote Development* (New York, Oxford University Press, 2007).

Katherine J. Cramer, *The Politics of Resentment: Rural Consciousness in Wisconsin and the Rise of Scott Walker* (Chicago, University of Chicago Press, 2016).

Liaquat Ahamed, *The Bankers Who Broke the World* (New York, Penguin Books, 2009).

Marcos Jank and Simao Silber, *Comparative Trade Policies: Organizational Models and Performance* (São Paulo, Singular, 2007).

Marie Lavigne, *The Economics of Transition: From Socialist Economy to Market Economy* (2nd ed.) (New York, Palgrave Macmillan, 2007).

Martin Ford, *Rise of the Robots: Technology and the Threat of a Jobless Future* (Oxford, Basic Books, 2016).

Martin Gilman, *No Precedent, No Plan: Inside Russia's 1998 Default* (Cambridge, The MIT Press, 2010).

Michael Trebilcock and Robert Howse, *The Regulation of International Trade* (4th ed.) (London, Routledge, 2012).

N. Gregory Mankiw, *Principles of Microeconomics* (4th ed.), p. 210 (New York, Thompson South-Wester, 2006).

National Bureau of Statistics of China, *Chinese Statistical Year Book 2009*, China Statistics Press (2009), available at: www.stats.gov.cn/tjsj/ndsj/2009/indexeh.htm.

OECD, *Looking Beyond Tariffs: The Role of Non-Tariff Barriers in World Trade* (Paris, OECD, 2006).

Oliver E. Williamson, *The Mechanisms of Governance* (New York, Oxford University Press, 1996).

Olivier Cadot, Antoni Estavadeoral, Akiko Suwa Eisenmann and Thierry Verdier (Eds), *The Origin of Goods: Rules of Origin in Regional Trade Agreements*, Centre for Economic Policy Research (New York, Oxford University Press, 2006).

Paul R. Krugman and Maurice Obstfeld, *International Trade* (10th ed.) (New York, Addison-Wesley, 2014).

Peter Gallagher and Andrew Stoler, *Viability of a Critical Mass Framework for Agricultural Trade Negotiations: An Alternative to the Single Undertaking Approach* (Sidney, Rural Industries Research and Development Corporation of Australia, 2010).

Peter Navarro and Greg Autry, *Death by China. Confronting the Dragon – A Global Call to Action* (New York, Pearson FT Press, 2011).

Peter Van Den Bossche, *The Law and Policy of the World Trade Organization* (2nd ed.) p. 308 (Cambridge, Cambridge University Press, 2010).

Richard A. Posner, *Economic Analysis of Law* (9th ed.) (New York, Aspen Publishers, 2014).

Robert E. Baldwin, *The Development and Testing of Heckscher-Ohlin Trade Models: A Review* (Cambridge, The MIT Press, 2008).

Roger B. Porter et al., *Efficiency, Equity, and Legitimacy: The Multilateral Trading System at the Millennium* (Washington, D.C., Brookings Institution Press, 2004).

Robert E. Hudec and J. Michael Finger, *Developing Countries in the GATT Legal System* (Cambridge, Cambridge University Press, 2014).

Robert J. Barro, *Determinants of Economic Growth: A Cross-Country Empirical Study* p. 1 (Cambridge, The MIT Press, 1998).

Ronder Wilkinson and James Scott (Eds), *Trade, Poverty, Development: Getting Beyond the WTO's Doha Deadlock* (London, Routledge, 2012).

Rudolf Dolzer and Christoph Schreuer, *Principles of International Investment Law* (2nd ed.) (New York, Oxford University Press, 2012).

Sabina Nüesch, *Voluntary Export Restraints in WTO and EU Law: Consumers, Trade Regulation and Competition Policy* (New York, Peter Lang AG, 2010).

Seev Hirsch, *Location of Industry and International Competitiveness* (Oxford, Clarendon Press, 1967).

Stephen D. Cohen et al., *Fundamentals of U.S. Foreign Trade Policy: Economics, Politics, Laws, and Issues* (2nd ed.) (Boulder, CO, Westview Press, 2002).

Surjit S. Bhalla, *Devaluing to Prosperity: Misaligned Currencies and their Growth Consequences* (Washington, D.C., Peterson Institute for International Economics, 2012).

The Concise Encyclopedia of Economics, *Bertil Gotthard Ohlin (1899–1979)*, available at: www.econlib.org/library/Enc/bios/Ohlin.html.

Vladimir Banacek and Mihaly Laki, *The Private Sector after Communism: New Entrepreneurial Firms in Transition Economies* (London, Routledge, 2013).

Vladimir Mau and Robert Skidelsky, *The Political History of Economic Reform in Russia, 1985–1994* (New York, New Series, 1995).

William Beinart, *Twentieth-Century South Africa* (New York, Oxford University Press, 2001).

William Poundstone, *Prisoner's Dilemma: John von Neumann, Game Theory, and the Puzzle of the Bomb* (New York, Anchor, 1993).

WTO, *Global Value Chains in a Changing World* (Geneva, World Trade Organization, 2013).

Xavier Sala-i-Martin, *Economía en Colores* [*Economics Through Colors*] (Barcelona, Rosa dels Vents, 2016).

Zuleika Arashiro, *Negotiating the Free Trade Area of the Americas* (New York, Springer, 2011).

Chapters in books

Aaditya Matoo and Pierre Sauvé, 'Services', in *Preferential Trade Agreement Policies for Development* (Jean-Pierre Chauffour and Jean-Christophe Maur Eds), Washington, D.C., The World Bank, 2011.

Acharya et al., 'Landscape', in *Preferential Trade Agreement Policies for Development, A Handbook* (Jean-Pierre Chauffour and Jean-Christophe Maur Eds), Washington, D.C., The World Bank, 2011.

Alan O. Sykes, 'International Trade and Human Rights: An Economic Perspective', in *Trade and Human Rights: Foundations and Conceptual Issues* (Frederick M. Abbott, Christine Breining-Kaufmann and Thomas Cottier Eds), Ann Arbor, University of Michigan Press, 2006.

Alan O. Sykes, 'Optimal Sanctions in the WTO: The Case for Decoupling (and the Uneasy Case for the Status Quo)', in *The Law, Economics and Politics of Retaliation in WTO Dispute Settlement* (Chad P. Bown and Joost Pauwelyn Eds), Cambridge, Cambridge University Press, 2014.

Alessandra Arcuri, 'The TBT Agreement and Private Standards', in *Research Handbook on the WTO and Technical Barriers to Trade* (Tracey Epps and Michael J. Trebilcock Eds), p. 485, New York, Edward Elgar Publishing, 2013.

Aluisio de Lima-Campos, 'In Agriculture, it is Time to Act with Plurilaterals', in *Tackling Agriculture in the Post-Bali Context* (Ricardo Meléndez-Ortiz, Christophe Bellmann and Jonathan Hepburn Eds), Washington, D.C., International Center for Trade and International Development, 2014.

Amelia Porges, 'Dispute Settlement', in *Preferential Trade Agreement Policies for Development, A Handbook* (Jean-Pierre Chauffour and Jean-Christophe Maur Eds), Washington, D.C., The World Bank, 2011.

Andrew L. Stoler, 'TBT and SPS Measures in Practice', in *Preferential Trade Agreement Policies for Development, A Handbook* (Jean-Pierre Chauffour and Jean-Christophe Maur Eds), Washington, D.C., The World Bank, 2011.

Anuradha R.V., 'Environment', in *Preferential Trade Agreement Policies for Development* (Jean-Pierre Chauffour and Jean-Christophe Maur Eds), Washington, D.C., The World Bank, 2011.

Bernard Hoekman, 'North-South Preferential Trade Agreements', in *Preferential Trade Agreement Policies for Development, A Handbook* (Jean-Pierre Chauffour and Jean-Christophe Maur Eds), Washington, D.C., The World Bank, 2011.

Bruno Ciccaglione and Alexandra Strickner, 'Global Crisis, the Need to Go Transnational Solidarity in the Struggle Against the Expansion of Free Trade', in *Free Trade and Transnational Labour* (Andreas Bieler, Bruno Ciccaglione, John Hilary and Ingemar Lindberg Eds), London, Routledge, 2010.

Caroline Freund and Joseph Gagnon, 'Consumption Taxes, Real Exchange Rates, and Trade Balances, Border Tax and Corporate Tax Reform', *PIIE Briefing* (Adam Posen and Chad Bown Eds), Washington, D.C., Peterson Institute for International Economics, 2017.

Carsten Fink, 'Intellectual Property Rights', in *Preferential Trade Agreement Policies for Development* (Jean-Pierre Chauffour and Jean-Christophe Maur Eds), Washington, D.C., The World Bank, 2011.

Dukgeun Ahn, 'Is the Chinese Exchange-rate Regime "WTO-legal"?', in *The US-Sino Currency Dispute: New Insights from Economics, Politics and Law* (Simon Evenett Ed.) p. 142, London, Centre for Economic Policy Research, 2010.

Edmar L. Bacha, 'Brazil's Plano Real: A View from the Inside', in *Development Economics and Structuralist Macroeconomics* (Amitava Krishna Dutt Ed.), New York, Edward Elgar Publishing, 2003.

Gregory C. Shaffer, Michelle Ratton, Sanchez Badin and Barbara Rosenberg, 'Winning at the WTO: The Development of a Trade Policy Community Within Brazil', in *Dispute Settlement at the WTO: The Developing Country Experience* (Gregory C. Shaffer and Ricardo Meléndez-Ortiz Eds), London, Cambridge University Press, 2010.

Ignacio García Bercero, 'Dispute Settlement in European Union Free Trade Agreements: Lessons Learned?' in *Regional Trade Agreements and the WTO Legal System* (Lorand Bartels and Federico Ortino Eds), New York, Oxford University Press, 2006.

James Van Alstine and Eric Neumayer, 'The Environmental Kuznets Curve', in *Handbook on Trade and the Environment* (Kevin P. Gallagher Ed.), New York, Edward Elgar Publishing, 2008.

Jean-Christophe Maur and Ben Shepherd, 'Product Standards', in *Preferential Trade Agreement Policies for Development, A Handbook* (Jean-Pierre Chauffour and Jean-Christophe Maur Eds), Washington, D.C., The World Bank, 2011.

Jean-Pierre Chauffour and Jean-Christophe Maur, 'Beyond Market Access', in *Preferential Trade Agreement Policies for Development, A Handbook* (Jean-Pierre Chauffour and Jean-Christophe Maur Eds), Washington, D.C., The World Bank, 2011.

Jean-Pierre Chauffour and Jean-Christophe Maur, 'Overview', in *Preferential Trade Agreement Policies for Development, A Handbook* (Jean-Pierre Chauffour and Jean-Christophe Maur Eds), Washington, D.C., The World Bank, 2011.

Joanne Gowa, 'Explaining the GATT/WTO: Origins and Effects', in *The Oxford Handbook of the Political Economy of International Trade* (Lisa L. Martin Ed.) p. 337, New York, Oxford University Press, 2015.

Kamala Dawar and Peter Holmes, 'Competition Policy', in *Preferential Trade Agreement Policies for Development, A Handbook* (Jean-Pierre Chauffour and Jean-Christophe Maur Eds), Washington, D.C., The World Bank, 2011.

Kamala Dawar and Simon J. Evenett, 'Government Procurement', in *Preferential Trade Agreement Policies for Development* (Jean-Pierre Chauffour and Jean-Christophe Maur Eds), Washington, D.C., The World Bank, 2011.

Kimberly Ann Elliott, 'Labor Rights', in *Preferential Trade Agreement Policies for Development* (Jean-Pierre Chauffour and Jean-Christophe Maur Eds), Washington, D.C., The World Bank, 2011.

Hunter Nottage, 'Evaluating the Criticism that WTO Retaliation Rules Undermine the Utility of WTO Dispute Settlement for Developing Countries', in *The Law, Economics and Politics of Retaliation in WTO Dispute Settlement* (Chad P. Bown and Joost Pauwelyn Eds), Cambridge, Cambridge University Press, 2014.

Laura Rovegno and Hylke Vandenbussche, 'A Comparative Analysis of EU Antidumping Rules and Application', in *Liberalizing Trade in the EU and the WTO: Comparative Perspectives* (Sanford Gaines, Birgitte Egelund Olsen and Karsten Engsig Sørensen Eds), Cambridge, Cambridge University Press, 2011.

Leslie Johns and Lauren Peritz, 'The Design of Trade Agreements', in *The Oxford Handbook of the Political Economy of International Trade* (Lisa L. Martin Ed.) p. 337, New York, Oxford University Press, 2015.

Luiz Eduardo Salles, 'Procedures for the Design and Implementation of Trade Retaliation in Brazil', in *The Law, Economics and Politics of Retaliation in WTO Dispute Settlement* (Chad P. Bown and Joost Pauwelyn Eds), Cambridge, Cambridge University Press, 2014.

María Victoria Daract, Mercosur, 'Antecedentes Históricos' ['Mercosur, Historical Background'], in *Estudios sobre el Mercosur* [*Studies on Mercosur*] (Juan F. Armagnague, Silvia Barón et al. Eds), p. 135, Cuyo, 2007.

Mario Marconini, 'Brazil' in *The Political Economy of Trade Reform in Emerging Markets: Crisis or Opportunity* (Peter Draper, Phil Alves and Razeen Sally Eds), New York, Edward Elgar Publishing, 2009.

Mark E. Mendel, 'Retaliation in the WTO: The Experience of Antigua and Barbuda in US-Gambling', in *The Law, Economics and Politics of Retaliation in WTO Dispute Settlement* (Chad P. Bown and Joost Pauwelyn Eds) p. 310, Cambridge, Cambridge University Press 2014.

Michael Trebilcock and Michael Fishbein, 'International Trade: Barriers to Trade', in *Research Handbook in International Economic Law* (Andrew T. Guzman and Alan O. Sykes Eds), New York, Edward Elgar Publishing, 2008.

Richard Baldwin and Caroline Freund, 'Preferential Trade Agreements and Multilateral Liberalization', in *Preferential Trade Agreement Policies for Development, A Handbook* (Jean-Pierre Chauffour and Jean-Christophe Maur Eds), Washington, D.C., The World Bank, 2011.

Robert E. Hudec, 'The Adequacy of WTO Dispute Settlement Remedies: A Developing Country Perspective', in *Development, Trade and the WTO* (Bernard Hoekman, Aaditya Mattoo and Philip English Eds), Washington, D.C., The World Bank, 2011.

Robert W. Staiger and Alan O. Sykes, 'Currency "Manipulation" and World Trade: A Caution', in *The US-Sino Currency Dispute: New Insights from Economics, Politics and Law* (Simon Evenett Ed.) p. 110, New York, Centre for Economic Policy Research, 2010.

Sébastien Miroudout, 'Investment', in *Preferential Trade Agreement Policies for Development* (Jean-Pierre Chauffour and Jean-Christophe Maur Eds), Washington, D.C., The World Bank, 2011.

Sherry Stephenson and Gary Hufbauer, 'Labor Mobility', in *Preferential Trade Agreement Policies for Development* (Jean-Pierre Chauffour and Jean-Christophe Maur Eds), Washington, D.C., The World Bank, 2011.

Tomer Broude, 'From Pax Mercatoria to Pax Europea: How Trade Dispute Procedures Serve the EC's Regional Hegemony', in *Economics of European Union Law* (Paul B. Stephan Ed.), New York, Edward Elgar, 2007.

Yasushi Ninomiya, 'Industrial Policy and the Post-New Brazil', in *The Post-New Brazil* (Ryohei Konta Ed.), Tokyo, Institute of Developing Economies, 2015.

Websites

2015 Turkey G20, http://g20.org.tr/

The Advisory Centre on WTO Law, www.acwl.ch/

ALADI, www.aladi.org/sitioAladi/index.html

Alianza del Pacífico, https://alianzapacifico.net/

The American Enterprise Institute for Public Policy Research, www.aei.org

The American Federation of Labor – Congress of Industrial Organizations, www.aflcio.org/

APEC, www.apec.org/

ASEAN, http://asean.org/

ASEM, www.aseminfoboard.org/

The Asia Digest, www.theasiadigest.com/

Asia Regional Integration Center, https://aric.adb.org/
The Association of Mining and Exploration Companies (Australia), www.amec.org.au/
The Australian Chamber of Commerce and Industry, www.acci.asn.au/
The Australian Federation of Employers and Industries, www.afei.org.au/
The Australian Food and Grocery Council, www.afgc.org.au/
Australian Unions, www.australianunions.org.au/
The BBC (British Broadcasting Corporation), www.bbc.com/
Berkeley University, http://eml.berkeley.edu/~webfac/trehan/e100b_sp05/chap4.pdf
Bloomberg, www.bloomberg.com/
Brazil Monitor, http://brazilmonitor.com/
The Brookings Institution, www.brookings.edu
The Cairns Group, http://cairnsgroup.org/
Cámara de Comercio de la Ciudad de México (Chamber of Commerce of Mexico City), www.ccmexico.com.mx/es/
CAMEX, www.camex.gov.br/
The Canadian Association of Petroleum Producers, www.capp.ca/
The Canadian Chamber of Commerce, www.chamber.ca/
The Canadian Labor Congress, http://canadianlabour.ca/
The Carnegie Endowment for International Peace, www.carnegieendowment.org
Cátedra UNESCO de Derechos Humanos de la Universidad Nacional Autónoma de México UNAM [UNESCO Cathedra of Human Rights at the UNAM], http://catedraunescodh.unam.mx/catedra/pronaledh/index70ed.html?option=com_content&view=article&id=148&Itemid=126
The CATO Institute, www.cato.org
The Center for Global Development, www.cgdev.org
The Center for Responsive Politics, www.opensecrets.org/
Central Única dos Trabalhadores, www.cut.org.br/
CEPA, www.cepa.gov.mo/
CEPAL, www.cepal.org/en/
Chamber of Commerce and Industry (South Africa), www.sacci.org.za/
China FTA Network, http://fta.mofcom.gov.cn/english/index.shtml
CNN (Cable News Network), www.cnn.com
Coalition of Services Industries, http://servicescoalition.org/negotiations/trade-in-services-agreement
Codex Alimentarius, international food standards, www.fao.org/fao-who-codexalimentarius/standards/list-standards/
Columbia University, www.columbia.edu
Colombian Ministry of Commerce, Industry and Tourism, www.mincit.gov.co
Comisión Económica para América Latina [Economic Commission for Latin America] CEPAL, www.cepal.org/
Commonwealth Network, www.commonwealthofnations.org/
Comunidad Andina de Naciones (Andean Nations Community), www.comunidadandina.org/
Confederação Nacional de Agricultura (Brazilian National Confederation of Agriculture), www.cnabrasil.org.br
Confederação Nacional da Indústria or National Confederation of Industry (Brazil), www.portaldaindustria.com.br/cni/en/
Confederación de Trabajadores de México (Mexican Confederation of Workers), www.ctmoficial.org
Constitución de los Estados Unidos de México [Constitution of the Mexican United States], www.sct.gob.mx/JURE/doc/cpeum.pdf

Constitution of India, http://indiacode.nic.in/coiweb/welcome.html
Coparmex (Mexico), www.coparmex.org.mx/
The Council on Foreign Relations, www.cfr.org
Countrymeters, http://countrymeters.info/en/
Court of Justice of the European Union, https://europa.eu/european-union/about-eu/institutions-bodies/court-justice_en
Department of Foreign Affairs and Trade (Australia), http://dfat.gov.au/
Department of Global Affairs (Canada), www.international.gc.ca/
Department of International Relations and Cooperation (South Africa), www.dirco.gov.za/
Department of Trade and Industry (South Africa), www.thedti.gov.za/
Diario Oficial de México, www.dof.gob.mx/
Diario Oficial Da União, http://pesquisa.in.gov.br/
Directory of Mexican Non-Governmental Organizations, http://ongs.com.mx/directorio/
Donald J. Trump official website, www.donaldjtrump.com/
The Economic European Area, www.efta.int/eea
The Economist, www.economist.com/
EFTA, www.efta.int/
Enforcement and Compliance, WTO subsidies notifications, http://enforcement.trade.gov/
Eurasian Economic Commission, www.eurasiancommission.org/
Eurasian Economic Union, www.eaeunion.org/?lang=en
Euro, everything related to Euro and European Union and Schengen Visa, www.euro-dollar-currency.com/
The European Banking Authority, www.eba.europa.eu/
The European Commission, http://ec.europa.eu/
The European Parliament, www.europarl.europa.eu/atyourservice/en/displayFtu.html?ftuId=FTU_6.5.3.html
The European Union, http://europa.eu
Eurostat, http://ec.europa.eu/
Export.gov, www.export.gov/
The Fair-Trade Association (Australia), www.fta.org.au/
Federação das Indústrias do Estado de São Paulo (Industry Federation of the São Paulo State), www.fiesp.com.br/
The Federal Assembly (Russia), www.gov.ru/main/page7_en.html
Financial Times, www.ft.com/
Financial Times blogs, http://blogs.ft.com/
The Fisheries Council of Canada, http://fisheriescouncil.com/
Foreign Trade Information System, www.sice.oas.org/
Fullfact.org, https://fullfact.org/
Fundação Getulio Vargas, observatory on exchange rates, http://ccgi.fgv.br/en/observatory-exchange-rates
General Administration of Customs (China), http://english.customs.gov.cn/
Generalized System of Preferences, http://ptadb.wto.org/
The Guardian, http://theguardian.com
Gulf Cooperation Council, www.gcc-sg.org/en-us/Pages/default.aspx
ICSID, https://icsid.worldbank.org/
The Independent, www.independent.co.uk/
India Brand Equity Foundation, www.ibef.org/
The Indian Patents, www.ipindia.nic.in/
The Inter-American Development Bank, www.iadb.org
The Inter-American Dialogue, www.thedialogue.org

The International Brotherhood of Teamsters, https://teamster.org/
The International Labor Organization, www.ilo.org
The International Monetary Fund, www.imf.org
The International Progress Organization, www.i-p-o.org
The International Trade Administration Commission (South Africa), www.itac.org.za/
The International Trade and Economic Development Commission (South Africa), www.thedti.gov.za/
Justice Laws website, http://laws-lois.justice.gc.ca/
Knoema, www.knoema.com/
Mercosur, www.mercosur.int/
The Mining Association of Canada, http://mining.ca/
Minister for Trade, Tourism and Investment (Australia), http://trademinister.gov.au/Pages/default.aspx
Ministry of Agriculture (China), http://english.agri.gov.cn/
Ministry of Commerce (China), http://english.mofcom.gov.cn/
Ministry of Commerce and Industry Department of Commerce (India), http://dgft.gov.in/
Ministry of Commerce and Industry (India), http://commerce.nic.in/
Ministry of Commerce, Industry and Tourism (Colombia), www.mincit.gov.co/
Ministry of Economic Development (Russia), http://economy.gov.ru/en/home
Ministry of Finance (China), http://english.gov.cn/state_council
The Moscow Times, https://themoscowtimes.com/
NAALC, www.naalc.org/
NAFTA Now, www.naftanow.org/
NAFTA Secretariat, www.nafta-sec-alena.org/
The Nation, www.thenation.com
The National Bureau of Economic Research, www.nber.org/papers/w17969.pdf
The National Confederation of Industry (Confederação Nacional da Indústria), http://admin.cni.org.br/
The National Development and Reform Commission (China), http://en.ndrc.gov.cn/
The National Economic Development and Labor Council (South Africa), http://new.nedlac.org.za/
The National People's Congress (China), www.npc.gov.cn/englishnpc/
The National People's Congress Standing Committee (China), www.npc.gov.cn/englishnpc/
The National Treasury (South Africa), www.treasury.gov.za/
NATO, www.nato.int/
The New York Times, www.nytimes.com/
NGOs Based in Canada, www.chatt.hdsb.ca/
Nikkei Asian Review, http://asia.nikkei.com/
The Nobel Prize Organization, www.nobelprize.org/nobel_prizes/economic-sciences/laureates/
Official Website of the United Kingdom Government, www.gov.uk/
Organization for Economic Cooperation and Development (OECD), www.oecd.org/
Parliament of Australia, www.aph.gov.au/
The Peterson Institute for International Economics, https://piie.com/
Planalto, Presidência da República, www2.planalto.gov.br/
Portal da Indústria – industry website, www.portaldaindustria.com.br/cni/en/
Portal Político – politics website, www.portalpolitico.tv/
Prime Minister of Canada, http://pm.gc.ca/eng/
Rainbow Nation, www.rainbownation.com/

RANEPA, The Russian Presidential Academy of National Economy and Public Administration, Russia in APEC, http://apec-center.ru/en/russia-in-apec/
REBRIP, A Rede Brasileira Pela Integração dos Povos, www.rebrip.org.br/
Reform the CAP, www.reformthecap.eu/issues/policy-instruments/export-subsidies
The Regional Trade Agreements Information System, http://rtais.wto.org/
Reuters, www.reuters.com/
Russia Direct, www.russia-direct.org/
Russia G20, http:// http://en.g20russia.ru/
Schengen Visa Info, www.schengenvisainfo.com
SICE Foreign Trade Information System, Organization of American States, www.sice.oas.org/ctyindex/BRZ/BRZagreements_s.asp
Southern African Customs Union (SACU), www.sacu.int/
Southern African Development Community, www.sadc.int/
Stop the Untouchables, Justice for Sergei Magnitsky, http://russian-untouchables.com/eng/
Theodora.com, www.allcountries.org/
Trade and Industry Department, the Government of Hong Kong Special Administrative Region, www.tid.gov.hk/english/cepa/
Transparency International, www.transparency.org/
UFCW Canada, www.ufcw.ca/
UK Government Web Archive, www.nationalarchives.gov.uk/webarchive/
The United Food and Commercial Workers International Union (Canada), www.ufcw.ca/
The United Nations, www.un.org/en/
The United Nations Conference on Trade and Development, www.unctad.org/en
The United Nations Economic and Social for Asia and the Pacific, www.unescap.org/apta
The United Nations Food and Agriculture Organization, www.fao.org
The U.S. Customs and Border Protection, www.cbp.gov/
The U.S. Census Bureau, www.census.gov/
The U.S. Department of State, www.state.gov/
The U.S. International Trade Commission, www.usitc.gov/
The USDA Foreign Agricultural Service, http://gain.fas.usda.gov/
The USTR, https://ustr.gov/
The Wall Street Journal, www.wsj.com
The Washington Post, www.washingtonpost.com/
The White House, www.whitehouse.gov
Wordnet Princeton, https://wordnet.princeton.edu/
The World Bank, www.worldbank.org
The World Bank Data, http://data.worldbank.org/
The World Customs Organization, Harmonization Work Program, www.wcoomd.org/en/
World Integrated Trade Solution, http://wits.worldbank.org/
The World Intellectual Property Organization, www.wipo.int/portal/en/index.html
World Population Review, http://worldpopulationreview.com/
World Top Exports, www.worldstopexports.com/
The World Trade Organization, www.wto.org/
The World Trade Organization Time Series, http://stat.wto.org/StatisticalProgram/WSDBViewData.aspx?Language=Eh
World Values Survey Online Database, http://worldvaluessurvey.org
Worldometers, www.worldometers.info/
Worldwide NGO Directory, www.wango.org/

WTO Agreements

1994 WTO Agreement.
Agreement on Agriculture.
Agreement on Antidumping Duties.
Agreement on Government Procurement.
Agreement on Rules of Origin.
Agreement on Safeguards.
Agreement on Sanitary and Phytosanitary Measures.
Agreement on Subsidies and Countervailing Duties.
Agreement on Technical Barriers to Trade.
Agreement on Trade in Civil Aircraft.
Agreement on Trade Facilitation.
Dispute Settlement Understanding.
General Agreement on Trade and Tariffs.
General Agreement on Trade and Services.
Government Procurement Agreement.
Information Technology Agreement.
Marrakesh Agreement Establishing the World Trade Organization.
Ministerial Decision on Dispute Settlement of 29 November 1982, L/5424, GATT B.I.S.D. (29th Supp.).
Rules of the WTO Committee on Rules of Origin (CRO) in Geneva and of the WCO Technical Committee (TCRO).
Russian Protocol of Adhesion.
Trade in Services Agreement.
Trade-Related Aspects of Intellectual Property Rights.
WTO, Report of the Working Party on the Accession of China, WT/ACC/CHN/49, October 2001.

International legal rules

Agreement of the International Monetary Fund.
Codex Alimentarius, International Food Standards.
Vienna Convention on the Law of Treaties.

Regional legal rules

Additional Protocol to the Treaty of Asunción on the Institutional Structure of Mercosur.
Protocol of Olivos of 2002.
Treaty of Asunción.
Treaty of Ouro Preto.

Preferential trade agreements

CAFTA.
North American Free Trade Agreement.
PTA United States – Colombia.
PTA United States – Chile.
PTA European Union – Chile.

Domestic legal rules

Treaties of the European Union

Regulation 978/2012, European Union
European Council Regulation No 3286/94, European Union.
Council Regulation (EC) No 384/96, European Union.
Regulation 738/94, European Union.
Regulation (EU) 2016/1037 of the European Parliament and of the Council of 8 June 2016 on protection against subsidized imports from countries not members of the European Union.
Regulation (EU) 2016/1036 of the European Parliament and of the Council of 8 June 2016 on protection against dumped imports from countries not members of the European Union.

Other domestic legal rules

Andean Trade Preference Act, United States.
Trade Expansion Act, United States.
Trade Promotion Authority, United States.
Trade Act of 1974, United States.
URAA Section 123 in the Federal Register.
Russia and Moldova Jackson-Vanik Repeal and Sergei Magnitsky Rule of Law Accountability Act of 2012.
Omnibus Trade and Competitiveness Act of 1988.
Brazilian Constitution.
Decree N° 9.029 (2017).
Decree N° 8.807 (2016).
Decree N° 4.732 (2003).
Trade Administration Act, South Africa.
1985 Investment Canada Act.
Australia's Tobacco Plain Packaging Act 2011 and its implementing regulations.
Decree 640, 2016, Argentina.
Res. 574/2000, Argentina.
The Sugar Act and the Navigation Acts, United Kingdom.
The Decision of the State Council on Amending the Antidumping Regulations of the People's Republic of China (2004).

WTO cases

DS467, Australia – Certain Measures Concerning Trademarks, Geographical Indications and Other Plain Packaging Requirements Applicable to Tobacco Products and Packaging.
DS458, Australia – Certain Measures Concerning Trademarks, Geographical Indications and Other Plain Packaging Requirements Applicable to Tobacco Products and Packaging.
DS456, India – Certain Measures Relating to Solar Cells and Solar Modules.
DS441, Australia – Certain Measures Concerning Trademarks, Geographical Indications and Other Plain Packaging Requirements Applicable to Tobacco Products and Packaging.

DS435, Australia – Certain Measures Concerning Trademarks, Geographical Indications and Other Plain Packaging Requirements Applicable to Tobacco Products and Packaging.

DS434, Australia – Certain Measures Concerning Trademarks and Other Plain Packaging Requirements Applicable to Tobacco Products and Packaging.

DS402, United States – Use of Zeroing in Anti-Dumping Measures Involving Products from Korea.

DS381, US – Tuna II.

DS379, United States – Definitive Antidumping and Countervailing Duties on Certain Products from China.

DS332, Brazil – Measures Affecting Imports of Retreaded Tyres.

DS322, United States – Measures Relating to Zeroing and Sunset Reviews.

DS321, European Communities – Trade Description of Sardines.

DS315, European Communities – Selected Customs Matters.

DS308, Mexico – Tax Measures on Soft Drinks and Other Beverages.

DS302, Dominican Republic – Measures Affecting the Importation and Internal Sale of Cigarettes.

DS294, United States – Laws, Regulations and Methodology for Calculating Dumping Margins (Zeroing).

DS285, United States – Measures Affecting the Cross-Border Supply of Gambling and Betting Services.

DS268, United States – Sunset Reviews of Anti-Dumping Measures on Oil Country Tubular Goods from Argentina.

DS267, United States – Subsidies on Upland Cotton.

DS257, United States – Final Countervailing Duty Determination with respect to certain Softwood Lumber from Canada.

DS246, European Communities – Conditions for the Granting of Tariff Preferences to Developing Countries.

DS241, Argentina – Definitive Antidumping Duties on Poultry from Brazil.

DS217, United States – Continued Dumping and Subsidy Offset Act of 2000.

DS135, European Communities – Measures Affecting Asbestos and Products Containing Asbestos.

DS121, Argentina – Safeguard Measures on Imports of Footwear.

DS108, United States – Tax Treatment for Foreign Sales Corporations, Resource to Article 21.5 of the DSU by the European Communities.

DS98, Korea – Definitive Safeguard Measure on Imports of Certain Dairy Products.

DS90, India – Quantitative Restrictions on Imports of Agricultural, Textile and Industrial Products.

DS70, Canada – Measures Affecting the Export of Civilian Aircraft.

DS58, United States – Import Prohibition of Certain Shrimp and Shrimp Products.

DS56, Argentina – Measures Affecting Imports of Footwear, Textiles, Apparel and Other Items.

DS52, United States – Standards for Reformulated and Conventional Gasoline.

DS44, Japan – Measures Affecting Consumer Photographic Film and Paper.

DS26, European Communities – Measures Concerning Meat and Meat Products (Hormones).

DS22, Brazil – Measures Affecting Desiccated Coconut.

DS18, Australia – Measures Affecting Importation of Salmon.

DS2, United States – Standards for Reformulated and Conventional Gasoline.

DS27, European Communities – Regime for the Importation, Sale and Distribution of Bananas.

Other cases

R (Miller) v. Secretary of State for Exiting the European Union, 2016] EWHC 2768 (Admin) Case No CO/3809/2016 and CO/3281/2016 3 November 2016 (United Kingdom).

UK Case Chemco Leasing S.p.a. v. Rediffusion plc [1983] (Engl. Q.B. Comm'l Ct.) (unreported) (Mr. Justice Vaisey) (citing Sir Robert Edgar Megarry): *aff'd* [1987] 1FTLR 201 (United Kingdom).

Arbitral Award on the dispute between Brazil and Argentine on the application of antidumping measures against the export of poultry coming from Brazil.

United States v. Eurodif S. A. 555 U.S. 305 (2009) (United States).

Other documents

UNCTAD's *World Investment Report* (2013: XXII).

WTO Dispute Settlement Body, Minutes of meeting held in the Centre William Rappard on 31 August 2015.

WTO Dispute Settlement Body, Minutes of meeting held in the Centre William Rappard on 22 June 2016.

WTO, *Making Trade an Engine of Growth for All, The Case for Trade and for Policies to Facilitate Adjustment.*

INDEX